DIS-
RUPT

Filipina Women: Leading with Intersectionality

5.0

DIS-RUPT

5.0

Filipina Women: Leading with Intersectionality

The Fifth Book
on Leadership
by the Foundation
for Filipina
Women's Network

Edited by
MARIA AFRICA BEEBE

San Francisco, California

"Break the mold"
(A Rap for DISRUPT 5.0)

Listen up, y'all, it's time to get woke
To the stories of women who've weathered each stroke
Filipina women leaders are changing the game
Breaking barriers daily, they're rising to fame

(Chorus)

DISRUPT 5.0, yeah, that's the name
Intersectionality is their claim to fame
Race, class, and gender, they've faced it all
But these women refuse to hit the wall

Verse 1:

First-gen, second-gen, they came to succeed
Faced with stereotypes, they paid no heed
In the corporate world, they're making their mark
Lighting up boardrooms that once were dark
They've got tales to tell, experiences to share
Of struggles and triumphs, of learning to dare
From poverty's grip to the executive suite
These women show strength that can't be beat

(Chorus)

DISRUPT 5.0, yeah, that's the name

Intersectionality is their claim to fame
Race, class, and gender, they've faced it all
But these women refuse to hit the wall

Verse 2:

To all the young hustlers, take note of this book
It's time to change how the world's gonna look
Diversity ain't just a box to check
It's about perspectives, so show some respect
For the DEI pros and the execs in suits
It's time to dig deep and examine your roots
These Filipina stories will open your eyes
To talent and wisdom you might otherwise miss

(Chorus)

DISRUPT 5.0, yeah, that's the name
Intersectionality is their claim to fame
Race, class, and gender, they've faced it all
But these women refuse to hit the wall

Outro:

So let's amplify voices, tear down the old ways
Create workplaces where everyone slays
DISRUPT 5.0 is the blueprint, you see
For a future where all can be truly free

CONTENTS

LEGACIES

SYNTHESIS

APPENDICES

FOREWORD

DISRUPT 5.0 -
The Intersectional Evolution
of Filipina Leadership

Five books ago, we ignited a movement. We declared that Filipina women are the ultimate global disrupters. Today, with "D5.0: Filipina Women Leading with Intersectionality," we're not just continuing that disruption— amplifying it, evolving it, and proving its indispensable value in the modern business world.

Let's rewind for a moment. In our first book, "DISRUPT. Filipina Women. Proud. Loud. Leading Without A Doubt," we established a fundamental truth:

Filipina women do not back down. Once they make up their minds that they will get behind a cause or an issue that will change how people live or aim for that promotion or leadership position, they don't stop. They're tenacious, firm, forceful, and don't give up.

This tenacity, this disruptive force, has been the through-line of our series. We've showcased how Filipina women have disrupted their lives through immigration, shattered glass ceilings in organizations, innovated in business, advocated in communities, and reshaped political landscapes.

With "D5.0," we're taking this disruption to a new level. We're not just proud, loud, and leading without doubt—we're leading with intersectionality, and in doing so, we're offering a masterclass in 21st-century leadership that every forward-thinking organization needs to pay attention to.

Why? Because in today's hyper-connected, rapidly evolving business landscape, the ability to navigate and leverage diverse perspectives isn't just a nice-to-have—it's a critical competitive advantage.

Consider this: The second-generation leaders we highlighted in our first book, who grew up "confused" in bi-cultural or multi-cultural families, have become the vanguard of global leadership. Their ability to embrace Eastern and Western values, develop new paradigms for managing conflict, and spark thoughtful conversations about multiculturalism are precisely the skills needed to lead in our complex, interconnected world.

Now, let's talk business. Think again if you're picking up this book expecting another feel-good narrative about diversity. What you hold in your hands is a roadmap to revolutionizing your approach to talent, leadership, and organizational success.

Through the lens of Filipina leaders across the globe, "D5.0" offers concrete strategies for:

1. **Talent Retention:** The "Crucibles" section isn't just about overcoming challenges. It's a blueprint for creating environments where diverse talent feels valued and stays committed.

2. **Innovation Catalyst:** Our "Glocal" perspectives aren't just exciting anecdotes. They're case studies of how diverse viewpoints fuel creativity and problem-solving, essential for staying ahead in a competitive market.

3. **Leadership Development:** The "Champions" we showcase aren't outliers. They represent the leaders organizations must cultivate to thrive in a global marketplace.

4. **Risk Mitigation:** In an era where cultural missteps can go viral, insights on navigating complex identities and addressing systemic biases are crucial risk management tools.

5. **Market Expansion:** The global perspectives shared here offer invaluable insights for companies looking to expand into new markets. They demonstrate how understanding intersectionality can be a key to connecting with diverse customer bases.

Let's address the elephant in the room: Yes, Diversity, Equity, Inclusion, and Belonging (DEIB) initiatives have faced backlash. But here's the truth—companies that view diversity as a checkbox exercise are missing the point entirely. What "D5.0" advocates isn't just diversity for diversity's sake. It's about leveraging the unique strengths that come from diverse experiences to drive tangible business outcomes.

This book does not ask you to implement DEIB initiatives out of obligation. It challenges you to see intersectionality as a powerful lens through which to view and optimize your business strategies. It invites you to embrace disruption not as a threat but as a catalyst for growth and innovation.

As you read these pages, prepare to be challenged, inspired, and maybe even a little uncomfortable at times. That discomfort is good. It is the feeling of your perspectives expanding, your assumptions being questioned, and your leadership toolkit growing.

"D5.0: Filipina Women Leading with Intersectionality" is more than a book—it's a call to action. It challenges leaders to step up, see the untapped potential within their organizations, and create workplaces where everyone can bring their full, authentic selves to the table.

So, here's my challenge: Read this book not as a passive observer but as a leader ready to take action. Engage with these stories, reflect on your experiences, and ask yourself: How can embracing intersectional leadership drive my organization forward?

The future of business is intersectional. Are you ready to disrupt the status quo and lead the way?

Remember: We are Filipina Disrupters, leading our communities and organizations without any doubt of our capacity to achieve results. Join us in this disruption, and together, let's reshape the global leadership landscape.

Marily Mondejar
Founder and CEO
Foundation for Filipina Women's Network

PREFACE

ISRUPT 5.0: *Filipina Women Leading with Intersectionality* stands as a powerful testament to Filipina women's strength, resilience, and brilliance.

The fifth book in this series serves as both a call to action and a celebration of the multifaceted identities that shape their journeys. By embracing intersectionality, it illuminates the unique challenges Filipina women encounter in leadership while pushing back against conventional narratives. This work empowers a new generation to envision leadership rooted in justice and equity.

Marily Mondejar, the founder and CEO of the Filipina Women's Network (FWN), radiates a powerful and inspiring energy that brings together diverse communities through the transformative power of technology and business. Under her visionary leadership, FWN has become a beacon of empowerment, leveraging innovation and strategic business practices to elevate the voices and influence of Filipina women.

I first met Marily Mondejar when I joined then-Mayor Gavin Newsom's staff as the Asian Community Liaison in the Mayor's Office of Neighborhood Services. I was introduced to Marily through my best friend Jason Chan, who was participating in a reading for *The Vagina Monologues*. I quickly saw Marily's dynamic presence in action. Her personality was infectious, embodying the strength and resilience of Filipina power.

As I got to know Marily, the late San Francisco Mayor Ed Lee and I recognized the qualities that made her a natural leader in the community. Her passion for uplifting Filipina women, particularly those affected by intimate partner violence, was evident in everything she did. Through her work at the FWN, Marily became a beacon of hope and empowerment for Filipina women in the United States and the 34 countries where FWN members reside.

Her unwavering commitment to addressing the challenges Filipina women face, from marginalization to violence, has had a profound impact on the global community. Marily's leadership continues to inspire a new generation of Filipina women to stand tall, disrupt the status quo, and reclaim their power.

This collection of stories forms a powerful chorus of strong voices, showcasing what is possible when a Filipina woman's talents, determination, dreams, and leadership are shaped and refined by the challenges of cultural norms, traditions, and expectations. Reflecting the breadth of the Filipino diaspora, these stories transcend borders, highlighting the global influence this leadership already has and the profound impact it is poised to achieve.

DISRUPT 5.0 is more than a collection of stories—it's a movement. It represents an enduring commitment to social justice and boldly declares the power of Filipina women to disrupt the status quo and create a more inclusive future.

I am honored to be an ally to FWN and hold the honor of being the first man in *DISRUPT 5.0.*

Francis Tsang, MPH
Strategic Communications Advisor, San Francisco International Airport
Former Deputy Chief of Staff to Mayor Edwin M. Lee
Former Deputy Press Secretary to Mayor Gavin Newsom

INTRODUCTION

Leading with Intersectionality

This book is about **Leading with Intersectionality**. Intersectionality recognizes that the individual realities and lived experiences of Filipina women leaders are shaped by many intersecting factors, including race, class, gender, sexual orientation, religion, ability, and other markers of difference. Intersectionality appreciates that multiple and intersecting identities shape individuals and groups. These identities often inform an individual's worldview, perspective, and relationship with others in society.

Pioneered by scholar Kimberlé Crenshaw, intersectionality originally focused on revealing the compounded disadvantages marginalized groups face. It has since evolved to explore how intersecting privileges shape the experiences of individuals in positions of power. By the late 1990s and early 2000s, the concept of intersectionality began to expand beyond its initial focus. Scholars and advocates examined how identities like being white, male, or wealthy could confer multiple layers of privilege. This broader application of intersectionality helped to highlight how social advantages are distributed and maintained. Intersectionality, therefore, attends to not only individual identities but also the systems wherein inequalities are reproduced across individuals, groups, and institutions.

It also became increasingly clear that traditional leadership frameworks often overlooked the complex, intersecting identities of both leaders and those they lead. This recognition, emerging in the late 2000s and early 2010s, drove the integration of intersectionality into leadership studies. By applying an intersectional lens, these studies emphasized the need to consider how race, gender, class, and other identities influence leadership styles, access to leadership opportunities, and the challenges leaders face.

This approach allows leadership theories and practices to more accurately reflect the realities of a diverse workforce and society, ultimately leading to more equitable and effective leadership.

Leadership development programs have increasingly embraced intersectionality in their initiatives, aiming to cultivate inclusive leadership that recognizes and harnesses all individuals' diverse perspectives and experiences. A key example of this commitment is the United Nations' development of an *Intersectionality Resource Guide and Toolkit*, designed to ensure no one is left behind. This toolkit is structured around core intersectionality enablers, including diverse knowledge, power relations, and reflexivity. These enablers are essential for addressing the "multi-level interacting social locations, forces, factors, and power structures that shape and influence human life" (Hankivsky, 2012)[1]. By integrating these principles, leadership programs can better equip leaders to navigate and respond to the complexities of a diverse and interconnected world.

At the 19th Filipina Leadership Summit held in Prague in 2023, the Filipina Women Leaders examined leadership using an intersectional lens. The narratives that make up *DISRUPT 5.0 Leading with Intersectionality* uncover how global complexities affect Filipina women's leadership and how leadership operates in different contexts.

---

1   Hankivsky, O. (Ed.). (2012). *An intersectionality-based policy analysis framework. Institute for Intersectionality Research and Policy.* Simon Fraser University.

Global Context

The Philippines Statistics Authority (PSA)[2] estimates the 2024 population to be 119.1 million, with women making up approximately 49.3% of the population and men comprising around 50.7%.

The Philippines ranks 25th out of 146 countries in the 2024 World Economic Forum (WEF)[3] Global Gender Gap Index and records a gender parity score of 77.9 percent, lower than its 2023 score of 79.1 percent. Among Asian countries, the Philippines ranked highest, followed by Singapore at 48th place, Thailand at 65th, and Vietnam at 72nd. Eastern Asia and the Pacific (including the Philippines) rank fourth, with an overall gender parity score of 69.2%. Northern America reports a gender parity score of 74.8%. The Global Gender Gap Index benchmarks gender parity across four key areas: economic participation and opportunity, educational attainment, health and survival, and political empowerment. According to the report, the Philippines' economy "has achieved full parity across all Educational Attainment indicators, although the shares of women enrolled at each level of education have not all consistently increased across editions of the index."

---

2   Philippines Statistics Authority. (2024). Population of the Philippines. https://psa.gov.ph/

3   World Economic Forum. (2024). Global Gender Gap Report 2024. https://www.weforum.org/publications/global-gender-gap-report-2024/in-full/benchmarking-gender-gaps-2024-2e5f5cd886/

The report indicates that as far as gender gaps in the skills of the future are concerned, men and women continue to showcase STEM skills disproportionately, with the share of women with STEM skills at 27.1%. Another key takeaway is that while women are close to occupying nearly half of entry-level positions, they fall short of representing just one-quarter of C-suite roles.

More Filipinas Migrate than Men

Filipino migrants encompass a broader category of Filipinos living abroad, including various types of migrants such as students, permanent residents, and naturalized citizens. Overseas Filipino Workers (OFWs)[4] specifically refer to Filipinos employed overseas for work purposes.

As of 2023, the Commission on Filipinos Overseas (CFO) estimated that 10.4 million Filipinos live abroad as permanent, temporary, or irregular migrants. This number includes people of Filipino ancestry and citizens who live in countries where they have jobs. The Filipinos are in more than 200 countries and territories worldwide.

In 2023, 58% of OFWs were female, and the majority were between the ages of 30 and 34, followed by those 45 and older.

In 2022, 80.8% of OFWs worked in Asia, with the top five destinations being Saudi Arabia (23%), United Arab Emirates (13.7%), Kuwait (7.7%), Hong Kong (6.1%), and Qatar (5.8%). Other destinations include Europe (9%), North and South America (6.3%), Australia (2.9%), and Africa (1%).

More Filipinos Live in the United States

The U.S. has the largest population of Filipinos outside the Philippines. As of 2022, the U.S. Census Bureau reported that 4.1 million Filipino Americans lived in the United States, making up 17% of the Asian American population.

The Migration Policy Institute (2023)[5] reports that the United States is home to most Filipinos abroad. About one in three international migrants from the Philippines

---

4   Commission on Filipinos Overseas. (2023). Number of Overseas Filipinos. https://cfo.gov.ph/

5   Migration Policy Institute. (2023). Filipinos Abroad. https://www.migrationpolicy.

resided in the United States as of the most recent mid-2020 United Nations Population Division estimates. Other top destinations for migration include Saudi Arabia (645,000), Canada (634,000), the United Arab Emirates (565,000), Australia (286,000), and Japan (275,000).

In 2015, the U.S. remained the primary destination for permanent migrants; emigrants are primarily female, the majority are single, young ages 20-39 (41%), below 15 years (21%), a third completed tertiary education and up, and most were not employed before emigration (OECD/Scalabrini Migration Center 2017).

Migration to the U.S. is linked to historical factors, such as when the Philippines, a Spanish colony since the 16th century, was ceded to the U.S. in 1898 following the Spanish-American war. The introduction to *DISRUPT 1.0. Filipina Women: Proud. Loud. Leading without a Doubt* (2015) provides a succinct summary of the socio-historical and socio-cultural factors that shaped the leadership of Filipina women leaders in the global environment.

Economic and Social Impacts of Migration

Over the past five years, the Philippines has consistently received substantial remittances from overseas Filipino workers (OFWs), a vital source of income for many Filipino households and a significant contributor to the country's economy. Remittances have shown a steady increase, driven by the strong global presence of Filipino workers in various industries, particularly in healthcare, domestic work, and construction.

From 2018 to 2023, annual remittances to the Philippines averaged around $30-35 billion, with a slight dip in 2020 due to the COVID-19 pandemic, as many OFWs faced job losses or reduced working hours. However, the following years saw a robust recovery, with remittances rebounding as economies reopened and demand for overseas labor surged. In 2022, remittances reached P1.9 trillion, about 8.9% of the Philippines' GDP. The Asian Bankers Association estimates that unofficial remittances, including illegal ones, could be 30–40% higher than the official figure.

In 2021, the Philippines' primary sources for remittances were the United States, Saudi Arabia, Canada, the United Arab Emirates, and Australia. The continued growth of remittances underscores the resilience of Filipino workers abroad and the critical role these funds play in supporting families and driving domestic consumption in the Philippines. (Statista, 2024).[6]

Personal remittances comprise personal transfers and compensation of employees. Personal transfers include all current transfers between resident and nonresident individuals. At the same time, the compensation of employees refers to the income of employees employed in an economy where they are not resident, as well as of resident employees employed by nonresident entities.

Remittances have been used for housing renovation or construction, schooling of children and relatives, scholarships, and business startups that generate employment. Undoubtedly, migration has contributed to the Philippines' economic growth, poverty reduction, skill development, knowledge transfer, educational opportunities, cultural exchange, global networks, and community development. However, the negative impacts include brain drain, family separation and children left behind, dependency on remittances, social costs, community disruption, and impact on children's development (Asis, 2006; Graham, 2011; Dominguez, 2022).

The narrative has shifted from the Philippines' longstanding labor migration to incorporating migration into long-term development planning and strategizing the return and reintegration of overseas Filipinos (Asis, 2017). Mina Roces (2021) focuses on Filipino migrants as global change agents, refusing to be marginal.

DISRUPT 5.0. Filipina Women. Leading with Intersectionality

Filipina women rose to leadership positions not only in the Philippines but also in the diaspora. As part of the strategy of FWN to recognize Filipina woman leaders in the global environment, FWN first established the US FWN100™ awards and, in 2013, the Global FWN100™ awards. About 165 awardees shared their leadership stories in the DISRUPT books published by FWN. The books celebrate Filipina women leaders who have had an impact beyond the boundaries of the Philippines. The FWN books aim to make the stories of women leaders accessible to next-generation leaders while contributing to the scholarship on women and leadership.

---

6   Statista. (2024). Annual value of incoming personal remittances in Philippines 2000-2023. https://www.statista.com/statistics/880780/philippines-value-of-remittances/

In January 2024, the Filipina Women's Network (FWN) called for abstracts on the theme of *Filipina Women: Leading with Intersectionality*. Of those who responded to the call, Global FWN100™ awardees shared their leadership stories about overcoming crucibles, becoming champions, navigating glocal leadership, and building legacies. The women authors reside in the Philippines, Canada, Japan, Switzerland, the UK, and the United States. Several maintain two homes, one in the Philippines and one in their adopted countries.

The DISRUPT Book Series

DISRUPT 5.0: Filipina Women Leading with Intersectionality weaves the individual realities and lived experiences of Filipina women leaders that are shaped by many intersecting factors, including race, class, gender, sexual orientation, religion, ability, and other markers of difference. Intersectionality recognizes that multiple, overlapping identities shape individuals and groups, influencing their worldviews, perspectives, and societal relationships. Through the lens of intersectionality, this book sheds light on the complex kaleidoscope of leadership, challenging conventional narratives and inspiring a new generation of globally engaged leaders. It serves as a testament to the resilient spirit of Filipina women, their steadfast dedication to social justice, and their power to challenge the status quo, forging a brighter future wherever they are in the world.

DISRUPT 4.0. Filipina Women: Being is the fourth book in a series on leadership by the Filipina Women's Network (FWN). The purpose of this 4th FWN leadership book is to reflect on her trajectory to BEING who she is now – a global Filipina woman leader demonstrating leadership in her profession or industry in the global workplace and community. The chapters are first-person narratives reflecting on personal and professional lives as a Filipina woman leader in her home country, as an expatriate, or as a migrant; first, a second or third-generation immigrant who is exercising leadership in the diaspora. The themes that will bind the chapters together are being a Filipina woman leader in the Philippines or her new home country overseas, her experience in migration, personal and professional development, and leadership challenges and successes. The narratives will highlight liberation, transformation, and changes that lead to social and economic changes.

DISRUPT 3.0. Filipina Women: Rising celebrates Filipina women who have emerged as global leaders despite varying levels of challenges. Some challenges were major setbacks while other challenges were minor. The same challenge was viewed as a failure by some and only an inconvenience by others. Filipina women discuss their responses to challenges and actions that led to success. They discuss the significance of their success and the implications of their leadership for their *kapwa tao* [fellow humans]. The readiness for the global leadership of Filipina Women Leaders consists of the dimensions of global competence identified by Hunter and Hunter (2018). These leaders are self-aware, open-minded, attentive to diversity, and risk takers; these leaders balance historical perspectives with global awareness, demonstrate intercultural capability, and collaborate across cultures. These leaders demonstrate their character strengths in virtues that are common across cultures (Patterson & Seligman, 2004). These are humanity, transcendence, wisdom, courage, temperance, and justice

DISRUPT 2.0. Filipina Women: Daring to Lead (2016) is an affirmation of the

leadership competencies of Filipina women leaders (FWL) with a global mindset. The global FWL referenced competencies that were relevant in various global settings. Using the "Benchmarks by Design" (Center for Creative Leadership (CCL, 2015)[7], the competencies can be organized into (1) Leading yourself – Filipina women leaders showed an awareness of their strengths and the capacity to adapt, learn, and cope in both the Philippines and in international environments; (2) Leading others – Filipina women leaders have shown that effectively leading others could be done as part of a team or as part of an organization; (3) Leading the organization – The Filipina women leaders have carried out their leadership roles for setting vision and direction, building commitment, and creating alignment.

DISRUPT 1.0. Filipina Women: Proud. Loud. Leading without a Doubt (2015) contributed significantly to redefining how Filipina women in the diaspora are perceived. The themes articulated by Filipina women in their leadership stories in *DISRUPT 1.0* concern the **how** and **why** of leadership that make up their leadership repertoires (Beebe, 2017)[8]. The **how** of leadership consisted of actions that emphasized

---

7   Center for Creative Leadership (CCL). (2015). Benchmarks by design. https://www.ccl.org/leadership-solutions/leadership-development-tools/leadership-assessments/benchmarks-360-assessments/

8   Beebe, M. (2017). DISRUPT 1.0. Filipina Women: Proud. Loud. Leading without a Doubt. Filipino Women's Network. CreateSpace Independent Publishing Platform. ISBN

the centrality of relationships, the significance of values, and self-transcendence. The **why** of leadership for most women referenced finding purpose and meaning in life, achieving impact in their work, and giving back to their local communities. At the center of their leadership repertoires is the Philippine cultural value, *kapwa*. Translations for *kapwa* include "shared humanity," "unity of the self and the others," "shared inner self," and "together with the person." *Kapwa* is the core value that guides all forms of interpersonal relations and social interaction among Filipinos. Therefore, it stands to reason that *kapwa* would play a central role in their leadership, resulting from human interaction and negotiations.

DISRUPT 5.0. **Book Organization**

DISRUPT 5.0. Filipina Women: Leading with Intersectionality has first-person narratives organized into four sections:

Crucibles come in various forms: a life-threatening diagnosis, a profound reversal like the death of a loved one, a period of suspension such as unemployment or graduate school, or the challenge of navigating new territory like an overseas assignment. Much like a crucible that refines metals under extreme heat, these experiences—though often hostile and identity-challenging—produce "gold" in the form of stronger, wiser identities. Rather than dissolving under pressure, the Filipina women leaders draw strength from their trials, challenging and refining their sense of identity. The authors share several critical incidents, focusing on particularly impactful early experiences.

Champions are more than just advocates; they are passionate and dedicated individuals who fight tirelessly for a cause or on behalf of others. These people stand up, often in the face of adversity, to drive change and support those who may not have the power or platform to do so themselves. Champions are not merely supporters; they are leaders who use their influence, voice, and resources to amplify the needs and rights of others.

Glocal leaders drive teams to achieve common goals by challenging the status quo, fostering creativity, and sparking innovation. They recognize that local efforts can have a global impact, and global trends can shape local strategies. This "glocal" mindset is crucial in cultivating leadership that bridges local action with global significance, leading to an enhanced social footprint. Glocal engagement refers to the intentional engagement with people, communities, cultures, and institutions beyond one's borders, fostering a deeper understanding of the complexities and interconnections that shape our world.

Building legacies is about creating a lasting and positive impact that extends beyond a leader's life, touching the lives of friends, colleagues, and even strangers. It is the culmination of a leader's personal values, achievements, and actions that leave an enduring mark on the world and resonate with those around a leader. A legacy is not merely about what leaders accomplish but how they live life—the principles they uphold, the kindness they show, and how they inspire and empower others. Filipina women leaders who build legacies mean living a life that contributes to the greater good, inspiring others to carry forward the values and ideals they cherish, and leaving behind a better world.

A **Synthesis** highlights the leading with intersectionality themes of being **Filipina**, being **Filipina women**, and being **Filipina women leaders**. Each influential Filipina shares her life experiences, considering the complex, intersecting identities of her leadership and those she leads. Their narratives emphasize the importance of understanding how race, gender, class, and other identities influence leadership styles, access to leadership opportunities, and their challenges as leaders. By applying an intersectional lens, leadership theories and practices could better reflect the realities of a diverse workforce and society, leading to more equitable and effective leadership.

Moreover, the book celebrates excellence by featuring stories of FWN's lifetime members, providing updates on the global achievements of recent awardees, and highlighting significant milestones of the Filipina Women's Network.

MARILY MONDEJAR

Founder and CEO, Foundation for Filipina Women's Network

Image Consultant, Institute for Image Management

Filipina Women Leaders: Disrupting Stereotypes

"In *Filipina Women Leaders: Disrupting Stereotypes,* Marily Mondejar boldly showcases how Filipina women shatter societal expectations through dynamic, intersectional leadership. Drawing on the rich experiences shaped by their identities—gender, ethnicity, class—these women break free from limiting norms to lead with power and purpose. As Kimberlé Crenshaw's concept of intersectionality reveals, Filipina women face unique and complex layers of privilege and oppression, both in the Philippines and around the globe.

Marily highlights the cultural pressures Filipina women encounter, particularly the stereotypes tied to traditional gender roles like self-sacrifice and domesticity. Yet, trailblazing leaders such as Corazon Aquino and Leni Robredo have smashed these molds, rising to the highest political offices and proving that Filipina women are more than capable of leading on the global stage. In the corporate world, the "bamboo ceiling" remains a formidable challenge, but women like Cora

Tellez and Sheila Lirio Marcelo have shattered that barrier, carving out powerful positions in male-dominated industries and defying expectations that seek to keep them invisible.

In fact, it was my own experience as a leader in the business world that led me to the Filipina Women's Network as I was navigating the male dominated industry of Food and Consumer Packaged Goods. After meeting Marily and understanding her vision for FWN, I became more involved later serving on the board from 2013 to 2018 as President and supporting the work of the organization as an Advisory Board Member.

Marily also uncovers the struggles faced by Filipina women working abroad, especially Overseas Filipino Workers (OFWs), who grapple with layers of discrimination rooted in gender, class, and nationality. Yet, even in the face of adversity, these women assert their strength, advocating for labor rights and challenging the global narrative that seeks to diminish their power.

Through an intersectional feminist lens, Marily shines a light on how Filipina women are not just breaking stereotypes but also leading the charge for broader social justice. From battling gender-based violence to championing labor rights, the Filipina Women's Network (FWN), led by Marily, is a force to be reckoned with. By dismantling stereotypes and recognizing the power in their multifaceted identities, Filipina women are rewriting the rules of leadership, inspiring change, and showing the world that intersectionality is their strength.

Susie Quesada
President, Ramar Foods
FWN President (2013-2018)

Introduction

As a Filipina woman deeply involved in the fight for equality and justice, I've witnessed firsthand the power of intersectionality in our lives and leadership. Our story is one of resilience, innovation, and transformative change. I want to share my thoughts on how we, as Filipina women, navigate the complex intersections of gender, ethnicity, class, and other social categories across the global diaspora.

Intersectionality is not just a concept—it's the reality we live every day. It shapes our experiences by helping us understand how different systems of privilege and oppression overlap. By embracing an intersectional approach, we're addressing our unique challenges and paving the way for more inclusive leadership across all sectors of society.

It's important to note that our understanding of intersectionality varies widely depending on where we are, our education, and our exposure to these concepts. I've seen this variation firsthand in my interactions with Filipina women from all walks of life, from the bustling streets of Manila to the diverse communities of the Filipino diaspora.

Understanding Intersectionality: A Filipina Woman's Perspective

While Kimberlé Crenshaw coined the term "intersectionality" in 1989, I've realized that Filipina women have long lived the experiences it describes. However, how we articulate and apply this concept varies greatly.

Judith Martinez, the founder of InHerShoes Inc. and an award-winning leader in intersectional social impact, stated:

"There is intersectionality in everyone's story. The fabric of our identities consists of intersecting shades of meaning from the past, realities of the present, and hopes for the future. In my quest for clarity about my own identity, I've discovered a deepened understanding that Asian Americans are not a monolith. No culture is. Ethnic and racial identity is a social construct, often defined by what meaning an individual brings to it."[9]

On the other hand, when I spoke with Filipina women in the Philippines, many weren't familiar with the term "intersectionality." Still, they understood the overlapping systems of oppression embedded in their everyday lives.

---

9   Filipina Women Leaders: Disrupting Stereotypes
Martinez, J. (October 2020). *When Words Create Worlds - Celebrating Intersectionality In Filipino American History Month.* Forbes. https://www.forbes.com/sites/civicnation/2020/10/26/when-words-create-worldscelebrating-intersectionality-in-filipino-american-history-month

Dr. Kristine Aquino, sociologist and urban ethnographer, explained how these women are often compelled to see themselves "through the eyes of others" and "through the revelation of the other world," a struggle that is both tangible and ongoing. She further pointed out:

> "Everyday racism is negotiated across different temporal and spatial contexts and through varying identity struggles... depending on the intersections of race, gender, and class."[10][11]

This varying level of familiarity presents challenges and opportunities as we work towards social justice and equality.

My Experiences in Different Countries

Through my travels and conversations with Filipina women worldwide, I've observed how our understanding and application of intersectionality differ based on where we are:

- ☐ **Filipina Americans** like me often lead the way in articulating our intersectional experiences, constantly balancing our Filipino cultural heritage with American social dynamics.

- ☐ **Filipina women in the Middle East** navigate complex intersections of gender, class, and nationality within the context of labor migration.

- ☐ **Filipina women in Europe** grapple with issues of race and cultural identity in predominantly white societies.

The International Labour Office's working paper titled *Philippines: Good Practices for the Protection of Filipino Women Migrant Workers in Vulnerable Jobs* clearly shows how deeply entrenched the challenges are for Filipina women. This paper underscores a harsh reality:

10   Aquino, K. (2017). Racism and resistance among the Filipino diaspora: Everyday anti-racism in Australia. Routledge. https://www.routledge.com/Racism-and-Resistance-among-the-Filipino-Diaspora-Everyday-Anti-racism-in-Australia/Aquino/p/book/9780367787219?srsltid=AfmBOopbop7ltXxILu-E37b_2JeofUuktqh8wyGBeDScu9J-wxHnqFrO.

11   Power, J. (2021). Everyday racism is real, and the research says it makes people unhappy and sick. Sydney Morning Hub. https://www.smh.com.au/national/everyday-racism-is-real-and-the-research-says-it-makes-people-unhappy-and-sick-20210624-p583y4.html

"Gender-based discrimination intersects with discrimination based on other forms of 'otherness'—such as non-national status, race, ethnicity, religion, economic status—placing women migrants in situations of double, triple, or even fourfold discrimination, disadvantage or vulnerability to exploitation and abuse."12

Intersectionality magnifies Filipina women's vulnerability, exposing them to layers of prejudice and exploitation that demand urgent attention and action.

The Origins of Intersectionality and Its Relevance to Filipina Women

Kimberlé Crenshaw's work on intersectionality, while not specifically about Filipina women, offers a powerful framework for understanding our experiences, especially regarding violence against women.

I remember attending workshops where Crenshaw's ideas were discussed. Her explanation resonated deeply with me:

"Intersectionality is a lens through which you can see where power comes and collides, where it interlocks and intersects. It's not simply that there's a race problem here, a gender problem there, and a class or LGBTQ problem. That framework often erases what happens to people subject to all of these things."13

"How we imagine discrimination or disempowerment often is more complicated for people subjected to multiple forms of exclusion. The good news is that intersectionality allows us to see it. We might have to broaden our scope of how we think about where women are vulnerable because different things make different women vulnerable."14

---

12   Villalba, Maria Angela Mayan C. Philippines: Good practices for the protection of Filipino women migrant workers in vulnerable jobs. No. 993662193402676. International Labour Organization, 2002.

13   Crenshaw, K. (2019). "Reach everyone on the planet….": Kimberlé Crenshaw and intersectionality. Gunda Werner Institute in the Heinrich Böll Foundation and the Center for Intersectional Justice (CJI). https://doi.org/10.25530/03552.11.

14   Crenshaw, K. (2013). Mapping the margins: Intersectionality, identity politics, and violence against women of color. The public nature of private violence. Routledge, 93-118. https://www.jstor.org/stable/1229039

Although Eve Ensler didn't originate the concept of intersectionality, her work has significantly contributed to raising awareness about violence against women through this lens.

I was struck by a passage in her book *"Insecure at Last: Losing It in Our Security-Obsessed World,"* which perfectly captures the intersectional nature of our experiences with oppression and violence. I vividly recall watching her TED Talk and being deeply moved by her words:

> *"I have traveled to more than 40 countries and met women and men*
> *who, through various circumstances – war, poverty, racism, multiple*
> *forms of violence – have never known security or have had the illusion*
> *of security forever devastated."*15

This statement perfectly captures the intersectional nature of our experiences with oppression and violence.

Relevance to My Experience as a Filipina Woman

Applying an intersectional lens to issues of violence against women in the Philippines has helped us develop more nuanced and effective strategies for prevention and support. I've come to realize that our experiences of violence are shaped not only by our gender but also by factors such as class, ethnicity, religion, and geographic location.

The intersectional framework developed by Crenshaw and the awareness raised by activists like Ensler have been invaluable tools for understanding and addressing the complex challenges we face in the diaspora.

This framework is particularly relevant when examining the experiences of Filipina migrants, especially the tension between traditional gender roles and the economic realities that drive Filipina women to migrate. As explored in *The Force of Domesticity: Filipina Migrants and Globalization* by Rhacel Salazar Parreñas, she explained:

> *"The Philippines sends mixed messages to women. It tells women to*
> *work outside the home, but at the same time, it maintains the belief*
> *that women's proper place is inside the home... In the migration process,*

---

15   Ensler. E. (July 2005). What security means to me. TED Talks. https://www.ted.com/talks/eve_ensler_what_security_means_to_me

*actions and institutions constitute and reconstitute the ideology of domesticity. Migrant women, as they face a segregated labor market, often perform the ideology of women's domesticity at work."*16

The powerful insight shared by Tria Marie Garcia, a Master of Science in International Development Studies, highlighted the cultural conditioning that shapes the global perception of Filipina women:

> *"In the Philippine culture, the caring roles of women are attributed to being self-sacrificial and altruistic. The silent and non-complaining ideal of a Filipino woman is one of the reasons Filipino women are model domestic and care workers around the world.*
>
> *This sacrificial and altruistic stereotype of Filipino women supports household and national economies. [Yet] these women stay silent about experiencing Violence Against Women (VAW) abroad because they fear being blamed or stigmatized and bringing shame into their family."*17

By applying an intersectional lens to issues of violence against women in the Philippines, we've been able to develop more nuanced and effective strategies for prevention and support. We now recognize that our experiences of violence are shaped not only by our gender but also by factors such as class, ethnicity, religion, and geographic location.

Our Filipino Context: History and Culture

To truly understand our intersectional experiences as Filipina women, we must look at our historical and cultural context. Our colonial past, religious influences, economic factors, and cultural norms have all shaped who we are today.

In *Filipino American Psychology: A Handbook of Theory, Research, and Clinical Practice*, Kevin Nadal highlights the paradox of Filipino-Americans being both highly populous and largely overlooked. Despite being the second-largest Asian American and Pacific Islander group in the U.S., they often find themselves marginalized and forgotten.

---

16   Parreñas, R.S. (2008). The force of domesticity: Filipina migrants and globalization. NYU Press. https://www.jstor.org/stable/j.ctt9qghg8.

17   Garcia, Tria Marie Rodriguez. "Violence against women in the Philippines." Master's thesis, Norwegian University of Life Sciences, Ås, 2020.

Nadal elaborates on the distinct identity of Filipino-Americans, shaped by over three centuries of Spanish and nearly 50 years of U.S. colonization. He describes them as "an ethnic group with a sociocultural and historical experience unlike any other."[18] Yet, despite this multifaceted identity, California state laws mandate that they be categorized separately as "Filipino."

This distinctiveness is frequently overlooked, leading to their unfortunate label as the "Forgotten Asian Americans." Nadal poignantly remarks on their "invisible presence in psychology, education, humanities, and other social sciences,"[19] emphasizing the profound underrepresentation and erasure of their contributions to American society.

This theme of colonial identity extends into other areas of research as well. I explored Almond Aguila's work on Filipino diasporic identity, which delves into the ongoing struggle for self-understanding among many Filipina women. Aguila discusses how complex influences and the lingering impacts of colonialism shape this search for identity. She observes:

> *"Tracing the evolution of Filipinoness, I argue that colonialism still influences our identity-making efforts... Diasporic Filipinos renegotiate cultural identities in the in-between of both worlds [host's culture and Filipino culture]. Constantly in flux are identities created through community building across time and space."[20]*

In my work and personal life, I've seen how these key factors influence our intersectional experiences:

- ☐ **Colonial History:** The impacts of Spanish (1565-1898) and American (1898-1946) rule still echo in our society today.

- ☐ **Religion:** Our predominantly Catholic faith, intertwined with indigenous beliefs, shapes our values and societal norms.

---

18   Nadal, K.L. (2020). Filipino American psychology: A handbook of theory, research, and clinical practice. John Wiley & Sons. https://doi.org/10.1002/9781118094747

19   Ibid.

20   Aguila, A.N. (2015). The Filipino, Diaspora and a Continuing Quest for Identity. University of the Philippine Diliman, 11(2). https://journals.upd.edu.ph/index.php/socialsciencediliman/article/view/4798

☐ **Economic Factors:** High poverty rates and labor migration significantly impact our life choices and opportunities.

☐ **Cultural Norms:** Strong family ties and communal values often intersect with our individual aspirations and societal expectations.

Dr. Linda Lumayag, a Filipina sociologist, posed questions that stuck with me:

> *"Why does international migration in the Philippines have a woman's face? Why is there a demand for Filipino domestic maids? Why is the aspect of gender-relevant in understanding the whole issue of migration and its role in developing strategies and practical actions to counter the deepening exploitation of women involved in the migration process?"[21]*

Her words perfectly capture the intersectional nature of the choices many of us face.

Profiles of Filipina Women as Intersectional Leaders

Throughout my journey, I've had the privilege of meeting and working with many Filipina women who apply intersectional approaches to their work and activism. Their stories inspire me daily.

Dr. Fatima Bustos-Choy, who has over thirty years of corporate, business management, organizational and leadership development consulting, said:

> *"From my own experience as an organizational development and leadership consultant for twenty-five years, I have seen fellow Filipino American men and women who are highly educated, hardworking, qualified, and intelligent, lag behind other Asian Americans in attaining management positions in corporate organizations.*
>
> *When asked about their career aspirations, many expressed their desires to move up in their organizations but said they felt less qualified and not ready—though by objective measure they were qualified. Others feared*

---

21   Lumayag, L. A lonely journey: Struggles of Filipino domestic worker in Malaysia. University Putra Malaysia: Institute for Community and Peace Studies and Women's Studies Unit. http://www.malrep.uum.edu.my/rep/Record/my.upm.eprints.30875.

their families would suffer were they to take on demanding careers, and there are those who simply settled for lesser positions or gave up."[22]

This situation was disconcerting, particularly among Filipino American women who felt the double-edged sword of being "contingently visible, as overseas contract workers, mail order brides and objects of a sexist ideology, yet remain[ing] invisible as subjects and agents,[23]" a concept drawn from Melinda L. de Jesús's work in Pinay Power: Peminist Critical Theory.

As the founder of the Filipina Women's Network (FWN), I've made it my mission to ensure that our organization's programming is focused on intersectionality. At FWN, we recognize that Filipina women face unique challenges that come from the intersection of our gender, ethnicity, and often our status as immigrants or children of immigrants.

The powerful words of Beverly Sarza, Professor of Philosophy at De La Salle University, resonates with me:

"This is the main point of intersectionality. Since the effects of discrimination are deeply embedded, intersectional feminism instigates an analysis that shall consider the multifaceted roots of discrimination. Systems of oppression continue to thrive up to this day precisely because these marginal aspects, such as race and gender, remain."[24]

These women and many others show us how an intersectional approach can be applied in various fields, from academia to activism to business leadership.

---

22   Bustos-Choy, F. (2009). Narratives on the impact of colonialism on the lives of modern-day Filipino American women in the workplace. California Institute of Integral Studies. http://rizalls.lib.admu.edu.ph:8080/proquestfil/3354490.pdf.

23   De Jesus, M.L. (2005). Pinay power, peminist critical theory: theorizing the Filipina/American experience. Psychology Press. https://catalogue.nla.gov.au/catalog/3562448.

24   Sarza, B. (2021). "Babae on Bikes: Intersectional Feminism and Public Policy in the Philippines." DLSU Research Congress. https://www.scribd.com/document/695026779/Babae-on-Bikes-Intersectional-Feminism-and-Public-Policy-in-the-Philippines

Our Sisters in Global Contexts: Challenges and Contributions

As a Filipina woman, I'm proud of the diverse and complex stories we share, whether as mail-order brides, Overseas Filipino Workers (OFWs), nurses, caregivers, doctors, entrepreneurs, or professionals.

Mail Order Brides: Navigating Stereotypes and Agency

The "mail-order bride" phenomenon is close to my heart. I've worked with many women labeled this way, and their stories are far more nuanced than the stereotype suggests.

In her compelling academic article *Mail Order Brides: Choice or Constraint,* Hannah Middle critically examines the complex motivations behind the decision to become a mail-order bride. She argues that these brides represent a "survival circuit," highlighting how they send remittances back to family members or friends in the Philippines. As Middle explains:

> *"Feminization of survival is increasing, as women's labor becomes imperative to the household due to growing male unemployment because of deindustrialization, globalization, and mechanization. Therefore, choosing to be a mail-order bride is an opportunity (albeit one born out of desperation) to gain profit, make a living, and escape poverty."* [25]

Middle's analysis reveals the harsh economic realities driving Filipina women, turning what might seem like a choice into a survival strategy in the face of systemic challenges.

Merzamie Sison Cagaitan, a scholar in Language and Literature who has also written about this issue, elaborated:

> *"When viewed through the lens of Intersectionality, it becomes even easier to understand how social constructs like the Filipino marriage migrants' race, class, and gender coalesce to produce situations of heightened vulnerability to violence for "Oriental Girls" who stay in and venture outside of Asia.*

---

25   Middle, H. (2020). Mail Order Brides: Choice or Constraint? Critical Reflections: A Student Journal on Contemporary Sociological Issues. Leeds Becket University. https://ojs. leedsbeckett.ac.uk/index.php/SOC/article/view/4602

I wish to inspire readers (who may or may not have ties to the marriage market or mail-order bride industry) to reflect on how they are nevertheless implicated in a conversation about bondage and liberation. I use "bondage" in terms of being tied to categories like race, class, and gender and "liberation" in terms of being able to break from narrative conventions that tie us down to fixed notions of the aforementioned social constructs of race, class, and gender."26

I've seen firsthand the challenges these women face, from stereotyping and objectification to vulnerability to domestic abuse. But I've also witnessed incredible resilience and agency. I've been honored to work with members of the Filipina Women's Network and the leaders of organizations like GABRIELA, V-Day, One Billion Rising, San Francisco Domestic Violence Consortium, and domestic violence agencies and shelters, especially in San Francisco, providing crucial support and advocacy for Filipina women.

Our OFW Sisters: Labor Migration and Family Separation

The stories of our Overseas Filipino Worker (OFW) sisters, particularly those in Europe and the Middle East, deeply resonate with me. Their experiences reveal how the portrayal of them as selfless migrant saviors often conceals the exploitation they endure, shedding light on the harsh realities of gender, class, nationality, and religious discrimination in Filipino migration.

Dr. Rodriguez, US FWN100 2009, whose work on Filipino migration I deeply admire, once said:

"The state has produced a discourse of "migrant heroism" representing overseas workers, particularly women migrants, as self-sacrificing, nationalist martyrs to normalize migration and migrants' faithful

---

26   Cagaitan, Merzamie Sison. "Behind the veils of industry: Contesting the victim discourse surrounding Filipino mail-order brides." The McNair Scholars Journal of the University of Washington 15, 2013.

remittance-sending to the homeland. At the same time, it produces discourses of Filipinas as having distinctive racialized and gendered characteristics, making them desirable forms of labor for foreign employers."27

I've seen the toll this takes—the vulnerability to abuse, the limited legal protections, the emotional cost of family separation. But I've also seen remarkable resilience and leadership. I think of Terry, a housemaid who moved to Dubai in 2012. She once said:

"Every Filipino here has problems regarding their family back home. So, we need to fight, fight, and fight for the future of our kids. You must be strong and patient. See, you're looking at us now, and we're all smiling and laughing, but on the inside, we are in deep pain, all of us. It's so difficult for us to see a future for our kids with our lives back home, so we are here to make sure that they have one."28

Our Nurses: Unsung Heroes of the Global Pandemic

As a Filipina woman, I've always been proud of our nurses' contributions to global healthcare. The COVID-19 pandemic only heightened this pride, exposing the challenges they face.

Dr. Catherine Ceniza Choy, whose book *"Empire of Care"* I often recommend, shared an insight that resonated deeply with me:

"Filipino Nurses in the U.S. are concentrated specifically in in-patient critical care services... Many of them are also caregivers at home, not only of children but also their parents and other elders. And so, part of the problem with the pandemic is these multiple layers of vulnerability and exposure."29

---

27   Rodriguez, R.M. (2017). Domestic insecurities: Female migration from the Philippines, development and national subject-status. University of California. https://ccis.ucsd.edu/_files/wp114.pdf

28   Terry is featured by Saleh, Zeina, "The Satwa Diaries: Dubai's Filipino Domestic Workers," Artefact Magazine, March 18, 2022, https://www.artefactmagazine.com/2022/03/18/the-satwa-diaries-dubais-filipino-domestic-workers/

29   Choy, C.C. (2003). Empire of care: Nursing and migration in Filipino American

I think of Zenei Triunfo-Cortez, RN (Global FWN100™ 2014), the first Filipina woman co-president of (NNU) National Nurses United, the largest U.S. union and professional association of registered nurses, and as the President of the California Nurses Association/National Nurses Organizing Committee (the state affiliate of NNU). Her words capture the complexity of their experience:

> *"Culturally, we don't complain. We do not question authority," Cortez said. Many Filipino Nurses feel a strong sense of group loyalty, or the importance of putting the welfare of the group over that of the individual; in Tagalog, the word is pakikisama. "We are so passionate about our profession and what we do, sometimes to the point of forgetting about our own welfare," she said. "We treat our patients like they are our own family."30*

Our Caregivers: The Global Care Chain

Our Filipina women caregivers form a significant part of the global care workforce. Their stories are often invisible, yet they're crucial to families worldwide. They are vital links in the global care chain, providing essential care in wealthier countries while being separated from their own families.

This separation creates a "care deficit" in their home communities, as Dr. Rhacel Parreñas discusses in her book *Servants of Globalization: Migration and Domestic Work*. The situation highlights global inequalities in the value and distribution of care work, where Filipina caregivers' labor is critical abroad but leaves gaps in care back home.

This exploitative dynamic is further critiqued in *Global Woman: Nannies, Maids, and Sex Workers in the New Economy* by Arlie Russell Hochschild and Barbara Ehrenreich. They argue that the economic disparities between wealthy and impoverished nations drive the demand for female migrant labor, particularly in caregiving roles.

---

history. Duke University Press, 272. https://doi.org/10.2307/j.ctv11hpnv7

30   Featured by Lee McFarling, Usha, "Nursing ranks are filled with Filipino Americans. The pandemic is taking an outsized toll on them," STAT, April 18, 2020, https://www.statnews.com/2020/04/28/coronavirus-taking-outsized-toll-on-filipino-american-nurses/

This system not only exploits these women but also deepens emotional and familial fractures in their home countries as they sacrifice their own family lives to care for others, highlighting the human cost of global inequalities.

I've seen the toll of emotional labor, the precarious work conditions, and the challenges of transnational motherhood. But I've also seen how many of our sisters have found ways to transform these experiences into sources of empowerment. I think of Edelyn, a caregiver in Canada, who said:

> *"The airport represents your dream for your family. Leaving the Philippines, even though it is hard for you to leave your family back home, you are going to other countries to give them a better life. We come to Canada as a caregiver; we have our profession; we have our abilities. In Canada, we can improve our skills rather than being deskilled."[31]*

Our Survivors: Resilience in the Face of Domestic Violence

Domestic violence is a critical issue that affects many of our sisters in diaspora communities. As a domestic violence survivor who has worked with many survivors, I've come to recognize the necessity of an intersectional approach to addressing this complex problem.

Ma. Alcestis Abrera-Mangahas, Global FWN100™ 2014, the former Deputy Regional Director of ILO's Regional Office for Asia and the Pacific, discussed this intersection of violence and migration, stating:

> *"In the past two decades, the Philippines has become the largest source of women migrant workers in Asia. At the same time, the increasing evidence of exploitation and abuse of female migrant workers in the host countries has built pressure to phase out the foreign employment of women.*

---

31   Edelyn is featured by Magkaisa Centre, https://magkaisacentre.org/arts-culture/picture-in-picture/#

For many women, the home and the workplace are the same. Violence at the workplace involves incidents where women are abused, threatened, or assaulted in circumstances involving an implicit or explicit challenge to their safety, wellbeing, and health."[32]

I've seen how economic dependence, cultural expectations, immigration status, and mental health stigma all play a role in shaping our sisters' experiences of violence. But I've also witnessed incredible strength and transformation.

I think of Nena Ruiz, a human trafficking and domestic violence survivor in California. She shared:

"Fighting my trafficking case made me a stronger person. Even when my rights were violated on the job, I had the tools and the community to fight for them—and for those of the countless undocumented domestic workers who can't speak out.

At 74 years old, I am back in the Philippines and finally retired. I have remained active with the Pilipino Workers Center (PWC) to help raise awareness of workers' rights in California and human trafficking issues."[33]

Poverty: A Crucial Lens in Our Intersectional Experience

Poverty isn't just a backdrop; it's the lens through which many of us, especially Filipina women, navigate the complexities of our lives. It shapes the very choices we make, the opportunities we chase, and the obstacles we face.

Intersectionality reveals how poverty compounds the challenges of gender, race, and other identities, creating a web of oppression that is especially pronounced in a

---

32   Abrera-Mangahas, M.A. (1998). Violence against women migrant workers: The Philippine experience. International Labor Organization. https://pssc.org.ph/wp-content/pssc-archives/Philippine%20Migration%20Research%20Network/Filipino%20Workers%20on%20the%20Move_Trends,%20Dilemmas%20and%20Policy%20Options/04_Violence%20Against%20Women%20Migrant%20Workers_The%20Phil.%20Experience.pdf

33   Ruiz, N. (March 2018). I Am a Survivor of Human Trafficking: Nena's Story. The   Atlantic.   https://www.theatlantic.com/business/archive/2018/03/human-trafficking-nena/554846/

globalized world. Economic inequalities at home and abroad push many of us to seek livelihoods far from our families, enduring sacrifices that wealthier women might never have to consider.

Addressing poverty isn't just an act of charity; it's a crucial step toward genuine empowerment for Filipina women everywhere. We cannot claim to uplift our sisters if we ignore the economic forces that shape their every move.

The Challenges and Barriers We Face

Despite our progress, Filipina women continue to face numerous challenges arising from the intersection of various aspects of our identities. In my work and personal life, I've encountered these challenges time and again:

- ☐ **Gender discrimination in the workplace**: Despite high levels of education, many of us face wage gaps and limited access to leadership positions.

- ☐ **Economic disparities**: Poverty remains a significant barrier, shaping our life choices and limiting opportunities.

- ☐ **Cultural expectations and stereotypes**: These often place additional burdens on us, particularly when balancing career and family life.

- ☐ **Challenges related to migration**: Many of our sisters working overseas face exploitation and abuse, yet their remittances are crucial to the Philippine economy.

- ☐ **Racial discrimination**: Particularly for those of us living abroad, navigating racial stereotypes adds another layer of complexity to our lives.

- ☐ **Limited access to healthcare and education**: These issues are especially pressing in rural areas of the Philippines.

- ☐ **Vulnerability to various forms of violence**: Domestic violence remains a significant issue exacerbated by economic inequality and cultural norms.

Dr. Cirila Limpangog, a philosopher who focuses on Gender Studies, once observed:

> *"Intersectionality provides a complex but highly fruitful approach to understanding migrants' identity disruption, reconfiguration, and*

reassertion. I argue that the women have reasserted their multiple identities as Filipinas, immigrants, Australian citizens, and skilled workers in their dealings with workplace discrimination and violence.

These intersectional boundaries, however, are not discrete but fluctuate according to the situation, producing reworked identities within and beyond the realms of gender, race, or culture.[34]

The Challenges of Migration and Diaspora

Many of our sisters work overseas as part of the global Filipino diaspora, often in vulnerable positions such as domestic work or healthcare. The challenges they face are close to my heart.

Dr. Robyn Rodriguez, US FWN100™ 2009, whose work on Filipino migration is eye-opening, uses the term "domestic anxieties" to describe different concerns about women's migration from the Philippines. She said:

"The overriding concerns that emerged about the migration of entertainers and domestic workers were that they faced specific sets of risks given the nature of their jobs, their migration had detrimental effects on their families, and that their employment brought some degree of shame to the Philippine nation."[35]

The Persistent Issue of Violence Against Women

Violence against women remains a significant issue, often exacerbated by economic inequality and cultural norms. The words of Dr. Leila Joudane, Country Representative of the United Nations Population Fund (UNFPA) and chair of the UN GTG, stay with me:

"Violence against women is a persistent, widespread, and worsening global crisis that demands immediate action. It is rooted in structural

---

34   Limpangog, C.P. (2013). Racialised and gendered workplace discrimination: The case of skilled Filipina immigrants in Melbourne, Australia. Journal of Workplace Rights, 17(2). http://dx.doi.org/10.2190/WR.17.2.e

35   Rodriguez, Robyn M. "Domestic insecurities: Female migration from the Philippines, development and national subject-status," 2017.

injustice and fueled by a male-dominated culture that denies women equality. Together, we must invest in prevention, support survivors, end impunity, and promote women's leadership to create a world free from violence against women."[36]

8. Our Strategies for Addressing These Challenges

In the face of these challenges, we Filipina women and our allies are employing various strategies to address these intersectional issues:

- ☐ **Policy Advocacy**: Pushing for laws and policies that address our intersectional needs, such as labor protections for OFWs and support for women in leadership positions.

- ☐ **Education and Awareness**: Implementing programs to educate our communities about gender equality and intersectionality.

- ☐ **Economic Empowerment**: Creating initiatives to improve our economic status and independence.

- ☐ **Cultural Change**: Working to shift cultural norms and stereotypes about women's roles in our society.

- ☐ **Transnational Activism**: Building support and advocacy networks across our global diaspora, recognizing the global nature of many of our challenges.

At the Filipina Women's Network (FWN), I've always emphasized the importance of femtorship (female mentoring):

> *"We focus on femtoring and supporting Filipina women leaders because we understand that our success is intersectional. It's not just about individual achievement but about lifting our entire community."*

---

36   Featured in the Press Release of United Nations Philippines, "U.N. agencies, Senator Pia partner for experiential exhibit raising awareness, action vs. violence against women," December 4, 2023, https://philippines.un.org/en/254688-un-agencies-senator-pia-partner-experiential-exhibit-raising-awareness-action-vs-violence

Breaking Glass Ceilings: Filipina Women in Politics and C-Suite Positions

Our Sisters in Philippine Politics

I'm proud of the many prominent women politicians who have emerged in the Philippines, including two female presidents. These leaders navigate complex intersections of gender, politics, and cultural expectations.

Key elected and appointed figures in our political landscape include:

1. Corazon Aquino: elected first female President of the Philippines (1986-1992)

2. Gloria Macapagal-Arroyo: elected second female President of the Philippines (2001-2010)

3. Gwen Fiel Garcia, Global FWN100™ 2018: elected Governor of Cebu; former Deputy Speaker, 17th Congress of the Philippines

4. Jeannie Sandoval, Global FWN100™ 2024: elected Mayor of the City Government of Malabon

5. Leni Robredo, Global FWN100™ 2016: elected Vice President of the Philippines (2016-2022) and presidential candidate

6. Dr. Maria Sheila "Honey" Honrado Lacuna-Pangan, Global FWN100™ 2022: Mayor, City Government of Manila; first woman elected Mayor of Manila

7. Margarita Gutierrez, Global FWN100™ 2019: Justice Undersecretary, former Undersecretary for Plans, Programs, and Communication of the Department of Interior and Local Government (DILG), both appointments by President President Ferdinand Marcos, Jr.

8. Miriam Defensor Santiago: elected Senator and presidential candidate

9. Nieves R. Confesor, Global FWN100™ 2017: first woman appointed by President Corazon Aquino in 1991 to become Secretary of Labor and Employment in the Philippines and first Filipino elected as Chair of the International Labor Organization

10. Susan Mercado, Global FWN100™ 2018: Co-Chair, Philippine Climate Change Commission, former Special Envoy of President Duterte for Global Health Initiatives

11. Wilma "Amy" T. Eisma, Esq., Global FWN100™ 2017: first woman Chair & Administrator, Subic Bay Metropolitan Authority (SBMA) appointed by President Duterte; first woman President and Chief Operating Officer, Philippine Amusement and Gaming Corporation (PAGCOR) appointed by President Ferdinand Marcos, Jr.

Senator Risa Hontiveros' words resonate:

"From 1998 to 2013, there has been a steady increase in women's participation. But when compared to men, the gap is overwhelming. The political language, behavior and values of our beloved country are still beset by a culture of misogyny and sexism that belies any statistic."[37]

Our Sisters in Politics in the U.S., Canada, and Europe

I'm equally proud of our Filipina sisters, who have made significant strides in politics outside the Philippines. They navigate complex intersections of gender, ethnicity, immigration history, and local political structures.

Notable elected and appointed officials include:

1. Chief Justice Tani Cantil-Sakauye, US FWN100™ 2007: The first Asian-Filipina American and the second woman to serve as California's Chief Justice (2011-2023)

2. Cynthia Alcantara Barker, Global FWN100™ 2017: Mayor, Brookmeadow, Elstree & Borehamwood Town Council, UK; first Filipina woman elected in British local government

3. Erica Mosca: Nevada State Assemblywoman

---

37   Featured by De Guzman, L.E.P. (May 2017). Female powerhouses sound off on what it's really like to be a woman. Business World. https://www.bworldonline.com/sparkup/2017/05/30/143807/female-powerhouses-sound-off-on-what-its-really-like-to-be-a-woman/#google_vignette

4. Genevieve Mina: Arkansas State Representative

5. Hydra Mendoza, US Global FWN100™ 2009, Global FWN100™ 2013, first and only Filipina elected to office in San Francisco, elected to the San Francisco Unified School District Board of Education in 2006, 2010 and 2014, and served as President of the Board

6. Junelle Cavero: Arizona State Representative

7. Juslyn Manalo, Global FWN100™ 2015: Daly City Mayor, first Filipina woman elected to the Daly City Council

8. Kris Valderrama, US FWN100™ 2009: Maryland State Delegate

9. Luz Bay: New Hampshire Representative

10. Malia Vella, Esq.: Alameda City Council Vice Mayor

11. Maria Cervania: North Carolina State Representative; first Asian American woman elected to the North Carolina General Assembly

12. Marily Mondejar: Chair, Commission on Community Investment and Infrastructure, San Francisco

13. Myla Dela Vega Arceno, Global FWN100™ 2022: Mayor and Councillor, Stevenage, United Kingdom; first Filipina woman elected in Stevenage

14. Rachelle Sumagaysay Pastor Arizmendi, Global FWN100™ 2018: Former Mayor and City Council Member, City of Sierra Madre, California

15. Nikki Fortunato Bas, Global FWN100™ 2021: Oakland City Council President

16. Rechie Valdez, Global FWN100™ 2022: Minister of Business and Member of Parliament, House of Commons, Canada

17. Rozanna Verder-Aliga, US FWN100™ 2009: Vallejo City Councilmember

18. Sofia Asuncion Anis Aragon, Global FWN100™ 2022: Mayor, City of Burien, Washington

19. Thelma Boac, US FWN100™ 2007: Berryessa Union School District Trustee

20. Trish La Chica, Global FWN100™ 2015: Hawaii State Representative

21. Wendy Lee Ho, Global FWN100™ 2018: Board Trustee, San Jose-Evergreen Community College District Board

Our Sisters in C-Suite Positions

I'm equally inspired by our Filipina sisters who have broken the corporate glass ceilings and have reached C-Suite positions in the Philippines and internationally. These leaders navigate complex intersections of gender, ethnicity, and corporate culture.

Some of our notable women in C-Suite positions include:

1. Astrid S. Tuminez, Global FWN100™ 2013: President at Utah Valley University

2. Conchita Labao Manabat, PhD, Global FWN100™ 2018: Independent Director, The Philippine Dealing System Group of Companies

3. Cora Doris Magsaysay-Ho: President and CEO of the Magsaysay Group

4. Cora Manese Tellez, Global FWN100™ 2013: Board Chair and Founder, Sterling Health Services Administration

5. Cymbeline Tancongco Culiat, PhD, Global FWN100™ 2022: President, NellOne Therapeutics Inc.

6. Dr. Eileen Patricia De Villa, Global FWN100™ 2022: Medical Officer, Toronto Public Health, City of Toronto

7. Jenette Ramos, Global FWN100™ 2022: Member, Board of Regents Washington State University

8. Evelyn Dilsaver, US FWN100™ 2011: Former President and CEO of Charles Schwab Investment Management

9. Josephine Gotianun-Yap: President and CEO of Filinvest Development Corporation

10. June Cheryl A. Cabal-Revilla, Global FWN100™ 2023: CFO, Metro Pacific Investments Corporation

11. Lisa Gokongwei-Cheng: President of Summit Media

12. Marivic Acosta, Global FWN100™ 2018: Executive Vice President – International Marketing, Megaworld Corporation

13. Minerva Tantoco, US FWN100™ 2011: First Chief Technology Officer, City of New York; Interim Chief Executive Officer, New York Hall of Science

14. Rosemarie Rafael, Global FWN100™ 2023: Chairwoman and President, AIC Group of Companies Holding Corporation

15. Dr. Rosannette Hernandez Rimando-Chareunsap, Global FWN100™ 2022: CEO, Seattle Colleges, Washington

16. Sheila Lirio Marcelo: Co-Founder and CEO of Ohai.ai, Founder of Care. com

17. Susie Quesada, US FWN100™ 2007, Global FWN100™ 2013: President, Ramar Foods International

18. Teresita Batayola, Global FWN100™ 2019: President and CEO, International Community Health Services; Commissioner appointed by U.S. President Joe Biden to The White House Initiative on Asian Americans and Pacific Islanders

19. Tessie Sy-Coson: Vice Chairperson of S.M. Investments Corporation

I've had the privilege of meeting many of these incredible women, and their stories never fail to inspire me. I remember a conversation I had with Cora Tellez, who shared:

> *"As Filipina women in leadership positions, we're not just representing ourselves or our companies. We're often seen as representatives of our gender and our ethnicity. This intersectional identity can be both a challenge and a strength."*[38]

---

38   Spoken words by Cora Tellez, Board Chair and Founder, Sterling Health Services Administration.

Her words resonate deeply with my experiences and those of many Filipina women leaders I know. We're not just breaking the glass ceiling but navigating a complex maze of cultural, gender, and corporate expectations.

Ginger Arboleda, the young Chief Operating Officer (COO) of Taxumo, highlights the profound challenges of intersectionality, where the struggles faced by marginalized groups often stem from the lack of connection between their unique experiences and the broader industry context:

> *"When we started our tech startup in 2016, the Philippine startup scene was largely male-dominated, with few female founders. As a woman entrepreneur, I struggled to find mentors and role models who shared my experiences and perspectives. This lack of diversity and representation reflected wider cultural biases that limit women's participation and leadership in the tech industry."[39]*

These women, whether in politics or business, demonstrate the power of intersectional leadership. They navigate complex identities and systems to create change and pave the way for future Filipina women leaders.

The Next Generation: Young Filipina Leaders and Intersectionality

As I look to the future, I'm filled with hope and excitement by the emerging young Filipina women leaders. They're bringing fresh approaches to intersectionality, often leveraging technology and social media to amplify their voices and create change. Their widespread use of pronouns in their email signatures is a sign of asserting strong identity and confidence in their sexuality.

Digital Natives and Social Media Activism

I'm continually amazed by how our young leaders use social media as a tool for intersectional activism. Maria, a 24-year-old human rights activist, feminist, and abolitionist towards liberation for all, bravely shared:

---

39   Featured by Chico, S.S. (2022). Breaking Barriers: The Rise of Filipina Founders with Unshakeable Confidence. PhilDev. https://www.phildev.org/news/breaking-barriers-the-rise-of-filipina-founders-with-unshakeable-confidence/

"It is a dangerous time to be a young climate activist in the Philippines. Nonetheless, I continue to fight for gender justice, promote the importance of mental health, and raise awareness of human rights.

To do this effectively and efficiently, I use social media to campaign for the causes I am passionate about. I post about our campaigns for climate justice by pushing for renewable energy, and I also spread awareness about how fossil fuels exacerbate the impacts of the climate crisis in our country."

Although social media platforms are used to communicate climate science, campaigns, and solutions, they are also a place where trolls try to hurt people, conduct smear campaigns, and destroy movements. This is the kind of political terrain young intersectional climate justice activists are navigating – and it is very scary."[40]

Intersectionality in Education

Our leaders are also pushing for more intersectional approaches in education in the diaspora communities. Dr. Patricia Espiritu Halagao, US FWN100™ 2009, Professor and Chair of the Department of Curriculum Studies at the University of Hawai'i, shared:

"Education is not a neutral venture. It has been used to 'mis-educate' the enslaved and the colonized. Likewise, education can also be used to liberate and decolonize. With the historical legacy of colonialism, educators from formerly colonized groups have begun looking at developing curricula and pedagogy with a decolonization framework in mind to emancipate students from ignorance and to ignite a commitment to social change."[41]

40   Published by Newsweek. (August 2023). Speaking Up Became a Threat to My Survival. Newsweek. https://www.newsweek.com/speaking-became-threat-my-survival-activist-philippines-1819167

41   Halagao, P.E. (201). Liberating Filipino Americans through decolonizing curriculum. Race Ethnicity and Education, 13(4), 495-512. h ttps://doi.org/10.1080/13613324.2010.49213 2

Entrepreneurship with a Social Impact

Many of our young Filipina leaders combine entrepreneurship with social impact, creating businesses that address intersectional challenges. Women like Natalia Romagosa, a trained fashion designer and journalist inspire me. She said:

> *"I also turned to intersectionality to reflect on how the identity categories of groups that have been historically dominant or dominated have shaped the fashion field and, by default, fashion and sustainability, thus impacting who gets to be part of conversations on sustainability."[42]*

These young leaders face unique challenges, from ageism to balancing activism with educational and career pressures. But they're also optimistic about the future. As Lauren, a young member of GABRIELA in Los Angeles, expressed:

> *"As a Filipino American, you can feel disempowered about what's happening in the U.S. and back home and what our government is doing abroad. We don't have to wait for a president to make changes. Everyone has a place in the movement."[43]*

Their energy, innovative approaches, and deep understanding of intersectionality give me great hope for the future of Filipina leadership.

Intersectionality in the Global Workplace

As a Filipina professional navigating the global workplace, I have witnessed how intersectionality shapes our experiences, opportunities, and challenges. The intersection of gender, ethnicity, culture, and other identity markers significantly impacts how we are perceived, how we advance, and the barriers we face in professional settings worldwide.

---

42   Romagosa, N. (2023). Care, action, change: fashion professionals' journey to engaging with sustainability. Stockholm University. https://su.diva-portal.org/smash/record.js-f?aq2=%5B%5B%5D%5D&c=6&af=%5B%5D&searchType=LIST_LATEST&sortOrder2=ti-tle_sort_asc&query=&language=sv&pid=diva2%3A1832888&aq=%5B%5B%5D%5D&s-f=all&aqe=%5B%5D&sortOrder=author_sort_asc&onlyFullText=false&noOfRows=50&dswid=-5207

43   Featured by Su,Y. (July 2020). Meet the Filipino Women Activists of GABRIELA," Mochi Magazine. https://www.mochimag.com/activism/meet-the-filipino-women-activists-of-gabriela/

Navigating Cultural Expectations and Professional Identity

In global workplaces, especially in multicultural environments, the intersectionality of our identities as Filipina women often requires us to navigate complex cultural expectations. For instance, the perception of authority and leadership can vary widely depending on cultural norms. As Filipina women, we may be expected to conform to certain stereotypes—whether it's being seen as nurturing and supportive or as deferential and compliant.

However, I've seen how embracing our intersectional identities can also be a source of strength. By bringing our whole selves to work, we offer unique perspectives that can enrich decision-making, foster inclusivity, and drive innovation. Our ability to bridge cultural divides and our deep understanding of the complexities of identity makes us valuable contributors in any professional setting.

Challenges in Leadership and Career Advancement

Despite our talents and contributions, many Filipina women professionals still face significant challenges in climbing the corporate ladder. Intersectionality often means that we must contend with multiple layers of bias—gender, racial, and cultural— simultaneously. For example, the "bamboo ceiling" is a well-documented phenomenon in which Asian professionals, including Filipina women, are underrepresented in leadership positions despite high levels of education and competence.

In my conversations with Filipina women leaders across various industries, many have shared stories of being overlooked for promotions, facing microaggressions, or questioning their leadership styles because they don't fit the dominant, often Western, leadership paradigms. These challenges are exacerbated by the intersection of gender and race, where stereotypes about both can limit perceptions of our capabilities.

Yet, I've also been inspired by Filipina women who have broken through these barriers. Leaders like Cora Tellez, who first broke the glass ceiling in corporate America, Sheila Lirio Marcelo, the founder of Care.com, one of the first Filipino-owned companies that went public in 2014 and has since become a serial entrepreneur; and Melanie Perkins, an Australian technology entrepreneur who co-founded Canva, valued over AUD1billion, have demonstrated that it is possible to leverage our intersectional identities as strengths. They have shown that our unique blend of cultural insights, resilience, and adaptability can redefine leadership in the global workplace.

Intersectional Advocacy in the Workplace

Advocating for intersectionality in the workplace isn't just about individual advancement; it's about transforming the workplace itself. By pushing for diversity, equity, and inclusion (DEI) initiatives that recognize and address the intersectional identities of all employees, we can create environments where everyone can thrive.

I've been involved in efforts to bring intersectionality into corporate DEI programs, emphasizing that gender equality cannot be fully achieved without considering the intersections of race, ethnicity, and other identity factors. This means advocating for more comprehensive anti-discrimination policies, creating mentorship programs that support women of color, and ensuring that leadership development initiatives are accessible to those who might otherwise be marginalized.

Intersectionality becomes not just a lens through which we view our challenges but a powerful tool for systemic change. By recognizing and addressing the unique barriers that different groups face, we can move towards a workplace that truly values and leverages its people's diversity.

The Impact of Intersectionality on Our Professional Lives

Reflecting on my journey and the stories of countless Filipina women professionals, I see clearly that intersectionality is a defining feature of our professional lives. It shapes the challenges we face, the strategies we employ to overcome them, and the unique strengths we bring to the global workplace.

The impact of intersectionality on our careers is profound, but it is not a burden—it is a source of power. By embracing our entire identities and advocating for inclusive workplaces, we are not only advancing our own careers but also paving the way for future generations of Filipina women leaders. We are redefining what it means to be a leader in the global workplace, making it more inclusive, equitable, and reflective of our diverse world.

As we continue this journey, I am confident that our collective efforts will lead to a world where intersectionality is acknowledged and celebrated—where every Filipina woman professional can thrive and lead with confidence and pride.

Intersectionality and the Power of Networks

One of the most impactful strategies I've observed for overcoming these intersectional challenges is the power of networks. Professional networks, especially those that understand and value intersectionality, can provide critical support, mentorship, and opportunities for Filipina women. Organizations like the Filipina Women's Network (FWN) play a crucial role in this regard, offering a platform where Filipina women professionals can connect, share experiences, and support each other in navigating the complexities of the global workplace.

Through these networks, we can amplify our voices, advocate for more inclusive policies, and build the confidence needed to challenge the status quo. I've seen how Filipina women who might have felt isolated in their struggles found solidarity and strength through these connections, leading to career advancements and the ability to impact organizational culture in meaningful ways.

My Role as the Founder and CEO of the Filipina Women's Network

I can only talk about Filipina women's leadership by mentioning the incredible work of the Filipina Women's Network (FWN) awardees and members. FWN has been instrumental in promoting intersectional leadership among Filipina women globally. FWN's approach recognizes our diverse experiences and challenges across different contexts. Programs like the US FWN100™ and Global FWN100™ (100 Most Influential Filipina Woman in the World Award), the DISRUPT Filipina Leadership Book Series, and the Filipina Leadership Global Summit celebrate and support Filipina leaders making a difference in various fields.

FWN's intersectional approach is clear:

> *"At FWN, we understand that multiple intersecting factors shape our experiences. Our programs are designed to address these complexities, whether helping a Filipina woman executive navigate corporate culture in the U.S. or supporting a community leader tackling bias and harassment in the Philippines."*

FWN's work demonstrates how an intersectional approach can be applied to leadership development and community empowerment on a global scale. It has been incredible to see how this network has grown and impacted so many Filipina women's lives.

Our Intersectional Future

I'm filled with pride and hope about our journey as Filipina women leading with intersectionality. Our story is one of resilience, innovation, and transformative change. From our historical context of colonialism and cultural norms to the contemporary challenges faced by our OFW sisters, nurses, caregivers, and domestic violence survivors, to the achievements of our women in business, politics, and C-Suite positions, and the emerging voices of our youth leaders, we have consistently demonstrated the power of an intersectional approach to leadership and social change.

Looking to the future, I see several key areas as critical for our continued progress:

☐ **Education and Awareness**: We must expand our understanding of intersectionality in global contexts where our sisters live and work.

☐ **Policy Development**: We must create and implement policies that address our intersectional needs, from labor protections for OFWs to support for women in leadership positions.

☐ **Economic Empowerment**: We must address the root causes of economic vulnerability that underlie many of our challenges. By empowering Filipina women economically, we enable them to make choices that uplift not just their lives but the lives of their families and communities.

☐ **Global Solidarity**: We should strengthen our support and advocacy networks across our global diaspora. Recognizing the interconnected nature of our challenges will allow us to build alliances and create systemic change on a global scale.

☐ **Intergenerational Collaboration**: We must foster dialogue and collaboration between our established leaders and emerging youth voices. This will ensure both continuity and innovation in our intersectional approaches, keeping our movement dynamic and responsive to new challenges.

As I look ahead, I know our work is far from finished. But the resilience, courage, and innovation displayed by Filipina women worldwide fill me with unwavering hope. Our story is one of triumph over adversity, a testament to the strength of embracing our multifaceted identities.

I believe the future is intersectional, and it is ours to shape. By leveraging the power of our diverse experiences, we are not just breaking barriers but redefining leadership itself. We are showing the world that true leadership is inclusive, equitable, and deeply rooted in understanding the complex realities we face.

We will continue to turn our challenges into opportunities, transforming the world one intersectional step at a time. The path forward is bright, and with every step, we are paving the way for a more just and equitable world—not just for Filipina women, but for all.

So, to the next generation of Filipina women leaders, I urge you to embrace your intersections, let them guide you, and never underestimate your power. The world is watching, and together, we will disrupt the status quo, challenge stereotypes, and lead with the kind of courage that only comes from knowing who you indeed are.

I will end my narrative with this challenge:

> *Our work is about individual achievement and lifting our global community. By embracing our intersectional identities and experiences, we're not just changing our lives – we're reshaping the world's understanding of leadership and creating more inclusive, equitable societies.*

> *Our future as Filipina women leaders is intersectional, and that future is bright. Together, we will continue to navigate the complex intersections of our identities, turning challenges into opportunities and paving the way for a more just and equitable world.*

Our future is intersectional, and it is unstoppable.

CRUCIBLES

"Extraordinary leaders find meaning in - and learn from - the most negative events. Like phoenixes rising from the ashes, they emerge from adversity stronger, more confident in themselves and their purpose, and more committed to their work.

Such transformative events are called crucibles — a severe test or trial. Crucibles are intense, often traumatic — and always unplanned."

— Bennis & Thomas, Harvard Business Review (September 2022)

"The truth is that challenge is the crucible for greatness."

—Jim Kouzes and Barry Posner

CHARINA AMUNATEGUI, MBA

Executive Director, Fund Finance Business Execution, MUFG Investor Services;
Treasurer, Board of Directors, Inspiring Girls USA
Global FWN 100™ 2023

I AM ENOUGH

"*No,*" *reverberated through her mind, a chorus of fear and caution, limiting Charina's boundless curiosity. As Charina shares her leadership journey from the haphazard streets of Tondo, Manila, to the bustling cityscape of Toronto, Canada, and New York City, she reflects on the obstacles she overcame. The countless "nos" she whispered to herself, the self-doubt that gnawed at her dreams, and the anxiety disorder that clouded her path—these were the battles she fought. Yet, from doubting her place in the world of finance, wondering what business a girl from Tondo had in the high-stakes streets of New York City, to ultimately embracing her ambitions and taking charge of her leadership journey, Charina's narrative is one of resilience and triumph over self-imposed limitations, proving she is more than enough.*

Edith Winterhalter, Ed.D.
California State University, Northridge

Code Red

As I wake and open my eyes each morning, a surge of panic and dread overwhelms me. Thoughts rush through my mind as I desperately search for reasons to justify my panic and worrying thoughts. First comes the feeling of threat, that something or someone is about to harm me, and then I try to search frantically for a reason why I feel this way. I am frozen, debilitated, helpless. What threat am I facing now? I need to brace for an attack. I feel like wild dogs are chasing me. It is as if I am always under threat. Even as I try to self-soothe and tell myself there is nothing to worry about, an inner part of my mind fights me and insists that I must panic and that there must be something that I need to worry about, a threat I must contend with.

This is my daily experience on high alert waking up with an anxiety disorder – every morning is code red. Living with this disorder, my fears are pronounced, and my thoughts are blown out of proportion. Worrying thoughts feel vividly real and magnified. I feel fear and feel threatened, but I find it hard to find a reason why.

After a moment, I take a deep breath and tell myself I am fine. I am not under threat or attack; nothing terrible will happen to me now. I am, in fact, safe and warm in my home. Long before I had the tools to cope with this daily moment of dread, panic, and overwhelming fear, long before I had the wherewithal to pause and tell myself nothing would harm me, I had a long journey of transformation dating back to childhood where I formed self-limiting beliefs that **I am NOT ENOUGH; not beautiful enough, not wealthy enough and indeed not smart enough** to a road of self-discovery and seek the help I needed, to where I am now an independent, resilient career woman.

Though it might sound strange to say it, I have realized that being diagnosed with anxiety disorder was the best thing that has ever happened to me. In 2008, I began receiving treatment in Cognitive Behavior Therapy (CBT), where I harnessed the skills to challenge thoughts that were holding me back from discovering my true potential: thoughts of **deep-seated doubt, insecurity, and the fear of rejection**. At first, I actively sought out these tools as ways to cope and survive, but I later learned to leverage these tools to achieve success. I realized that leadership starts with yourself and begins with building emotional intelligence, self-awareness, and a solid relationship with the person who matters most: YOU.

Heart Palpitations & Puppy Love

I must have been about 13 years old when I started feeling constricted feelings in my chest. I could feel my heart racing, palpitating like my chest was about to explode, and my head was spinning with panic and confusion. Imagine how it would feel after drinking five cans of Red Bull. I did not know what was happening to me physically and emotionally. As my family was preparing to go through the immigration process to Canada, we had to undergo a medical exam, and the examiner noticed that my heart was racing abnormally. Many examinations followed; electrodes were attached to me for several days at a time to track my heartbeats; doctors declared I had a heart condition called mitral valve prolapse. Then began a slew of drugs to treat my heart condition Everyone around me indeed treated me as the "girl with the heart condition." That convinced me I was weak and sickly. I started to develop a view of myself that I lacked physical, psychological, and emotional strength.

Looking back and trying to remember what was happening at that age, the truth was that boys started entering the picture at this age. Since I attended an all-girls catholic school, there was little opportunity to meet boys. Our school did have some controlled, highly supervised activities with an all-boys school in the general neighborhood. I had a lot of anxiety as I worried about what it would take to be attractive to boys. I had short boy-cut hair and felt uncomfortable in my own skin. I mean, who did at that age?! The proverbial butterflies in my stomach manifested as heart palpitations and cold sweat. I was alone and had no one to share my feelings and struggles with. I recall liking this boy, but he did not reciprocate. He did not like me. I remember he called me a few times on my house landline to chat, but suddenly he stopped. I think he fancied another girl in my school. Yes, my dear friends, I was ghosted at 13, long before ghosting was a thing. The New York Times says ghosting is "when someone cuts off all communication without explanation." While this behavior may now be the norm, and some would say it's a way of life when dating in New York City, where I now reside, my 13-year-old self was wounded and scarred! I was utterly devastated, and I immediately jumped to the conclusion that he must not like me because I was fat, ugly, and not good enough. The heart palpitations are now exacerbated by uncontrollable tears and rising feelings of rejection, which was not a good combo. It was the eighties in the Philippines; if you were not 4'11" and weighed less than 100 lbs (I was neither), you were considered 'fat.' Rejection is a salty bitch. It still stings thinking about it over 30 years later as I write this. I had to be nudged by a friend to write about this experience. My first reaction when my friend brought it up was that there was no way I would want people to know this about me. I was willing to talk about any other experience of rejection in life, except this one! Pick something else, I said! My first experience with rejection at 13 is out of bounds! If only I could go back and tell my 13-year-old self not to sweat it; that one day, I would gain all the confidence needed to overcome much bigger dilemmas. I allowed this young boy's rejection of me to shape my views of myself, and for that, I feel a tremendous amount of regret.

13 Going on 30

It was not until decades later that I discovered the heart prognosis was inaccurate. I was 30 years old when I learned that I suffered from Generalized Anxiety Disorder (GAD) and had no heart ailment whatsoever. I lived in Canada then, working long hours at the office in a stressful role as I amassed managerial duties. I woke early in the morning at home in my apartment in Toronto. I was alone. I could feel this heaviness in my chest as if a heavy weight was on top of me. My thoughts were racing. I was confused about what was happening. Every breath was difficult. I was wondering if this is what it feels like to have a heart attack. At first, I refused even to consider getting help; I was afraid that paramedics would think I was being dramatic. I doubted my worthiness in seeking the help I needed. I did not want to call for help because I was worried that I was wrong about my feelings of chest pain. The heaviness in my chest got so unbearable that I finally called 911. By the time the paramedics came, I had passed out on the floor of my apartment. I do not recall their faces as I could not open my eyes. I remember hearing them come in, and I recall being lifted onto and wheeled out on a stretcher down my building into an ambulance.

Finally, gaining consciousness at the hospital alone; the doctors were poking and prodding me, trying to figure out what was wrong with me; they considered things like blood clots in my lungs. However, the doctors could not find anything physically wrong with me. Finally, the emergency room doctor sat down and, in a very guarded manner, asked me if I was willing to see a psychiatrist. I was open to it and up for the help I needed to heal. A few days later, I went back to the hospital for an initial assessment; I met with a psychiatrist for about an hour who asked me a lot of random questions, which I now cannot recount. I was eventually diagnosed with Generalized Anxiety Disorder (GAD), and the experience I recently endured was a panic attack.

Now that the doctors and I knew what we were dealing with, we could devise a game plan for moving forward. The doctors recommended that I undergo Cognitive Behavior Therapy (CBT). I immediately started weekly sessions at St. Michael's Hospital in Toronto.

In CBT, I learned that our thoughts drive and shape our feelings. Think of a horse-drawn carriage. The horse leads and is in charge, and the carriage follows and is there for the ride. The horse is the thought, and the carriage is the resulting feelings and emotions driven by that thought. At first, I did not believe the therapist when she told me that we have the power to change our thoughts or how we look at situations – and therefore, we ultimately have the power to change how we feel about things and how to manage our emotions best. So many of our thoughts are automatically derived from experiences we accumulate throughout our lives, and although they feel genuine, they are just thoughts. We can reframe our thoughts by challenging them and putting them to the test, as in putting our thoughts before a judge, jury, and real-life evidence to see if they stand.

One of the tools I learned was to write out 'Thought Records.' I had to fill out seven columns on a printed sheet of paper whenever I encountered a problematic situation. The columns were:

1. Describe the Situation
    a. Who? What? Where? When?
2. Moods
    b. What did you feel?
    c. Rate each mood (0-100%)
3. Automatic Thoughts (Images)
    d. What was going through your mind before you started to feel this way?
    e. Circle the hot thoughts
4. Evidence that supports this hot thought
5. Evidence that does not support the hot thought
6. Alternative / Balanced Thoughts
    f. Write an alternative or balanced thought
    g. Rate how much you believe in each alternative or balanced thought (0-100%)

I will share one of my actual thought records, which I completed in 2008 when I first started CBT. At the time, I took on my first managerial role and looked after a team of fund accountants. We were a bustling group with many clients and deliverables. We were reeling from the Global Financial Crisis, which caused instability and many layoffs across the industry. We worked long hours at the office, eager to prove ourselves. While several team members were challenging to work with, I did have a boss I learned so much from and enjoyed working for.

1. Describe the Situation
    a. It was a Friday afternoon after a very long and hectic week at the office. A problematic team member still needed to catch up and was behind on their deliverables, and a client had just called to complain. I raised the issue with my boss that we needed to terminate this employee based on their track record of poor performance, and my boss disagreed with this course of action. I was furious that this underperforming person yet again seemed to get away with murder.
2. Moods
    b. 100% Full-throttle Angry and Frustrated!
3. Automatic Thoughts and Images going through my mind
    c. This is not fair! My boss never listens to me. Why are we giving special treatment to poor performers?! Why is it that no one ever listens to me? My opinion does not matter to anyone. It must mean that **I do not matter and am not significant** (circle this HOT THOUGHT).
4. Evidence that supports this hot thought
    d. I have raised many such issues in the past, but no action has ever been taken.
5. Evidence that does not support the hot thought
    e. I was part of the selection committee and interviewed new potential hires.
    f. I was promoted to Deputy Group Head within six months of joining the firm.
    g. I was then promoted in rank to Associate Director 12 months later.
    h. Colleagues in the group turn to me for help solving complex client issues.

6. Alternative / Balanced Thoughts

    i.   Once I have challenged the hot thought, it is evident that I matter to the organization. I have been promoted several times and am deeply involved in the team's day-to-day management. I cannot control my boss's actions, nor am I privy to her pressures. A more extensive picture outside my purview prohibits her from terminating employees. The only action I can take is to escalate matters to her and provide her with a written factual and quantitative account of the situation. Although situations at work may be frustrating, I can still appreciate that I have a big life outside of work; I matter to my family and friends, and I have enriching activities such as salsa dancing to look forward to, among many hobbies!

    j.   After coming up with this alternative thought, I felt less furious. I went from 100% full-throttle angry and frustrated to 50%

While at first, I would write thought records to help me with issues at work that made me feel anxious, I also started to use this tool to challenge deep-seated self-limiting beliefs I developed in my childhood.

Travel Back In Time

As a young child, I started to shape my belief that I was incapable of taking care of myself, that I was helpless, and that I needed to be fearful to live and survive in the world around me. I formed self-limiting beliefs that I did not have the faculties to be independent. I took the physical limitation of independence a step further in my mind to mean that I could also not be intellectually independent. I translated my childhood experience into my young mind, meaning I was prohibited from independent thought and actions. As a result, I did not naturally develop a confident voice. I was convinced I was not smart, not intellectually competent, and had no outstanding abilities to share with the outside world.

I was born in Tondo, Manila, in the Philippines, to parents Hilario and Elizabeth. Tondo is one of the poorest neighborhoods in the country, known for its overpopulation, bustling activity, and noise. The area is filled with slums, where thousands of people live without adequate access to basic necessities, like housing, electricity, or clean water. The honking noises of cars, taxis, and jeepneys could be heard at all hours of the day. The clanking sound of horse hooves as two-wheeled horse-drawn carriages called *kalesas* went up and down the street, transporting people was hard to miss. Walking street vendors yelling *balut*, a local delicacy which is a fertilized duck egg, and *taho*, a warm silken tofu snack with sweetened syrup, endures in my memory.

My father passed away unexpectedly when I was only eight months old, and my mother was a few months pregnant with my brother. We went to live with my grandparents, Benjamin (Lolo Ben), an Engineer, and Rosalina (Mama Chi), an English Schoolteacher, who, despite their humble beginnings, started a small industrial machine-rebuilding business. This venture gave them the means to provide us with a safe home and an education at highly regarded institutions.

Growing up, I remember the neighborhood as dangerous and riddled with crime. I was told it was unsafe to go outside; it was downright forbidden to step outside our home unless accompanied by an adult. Often, I could hear the adults talking about horrific stories of crime surrounding us, of drug dealers, murderers, and rapists. The mere thought of learning to cross the street alone was not a consideration. The concept of developing independence did not exist. While I had my siblings and cousins to play with inside the house, we were never allowed to play outside our home or galivant around the neighborhood. Unlike the norm in parts of the United States, we were not allowed to play with and make friends with other kids in the neighborhood. I understand now as an adult that my grandparents and parents were protective and vigilant only to ensure our safety. As a young girl, this was lost on me; all I heard was the resounding 'no' to every request I made to step outside and the feeling that I had no control. I felt frustrated and angry. I felt left out of the world. I had no agency, no control, and nowhere to channel my energy. I was not strong enough to change my situation.

Big Bad Bully

My insecurities kept building like a boulder descending a mountain, amassing momentum and gathering more rocks downhill. The resounding thought of **'I am not enough'** felt like it was there screaming at me everywhere I turned. Many children experience bullying, but fewer children take on that role for themselves. I relentlessly criticized myself for not having or being enough. I was convinced I was less than because I did not have all my classmates' material possessions. I was not from a fancy neighborhood, was not brought to school in fancy cars, and did not wear fancy clothes.

Our beat-up family vehicle and the daily scenic drive through a mountain of garbage meant to me, in my young mind, that I must be from a different social class than my schoolmates. I started to form thoughts of inferiority in comparison to them. I became hyperaware of signals of wealth they had access to that I did not. While my friends got dropped off every morning in expensive air-conditioned imported cars, I lived through the "drive of shame." Each morning, I would bear witness to poverty and squalor on my way to school; by the homeroom bell, I was in class rubbing shoulders with the upper class.

I was enrolled at St. Scholastica's College, an all-girls school run by Benedictine nuns in Manila, starting at age 7. The school is recognized for its prestige and its intensive curriculum. The young girls in my class came from wealthy families and extremely affluent neighborhoods. Some had renowned surnames that, when name-dropped in a room, would turn heads in Philippine society. Although we were all dressed the same in school uniform-- white socks, black leather shoes, and a mid-calf length navy blue jumper -- my young mind believed there was a big divide between us.

The drive to school in my grandfather's beat-up jeep in the morning often took us through Smokey Mountain. For the uninitiated, Smokey Mountain was a slum area where garbage was piled so high that it resembled a mountain range. The smokey part of the name came from garbage being burned at all hours of the day. Although a few kilometers from home, out of sight, the pungent smell of burning garbage was a daily part of life. Thousands of people, families, and young children lived on this mountain of trash. The jeep did not have doors nor glass windows, creating an open-air experience, and by open-air experience, it meant being exposed to the dusty, muggy air mixed with black smoke from cars' tailpipes. The air pollution was out of this world. Facemasks, although not in vogue then, could have been useful.

My classmates often invited me to their birthday parties in their elegant homes in their exclusive gated communities or at the country club's swimming pool their parents were members of. They would often talk about shopping at Benetton and Esprit, fashion brands afforded only by the upper class then. I did my best to blend in. We spoke with each other in a mix of English and Tagalog, one of the country's official languages. To speak in English is to speak the language of the country's elite. Since my grandmother was an English schoolteacher, she gave me lessons at home. She was very strict with pronunciation and emphasized the importance of having an extensive vocabulary.

Despite this social class divide, my schoolmates never mistreated or looked down on me. They were kind and loving, and to this day, I am secretly grateful to them for being kind to me when I was not even kind to myself. I judged myself so harshly over status and material possessions I did not have control over. I am still in touch with most of them even if we now live scattered across the world, and I hope someday they will read this and know how much their kindness has meant to me.

I wish I had known then what I now know and believe with all my heart: that integrity defines a person and that money and possessions are the poorest measure of one's worth. Nevertheless, I am grateful for the long road and journey to healing and the opportunity to build strength and tenacity. For most of my life, I felt like I was never enough, and now I know that it is never too late to challenge thoughts, even if you have lived with them for decades.

Yale? Yes, Yale!

The self-limiting beliefs I developed as a young child haunted me when I entered the University of Waterloo in Canada for my undergraduate degree at the age of 18. Although physically independent and living on my own for the first time, I had trouble believing I could be smart enough and astute enough. Fear and anxiety gripped me when studying for my courses and taking exams. I struggled big time. I was not even an average student getting C's. I am not exaggerating when I say I was a poor student: I got a lot of Ds and Fs. It took me much longer than expected to graduate as I retook many classes. I carried this embarrassment like a deep, dark secret for so long. My transcript is like a ghost of my past, and I cannot shake it off. When I was applying for my US Green Card a few years ago, my immigration lawyer looked at my transcript, a requirement in the application process, and said, "Well, at least you had fun!" I wished then that the world would open up and swallow me whole – he unknowingly hit upon a wound that could not handle any more salt. The truth was that I struggled to focus during my undergraduate degree as I had difficulties adjusting to my new life in Canada.

Right then and there, I decided it was time to challenge the giant gorilla in the room— **my self-limiting belief that I was not smart enough**. I had lived like an impostor trapped in my self-deprecating thoughts for far too long. It was time for fear to end its reign. I was a woman on a mission to redeem myself from my past. I researched many different programs in law and business schools and thought deeply about what I wanted my career to look like in the next 20 years. A friend suggested I investigate Yale University's Executive MBA program—Yale?! Why in the world would Yale University ever look twice at me, was my first reaction. It was time to call up an old friend, the good old thought record.

At this juncture, I asked myself, why would Yale University want to look twice at me? I am not good enough for Yale. Circle this hot thought! Yes, on the one hand, I had this indescribably horrific transcript that should not see the light of day once more. On the other hand (aka evidence that does not support this hot thought), I have 20 years of hard work learning the ropes and working my way from the ground up in the finance industry – surely real-life work had to count for something! The alternative thought I came up with was that I am not who I was when I was 18 years old; why should I let the past define me? I am now more focused and have real-life industry and management experience. Indeed, it would not hurt to try and test the waters.

I mustered the courage to contact Yale's admissions team for a preliminary conversation, and lo and behold, they responded and welcomed me to apply. As soon as I attended the first Yale recruitment event online, I never wanted anything more. So, after 20 years of being away from the books, I signed up to take the Executive Assessment (EA) exam, a version of the Graduate Management Admission Test (GMAT) geared towards experienced professionals. The exam was shorter than the GMAT, but the questions weighed more, and there was little room for error. My old friends, fear and anxiety, reared their ugly heads every step of the studying process. I took an exam preparation course and hired a tutor. Even then, I took the exam three times to come close to an acceptable score! Nevertheless, I was determined. Each time I received a bad score, nagging thoughts would come to mind. Why am I putting myself through the fire like this? Each time these negative thoughts came up, I would challenge them and list in my mind all the times in my life when I persevered. I would remind myself that I could do that again.

I even wrote a supplemental essay in my admission application explaining why I did not excel academically in my undergraduate years; I provided context regarding my frame of mind when I entered university in my late teens. My parents, four younger siblings, and I packed up and migrated to Canada from our home in the Philippines only four years before starting college. The world as I knew it changed overnight, and I found myself in starkly different surroundings. I devoted most of my time to building new relationships, growing my circle, and emotionally and financially supporting my family. I mismanaged my priorities, and as a result, my grades were adversely affected. In a way, I was asking for a second chance to prove that I could do better. In a more profound sense, I was also asking myself for permission to give myself a second chance.

That is precisely what I did: I poured my heart and soul into the MBA for Executives program for the next two years. On the first day of class, I met 50 new classmates. Of those, 56% already had advanced degrees, and 15 were medical doctors. The program's rigors were no laughing matter, each day was like climbing Mount Everest one small step at a time, proving to myself I was good enough to be in the room. It was the most challenging task I have had to do in my life to date. Whenever I doubted myself in class or when completing an assignment, I would go through a thought record in my mind and challenge my thoughts. There were many bumps and sleepless nights along the way, but I now have a transcript I am so proud of, filled with High Honors and Honors grades in courses like Macroeconomics, Game Theory, and Investment Management. It was a long, arduous process, but I proved myself smart and intellectually capable.

A few months before graduating, I spoke on a panel at the Yale School of Management on International Women's Day. At the Q&A, a classmate raised their hand and asked, "If you could go back, what would you tell your younger self?" I surprised myself that I was choked up and almost burst into tears. I held back and said, **"I would tell my young self, I am enough."** I could not elaborate further as I was holding back a surge of emotions; tears I could let pour down my face now as I thought about how far down the feelings I have buried go and how long I have suffered thinking that I was not smart enough when all along, it was not even remotely true. It's taken half my life to solve the mystery, but I am grateful that it is now solved, and there is no more doubt.

Who I Am Now

I am a Senior Executive for one of the largest banks in the world. In 2014, my dream to live in and grow my career in New York City came true. I have a 4-year-old Cavapoo who I absolutely adore—little love Ketchup is her name.

For over two decades, I have worked my way up the global financial industry in the United States, Canada, the United Kingdom, and Bermuda. I recently graduated with a Master of Business Administration from Yale University, specializing in Asset

Management. I have built a brand as an industry and community leader. I have engaged with large audiences and empowered hundreds, speaking about personal branding, self-advocacy, and confidence building. As Treasurer on the Board of Inspiring Girls USA, I support development and leadership programs for young girls across the country.

Outside my professional life, I am a fitness enthusiast. I love going to the gym five days a week to lift weights. I have entered several bodybuilding competitions in the Wellness category and plan to train for more in the future. I adore the discipline of prepping daily meals, waking up at the crack of dawn, and doing intense workouts.

I am a fan of the arts, history, and culture. On weekends, I frequent the Metropolitan Museum of Art and many pop-up exhibitions throughout the city. I have many friends in the city and love meeting them at local restaurant hot spots and wine bars.

In 2024, I was appointed the Grand Marshal of the Philippine Independence Day in New York City, the largest commemoration outside the Philippines. Tens of thousands of people came to support and celebrate our history and culture.

I now lead my life precisely as I envision: the career, the big city, the friendships, and most of all, the freedom to pursue my dreams. To get there, I challenged my self-limiting beliefs that were holding me back one by one. Each was like wrestling with a giant gorilla, but I survived. Going through Cognitive Behavior Therapy and using thought records changed my entire life trajectory. By challenging my self-limiting beliefs and deep-seated insecurities, I gained freedom from thoughts that were holding me prisoner.

SOFIA ARAGON, JD, BSN, RN, FAAN

Executive Director, WA Center for Nursing and former Mayor, City of Burien, WA
Global FWN100™ 2022

Wandering Off the Plantation: How racism and gender bias show up as incivility

The phrase *"Grow Where You Are Planted"* carries profound meaning in Sofia Aragon's journey. Sofia is a Filipina immigrant navigating the complexities of race, gender, and leadership in public policy and nursing. *From a young age, Sofia was acutely aware of the challenges she would face as both a minority and a woman. This realization did not deter her but rather fueled her determination to succeed. As she advanced in her career, Sofia found herself in leadership circles where she was often one of the few Filipinas or the only Filipina, confronting both racial and gender biases. Despite these obstacles, she remained grounded in her cultural heritage and the family tradition of nursing, which was always her home base. What she didn't anticipate was how her career would evolve to intersect with public policy. In this field, her unique perspective as a Filipina and a woman added depth to her leadership. Throughout her journey, Sofia was influenced by a diverse group of mentors, teachers, and allies—both intentional and unintentional—*

who helped shape her professional identity. Her experiences growing up an immigrant, , and witnessing her mother break the mold with political interests all contributed to her understanding of leadership and advocacy.

Velma Veloria
Former Washington State Representative
First Filipina elected to a state legislature in the continental United States

Mom and the Plantation

I would take Mom with me on business trips because I didn't have the time nor could afford to take a trip to historic places for travel's sake. Mom couldn't travel independently. Dad had left, and she lived alone in the house where I spent my formative years in high school. My parents taught me that relationships were fickle and that the only person who could envision a vision of the future for myself was me.

We were in San Antonio, where I would receive an award from the American Association of Nurse Practitioners for excellence in state advocacy. Artifacts from the Spanish-American War in the bar of the historic Menger Hotel surrounded us. Lieutenant Colonel and future United States President Theodore Roosevelt set up an enlistment table in this old-fashioned bar made with mahogany wood. Over 1250 men signed up to form the Roosevelt Rough Riders, the 1st United States Volunteer Cavalry established in 1898 to fight in the Spanish-American War.

"My grandfather would house soldiers at the hacienda," Mom casually announced while sipping iced tea. The word "hacienda" conjured up vivid images of acres of lush vegetation. An operation that could feed hundreds through the science of agriculture and the hard work of laborers. I imagined a hierarchy of foremen and field hands working the soil. The opportunity of harvest occurring in a specific window of time each year. I saw mom as the grandchild of a farmer running through stalks of growth much taller than she as she ran in a frilly dress. Would the presence of soldiers cause fear? How disruptive were they? Another military disruption would occur in her life during the declaration of martial law the year I was born in Manila. My parents would decide to leave for America three years later.

"You know, one time I traveled to support a campaign." This mahogany bar, protecting us from the heat, inspired another story from her life that I was hearing for the first time. "While my nursing education was on hold because my father needed to earn more money to continue putting me and my siblings through college, I decided to join a campaign for a candidate for Senator on the Island of Romblon. I imagined her getting on a modest sailboat from Luzon to journey to Romblon. Today, a ferry is nearly a 30-hour trip from Manila. That explains her recollection of sailing in the darkness of night. I sat stunned. She looked down at the paper napkin with the Menger logo and carefully tucked it into her purse as a souvenir. To this day, I can't believe that was the first time she shared that story. I thought to myself clearly, the mango doesn't fall far from the tree.

She introduced me to the political process when she brought me to a democratic caucus at the local middle school. George W. Bush was running for re-election, and she wanted to add her voice to the debate about t who would be the democratic nominee. A few people approached us to advocate for John Kerry because he was sensible. I remember not feeling compelled as a teenager; I expected more rigorous advocacy for a potential president of the United States. She told organizers that she would vote for Howard Dean because her union said so.

Mom was the quintessential swing voter. A fan of George Herbert Bush, she laughed at his son, George W. Bush, and the daily jokes that made fun of his lack of intelligence. She was relieved to vote for Barack Obama, believing the country deserved at least a smarter president.

In 2016, I was active in local democratic politics during a year of high stakes in who would be the democratic nominee for president. Hilary Clinton was the establishment favorite, but I gravitated toward Bernie Sanders, the Senator from Vermont. He messaged about access to a college education, the need for a well-educated workforce, the burden of student loans, and rampant income inequality. He understood the struggles of young professionals, such as me, who put in the time to educate themselves into professional roles only to struggle to afford housing and manage student loans.

It was my turn to participate in the local democratic caucus as an adult. A process as old as the United States itself, my husband and I attended the local democratic caucus meeting at a nearby middle school. We ran into neighbors there, including my acquaintance in governmental affairs circles. I was the governmental affairs director of the WA State Nurses Association, and he was the education policy analyst for the State House of Representatives. After exchanging enthusiastic greetings, we paused to listen to instructions from the event facilitator on the microphone, trying to get the attention of a crowded room. We were to divide ourselves into two groups: one side of the room for Hilary supporters and the other for Bernie Sanders supporters. As Brian and I joined the Sanders contingency, I realized I was moving away from my colleague who stepped back to join Hilary Clinton supporters. He looked at me with confusion as we separated into our chosen crowds. The room appeared to divide equally, and we stood on both sides of a significant space divide as volunteers counted the number of supporters for each campaign. Once the counting was done, the room cleared in silence as we left to head back to our car. It felt unexpected. Odd. Awkward. Like an unresolvable disagreement forming an invisible wall. Bernie Sanders would win Washington State, and I headed to the Democratic National Convention as a Bernie Sanders delegate.

I attempted my own run for office about six years before, to the state House of Representatives. Mom was the first person to call me a politician.

Leading as The First Woman of Color Mayor

I call myself an Accidental Mayor because this is not the assignment my parents gave me in life. Nor did I have to use my lobbying skills to convince those with the necessary votes to land the job. Headlines on my appointment read Burien elects the first woman of color mayor. I was simply the right person at the right time. The political powers wanted my outward appearance and identity, and voters agreed with them.

I had already served two years on the Burien City Council, and my service began in 2020, the year of the COVID-19 pandemic. Until I was elected mayor, meetings were held online. I was the least likely to grandstand on the dais. Besides, the other council members were more willing to fill the air than I was. My policy background demanded a deep dive into the issues at hand. What are we trying to accomplish? Who in the community benefits? Who will suffer unintended consequences from the legislation we pass? What resources are required?

Councilmember and immediate past mayor Jimmy Matta was a great role model and collaborator in the politics of the work. I developed a habit of observing leaders in their fields, finding opportunities to work with them, and learning from their approaches. I recognized Jimmy to be one of them. The son of a Guatemalan immigrant who was fluent in Spanish, he was the first Latino to serve as mayor of Burien. He was a quintessential politician. At political events, you would see him work the room, shaking hands as he made his way through packed ballrooms. He wore a suit and tie to political functions, looking like the owner of a construction business that he was. His social media posts were full of selfies of him in a hardhat and a construction crew, documenting the several projects he oversaw. Explanations were both in English and Spanish.

He built strong relationships with county leadership, which allowed him to address large crowds and grow a reputation as the next leader of higher office. His political roots were in the labor community. I remember another elected official of color counseling me, "You have to have labor's support to win an election." Most of all, I saw Jimmy Matta as an expert organizer of people. He knew how to mobilize others into action.

A memorable piece of legislation proposed during COVID-19 was to allow food trucks into the City of Burien. Small businesses struggled during COVID-19, and a strong contingent was Latino small businesses. Many of them were family-owned restaurants that struggled to keep doors open during the shutdown. Allowing food trucks into the City of Burien threatened the survival of these restaurants.

While other cities have successfully piloted food truck regulations to balance the needs of these mobile businesses with those of brick-and-mortar restaurants, legislation during the pandemic deserved special consideration because these were not "normal" times.

Mayor Matta and I were part of the progressive Democratic majority on the city council, with a commitment to racial equity and to eradicate racism because of the murder of George Floyd.

I was taken aback by how white progressive women on the council represented and spoke for people of color, including Latino business owners, as if their authority matched the lived experiences of these residents. Why did this make me uncomfortable while admiring their confidence? I wanted to see their support for their colleague, Council Member Matta, who proudly represented the Latino community. A heated argument erupted over whether we refer to the community as *"Latino, Latina, or Latinx."* *"We've had this conversation,"* said one of the white-progressive-democrat council members. I sat there thinking, *"Who is 'we'?"* Mayor Matta crossed his arms and firmly suggested, *"I think we should consult the community about what they want to be called."* Seizing the moment, I supported his stance. *"I think the mayor makes a good point."* I could see the dismissive and annoyed expressions. Was I witnessing white privilege? Why did their advocacy for people of color make me feel so uncomfortable? I often felt the sting of a microaggression before identifying it with words in my consciousness.

An impressive show of dozens of Latino business owners, including the US Hispanic Chamber of Commerce, signed up to testify on the legislation for a food truck pilot. Without a doubt, Mayor Matta organized them. After all, he founded *Empresarios Unidos*, the local Hispanic Chamber of Commerce. Unanimously, they had respectfully requested a one-mile radius between any food truck and the downtown core, where most restaurants were located.

I argued that the council could walk the talk of promoting equity and not implement a food truck pilot at a time when brick-and-mortar businesses were struggling. While we all supported fair competition, this was not the right timing to implement this pilot program, as the city was still struggling with the economic impact of COVID-19.

Despite numerous testimonies and arguments from the community itself about how a food truck pilot would further put their businesses at risk, one of the white progressive female council members accused me of making arguments devoid of fact. I was stunned that she would make such an assertion in the face of dozens of community members expressing concern by sharing their very real struggles trying to survive the pandemic. I began to wonder how sincere my colleague's arguments were about food trucks being a tool to advance equity, especially in the face of Latino business members' arguments against hardship. Were people of color being tokenized in their arguments? In addition, I was highly offended that a person would accuse me, an attorney, of advocating an argument devoid of facts. The facts were being pleaded in front of our faces.

While contradictory arguments about equity didn't end on the City Council, I appreciated being able to discuss my concerns with the mayor. Elected people of color need peers who are willing to be sounding boards. We have an opportunity to have an elevated level of awareness to address bias and privilege in the political system. Bias and privilege are products of lived experiences. Coming from a place of lived experience is an aspiration placed on elected officials today. It's incumbent on those in office to own biases and privileges resulting from personal experiences. The additional challenge I faced was to call out my colleagues, who may unknowingly act in a biased manner in the guise of good intentions to further an agenda.

Another example was the debate on hazard pay for essential workers during the pandemic. I advocated for more time to deliberate on the proposed legislation because, as a lawyer, I was concerned about a clause for a private right of action. One of the white progressive female councilmembers took it upon herself to be lead on the legislation. This meant she would be responsible for educating the council on any aspect of the legislation. I asked her to explain the purpose of a private right of action. She could not answer. Not being able to give a response, I abstained due to a lack of information. The backlash against me was posted on social media the next day. A labor leader and close supporter of the council member posted how those who voted yes for the legislation were like the black protesters who crossed the Edmund Pettus Bridge in 1965 to demonstrate against the denial of voting rights to African Americans and the murder of 26-year-old Jimmie Lee Jackson by police just days before. Compelled to call her, I asked whether her statement was calling me a racist. Me. An Asian American immigrant. She said, "*No*," and subsequently took down the post. However, our relationship has remained strained.

I continue to struggle with how statements using race to advance an agenda land on my ears as incivility. They feel rude, impolite, and offensive. My concern for civility arises out of my two professions. Both nursing and the law have a code of ethics. Moreover, the law expects decorum. While there are legislators who are nurses and lawyers, there are no professional prerequisites for public office.

Public concern over incivility in politics is all over the news. How would an expectation for civility be created or enforced? Most professions are self-regulating, and it's up to its members to adopt and implement civility as a value. One of my most significant contributions was to draft and advocate for adopting Rules of Civility as part of the Council Rules of Order. Sadly, but not surprisingly, not all council members voted in support. The rationale? They did not want to be held to such a standard. My colleague, Mayor Matta, foresaw that voters would ultimately decide whether a council member would continue to serve on the council. One council member who opposed my views on the food truck initiative and did not sign onto the Council Rules of Civility was not re-elected.

Managing politics is the more significant challenge when it comes to politics versus policy.

Beginnings in Policy and Not Politics

For over a decade, I worked as a legislative advocate representing the interests of registered nurses and their agenda to provide access to quality care to benefit all residents of the state of Washington.

I fell in love with public policy while working as a fiscal analyst for the Local Government Fiscal Note Program in the WA State Department of Commerce 20 years ago. It was my first job out of law school. I commuted an hour and a half each way from my parent's home to the state capitol of Olympia to work long hours analyzing legislation costs to local governments. Due to my experience as a registered nurse, my primary assignments were in public health districts. The legislative session was a 24-hour, seven-day week operation for 120 days when it was a long session or 60 days when it was a short session for our part-time legislature.

Our small group of four analysts reviewed hundreds of bills in the basement of the old General Administration Building: a grey, concrete behemoth built in the 1950s. Entering the building every morning, the portrait of Governor Gary Locke, the first Asian American governor in the continental United States, welcomed me. I was proud to know we both attended Benjamin Franklin High School in Seattle in Seattle's Rainier Valley. It was the last year of his term, and I was beginning my career in public policy.

I enjoyed every minute of working in that makeshift office, which was only inhabited by staff when the legislature was in session. The smell of bacon grease trapped in the hallway greeted me, and as a morning person and usually the first to arrive in the office, this didn't bother me at all.

The director of the Local Government Fiscal Note Program was a fellow Asian American attorney named Louise. She was competent, with a law degree from a highly-ranked school. She was kind, personable, and quiet, but my colleagues found her odd. Maybe they found me odd, too.

As a city council member, a day job while serving in public office was necessary because I am neither independently wealthy nor retired. I remained the Executive Director of the Washington Center for Nursing (WCN), a statewide nursing workforce center. Success there required navigating the world of nursing leadership in WA state.

It took all my lobbying skills to earn the support of the Board of Directors to be only the second executive director of the organization: persuasion as a lawyer by drafting arguments disguised as letters of recommendation from willing colleagues and leveraging key relationships to position myself as the best person for the job.

Moving on, Not Resting on My Laurels

The WA State Nurses Association (WSNA) leadership had mixed feelings about supporting my move to the WCN. In the seven years I headed governmental affairs at WSNA, I expanded the organization's lobbying representation to include the School Nurse Organization of WA and the Advanced Registered Nurse Practitioners United of WA State. These expansions made WSNA a lobbying firm.

I also created an organizer position, convincing management that mobilizing our 11,000 members needed more than a few hours of the front desk receptionist's time on the phone. This position made it possible to grow WSNA's political organizing program. There were eight registered nurses in the state legislature then, and we worked to support their re-election bids. In addition, this enabled us to build relationships with other legislative candidates and candidates running for statewide offices that heavily influenced state health policy, such as governor, insurance commissioner, and the Office of the Superintendent of Public Instruction for school health.

I grew our contract lobbying team. I added one contract lobbyist who focused on health care, another who focused on our relationships with the United Labor Lobby, and another who focused on federal health reform implementation.

I enhanced legislative training for WSNA members to sharpen their skills in developing talking points for meetings with legislators. My simple formula was to use data complemented by compelling personal stories of nurses in the field.

Member participation continued growing until we needed more meeting space than the Washington Performance Center could provide. The Great Wolf Lodge, located 10 minutes outside the capitol, provided the needed lodging and training space for the nearly 750 nurses and nursing students eager to descend on Capitol Hill. Nurse Lobby Day was the most prominent citizen advocacy day year after year.

My first long session with the WSNA was during the Great Recession, the worst economic downturn in the US since the Great Depression. The housing market crumbled under the subprime mortgage crisis, causing home foreclosures across the country. The impact on Washington state was a shrinking budget, putting into jeopardy higher education and the ability of nursing schools to admit students needed to combat a nursing shortage. I used data from the WA Center for Nursing to show that the state could not afford to cut funding to higher education. Doing so would exacerbate a nursing shortage. Who would be caring for our rapidly growing population of residents over 65?

Those were some of the longer days of lobbying, and hundreds showed up to testify. It was back to the basement, as many of us filled overflow rooms, waiting 2 to 3 hours to give 3 minutes or less to testify in the hearing room upstairs.

Unlike Medicaid spending, higher education funding was considered discretionary, subject to cuts first or to fill holes in funding gaps with solid programs in a severe budget shortfall. For programs to survive, strong advocacy had to be behind them. Armed with data from the WA Center for Nursing, I built a solid case to say that maintaining higher education was necessary to maintain nursing graduation rates.

Lobbying in Coalition for Racial Equity in Public Policy

Leading legislative and political efforts at the WSNA gave me the on the ground experience I wanted. I learned the nuts, bolts, and strategy of legislative lawmaking. I created important relationships with legislators and made it a point to gain credibility with legislative leadership.

In one legislative session, I found myself with more flexibility to take on more issues. Few legislative advocates were from diverse racial backgrounds at the time. I could count on one hand the number of colleagues who came from a racially diverse background as I did. There was camaraderie, and with very little intention, we became a coalition.

The organization OneAmerica came to our attention. I learned about their mission and agenda to protect immigrant rights in the state of Washington. Their founder, Pramila Jayapal, created the organization to advocate against racism against the Muslim community after 9/11. It was then called Hate Free Zone. Pramila would later become the first Asian Indian to be elected to Congress. The OneAmerica lobbyist came to us for advice on how to defeat racially discriminatory legislation that would require social security numbers to be printed onto Washington drivers' licenses. The impact would be to create additional burdens for undocumented people in the state.

The lobbyist was young and was only beginning to cultivate relationships for an effective coalition. This requires strong connections to legislators and House and Senate leadership. The head of the state nurses' association frequently said that coalitions accomplish two things: collectively passing legislation or collectively defeating legislation.

I offered to bring concerns about the driver's license legislation to a meeting I had coming up with the Speaker of the House. With One America's factsheet clearly describing the legislation's potential discriminatory impact, I included it with my meeting. The Speaker shared his concerns and had been looking for documentation included in the factsheet. A strong advocate for higher education, he was concerned about the impact on undocumented students. Years later, he would be instrumental in passing the Washington Dream Act, providing more state support to undocumented college students.

Given the issues I advocated for on behalf of the Washington State Nurses Association, I built relationships with legislators with various interests. The circumstances where undocumented persons enter and settle in the US illegally had the perception of, at the least, intent to do wrong and, at the worst, criminal intent, which was clearly the bias our coalition was fighting against. Doing research, I learned that people become undocumented for a variety of reasons not publicly well known. Examples are obtaining undocumented status to protect oneself from domestic violence. Another situation involves international students in higher education whose visas lapse. Unintended consequences of this legislation would also negatively impact the children of undocumented persons, a group that even legislators sponsoring the policy did not intend to affect.

I enjoyed supporting this coalition of young advocates. I lent my expertise and experience as a volunteer lobbyist by crafting key messages for testifying against the bill, assigning members to speak to certain legislators based on political or special interest affinity, taking turns talking to the same legislators with consistent messages, and counting votes. Our coalition is comprised of the Washington State Nurses Association, the State Labor Council, the ACLU of Washington, a teachers union, social justice organizations such as the Children's Alliance, Washington Community Action Network, and a faith-based coalition. We demonstrated a broad representation of interests working in unison.

One night, when legislators were grinding through the phase of floor debates on the final passage of legislation, we gathered in a conference room, talking through a strategy to kill the bill during floor debates if necessary. I'd become an expert in crafting deadly amendments to arm legislators willing to be our champions during floor debate. I'd battled many harmful amendments proposed by the opposition seeking to block legislation by the nurses' association. *"Killing with kindness,"* is how one experienced legislative staffer described this strategy: creating floor amendments designed to weigh legislation down but designed as having good intentions to "clarify" or create more "comprehensive" legislation.

We were successful in defeating the legislation. After the session ended, our efforts were celebrated, and we were formally recognized by the Children's Alliance, the Minority Executive Directors Coalition, the American Federation of Teachers-Washington, the King County Social Services Coalition, and others.

From the nickname the Speaker gave us of the "Driver's License Coalition," we would formally adopt the name Racial Equity Team lobby. We grew from a handful of lobbyists of color leveraging the influence of our organizations to a coalition of over a hundred organizations still working together today.

That was my first meaningful experience advocating for racial equity. I look back fondly on this time when I was called upon to represent, even if that was not my formal expectation.

Shifts In Power Jeopardizes the Value of a Balanced Approach

The Tea Party Movement in the United States also rose around 2009. The Tea Party generally opposed excessive taxation and government intervention in the private sector while supporting solid immigrant controls.

In response to social service funding cuts, advocates proposed an increase in the sales tax. Polling showed the public to be tolerant of this approach. Washington's revenue system rests precariously on a three-legged stool of property taxes, sales taxes, and a smaller budget of fees dedicated to specific purposes.

An increase in sales tax was the only revenue source available that the legislature could consider to keep existing state programs afloat. Notorious advocate Tim Eyman capped property tax increases through the ballot initiative process through Initiative

722 in 2000. He became the darling of conservatives in the state after successfully passing Initiative 695, limiting the cost of car tabs. Car tab revenue supports essential services like public health. Advocates for public health continue to re-establish a stable funding source.

Eyman added theatrics to those budget hearings, showing up in a Darth Vader costume and swinging a lightsaber.

In 2010, voters supported a Republican wave of candidates nationally. When I began my role at WSNA, the state legislature had a supermajority of Democrats. I didn't have to talk to Republicans to get my votes to pass bills. That started to change when the margin between Democrats and Republicans narrowed.

For years, center-leaning Democrats complained that progressive Democrats were too liberal for their constituents. Ironically, many of these legislators were responsible for the Democratic supermajority. Collectively, they called themselves the Roadkill Caucus because they felt caught in the middle of an ideological divide, and as a result, their legislative initiatives often died.

In 2012, Republicans gained one seat in the WA State Senate. Then, two conservative Democrats, Tim Sheldon and Rodney Tom, agreed to caucus with the Republicans to create a Republican Majority Caucus in the Senate, allowing Republicans control over the change and determination of the leadership of all Senate committees.

I was lobbying for a bill to allow school nurses to carry out needed medical treatment for children in schools. A school nurse raised the alarm when a principal interfered with her decision to call an ambulance for a student she determined needed emergency care. Parents, concerned about costs, complained to the principal. This incident and similar incidents of non-clinical school nurse supervisors interfering with the clinical judgment of school nurses have resulted in barriers to care that put students' health and lives at risk.

With a registered nurse serving as Chair of the House Healthcare and Wellness Committee and held as the lead for healthcare issues by the Democratic majority, the legislation passed the House of Representatives. The next hurdle was passage through the Senate. In the Senate Education Committee, I eagerly awaited my turn to testify in support of our school nurse bill, listed 3rd on the agenda. I was used to arguments outlining the pros and cons of a proposed policy. Drama usually came from those testifying. I did not expect theatrics from the committee itself. Only on the first bill on the agenda, the legislators began to argue. Comments thrown out of turn, voices to the point of yelling. The Chair struggled to control the debate until he lost patience. The hearing quickly devolved into chaos before advocates even had a chance to speak. Was this a hearing or a reality show? Being used to civil debate, I didn't know how to feel. The chairman quickly adjourned the meeting in what appeared to be a last-resort move.

Time is of the essence during the legislative session. The state legislature considers thousands of bills annually, and only a fraction makes it through. A bill has only so much time to make it through the sausage machine.

I knew any bill awaiting to be heard in this meeting was dead. Worse, the bill died not because of the proposed policy's merits but because of obstructive incivility. I want to see progress because of efforts made. I began to see my future as a legislative advocate as being like a hamster on a wheel—working fast and hard but going in a circle and going nowhere fast.

I felt a change needed to come, and I began thinking about opportunities to increase my leadership skills. I soon received an e-mail from the Washington Center for Nursing Executive Director. I'd made a short list of people she wanted to notify of her impending retirement.

Being A Risky Hire and Navigating Nursing Leadership

I became the second Executive Director of the Washington Center for Nursing. I was also the first woman of color to lead a statewide nursing organization. The circle of nursing leadership is small in the state. As the face of the state nursing association's legislative advocacy, I often challenged the positions of the Board of Nursing and was seen as a competitor by other nursing unions. Because I advocated for staff nurses, I regularly challenged hospital nurse executives' positions. My past role created a reputation vulnerable to bias against me, making a challenging transition into the Executive Director role.

Success in a highly political environment depends on relationships rather than tactics, strategy, or ability to compete. Higher education misses this point: the importance of socialization into roles. Navigating my way as a member of nursing leadership would teach me this valuable lesson.

Nursing leaders advocated for a state nursing workforce center in the early 2000s in response to a severe nursing shortage. There was consensus that data that described the nursing workforce and gaps that created persistent shortages were fragmented, and there should be one entity to house that information. As a result, the state legislature created a not-for-profit state nursing resource center in 2003, with a funding source in the form of a surcharge, or an additional fee, on licensed practical, registered, and advanced practice nurses. The WA State Department of Health receives those funds and disburses them to the nursing resource center through a contract laying out deliverables or activities the WCN agrees to perform. The activities must be consistent with the statute that outlines the center's role.

The WA Center for Nursing is a not-for-profit state nursing resource center. As stated in the statute, it is governed by a board comprised of and led by nurses. My window into nursing politics is the result of the powers that be at the time, including three of the leading nursing unions: the WA State Nurses Association, United Food and Commercial Workers 141, Service Employees International Union 1199NW, as well as the Northwest Organization of Nurse Executives (hospital nurse executives), advanced registered nurse practitioner representatives, the Council on Nursing Education in WA State, which includes a representative from community colleges, and a representative for four-year colleges and universities.

Diversity in nursing is inversely related to a nurse's educational attainment. Licensed practical nurses are the most diverse group, followed by registered nurses. However, diversity among registered nurses generally lags behind that of the population at large. Diversity decreases further among nurses with graduate degrees. One of the critical functions of a nursing workforce center like WCN is to establish data that could describe key characteristics of the workforce, such as demographics, educational attainment, and practice role. Nursing leaders of organizations typically have graduate degrees. Their authority influences budgets, hiring practices, availability of training, and workplace policies that directly impact the diversity of the nursing workforce.

Like many professions, socialization occurs when a member learns the rules of the road and ways of conduct. Entering nursing leadership poses unique challenges in a profession where females are over 88% of the population. There are studies and a variety of commentary about indirect aggression among women. Examples of indirect aggression include exclusion from a peer group, spreading rumors behind a woman's back, and other tactics to undermine a woman's leadership. In contrast, men are socialized to compete more directly. As a result, they tend to be direct and open about conflict.

The Board of Nursing (BON) historically resided under the WA State Department of Health as one of the dozens of health professions the DOH regulated. Over the years, the BON gained independence over its budget by legislation. Unbeknownst to my predecessor and me, the BON negotiated with the department. to have oversight over the WCN contract. The BON was working on revising nursing education regulations for schools of nursing. Licensure fees had been stagnant for years due to advocacy by the nursing unions, and the BON budget remained stagnant. There has been a historical tension about whether the BON or state's nurses own the nurse licensing dollars. A vast majority of Washington's nurses are in a union, giving a significant voice to these organizations. A consistent union agenda is to keep licensure fees low.

The state boards of nursing have one job: regulating the nursing profession in the state. They set standards for nursing schools and determine criteria for students to graduate, administer the licensure exam, and restrict or revoke a nurse's license if they are shown to be a risk to patient safety.

After the Board of Nursing received more independence over its resources, there was an observable drift in its policy priorities away from being aligned with the WA State Department of Health. Instead, Washington's Board of Nursing sought alignment with their national organization, the National Council of State Boards of Nursing (NCSBN). The NCSBN had an ambitious agenda to create a national database of the nearly 4 million registered nurses in the United States to track nurses across state lines. The momentum behind a nurse licensure compact was growing. When I joined the WCN, there were less than 25 states in the compact. There are now 42, spurred on by the pandemic and the rise of travel nurses.

Each state regulates the nursing workforce within its borders by issuing licenses to practice. Before the nurse licensure compact, a nurse had to apply for a license to practice in a particular state. If a nurse wanted to practice in multiple states, the nurse would have to apply for an endorsement in each additional state. Endorsement fees are a significant source of income for the WA Board of Nursing and rose significantly during COVID-19 due to the influx of travel nurses.

The NCSBC is one of the US's most highly resourced national nursing organizations, with funding coming from each state's board of nursing and a few international members. The NCSBN also controls the licensure exam, the NCLEX-RN, which both US and internationally-educated nurses must pass to practice in the US. A few countries have also adopted the NCLEX-RN to license their registered nurses.

One or two states housed their nursing workforce centers within their state board of nursing. The WCN founders opted for a private, not-for-profit model.

WCN pioneered establishing and regularly convening the Council on Nursing Education in WA State (CNEWS). By having all nursing schools in four-year colleges and universities and community colleges convene in one forum, the group was well-positioned to collaborate on initiatives to support the schools and benefit students. The Board of Nursing, as regulators of nursing education, had its own ideas on how to improve nursing education and worked to revise nursing education regulations. WCN supported CNEWS convenings over the years and co-authored a Master Plan for Nursing Education, which outlined the strategies needed to improve nursing education to address the nursing shortage, including continuing competency, increasing the supply of nurses, promoting diversity, and enhancing educational access.

I first stepped into the role in 2015, and the budget of the WCN was a little over half a million dollars. I joined the National Forum of State Nursing Workforce Centers, the national association for nearly 40 organizations nationwide. There, I learned about state nursing workforce centers, such as WCN's unique role in contributing to state nursing workforce development. Like the almost 40 sister organizations, our role was to develop a data collection and analysis system to describe the nursing workforce accurately, the distribution of nurses across specialties, and geographic distribution. The goal is to more accurately describe gaps in the nursing workforce and potentially prevent shortages. Data could also inform targeted strategies to address workforce shortages beyond the number of nurses needed. I became active in the Forum's research committee and gained expertise in data collection and analysis of nursing workforce data. I served as President of the Forum to increase staffing support for the Forum for the purpose of building partnerships and supporting strategic initiatives to enhance the influence of our members and that of the association nationally. One statutory charge of the center was to evaluate nursing education and support the mobility of nurses throughout their careers. The WCN was to pay particular focus to underrepresented nurses across its efforts.

As the new Executive Director of WCN, I took the time to learn what nursing workforce centers did around the country and where WCN could further fulfill its role in nursing workforce development in Washington State. I identified significant gaps in data collection, analysis, and evaluation of nursing education. This type of research took considerable resources, and the first thing I did was leverage an existing Robert Wood Johnson Foundation grant for Academic Progression in Nursing. One of the grant's goals was to understand better how to improve diversity in the nursing workforce. Part of the grant funds was used to access a University of Washington researcher whose time and expertise were secured with grant funds.

My predecessor did some work on diversity in nursing education by surveying the deans and directors of nursing schools. The goal was to survey deans and directors on effective strategies to increase the diversity of the nursing workforce. Their response generally was the need for more funding or resources to support student nurses of color. A common theme among comments was difficulty working with students of English as a second language.

Nurse educators tended to be older and less diverse than other nurse practice groups. I learned this from national data from the National Forum and the NCSBN. This led me to believe that WCN would benefit from gathering student nurses' perspectives. I saw the benefit of gleaning the perspective of nurses of a younger generation. A school's diversity affects students as much as faculty. There should be curiosity about strategies students identified and how they differ from the deans or directors of their schools. Results showed differences in key areas, especially among underrepresented students. Diverse students viewed the importance of family as the top influence of their decision to become nurses. In contrast, deans and directors rated outreach to families low. In addition, students from underrepresented groups valued face-to-face instruction. In contrast, white students valued the flexibility of remote learning. While this study is almost ten years old, I've found the results resonate when I present these results to nursing students of color and other diverse groups of nurses.

Having spent years as a visible advocate for a nursing union, I wanted to establish a reset with the Executive Director of the state Board of Nursing. I communicated my desire to be in a different type of relationship. At least one different from our past adversarial encounters. I wanted her to understand WCN's role was different from that of the WSNA in the nursing community and that I wanted my approach to the BON to be more consistent with this new way of working together.

I experienced the Board of Nursing exerting more control over the WCN's work through its newly acquired role as contract manager. The statute establishing the WCN explicitly states that the DOH was to grant the organization funds. Yet, the DOH deferred to the BON on how dollars were distributed fundamentally. Funds would no longer flow to us like a grant, as the statute required, but as a contract for goods and services. I raised concerns. I recommended that the contracts office of the DOH be consulted about the implications of the WCN being a sole source contractor. Sole source contractors are uniquely qualified to implement the required work, and this was the mechanism by which legislators designed a funding stream for the WCN. The WCN was the only organization in the state that qualified due to the composition of its Board of Directors. However, the Board of Nursing's viewpoint was that they had the authority to determine whether WCN would remain a sole source contractor or not as the new contract manager.

As the new contract manager, the BON capped the funds we would receive at the amount the organization spent over the last two years. The consequence was that growth in surcharge funds would remain fixed, even if surcharge revenue grew.

I remember walking into a room of DOH staff with my board chair to discuss these new contract terms imposed on us. We were outnumbered by the Board of Nursing staff who laid out these new requirements, while DOH staff sat in silent complicity. I was disappointed because I had a working relationship with DOH contracts department staff that went back years.

I look back on that experience, where I felt coerced and angry and perceived attempts to intimidate me. I usually assume the good intentions of others and have no problem making a case as an advocate. I did want to believe that the BON wanted to bring me down or saw me as less than. Yet it was a David and Goliath situation, with the Board of Nursing having a more significant number of staff and a budget ten times that of WCN. I took this strong-arm tactic very personally.

BON staff lobbied the legislature with data WCN collected to argue a nursing shortage among nurse faculty and advocated for more funds to raise nurse educator salaries. This argument crossed purposes with the WA State Nurses Association advocating for hospital-patient ratios. The hospital association used the argument by the BON to oppose the nurses' association, arguing that schools were not in a position to graduate the number of nurses for mandated staffing ratios needed given a nurse faculty shortage. WSNA confronted the BON. WSNA approached me, concerned that I armed the BON with the data for their agenda. WCN's statutory authority did not allow surcharge funds to be used for lobbying purposes. Besides, we were a 501(c)(3), significantly limiting our ability to lobby. However, the data WCN gathers is public information, and our efforts highlighted the gap between nurse faculty salaries and nurses in clinical roles. This gap created a challenge for nursing schools, which could not compete with salaries offered by hospitals and clinics.

Having been the legislative and political director for WSNA the previous seven years, I maintained a strong relationship with WSNA leadership and governmental affairs staff. I could speak with the WSNA executive director frankly and share my concerns about the BON's control over our contract and, therefore, their use of our data to support their nursing education agenda. Shortly after that, BON staff engaged in lobbying resigned from the Board of Nursing. I'd outlived incivility, for now.

The BON was successful in advocating for more state funds to support nursing education programs in Washington State with 44 million additional dollars a year going to nursing programs within community and technical college. A persistent methaphor for legislating is sausage making, which results in unintended consequences. I learned after legislation passed that the 44 million dollar figure was meant to cover a gap for both four year college an university nursing programs and nursing programs administered by community and technical colleges. The additional 44 million dollars were allocated through a bill limited to funding community and technical colleges. As a result, nursing schools within four-year colleges and universities did not receive additional funding to support higher salaries for their educators. I don't know how the BON conducted their advocacy to legislators which resulted in leaving out four-year colleges and universities. These institutions are half of the state's capacity to graduate nursing students. Further, colleges and universities are the only nursing education institutions that could graduate future generations of nurse educators. This inequity persists today, and Washington continues to suffer from a shortage of nurse educators. Four-year colleges and universities now face increased challenges in recruiting and retaining faculty because they now must compete with the higher salaries offered at community and technical colleges. A problematic competition and tension between four-year colleges, universities, and communities was created at a time when we need more faculty across the board because it is a statewide problem. The result also undermined work by WCN, CNEWS, and the Board of Nursing through an academic progression grant, which aimed to promote nurses earning higher degrees by progressing to from community colleges to four-year colleges and universities.

I was concerned about how the BON conducted its advocacy with WCN's information without acknowledging our role in providing the data. As someone experienced in governmental affairs, I was concerned that the BON disregarded my advice to collaborate and coordinate with the nurses' association on their legislative efforts to avoid undermining each other's work. I turned to my board of directors. They saw a pattern of bullying behavior and felt compelled to address it.

In the darkness of COVID-19, the BON decided to conduct bidding for a new organization to take on the work of the state's nursing workforce center. They insinuated that organizations such as the National Council for State Boards of Nursing and the WA Board of Nursing had the expertise to do this work. The BON used its power as contract manager to put another in charge of the work. Another organization that wouldn't challenge their actions.

It was 2020. Television and social media highlighted racial inequities and resulting injustices after the murder of George Floyd. The vibrant discussions online helped me process my feelings related to observations of the WCN being used by the board of nursing. Kym Ali, a vocal African American nurse consultant in DEI, shared her own story of marginalization while working for a Fortune 500 company. She described her experience as efforts to silence her voice, public character insult, and being dehumanized into a stereotype. She was treated possessively; she felt defenseless, humiliated, and emotionally exhausted. I didn't want to believe that I was experiencing bias, let alone racism. During a discussion about my challenges with the Board of Nursing, a WCN board asked me, "*Why are you being treated differently?*" We compared my approach with the previous Executive Director, who had a much better relationship with the Board of Nursing despite her reputation for being a strong and challenging personality. The board members said out loud what I did not want to be true. She concluded that the primary difference between the previous Executive Director and me was that I am a person of color. From my perspective, I felt the Board was coercive, undermining, and not operating in good faith.

When the House Health Care & Wellness Chair of the state legislature legislator heard about the board of nursing's attempt to end our contract, she reached out directly to the Secretary of Health. She ended that passive-aggressive attempt to close down the WCN.

The Secretary assigned one of his staff to oversee a facilitator to mediate differences between the Board of Nursing and the WCN and to help us create a plan to get us back on track to working together. This involved several meetings led by a facilitator. She would interview me, WCN, and the Board of Nursing members separately. There would also be meetings where she convened the entire group to help us design a path forward.

After one of those meetings, the facilitator sent me an e-mail documenting her observation that the BON interrupted me the most often during meetings. I sought her help in bringing these microaggressions to light for discussion in upcoming meetings. To my disappointment, she didn't act on my request that she facilitate a discussion and confront the person committing the microaggressions.

The facilitator did document her concerns in an e-mail to me. I forwarded the e-mail to my board members and sought advice on what to do next. Although they did not respond with a plan of action, they openly agreed that they would be complicit in allowing this behavior if they did nothing. This evidence in writing proved to be what was needed to address this damaging dynamic.

The facilitator also recommended I read *In the Company of Women* because of her simple observation that all players in this situation were women. This book would be essential in helping me understand the roots of the dynamic between myself and the BON staff. This book researched female-to-female aggression in the workplace, which has increased significantly over the years. It described research on how women have been socialized since childhood to promote egalitarianism. When a woman takes on a leadership role, this creates a power imbalance that results in behavior described as indirect aggression. One example is exclusion from a peer group. Despite having 13 years of legislative experience, BON staff did not consult with me or acknowledge my skill in legislative advocacy. It is true that WCN could not lobby as an organization based on statutory and 501(c) 3 statutes. However, my skill in putting together information factsheets, who would be the right collaborators like the nurses' association, or my knowledge of the legislative process was never acknowledged. It was downplayed. Early on, I connected the BON with WSNA's new legislative director. I knew that the WSNA would continue to maintain expert governmental affairs advocates on staff and that the BON would benefit by using them as a soundboard, if not a coalition partner. Another example of indirect aggression is talking behind another's back. I heard from WCN board members that the WABON approached them to let them know they lacked confidence in my skills and abilities. *In The Company of Women* argues that women are socialized to use indirect aggression in a power imbalance. According to a "Power Dead Even Rule," women need to come across as having the same amount of power and self-esteem as the woman or group. In addition, there needs to be an equal give and take of small favors. As a nurse and an attorney, did I create a violation of the Power Dead Even Rule? My intentions in carrying out the actions of the WCN were to be in alignment with our legal obligations by statute, operating as a granted entity and fulfilling the role of the state nursing workforce center. What seemed to matter to the BON is that they wanted the power to be an influencer in the realm of nursing workforce development. Given that the legislature created the WA Center for Nursing, this was a role the WCN was to lead and was out of the Board of Nursing's scope.

Without being personally involved in any more group discussions about this issue, the aggression towards me and the WCN seemed to stop. I continued to meet with BON leadership monthly, but based on the facilitator's recommendations, we had staff in the meetings with us. There was no trust to have one-on-one conversations.

I'm thankful to the WCN board members who clearly advocated behind the scenes on my behalf. Today, I'm not sure who did what. In particular, my board chair, an African American woman who once served on the board of nursing and led the WCN's Diversity, Equity, and Inclusion initiatives, and another board member and union leader passionate about racial justice and defeating racism and bias in her advocacy of the WCN.

Diversity, equity, and inclusion remain at the top of WCN's priorities. As Board Members step down due to retirement, WCN recruits new members from diverse backgrounds, and we are now one of the most diverse boards. Within every research project, we explore the impact of racism on the well-being of nurses. I hire full-time staff to develop and implement WCN's Diversity, Equity, and Inclusion initiatives and form a coalition of nursing organizations committed to serving nurses of color.

There is a substantial body of research on incivility and racism in nursing. Resolving this issue is daunting, but the George Floyd's events and the rise of diverse nurse leaders provide the opportunity to work toward a more civil and inclusive workplace for nurses and those we serve.

Some believe that commitment to diversity, equity, and inclusion in the workplace is waning. At WCN, I ensure that efforts continue and evolve with the needs of the time. I support the importance of continuing to spread knowledge about the damage implicit bias causes in health care. Bias in health delivery systems and research result in significant health disparities, causing needless injury and death. I work with the WCN Board to ensure that increasing the workforce's diversity remains a critical strategy in providing culturally competent care. We identify and partner with allies in the greater nursing community to continue this mission.

What's Next

As I stated in my law school application years ago, one of the most essential things a diverse lawyer can do is to be a positive example of their community. At times, I struggle with what battles to fight, and I have just begun recognizing the biases that surrounded me during my term on the city council and in my work as a nurse leader. Moving forward, I am committed to using my experience to promote good by:

☐ Supporting diverse candidates running for office gets us closer to the cultural representation of our communities, particularly those who can demonstrate using a balanced and thoughtful approach to policy. Our current system is suffering from polarization due to extreme viewpoints

☐ Finding ways to support the mentoring of elected officials in office as a buffer against the isolation and bias that get in the way of effective lawmaking.

☐ Mentoring and developing young professionals from diverse backgrounds as the next generation of leaders and developing programs to reach out to underrepresented youth.

☐ Promoting civility in politics through the American Association of Nurse Attorneys and other groups that I engage with.

☐ Search, join, and support groups of women representing the many facets of my interests to share challenges, mentor each other, and form a community.

A nurse leader who helped jump-start my career in public policy nearly 25 years ago had a sign in her office that said, "*Grow Where You are Planted*." I think back to that fantasy of a plantation that Mom inspired. I think of farmers who grow crops with intention and weed out unwanted growth. I think of plants that seed and grow in places far from their origin. Such new growth results from seeds carried by the wind into new territory. Establishing roots in new places is also a function of survival and migration into new growth areas. Where seeds are planted, growth can be difficult and not always welcome or encouraged. My husband would say to me, *"Honey, you've wandered off the plantation,"* to help me reflect when I face challenges. My Filipina identity often makes me a new player to the table, one that those from established groups are not used to seeing or interacting with. I've been fortunate to be able to grow where I've been planted and committed to using what I've learned to benefit others.

MARIA SANTOS-GREAVES

President and Founder, Surrey Hearing Care, Inc.
Owner and Founder, Minamar
Janitorial Services
Global FWN 100™ 2015

Mastering the Mind: Harnessing Inner Power to Overcome Adversity

T his *narrative offers a profound exploration of the intricate relationship between the mind, emotions, and life experiences, particularly in the context of clinical depression. The narrative is rooted in the personal experiences of the author, who navigates through the complexities of mental health challenges exacerbated by significant life changes, such as relocating to a new country and facing professional setbacks. The narrative is a compelling testament to the strength of the human spirit, particularly within the context of the Filipina experience. It advocates for openness, vulnerability, and the transformative power of shared struggles. The narrative reinforces the importance of acknowledging and addressing our thoughts, not just our actions, to pursue personal growth and healing. Through sharing this journey, Maria Greaves offers hope and inspiration to others facing similar challenges, underscoring the enduring power of the mind when guided by faith and love.*

For much of my life, I believed that my actions were the sole architects of my destiny. We grow up with stories of perseverance and triumph, told that if we work hard enough, we can carve out any future we desire. It's a comforting narrative that gives us a sense of control in an unpredictable world. But as I grew older, I saw the cracks in that story. I realized that our thoughts—the silent, often unexamined voices in our minds—play a profound role in shaping our actions and, thus, our reality. This realization wasn't born from a moment of clarity but forged in the crucible of my struggles with clinical depression. During those darkest hours, I started to understand the immense power of the mind and how, when guided by faith and determination, it could lead me from despair to hope.

My journey began in the Philippines, a country of vibrant culture and deep-rooted values, where I grew up in a humble home. Life there was simple, unadorned by luxury, but rich in the things that truly matter—family, faith, and hard work. My parents, particularly my father, were embodiments of diligence and sacrifice. They weren't wealthy but resourceful, doing everything in their power to provide for us. Their efforts were not just about putting food on the table but also laying the foundation for our future. From them, I learned that no one hands you success—it is something you earn through persistence and sheer will.

This unwavering belief in the power of hard work gave me the courage to leave everything I knew behind and start anew in Canada. It was a decision that filled me with excitement and fear, a leap into the unknown that held the promise of a better future for myself and my family. The Great White North became my new home with its vast landscapes and endless possibilities. But the transition could have been more seamless. The initial years were tough, marked by uncertainty and the constant pressure to succeed in a land where I was, in many ways, a stranger. Yet, I did as my father had taught me—I worked hard, kept my head down, and persevered. Slowly but surely, I began to find my footing. I took risks, built a network, and eventually, with much effort, established my hearing clinic. The sense of achievement was immense.

My family back in the Philippines was proud, and it seemed that all the sacrifices had paid off for a while.

But life has a way of throwing shadows even on the brightest days. As I settled into my new role as a businesswoman, the pressures of my responsibilities began to weigh on me. The distance from my homeland, the cultural differences, and the isolation of being in a foreign land started to take their toll. The echoes of my past, combined with the stresses of my new life, often collided, leading to bouts of depression that were as unexpected as they were overwhelming.

Battling clinical depression feels like waging war against an invisible enemy, especially in the unfamiliar territory of a foreign land. The loneliness was suffocating, and the sense of isolation was sometimes unbearable. It had been years since I had experienced a major depressive episode, but in 2020, I lost my mother. She had been my anchor, the one who had stood by me from the very beginning of my journey. More than I realized, her death left a wound that I could not heal, a void that no amount of success could fill. Yet, in my grief, I found a renewed sense of purpose. I had to be strong, not just for myself, but for my father and my son, who had become my beacons of hope. I continued to dedicate myself to growing my business, pouring my heart and soul into achieving success and garnering recognition, all to secure financial stability. In doing so, I found that immersing myself in work was a convenient distraction, allowing me to evade the lingering shadows of my past. The accolades and financial rewards became a shield, protecting me from the emotional struggles I preferred to keep buried, deep within the depths of my mind.

But fate had more trials in store for me. A year before my mother's passing, my father received the devastating diagnosis of liver cancer. By then, it had already advanced to the third stage and had spread to other parts of his body. Yet, he remained resilient, greeting each day with joy as if the pain couldn't touch him. Alongside his battle with cancer, he was also struggling with dementia, his memory slipping through his fingers like sand on certain days. Knowing he was the only parent I had left ignited a fierce resolve in me to do everything in my power to keep his spirits alight. I became his steadfast companion, tending to him with unwavering devotion, day and night, placing his comfort and happiness above all else, even my own. But before I could fully come to terms with the loss of my mom, I was faced with his passing. His death was a blow that shattered me in ways I hadn't anticipated. I tried to maintain a brave face, to project an image of fortitude, but inside, I was crumbling. The weight of my grief, which I had tried to suppress for the longest time, combined with the pressures of running a business, brought me to the brink. Each bout of depression felt like a wave threatening to drown me, pulling me deeper into a sea of hopelessness.

Despite the crushing despair, I discovered a strength within myself that I hadn't realized existed. In my suffering, it was as if I had unearthed a hidden source of tenacity. I realized that my father's lessons of perseverance were not just about hard work—they were about enduring adversity and finding light even in the darkest times. And so, I kept going, one day at a time, driven by my parents' memory and my love for my son.

By the time last year came around, I found myself standing at a crossroads. I had been through so much, yet I was still here, fighting. But depression has a way of descending upon you when you least anticipate it.

My most recent episode was, without a doubt, the most harrowing one I've endured—a relentless storm that swept in at a time when I should have been celebrating the milestones of life. It was as if the universe had conspired to juxtapose joy and despair, setting them on a collision course that left me reeling. I had been eagerly anticipating a family reunion in the Philippines, a gathering that would be my year's highlight. The reunion was an opportunity to reconnect with loved ones and bask in the pride of receiving an honor from my alma mater. This was a moment I had been waiting for, a beacon of hope after years of upheaval, change, and uncertainty. The reunion felt like the light at the end of a long, dark tunnel, a much-needed respite that would allow me to catch my breath, reset, and find joy in the simple pleasures of life once more.

Alongside the anticipation of the reunion, I had just realized a long-held dream—one that I had nurtured for years: purchasing a property. It wasn't just any property; it was a condo unit I had envisioned for so long, one that could serve as both a business venture and a personal sanctuary. Owning a place of my own had always been a dream, a symbol of stability and achievement, especially after the years of uncertainty I had faced. I saw the condo as a space where I could find solace, a retreat from the chaos of life, and a venture that would allow me to build something tangible, something lasting.

Securing the property was grueling and more complex than I had anticipated. It required numerous visits to the bank, a mountain of paperwork, and more prayers than I could count, hoping for the mortgage approval that seemed perpetually out of reach. Each step felt like a battle, but I was determined to win. When the approval finally came through, it felt like a divine sign, as if all the obstacles had been placed in my path to test my resolve, and now, at last, I was being rewarded for my perseverance. Holding the keys to my little corner of the world felt like holding the keys to my future—a future filled with possibilities and opportunities I had only dared to dream about.

Eager to make the most of this new chapter in my life, I immediately began transforming the condo into a welcoming space. My plan was simple: I would turn the unit into a rental property, generating passive income that would provide me with financial security and a sense of accomplishment. At the same time, the condo would remain a personal retreat—a place where I could escape when the pressures of life became too much. I threw myself into the project with an enthusiasm that I hadn't felt in years. Each day, I visited the condo, making minor adjustments, adding personal touches, and slowly transforming the space into a reflection of my vision. The process was both exhausting and exhilarating—a creative outlet that allowed me to pour my energy into something positive, something that felt like progress.

After weeks of hard work, the condo was finally ready. I took a step back, admired what I had created, and felt a deep sense of satisfaction. This was more than just a property; it was a testament to my resilience, a physical manifestation of my dreams and efforts. Confident in my plan, I advertised the unit online, fully expecting a flood of inquiries to come rolling in. I was confident that the condo would be snapped up quickly and that my vision would soon pay off in tangible ways.

But as the days turned into weeks, the excitement began to fade, replaced by an insidious doubt that crept into my thoughts. The inquiries trickled in, but they were few and far between. Each one that fell through chipped away at my confidence, leaving me to question my decisions. Had I been too ambitious? Was this dream destined to slip through my fingers just as it had started to take shape? The uncertainty gnawed at me, fueling a growing sense of unease that I couldn't shake.

To add to my anxiety, my departure for the Philippines was fast approaching. I desperately wanted to secure a tenant before I left so that I could enjoy my time with family and friends, without the nagging worry of an empty property hanging over me. Each day brought a new wave of stress as the clock ticked down, and I grew increasingly anxious and irritable. My mind, once filled with excitement about the reunion, was now consumed with thoughts of failure and frustration.

Then, when my hopes were starting to dim, I received an inquiry that seemed like the answer to my prayers. An eager tenant expressed interest in renting the space long-term with his family. The space fulfilled every requirement on their list and fell within their budget. It seemed to be a flawless match. The relief I felt was immediate and overwhelming, like a heavy weight had been lifted from my shoulders. I was over the moon, convinced that my plan was finally coming together and that all the struggles and doubts were about to pay off. The renter visited the property and liked what they saw. After some discussion, we quickly came to a mutually favorable agreement. All that was left was for them to move in, and I could finally relax, knowing I had accomplished what I set out to do.

With my worries eased, I turned my attention to my upcoming trip, filled with renewed excitement and anticipation. I went on a shopping spree to pick out gifts and spent hours on the phone making plans with people I hadn't seen in years while imagining the joy on their faces when we reunited. The thought of being surrounded by family, celebrating life's milestones, and basking in the warmth of their love filled me with a sense of contentment that I hadn't felt in a long time.

But just days before my flight, everything came crashing down. I received a shattering message from the prospective tenant: they had found another place and were backing out of our agreement. In an instant, the euphoria I had been feeling evaporated, and my world seemed to collapse around me. Once a symbol of my achievement, the condo now felt like a burden. The dream that had seemed so close to realization was slipping away, leaving me to grapple with the stark reality of what I had lost.

For many Filipinos, moving overseas is often equated with success—a narrative that I had internalized, even as I struggled to reconcile it with my own experiences. But the reality is far more complex, a truth I have lived firsthand. As a Filipina, I faced numerous obstacles, often compounded by societal pressures and personal aspirations that created a delicate, precarious balance. The failed investment was more than just a financial setback; it was a blow to my mental health, unearthing emotions and fears that I had buried deep within after the loss of my parents. It was a blunt reminder of how quickly life's fragile balance can tip, leaving us to navigate the darkness once again.

My ego, insatiable and relentless, drove me into an endless cycle of pursuit. I became obsessed with the idea that I needed more—more success, more recognition, more proof that I was on the right path. When the ground beneath me started to tremble, I did what I knew best: I distracted myself. As I flew to the Philippines, I drowned out the inner turmoil with trivial activities, filling my days with shopping sprees and visits to unfamiliar places, hoping to escape the weight of my crumbling situation. But underneath these surface-level distractions, my sense of self-worth was eroding, slowly but surely, just like the foundation of my financial security.

On my third night back home, I had planned a reunion dinner for my family. It was supposed to be a night of joy and reconnection—a time to reminisce, laugh, and bask in the warmth of familial love. I wanted everything to be perfect, to recapture the simple happiness that had always been a part of our gatherings. But as the night approached, a strange feeling began to settle in—a growing unease that tugged at the fringes of my mind. What should have been a night of celebration slowly morphed into something else entirely—a confrontation with the darker issues that had been hidden in my mind. As I made my way to the venue, I found myself feeling more anxious than excited. Thoughts of fear that had been simmering under the surface now surged to the forefront, overtaking my mind and clouding my emotions. It was as if an invisible force was actively working against me, trying to prevent me from finding any joy in the moment. When I finally arrived, the emotions I had been trying so hard to suppress overwhelmed me completely. I broke down outside, tears streaming down my face, as a flood of negative emotions poured out.

I stood there, vulnerable and exposed, unable to hide from the pain any longer. The weight of years of suppression—years of shoving down my emotions, pushing them aside in the name of progress—had finally caught up with me. The burden had become too heavy to bear, and now it was crushing me. At that moment, I didn't see it for what it was: depression, creeping in quietly and stealing the joy from my life, leaving me feeling trapped and smothered. The despair was suffocating, and for the first time, I was forced to confront the truth that I had been avoiding for so long.

They say that fear is the mind-killer, and in my experience, it paralyzes me, amplifying every sense of despair that I had tried so hard to ignore. Fear became my constant companion, always lurking just beneath the surface, waiting for the right moment to strike. My ego, too, was locked in battle, trying desperately to maintain control over my mind, to keep me from acknowledging the reality of my situation. Despite the mounting darkness, I stubbornly refused to face the truth. I told myself I could handle it and did not need help. But as the hours grew darker, a glimmer of hope began to emerge—a bleak but steady light that signaled the possibility of reclaiming control over my mind.

It started with a single act of courage: opening up about my struggles. It was the first step; as is often the case, it was the hardest. Shame and the fear of judgment loomed large, with my ego standing as a barrier between me and the help I desperately needed. But with each conversation—with family, friends, and even colleagues—the faint light in my mind grew stronger.

Each conversation was like peeling back a layer of the darkness that had enveloped me. I had always prided myself on being strong, independent, and self-sufficient. Admitting that I was struggling, that I was in pain, felt like admitting defeat. But as I spoke, I realized that my strength didn't lie in pretending everything was okay. It lay in my ability to confront my fears, to allow myself to be vulnerable, and to accept help when I needed it.

Through these exchanges, I discovered the transformative power of vulnerability. Sharing my truth not only lightened my burden but also allowed others to offer their wisdom, strength, and love. I am forever grateful for the lifelong friends who emerged from this journey—friends who, as it turned out, possessed the expertise that could help me in profound ways. My childhood friend Deng, a doctor, was among the first I confided in. Having known me since my first major depressive episode, I felt comfortable laying bare my soul to him. He listened without judgment, his compassion palpable, and he took it upon himself to retrieve my medical records from decades ago in the Philippines. He put me in touch with a reliable colleague, and within days, I secured an appointment with a psychiatrist.

Even as everything seemed to fall into place, doubt persisted. I found myself asking, "What will be different this time?" Despite my apprehension, I mustered the courage to attend my appointment. I spoke candidly with my psychiatrist, unburdening the emotions I had felt and suppressed over the years. At work, I am usually the listener, absorbing clients' troubles and concerns. Finding myself on the receiving end of someone's attentive ear was a rare and comforting shift. By the end of our conversation, she had prescribed medication and arranged for future sessions. With her help and the sympathy and determination of those around me, I found myself on the path to recovery. The support I received was overwhelming, transforming how I viewed my situation.

This humbling experience taught me a vital lesson: the closer we are to fear, the farther we are from love. Concealing my struggles had only delayed my healing. It was only when I faced my fears and set aside my ego that things began to improve. My family, always my anchor, stood by me with unwavering support. Their love was the bedrock upon which I started to rebuild my life. My friends were there, offering their shoulders and ears, reminding me that I was not alone. Even when I was away, and after I returned, the community I had built in Surrey and my friends from church rallied around me, providing both practical help and spiritual support.

As the days turned into weeks and weeks into months, I began to see the changes in myself. The darkness that had once consumed me started to recede, replaced by a growing sense of peace and acceptance. It wasn't an overnight transformation— recovery is rarely a straight path. There were still days when I felt like I was teetering on the edge, but each time, I found myself better equipped to pull back, to ground myself, and to remember the love and support that surrounded me.

I started to rebuild, not just my life, but my sense of self. The person I had been before— driven by ego and fear—began giving way to someone new. Someone who understood that true strength isn't about never falling; it's about getting back up, time and time again, no matter how many times you stumble. It's about embracing vulnerability, admitting when you need help, and recognizing that you don't have to do it all alone. My years-long fight with depression also transformed me from within. I was no longer just the woman who believed that hard work alone could shape her destiny. I had come to understand that it was my thoughts and mindset that determined my path. Although thoughts can often feel uncontrollable when grappling with depression, the willingness to seek help remains firmly within your grasp. In embracing the help offered to us, we find our true strength.

In the end, I realized this: my ego had been my greatest obstacle, but it was also my greatest teacher. It showed me the importance of humility, of accepting that I am human and that to be human is to be imperfect. It taught me that the pursuit of more—more success, more recognition, more validation—was a path that led only to emptiness. True fulfillment, I learned, comes not from what we achieve, but from who we are, and how we choose to live our lives.

As I stand now, on the other side of this journey, I am not the same person I once was. I am stronger, yes, but I am also softer, more compassionate, more understanding. I have learned to be kinder to myself, to forgive my mistakes, and to embrace the person I am becoming. And in doing so, I have found a sense of peace that I had long thought impossible.

My journey is far from over, but I know now that I am not alone. I have my family, my friends, and a community that stands with me. And most importantly, I have myself—the person I have fought so hard to become. And for that, I am eternally grateful.

As I navigated the depths of this challenging period, I began to recognize a profound truth: the mind, when harnessed with faith and love, can transcend even the darkest moments. My journey was no longer just about surviving depression; it evolved into a transformative path of personal growth and healing. I realized that my thoughts were not merely fleeting whispers—they were the architects of my reality. By consciously nurturing positive thoughts and surrounding myself with a community of supportive, compassionate people, I found that I could begin to shape a brighter, more hopeful future.

Amid this inner turmoil, I found an anchor in my faith. Though it had always been a guiding force in my life, it became a wellspring of immense strength and comfort during this particularly turbulent time. Prayer and meditation became my daily rituals, calming the turbulence in my mind and providing moments of peace amid the chaos. My faith gently reminded me that I was not alone in my struggles and that a higher power guided my steps, even when the path ahead seemed unclear.

I discovered the healing process was a gradual journey with ups and downs. There were days when the simple act of getting out of bed or taking a shower felt like a monumental achievement, and the weight of despair threatened to pull me under. Yet, each small victory—a genuine smile, a burst of laughter, finishing a simple task—became a sign of hope, marking my gradual progress toward recovery. I learned to celebrate these moments, however trivial they may have seemed at the time, understanding that they were crucial steps in my journey back to wholeness.

Approaching this journey with renewed hope, I am discovering the profound value of self-compassion. For years, I had been my own harshest critic, driving myself relentlessly to achieve more, to be better, and to meet an impossible standard of perfection. In doing so, I had overlooked my own needs, neglecting the very essence of who I was. It took time, patience, and a great deal of introspection, but eventually, I began to treat myself with the same kindness and understanding that I so readily extended to others. I learned to acknowledge my efforts. To honor my resilience. To forgive myself for my perceived shortcomings. This shift in mindset was not just healing—it was transformative, laying the foundation for my continued growth.

As I share my story, I desire to inspire others facing similar battles. Depression is indeed a formidable adversary, but it is not invincible. By acknowledging our thoughts and seeking out the support of those around us, we can find our way through even the darkest times. I have learned that the love and support from the people around us hold a power far greater than any fear, shame, or despair. Through these connections, we find strength, healing, and, ultimately, a way forward.

The enduring spirit of the Filipina—a spirit characterized by resilience, faith, and an unwavering capacity for love—is something I carry with me, a testament to the strength and determination that resides within us all. By embracing openness and vulnerability and by daring to share our struggles and truths, we can transform our pain into sources of strength and inspiration, not just for ourselves but also for those who walk alongside us.

This chapter of my life is a powerful reminder that true healing and empowerment come from within. We can achieve profound personal growth by addressing our thoughts and actions with holistic care and nurturing our bodies, minds, and spirits. The journey is not easy, but it is in facing these challenges that we discover our true strength and the depths of our resilience.

As I look back on my journey, from my humble beginnings in the Philippines to my current life in Canada, I am filled with a deep sense of gratitude. Each experience, whether filled with joy or laced with pain, has played a crucial role in shaping the person I have become. I continue striving for a meaningful future, guided by the knowledge that my thoughts, my faith, and the love surrounding me are powerful tools in shaping my reality.

The power of the mind, when aligned with faith and love, can lead us to light, healing, and a future filled with possibility. Let us embrace our thoughts, seek the support we need, and always remember that we are never truly alone in our struggles. Through this, we can find deep empowerment, profoundly transforming ourselves and touching the lives of those around us.

ISABELITA T. MANALASTAS-WATANABE, M.A.

President, Speed International Finance

President, Speed Consulting Services, Inc.

President & Representative Director, Speed Money Transfer Japan Kabushiki Kaisha.

Global FWN 100™ 2013

Navigating the Labyrinth of Race and Gender In Japan

I have known Lita since we were both Japanese Ministry of Education scholars here in Japan. We became very good friends, sharing a common bond of being sorority sisters at the University of the Philippines and being students in the Japanese education system, grappling with the Japanese language. Although Lita and I had totally different fields of study, we became close by sharing each other's joys, struggles and triumphs. I have seen Lita rise from struggling student to director of the ASEAN-Japan Centre in Tokyo, and then head of the Philippine National Bank Tokyo Branch. While she was the top person in these organizations, she remained very unassuming and firmly rooted to the ground. These positions never went to her head even as she expertly performed her roles. Despite all that she has attained professionally, she has also had personal problems, which she openly shared with me. I saw her go through some of these battles, during which she remained steadfast and strong. Able to overcome all of them in her own right, she *is now the person that she is. She has fought hard and won, showing that she is indeed a true warrior, battle-hardened and triumphant.*

Ms. Leith Casel-Schut

Linguist

In FWN's Leadership Book 4.0, BEING, authors were asked by the Editor to write three words that best described themselves. I was the only one who chose WARRIOR as one of my three words. The book editor herself was the only one who wrote KATIPUNERA. It is probably because she and I are *Kapampangan.*[44] Arguably, Kapampangan women have asserted their individuality and influence since the 300s and 1400s, even though one sees only a few women in Kapampangan history. Take, Luisa Gonzaga De Leon of Bacolor, Pampanga. She wrote "Ejercito Cotidiano: "*iti amanu yang Castila bildug ne quing amanung Capampangan nang Dona Luisa Gonzaga de Leon, India quing balayang Baculud*," (*Daily Devotion*) (Translated from the Spanish language to the Kapampangan language by Doña Luisa Gonzaga de Leon, India of the town of Bacolor) which was published in 1844 (a year after her death) and made her the first woman author in Philippine history. This pioneer chose to identify with her Kapampangan lineage as "India" (a native woman) instead of Chinese, as custom dictated, since her paternal grandfather was Chinese. And, of course, I must mention the women of the Revolution: Praxedes Fajardo y Puno, Nicolasa Dayrit y Pamintuan, Matea Sioco, and Adriana Hilario. Equally commendable are the women who fought in the armed struggle against the Japanese and later against social injustice, such as Felipa Culala, also known as Kumander Dayang-Dayang, Elena Poblete, known as Kumander Mameng, and many other Kapampangan women.

Thus, I believe that when we are born, and I was born a *Kapampangan,* we are already destined for a future, although still unknown. Only God knows where we will be and what we will be until we leave this earth to join our creator. I have the same blood flowing in my veins as those powerful *Kapampangan* women who did not stay home while their men were out, changing the world.

"Warrior" can be a misunderstood term if not seen in my intended context. When I describe myself as a warrior, I mean a fighter who does not give up despite significant challenges hindering my success. Like bamboo that bends but does not break during

---

44   Kapampangan is a language in the province of Pampanga, located in Central Luzon, the Philippines. As many think, it is not a dialect, but it is classified as a language, as it is not mutually intelligible with other Philippine languages like Tagalog.

harsh typhoons and strong winds, I stand up even after falling, ready to rise and fight again, embodying the true spirit of the warrior that I am.

During the UPCAT (University of the Philippines College Admissions Test) that I took in 1970, I heard one sophisticated, rich-looking girl who was there to take the test say, *"Palulubugin natin ang mga probinsiyanang iyan" (We will ensure these people from the provinces go down the drain)*, looking at me directly. It was good my mother made me take valium before the UPCAT to ease my nerves. Of course, I made it to UP, the top-rate state university in the Philippines.

My time in the university, 1970-1974, was a milestone that only we in that generation were privileged to experience Martial Law and to see and hear first-hand the military firing their guns in various colleges in U.P. to force student activists to surrender. It was the time when friends in high school suddenly were not seen and were unheard of for years, and joy when they finally surfaced to rejoin society. I am so envious of the courage of those young men and women who fought for their principles despite the personal sacrifices and hardships that they knew they would experience by going underground. Me? I did what I thought was enough to contribute to the "movement," but perhaps "my enough" was not enough. It was not my warrior moment.

Maybe it was destiny that I continued studying, despite the many political upheavals during my youth, and then moved head-on, with solid determination, to realize my dreams of finishing my studies, even though I could not realize what I originally wanted for a career. I could not be a medical doctor but became a successful economist.

My decision to take my research and graduate studies in Japan and not in any other first-world country shaped my future. It made me what I am today, personally and professionally. While doing my M.A. in Economics at Tsukuba University on a full scholarship from the Japanese government, I almost gave up as I was illiterate in Japanese - **I could not read, write, or speak Japanese.** My Japanese classmates' computer ability and math levels were superior to my training. I never saw a computer during college, much less used one, and I never saw those economic equations in my econometrics class! One day, while riding my bike from my dorm to my class, I suddenly stopped at a park, cried, and asked myself, "What am I doing here?" At that moment of despair, I thought I should go home, give up my studies, and return to the comfort of my job as an economic researcher at the National Economic and Development Authority (NEDA). The crying and the thought of giving up lasted only 15 minutes. I stood up, bravely attended class, and talked with my guide-professor.

It is in realizing one's weaknesses and being honest about one's lack of ability or shortcomings that one can move to the next step. You know where you stand, and then do something about it! I told my guide-professor I needed a math tutor and wanted computer training. Voila! My guide-professor assigned a PhD student to help me with my aRithmetic (Math), and he sent me to Fujitsu Institute in Tokyo for a computer training course.

I read Samuelson's requisite Econ—101 book in Japanese. So, my Reading was alright, although, in Japanese kanji, one may know the meaning of a kanji character or a combination of more than one character. Still, you may not necessarily know how to read and pronounce the character or combination of characters. Anyway, it was only my aRithmetic and wRiting that I had to work very hard on.

I should have added Speak to those 3Rs I have mentioned. My advice to international students in Japan has always been, and still is, SPEAK in JAPANESE, no matter if you make many mistakes. Since Filipinos have good English-speaking ability, we switch easily to English when faced with difficulty speaking Japanese. It was a costly mistake for me to have that fear or worry to be laughed at, making mistakes in my spoken Japanese that made me less fluent than I would have if I had swallowed my foolish pride.

I spent three years in Japan—one year as a research student and two years as an M.A. student. Then, I returned to NEDA to serve.

But then Japan beckoned me to return to the land of the rising sun. As fate had it, a letter from the Philippine Department of Foreign Affairs (DFA) asked various government offices to nominate a candidate for a very high-ranking head of investments post at the ASEAN-Japan Center in Tokyo. ASEAN Promotion of Trade, Investment, and Tourism was an interregional governmental organization funded 90% by the Japanese government and 10% by the then-six ASEAN countries—Indonesia, Malaysia, the Philippines, Singapore, and Thailand. It still exists with its headquarters in Tokyo, and all current ASEAN member countries are members.

In my written response, I listed my ability to speak the Japanese language and familiarity with doing business with Japanese as an "added advantage."

Although I had no investment experience at the NEDA, I told my immediate boss I could do it. I could learn how to do the job and do it even better than the more experienced ones. I was in my warrior mode when the head of the Board of Investments of the Department of Trade and Industry interviewed me. I got the job!

I tried to find out who from DFA wrote that "added advantage" requirement. Again, my destiny was becoming clearer and clearer – he was a former Ambassador in Austria who was then a member of NEDA's inter-agency committee on trade, tariffs, and related matters (TTRM) for which my office served as secretariat. At the very tender age of 21, NEDA gave me the opportunity to meet and work with many much more senior officials from various government offices who were members of the TTRM. Speaking of fate!

At only 27, a female, and a Filipina, I had all the attributes for NOT becoming successful in Japan. Youth is not respected. Japanese women take a subordinate role and are famous for the "M curve." Japanese women join the workforce, starting from the bottom, slowly going up the ladder, then going down when they get married and are expected to resign to raise kids as *kyoiku* (education) mamas. When they rejoin the workforce, it is no longer for a career path but to earn financially (as part-timers), then down again when they get old and no longer in demand in the job market.

I needed to be a much stronger and much wittier warrior. Instead of informing organizations, universities, and other institutions requesting a lecturer on promoting Japanese investments to ASEAN countries that Ms. Manalastas would give the talk, I instructed my staff to refer to me as Manalastas Jicho, which means Deputy Director in Japanese. In Japan, it is customary to address someone by name, followed by their official designation, without indicating gender. This decision stemmed from a past experience where I was mistaken for a tea server or a simultaneous interpreter rather than being recognized as the main speaker at an investment seminar in Nagoya, southwestern Japan. At the presidential table, my nameplate read Mr. Manalastas.

During my initial career in Japan, I faced numerous frustrating experiences and considerable discrimination. However, I never gave up. I worked tirelessly to be recognized for my capabilities and abilities. Believing that God helps those who help themselves, I adopted a professional appearance by wearing dark, conservative suits, styling my long hair in a bun, and switching to dark, black-rimmed glasses.

Despite my efforts, I continued to be a curiosity. I graced the covers of Japanese magazines, appeared on the state television station, and was frequently interviewed. Remarkably, I was chosen as one of Japan's ten most beautiful professional women by *Shukan Bunshu*, a highly popular Japanese magazine featuring our photographs. This only heightened the curiosity about me, turning me into a sensation. I worked tirelessly, often putting in long hours six days a week. Yet, I relished every opportunity to surprise my hosts at various seminars and conferences with my youth, gender, and, of course, my abilities.

I am confident the ASEAN countries did not make a mistake in choosing me to represent all the member countries at promoting Japanese investments in the region. The Thai Board of Investments representative at the Centre nominated me for a second three-year term, and finally, I was extended for another three-year term, totaling nine years--unheard of in the history of the Centre. Being the highest-paid Filipina professional in Japan is something I still find unbelievable.

For my country, the Philippines, I take pride in being instrumental in Yokohama Rubber's decision to locate in the Philippines. Yokohama Tires, the Philippine subsidiary of the parent company in Japan, has expanded its operations over the years, occupying a huge tract of land in Clark, Pampanga, my home province, and now employing almost 3,000 workers.

I vividly recall diligently preparing to brief the executives of Yokohama Rubber about the advantages of locating in the Philippines compared to other Asian countries, only to discover they had already done their homework (as the Japanese always do). Despite this, I was taken aback by the unexpected questions they asked me, such as:

1. "If some officials ask for bribe money, what shall we do?"

2. "How much?"

3. *"If one employee asks one of our Japanese staff to be godfather to an employee's wedding, shall we agree?"*

4. *"Is it good to employ Filipinos living in the same area/barrio?"*

5. *"What can we do for the community so that they will appreciate our presence in the country and be loyal to our company, but will not cost us too much money?"*

At least, that is how I remember what happened during my briefing decades ago. I also recall my answers to those unexpected questions.

1. "YES. Anyway, in any country you go to, there will be corruption. Just be prepared for it;

2. *"It depends on how big-a-favor you want;*

3. *"No. Otherwise, you cannot refuse any succeeding requests to be ninong to hundreds of potential weddings among your employees;*

4. *"Definitely Yes. You will cultivate a lot of goodwill from that one area, and those local people there will be forever grateful to you;*

5. *"Basketball courts."*

I still keep a handwritten copy of a letter from one of the Yokohama executives who was present during my talk. In it, he thanked me and even read my horoscope. I recently contacted him. He is now more than 80 years old and not quite well health-wise, yet I still hope to meet him again in person and take him for a drink or two.

During my nine years at the ASEAN-Japan Centre in Tokyo, I had the opportunity to meet various heads of state, government ministers, and ALSO many DOMs - **D**irty **O**ld **M**en who think I will curry favors from them, need their influence to make me go up higher in the ladders of a successful career, and so agree to go out on dates with them. I could name the names of those who tried, but I will not, of course, because there is no need to shame them. Many are still alive but are probably already moving closer to their 6-foot-deep underground home. Offers of Mercedes Benzes, condos, and jewelry. Why be tempted? I know my abilities, and I am super qualified for what I was doing. I did not need any DOMs to push me up to greater heights.

My next professional experience in Japan was completely different, and like my previous job at the ASEAN-Japan Centre, I was again the head. I did not have banking experience, but once again, I told myself, *"I can do this!"* I accepted the challenge of opening the Philippine National Bank's (PNB's) Representative Office in Tokyo. It is the first step to establishing a full banking presence in Japan.

I was already in the U.S. at that time, thinking of what I would do as my next professional challenge after finishing my extended term at the ASEAN-Japan Centre. PNB's then Executive Vice President, who was also my immediate boss at the NEDA, called to ask me if I would re-open PNB's Tokyo Representative Office. It was closed when the bank was restructuring to reduce costs. I not only accepted, but I went further and upgraded the Representative Office into a fully licensed bank when the opportunity to do so came.

Japan applies the reciprocity rule when deciding to allow a foreign bank to set up a presence in the country. Two Japanese banks were initially granted permission by the Philippines' Central Bank (*Bangko Sentral ng Pilipinas*) to open a full banking presence in the Philippines. In return, the Japanese government also allowed two Philippine banks to open full banking in Japan. PNB was one of the two.

PNB's interest in having a presence in Japan is to serve our Overseas Filipino Workers (OFWs) in their remittance and other banking needs. At that time, only fully licensed banks were allowed to engage in the money transfer business, accept deposits, and offer loans.

It was my most fulfilling job to assist Filipinos with their banking, saving, and remittance needs. It was also a relatively much easier job, as I now conducted business with my own *kababayan* (countrymen) in my own language.

In April 2010, the Japan Payments Act was enacted, allowing non-banks to engage in the business of money transfer. Previously, only banks with full banking licenses were allowed to tackle. I plunged in despite the huge capital requirements and knowing how the Goliaths in the industry dominated the business; dominated the industry. I was in my warrior mode, a David ready to slay the Goliaths in the industry and win! My Japanese company continues to operate and soldier on. We have started outgoing money transfers from Japan, starting with only the Philippines as our remittance corridor. Now our main markets are Indonesia, Vietnam, Nepal, and India. Furthermore, forging a tie-up with another company with a worldwide presence enabled this little David to now serve 200 countries. Soon, I will be training for Japan inbound remittances, once again from around 200 countries worldwide. This is relatively more lucrative than the processing of outbound transactions.

Now, I can continue to give back not only to our OFWs but also to all migrants in Japan, no matter their nationality. "A company for Migrants, by Migrants" is our vision, and we have invited our OFWs to become shareholders in the company's preferred shares. It continues to be a challenge to fight the Goliaths. Looking back, I was actually very brave to enter this high-capital-intensive industry, but I am a warrior, remember?

The David amongst the Goliaths in the industry was still soldiering thirteen years after I set up a business. Our Japanese company has the slogan *"Isang Barya, Hatid ay Saya."* One Coin, Bringing Happiness refers to the JPY500 yen coin, which is my lowest remittance fee, compared to the JPY2,000 of the two Philippine banks', and the minimum JPY4,000 of Japanese banks. My main problem I face now is who will take over if I ever decide to retire.

I continue my mission to serve and give back to our OFWs. When our OFWs have problems, they ask for my advice in my *Dear Tita Lits,* a column I write in Jeepney Press (JP), an online non-profit and non-commercial publication run by a staff of volunteers who work towards making a unified, diverse, and responsible Filipino society in Japan. The dilemma of Intersecting identities and navigating the labyrinth of race and identity are woven in the questions and comments from my readers during my long years being their *Tita* Lits:

- ☐ "How do you handle discrimination when it happens to you? Have you experienced discrimination during your many years of stay in Japan?"

- ☐ "My son from my Japanese husband avoids being asked about my nationality and where I work. I work nights as a singer, just like before I married his father, as I have to help augment the meager pension my husband receives. He avoids being with me on many occasions where we will have the chance to meet his Japanese friends, as he feels ashamed and embarrassed about my being a Filipina and working as an entertainer. What can I do, Tita Lits?"

- ☐ "I was so happy and proud to graduate from a teachers' course in Tokyo, run by a Filipino Christian missionary. It was the first time for me to up the stage, receive my diploma, certify I am a teacher now, and even open my own Montessori school! I am now a "Sensei," everybody in my local community calls me this honorific. My Japanese husband and my Japanese parents-in-law changed their former attitude to me. In the past, I was looked down on as a Filipina who worked at night. Thank you, Tita Lits, for your kind words and encouragement during our teachers' training course's graduation ceremony."

I have been writing the advice column for more than twenty (20) years now and hope to continue doing so *gratis et amore* for many more years.

My Ima and Deng (my father) must be smiling in heaven as their strong-willed, warrior-minded daughter continues to explore ways to contribute to the welfare of her country and its people.

Lita is now an aspiring farmer. She believes that no Filipino should ever go hungry. She is currently developing Thanks Nature Farm in Pampanga, a 10-hectare integrated farm with 1,000 mango trees, to become a Learning Farm and a place for silent retreats. She has added two fish ponds, is raising free-range chickens, rabbits, goats, and pigs, planted various vegetables and trees like *calamansi*, uses bamboo to fence her farm and harvest bamboo shoots regularly, and has started planting rice.

Lita, the *Kapampangan* warrior, is finally back to her roots and where she was born. But don't bet on her retiring soon! She believes we all have an *ikigai—the Japanese word for a reason to live, a purpose in this world.*

Luid ya ing Babaing Kapampangan
Long life Kapampangan Woman
Long life Kapampangan Woman Warrior

GRACE JAMON

President/CEO Lapu-lapu Cebu International College
Global FWN 100™ 2022

By Grace, through Grace

A
mazing Grace. That was my monicker for this childhood BFF of mine from the homeland. Although a year or so older than her, I've never ceased to be amazed by Grace—her capacity to draw people of all walks of life to her, navigate spaces both humble and exalted, cause sworn enemies to rally together for a cause she champions, and doing all she does with ease, confidence, and—true to her name—grace. One of the things I most admire about her is her capacity just to *be*. In every sense of the word, she is a natural—with absolutely no affectation or self-consciousness. Around her, you're invited then also to just be—to take off the mask, let go of artifice. Quite apart from her myriad professional talents, I see this as her most precious gift to the world: the uncolonized indigenous *loob* that's able to just be—able to connect with anyone and everyone, to speak what is truly in the heart, extremely expansive and generous (sometimes to a fault!)—what we mean by magandang loob or beautiful Self. Those of us privileged enough to be in her intimate circle of Kapampangan friends often say that when the time comes, they'll have trouble finding a venue big enough to fit all the people whose

lives she's touched and who would, for sure, insist on paying tribute to her at her funeral. I have not known anyone with a bigger heart, with an infinite capacity to be there for others and care genuinely. Even across the distance (with me having now relocated to Turtle Island), she remains my dearest, most precious friend—my Amazing Grace. That's her. By Grace, Through Grace.

S. Lily Mendoza
*Professor, Oakland University; Executive Director,
Center for Babaylan Studies*

I Am Where I Am

I am currently in Vietnam to persuade universities in Hanoi and Ho Chi Minh City to collaborate with our Center for Language Studies at Lapu-lapu Cebu International College (LCIC). We specialize in teaching English as a second language, and over the past two years, we've developed a teaching style that instills confidence in foreign students, bringing them unmitigated joy. Within just four weeks of immersion, we've seen Japanese, Korean, and Taiwanese college students transform from timidity to confidence, leaving with inspiring stories shared in English. They describe their experience as an epiphany they will cherish forever.

As I speak to welcome and bid farewell to our students, often with tears, I know that **I am exactly where I am meant to be.** I am deeply grateful for this opportunity to serve, which feels like my destiny. As President, I have traveled tirelessly from Cebu to Manila every weekend to be with my family and three grandchildren. I survived COVID-19 twice and endured a knee osteoarthritis episode that disabled me from walking for a week. Through it all, I have never wavered in my belief that I am where I am meant to be. Grace has followed me, and I believe that God has supplied all I needed "according to His/Her manifold riches in glory." I am about to complete four years at LCIC.

Now, I hope to welcome Vietnamese students to our center. After this visit, I am confident we will attract as many students from Vietnam as we have from other countries. During this trip, I visited the University of Hanoi, Vietnam National

University, University of Social Sciences and Humanities Van Lang, University of Social Sciences in Ho Chi Minh, University of Economics and Finance, Ho Chi Minh City University of Technology, and Vietnam Aviation Academy University in Ho Chi Minh.

I retired after 45 years as a faculty member in the UP Department of Political Science. However, my retirement was short-lived, as I was tapped to establish Lapu-lapu International College (LCIC) in Cebu. LCIC fosters internationally minded talent equipped with the advanced knowledge and skills necessary to become active contributors to the international community.

In my inaugural address, I acknowledged the unprecedented challenges facing LCIC and exhorted, "*Nevertheless, we will power through with courage and conviction to achieve our purpose of bridging communities through learning excellence.*"

At LCIC, we believe in building better lives through a purpose-driven mission focused on excellence, diversity, and community, bringing higher learning into the digital age. LCIC stands for five hallmarks:

☐ Social Relevance-- A multi-model, learner-centric, multi-lingual mode of instruction, aligned with international standard learning and outstanding facilities, scholarships for deserving underprivileged youths, and a robust international internship program with our industry partners all over Asia;

☐ Passion for Student Success--Commitment to deliver what students want and need in a feasible manner;

☐ Agile Processes-- Smart investments to deliver programs responsive to the needs of the international economy in a consistent learning environment and experience;

☐ Continuous Innovation-- Remain competitive by striving for growth through innovation; and

☐ Driven Inspiration--Push the status quo to address unmet needs of industries in the Philippines.

Kapampangan and Tagalog Roots

I grew up in San Fernando, Pampanga. We are three siblings, and I am the only girl among them. My father eventually became a lawyer. He started as a firefighter at Clark Air Force Base. My father earned a dollar-denominated salary working at the American base, a socially well-regarded position in Pampanga society during that time. This allowed us early access to American products and exposure to the English language from birth. I vividly remember my father and relatives speaking to me in English, which was a novelty since they were native Kapampangan speakers. Despite the economic uplift his dollar-denominated salary brought to our family, he resigned after realizing the inequality in the treatment of natives by the Americans.

My father, despite being engaged for six years to a "*sarado Katoliko*" schoolteacher, married my mother instead—a beauty from Nueva Ecija with only a fourth-grade education but an immense entrepreneurial spirit. My mother, a talented dressmaker, epitomized hard work, grit, and grace. She was a true "steel magnolia," strong and beautiful.

Together, my parents modeled resilience and determination, shaping my values and career.

Unlike the poverty my father experienced growing up, our family was uplifted economically when my father and uncles began working at Clark Air Force Base. This job, coupled with our Methodist Protestant faith, introduced our family to a life of privilege within the Clark environment. I became the prototype of a "*colonized middle-class Filipino family.*"

Education for Life

I was a fresh graduate from Jose Abad Santos High School, formerly Pampanga High School, where I served as editor-in-chief of the school paper, Pampangan, and graduated with honors. In high school, I was a simple, non-competitive, yet joyful teenager who enjoyed school life. Gifted with a good voice, I participated in singing contests. In college, I was a member and soprano of my choral group under the baton of Professor Romulo Pesania, who called me his "royal soprano." We competed and won in choral competitions both locally and internationally.

My college years were enjoyable. During this time, I remained joyful and easy-going, considered "*Ate*" (big sister) by everyone. I was also a member of the State Christian Fellowship (SVCF), which partnered with The Navigators and Campus Crusade for Christ. These organizations were important during my time at UP, especially given the tumultuous decades of martial law in the Philippines. This period marked my gradual politicization as a political science student. The challenge was to take an informed personal stance on the competing polar ideologies at that time, which were communism versus democracy or godless communism with Christianity. My positions slowly shifted, reading and later teaching Marx and his influence on Latin American liberation theology. Finally, the church took the preferential option for the poor, partly settling the philosophical and political dilemma of my being Christian. This epiphany defined why I am open, accommodating, non-judgmental, and ready to participate. I learn from people and situations respecting their diversity rather than simply tolerating differences. As a professor, friend, and colleague, I personified this outlook with my students, colleagues, and friends for 45 years.

Life while getting a formal education was relatively smooth during this period. I started my college journey at UP Baguio, where I learned independence and launched my career in education. I excelled as a student and eventually progressed from an instructor to a professor at the Department of Political Science in Diliman, consistently receiving the highest commendations for my teaching. During this time, I completed my master's degree and eventually earned my PhD, all while teaching at UP.

Navigating Married Life

I married a classmate after completing our studies—me with my master's degree and him with his Bachelor of Laws from the UP College of Law. We married after he passed the bar exam. My mother-in-law often remarked that it was about time for him to settle down. My husband, a true-blue Filipino and a former student political figure, was raised by a strong, authoritarian, tough, and colorful mother who single-handedly supported the education of all six children in Manila, although she was married. Unfortunately, my father-in-law struggled with alcoholism and fathered many children outside of his marriage. This caused my husband to grow up hating his father, a trauma he confronted but never fully resolved until his passing. This unresolved trauma inevitably impacted our marriage.

Despite these challenges, my husband became a successful practitioner and a corporate lawyer for UNILAB in Asia and Asian Pharmaceuticals for ten years. He remained a trusted lawyer until he felt a calling to return to teaching law—a desire his direct boss did not support, leading to his resignation and acceptance of a teaching position at UP. The discounted tuition provided by UP, where all our children studied, was a significant help.

Our marriage, with its clash of cultures and ideologies, truly challenged the core of who we were, especially me. However, this experience became an opportunity for both of us to learn more about ourselves and make everything work for the sake of our children. Our marriage, though rocky at times, became the context for our growth and the foundation for making everything work for our kids as we navigated the rock and tumble of life together.

Career Trajectory

My teaching career included serving as Director, UP Diliman extension program in Pampanga and Olongapo. It was also punctuated with introducing and implementing Partnership and Programs:

- Social Enterprise Program "Entrepreneurial Leadership for Social Enterprise Competitiveness" funded by Citi Foundation, 2017-present.

- UPDEPP as A Center for Human Rights Training and Education, Partnership with the Commission of Human Rights, 2016-present.

- Research Partnership with UP Korean Studies Program "An Uncomfortable Embrace: Hanjin Philippines' Shipbuilding Operations and Government Regulations, published in the Korean Studies Journal

- Indigenous Studies Program with The Center of Babaylan Studies, Sonoma State University, 2017-present

- United Nations Asian and Pacific Training Centre for Information and Communication Technology for Development (UN-APCICT/ESCAP), Consultant for the Women and ICT Frontier Initiative (WIFI) Program, Incheon, Republic of Korea, April 14-15, 2016

☐ Philippine Commission on Women-UPDEPP, responsible for the implementation of a Capacity Development Program on Women Economic Empowerment for partners and women's microenterprises of GREAT Women Project 2, November 2016-November 2017.

☐ Great Women Facebook Training for Social Enterprises, November 10-12, 2016

☐ Multi-Sector Advisory Board of the Training and Doctrine Command TRADOC, part of the Multi-Sectoral for the training of Army Training in Capas, Tarlac

Destiny once again guided my path during those years when I was seconded from UP to various significant roles. I was invited to serve as the Dean of the Development Academy of the Philippines' (DAP) Graduate School for Public and Development Management. DAP operates directly under the Office of the President of the Philippines, serving as both a presidential think tank and a training ground for the nation's bureaucrats. However, I resigned after a year when the President began filling the bureaucracy with corrupt and unfit appointees, including her hair stylist.

During my tenure as Dean at DAP, I was elected President of the Association of Schools of Public Administration in the Philippines (ASPAP), a prominent network of over 100 public administration schools across the country. The influx of foreign projects from international development organizations like the World Bank, UNDP, and IFES came effortlessly. These institutions cited our strong networks and principled leadership as key reasons for choosing ASPAP. I served two terms, totaling six years.

My leadership roles within these organizations significantly enriched my teaching in the fields of politics and governance. I became an advisor to various public institutions, including the Office of the President, and a consultant to international organizations. My consultancy work with The Asia Foundation, where I was engaged for many years, introduced me to the realm of political and development advocacy. There, I mastered Development Entrepreneurship, a highly effective approach to guiding public policy reforms.

Following my time at DAP, I also served as a Director at the Philippine Social Science Council (PSSC), a private organization representing various social science institutions. During this period, we secured a book project funded by UNDP, resulting in the publication of *Chasing the Wind,* a two-volume book on politics and governance, awarded specifically to the Philippine Political Science Association as an institutional member of PSSC.

Though I was invited to join the Communist Party in the early 70s, I refused. I realized that we need not be boxed into rigid ideologies but instead appreciate the evolving nature of the world. This epiphany shaped my approach to teaching, where I learned from people and situations, respecting diversity rather than merely tolerating differences. As a professor, friend, and colleague, I personified this outlook for 45 years. Now, at almost seventy, I am still active politically and socially while working to give LCIC the chance to progress.

Living with Gratitude at 70

Today, I continue to work tirelessly to see LCIC progress while balancing my roles as a mother, grandmother, and social advocate. My life has been defined by the resilience, hard work, and grace I witnessed from my parents, and I strive to pass those values on to future generations.

At 70, I live with profound gratitude for every opportunity to offer comfort to the sick, hold hands, and visit those in the hospital, especially those battling cancer. Each weekend moment spent with family is cherished as I strive to make the most of my weekdays in Cebu, where I lead LCIC.

My children are now adults, each a leader in their own field, and my three grandchildren are an unmitigated source of joy. I am blessed to still be able to watch them grow and experience the fullness of life alongside them.

Discovery and Faith: My Journey with Breast Cancer

I was 34 years old when I discovered a lump in my breast, just after attending a month-long National Security Course in Kiel, Germany. At the time, I was a lactating mother, having left my 8-month-old daughter, Tin Tin, in the care of my aunt. It was a perplexing period in my life—why, at this stage, had I chosen career over family? This was in 1989, just two months before the Berlin Wall crumbled, marking the reunification of Germany. Our own EDSA Revolution had recently ignited democratic movements worldwide.

Upon returning home after a month, I found a hard lump in my breast. It was the greatest scare of my life. I remember wandering around the University of the Philippines, lost and unable to shed a tear. For the first time, I was truly scared. The thought of leaving my young children was overwhelming and unimaginable. When I got home, I went straight to my room and remembered a verse from a hymn that invites every believer to pray, promising that *"the peace of God shall dwell in your hearts forever."*

The next day, I was scheduled to receive the test results. I went to my room and, with all my heart, pleaded, *"Lord, please talk to me. Reassure me that I will be okay."* I sat on my bed and turned on the TV. The 700 Club was on air, and Pat Robertson was interviewing a woman who had been in remission from stomach cancer for 10 years. Her doctors had initially given her only six months to live, as the cancer had spread so extensively. She was testifying about her miraculous survival. When Pat Robertson asked the doctor what had happened, the doctor simply said, *"We were sure of what we saw... we can only attribute her recovery to a miracle."*

At that moment, I found myself on my knees, crying like a child, overwhelmed by the privilege of receiving an answer right when I needed it. I raised my hands in awe of God's love, grateful for His intercession and the peace He had given me. My mourning turned into joy. From that moment, I was certain that I had seen the face of the Lord, and that certainty never left me. All fear was gone; His love was more than enough.

The next day, I called my doctor. He confirmed that it was cancer. I responded with unexpected happiness, saying, *"I know."* I had already packed my bags for the hospital. My husband was in tears, but I shared with him my encounter with God's amazing grace the day before. For me, all fear was gone. The flowers I received during my hospital stay became a celebration of God's faithfulness and love.

I was blessed to have faced this challenge at 34, and it shaped how I approached my work. Every role I took on, I did so with great dedication, respect, and love for the institutions and the people we served. By grace, through grace, we live.

Grace and Destiny

Destiny is certain. I was meant to be exactly where I needed to be, guided by grace through every step. The universe convinces us that we are placed where we are for a reason. Life challenges us to believe that we are designated to accomplish our tasks dutifully, passionately, and lovingly. We will never run out of grace to see it through when we embrace this purpose. For by grace, we have been saved through faith. By grace and through grace, we live. I am sure we all have a story to tell—this is mine. GRACE. May you live with grace.

CHAMPIONS

"We all have a responsibility to try and make this world better, whether it's through our work, the causes we champion, the way that we treat people, or the values we impart to the next generation."

—Daniel Lubetzky

"I truly believe that it's all of the hard times that make you step up to the next level, and that's what makes you a champion."

—Caroline Buchanan

REGINA BERBA, MD. MSC
Professor 3 University of the Philippines Manila College of Medicine
Global FWN 100™ 2022

People Giving Hope: Ten PGH Champions during COVID-19

r. Regina Berba offers a compelling story about PEOPLE GIVING HOPE and HEALING, about ten Filipino women champions at the Philippine General Hospital (PGH) during the COVID-19 crisis. As one of the ten, Regina recounts the experiences of doctors and nurses, who became the heart of the hospital's response. PGH, a 1,500-bed hospital known as a lifeline for the nation's poorest, was suddenly designated a COVID-19 referral center, a role it had never anticipated. This chapter not only recounts the hospital's struggles but also highlights the intersectionality of gender, profession, and cultural identity, showcasing the unique challenges and strengths these women brought to the forefront. "People Giving Hope " is more than a story of a hospital and its staff during the pandemic; it is a narrative that highlights the power of intersectionality, showing how diverse identities and experiences can come together to create a powerful force for change. Through the lens of these ten women, the reader gains a deeper understanding of the complexities of the global pandemic and the extraordinary resilience of those who fought on the front lines. As they navigated the pandemic's physical, psychological, and emotional demands, these women juggled professional duties with personal fears, all while keeping hope alive for their patients and colleagues. Their story embodies the Filipino spirit of Bayanihan—community and cooperation—demonstrating how diverse experiences can unite in the face of a common enemy. "People Giving Hope" is a tribute to resilience and unity, capturing how these ten women turned the overwhelming challenges of the pandemic into a testament of strength, compassion, and innovation. As participants of an historical moment in the world and in our country, the stories of these 10 women are incomplete without acknowledging their internal struggles, their dilemmas, their personal sacrifices (as well as their families), and their conviction that the time they spent taking care of COVID-19 patients is the best use of this valuable resource. "Bayani's" are not born; they painstakingly evolve under extreme pressure, as shown by these extraordinary human beings.

Liberty Fajutrao, MD MSCE
Stockholm, Sweden

Introduction

Every Filipino knows what the "PGH" stands for. It is the Philippine General Hospital, the bastion of health service for the poor. PGH is the 1500-bed University of the Philippines hospital. It is a government-funded tertiary referral hospital where the poorest of the poor and the sickest of the sick line up for days at the Emergency Room (ER) to get admitted. The rarest cases, the most baffling syndromes, or the most complex human suffering end up here. The best doctors, nurses, and trainees line up to get a chance to work or train at the PGH. During the COVID-19 pandemic, which started in 2020, PGH was dubbed a new nickname, and now it is sometimes fondly referred to as "**P**eople **G**iving **H**ope."

On ordinary days, PGH is the hospital where you bring patients who are dying, who are very sick, who have no money, and who have lost hope.

During the extraordinary period of the COVID-19 pandemic, the national government chose PGH to be a "COVID-19 Referral Hospital," naturally driving away the "other" usual patients with heart attacks and diabetic feet. This situation obliged the hospital to temporarily abandon its "General Hospital" functions to become the go-to health facility for SARS CoV2 infections. For us health workers, it meant we did not just manage the SARS CoV2 viral infections; we also helped navigate through many psychological and socio-cultural dimensions of the illness like the sheer fear, panic which paralyzed, the desolation of isolation, the stress of logistical nightmares, and preparing for the inevitability of dying alone.

There was also something about PGH and the pandemic. It brought out the best in each one of us. The prevailing spirit of *Bayanihan* was palpable across the hospital, vertically and horizontally. Bayanihan from the root word "*bayani*" is the Filipino term for "hero." Early and throughout the pandemic were nine other Filipina women whose lives got entangled into my life as all ten of us tried to patch a path to surviving the pandemic. This chapter is not just my story but also the story of the other nine Filipina women. This is our PGH Pandemic story. I share with you how the ten champions, myself included, learned about pandemic resilience and compassion. Individually and united, we fought our battles and survived the daily struggles, one patient each time, one day at a time. We kept the flames of hope burning among our patients, staff, and communities. Our team of ten of the bravest and most innovative women doctors and nurses helped keep the university hospital through the most difficult crisis of our times.

March 29, 2024: The First Good Friday Post-Pandemic

I started to write this story on Good Friday of 2024. Like most Good Fridays in Manila, the day started slowly and quietly, as if the entire creation was in quiet prayer reflecting on the passion of our Lord. There was almost no noise on Good Friday, only whispered conversations, subdued laughter, and peaceful psalms. There was not even traffic in the streets; the malls were closed. Most people stayed at home or went home to their provinces. Very few people must go to work on Good Fridays. It's a day of prayer and sacrifice. This 2024 felt like a special Good Friday. I was glad I did not have to work and had the whole day to go back and relive the moments of the pandemic: a mix of intense fear, anxiety, grief, relief, loneliness bordering on despair, disbelief, gratitude, chaotic happiness, and ecstatic joy. And I closed my eyes in silence and savored the blessing of life, family, time, and another day. During the pandemic, there was almost no time to think profoundly about myself, my life, my faith, and my relationships. And now I have time. There's still that huge lump on my throat. Who would have thought we would ever reach this post-pandemic point.

January 15, 2020: Naïvely Miscalculating the New Virus Called 2019-NCoV

I, Dr. ***Regina Berba (#1),*** am a doctor of the PGH. On ordinary days, the PGH boasts 1500 beds, a tertiary academic center with the country's best physicians, nurses, and all health staff and services. Our history is rich with stories of heroism and excellence in providing the best medical care possible. We are the university hospital of the University of the Philippines with the mission to serve the poorest of the poor Filipinos and teach the doctors of tomorrow. Some people started giving PGH the nickname of "**P**ersons **G**iving **H**ope."

At the PGH, I have been the head of Infection Control for a long time, as far back as most people will remember. I succeeded the very first Infection Control Chair, Dr. Melecia Velmonte. We fondly called her "Doktora Vel" and hailed her as the "Mother" of Infection Control in the Philippines. I was her most dedicated disciple. So, I was more than thrilled that upon her retirement, Dra. Vel chose me as her successor! I was then a fresh graduate from our Infectious Diseases (ID) Fellowship.

Infection control is a crucial branch of medicine dedicated to enhancing hospital safety for both patients and staff. It aims to minimize the risk of acquiring new infections during hospital stays or while working within the facility. Although it might seem ironic, the possibility of catching a new infection in a hospital setting is real and necessitates rigorous preventive measures. It's a really serious problem requiring focus, planning, and a lot of patience. Under the usual pre-pandemic era, our office called the HICU (Hospital Infection Control Unit) would be doing never-ending surveillance, training, inspections, and outbreak investigations to make sure risks for infection were low despite the many inefficiencies and lack of resources typical in big public hospitals.

Working in Infection Control is like being in a war zone every single day. The war is against bugs, bacteria, viruses, and other germs. Our battle gear consists of alcohol and disinfectants and the proper use of gloves, hospital gowns, and the five moments of hand hygiene! Sometimes, we have an ongoing war against the problematic nonfollowers of infection control policies like difficult staff, lazy students, impatient patients, and adamant patient watchers or the ever-important presence of a patient community called the "PGH *bantays*." When COVID-19 came, it felt like we were going through real-life final exams day after day after day. COVID-19 kept yelling at us: "Okay, HICU team- so you think you are good, huh! Then show me everything you've got!"

Fortunately for me, I have three incredible women in my team: Miss Merlita Maat as our Chief Nurse, Miss Germie Lucas as our Head Nurse, and Miss Mary Garrido as our Surveillance Officer. These three strong women soldiers kept the fortress united and solid. **_Merlita Maat (#2)_** was our HICU Chief Nurse during the pandemic. She is a mother figure to all of us. She used to be the Boss of the neonatal ICU and recognized all nursing and medical personnel tactics. She organized our scrambled schedules and dealt with the "authorities" in our hospital.

When we started to hear the news about the strange series of infections, then still called the novel coronavirus or the "NCoV-19 from Wuhan, China, in January 2020, HICU was not particularly disturbed. Our clients in PGH were not foreigners or travelers so the probability of having that virus was distantly remote. PGH is not the go-to hospital for wealthy tourists from China. Nevertheless, we so naively prepared five pay rooms for isolation, as well as another three single rooms and eight ward beds on the charity floors. You know, "just in case" the tourists do come and knock at our emergency room. Many emotions needed to be managed here specially complaints from nurses. Behind the composed faces during meetings and post-meeting huddles, all the anxieties, fears, and tears came out; a long list of complaints compressed to "Why us?"

Our HICU Head Nurse **_Germilyn Lucas (#3)_** was the angel-hero-counselor-educator all rolled into one persona. It's a cute paradox that her name is Germie, we call her Mam Germs, and she is our Infection Control nurse. She later said that the feeling of urgency during those early preparatory days was very similar to what she felt when trying to escape the Iraqi Gulf War when she worked as an Overseas Foreign Worker (OFW) in the Middle East. Germie possesses a tough, battle-strong, war-ready exterior with her stern high-pitched voice, yet she has a gentle core. Her wise and reassuring responses to the anxious nurses helped them feel increasingly prepared, both physically and psychologically, to manage the COVID rooms.

Our surveillance officer, Nurse ***Mary Grace Garrido (#4)*** would be like the calming wisp of air amidst the chaos. She would always be the person to make sure our innovations were based on science or at least supported by some administrative memo from WHO or the DOH. She would be the last woman standing, always there, untiring, kind, and gentle.

At some point, we became increasingly paranoid about the brewing pandemic from China. We even made signs in foreign languages, particularly in Chinese dialects so we might be able to suspect their contagiousness earlier. In preparation for the wave of the virus coming in, we had simulation activities of Chinese people flocking to our ER and how our staff was supposed to respond. In January 2020, these simulation activities were light and riotous, as if the infectious threat was so far away and would never reach our shores. Every time we would make-believe and became actors pretending to be patients with fever, the activity would end in hilarious scenarios. Mam Merly and Mam Germs would be strict and not give in to joking and remind us that these risks were serious!

Despite the initial reluctance to prepare for COVID-19 by renovating an old spine unit into a new Isolation Unit, the HICU was determined and made it happen! We felt a sense of relief, believing we were ready for the challenges ahead. However, we soon realized that this 16-bed setup was the beginning of what was yet to come. This was only a teaser!

February 1, 2020: The Threat Felt Closer Yet still Distant.

Rapid national events shifted our perception of the emerging pandemic from indifference to sheer panic. When the first cases of COVID-19 were confirmed in a Chinese couple vacationing in our country on January 30, 2020, we began to believe the threat was real. Many of us started to feel anxious and afraid. The virus is here! We began to talk about it more, discussed with the trainees what to do, and debated forever on who is supposed to screen the COVID-19 suspect patients. "Why me?" the staff would ask when we gave tasks. "No, they will not come to our hospital." When we re-started to do our simulation exercises, nobody laughed anymore. We were now all dead serious.

March 14, 2020: I Carried the First PGH COVID Hotline, And My Phone Died From Overheating

The day after Philippine President Rodrigo Duterte announced the lockdown on March 12, 2020, we discussed what we needed to do in a virtual huddle. The huddle began with the PGH COVID-19 Information and Education Committee (IEC) group, another influential group whose communications output became a defining feature of our institutional COVID action. Because the declaration of the lockdown was so unexpected, we were certain many of our hospital staff had unanswered questions. So, we decided to have a telephone number printed onto one of our infographic posters to inform PGH staff that there was a way to get through if they had questions. Of course, I volunteered to be that phone contact. I did not think much of it and felt confident I could handle the questions to be texted or phoned.

But I miscalculated again! As soon as we released the first poster dated March 14, 2020 with my number, I was deluged with phone calls. I was again totally caught off guard. My phone would ring constantly. "Hello, PGH po ba ito?" (*"Hello, is this PGH?"*)

And they weren't simple questions. They were consultations. And they weren't just from our PGH community! They were from all over the city and, days later, from all over the country! There was a call from a child asking for help to bring her mom to PGH. Another was from the ER of another hospital, and eventually, I could hear the grief and crying and the brief sobs saying *"Wala na si* Mama." *"Mama is gone."* Were all these calls related to COVID-19?? I couldn't drive far enough because I needed to answer my phone every so often. It came to a point where I couldn't sleep long enough as I had to answer my incessantly ringing phone!

The lack of information was a significant problem, far beyond my control, larger than me, and it posed a serious threat to our countrymen. We needed to organize quickly and begin educating the public. Then, my cellphone died. It wouldn't turn on or charge. I remember leaving it to charge at the donning station before putting on my PPE to make rounds in the COVID wards. When I returned, it was unresponsive. Other staff tried to revive it, but my loyal cellphone had succumbed to exhaustion and overheating. This was worrisome—I needed a new phone, but where could I buy one amid a lockdown? By the time I got off work, it was already dark outside. As I drove, I noticed an eerie emptiness—no cars, buses, or people in sight, both ahead and in my rear-view mirror, as far as my eyes could see, along Epifanio delos Santos Avenue or EDSA, what used to be the most congested main highway in the whole of the Philippines before the lockdown. The desolation was unsettling, sad, and depressing. What was happening?

For more on this experience, visit "How the PGH COVID Hotline Changed my Life?"

< https://www.facebook.com/pghhsp>

Just as the sound of choppers signals the arrival of rescue forces, I welcomed the **launch of Bayanihan Na!** On March 30, 2020, the COVID-19 Operations Center introduced its Hotline Number 155-200 to address all sorts of queries related to COVID-19.<https://up.edu.ph/bayanihan-na-up-pgh-launches-covid-19-ops-center/> The best part was that it was open 24/7 and staffed by several trained volunteers at any given time. University Chancellor and Professor *Carmencita Padilla (#5)* was the brilliant mind behind this. Hundreds of students, faculty and staff could volunteer to participate. Millions of pesos worth of donations reached PGH through this Bayanihan Na! Operations Center (or the BNOC). Due to the overwhelming volume of donations, BNOC established a system of accepting cash and in-kind contributions. BNOC brought order. Even large food donations had to be scheduled among the health workers. Most importantly, BNOC created a sustainable system to answer questions and facilitate clinical consultations. We recognized the importance of providing patients with someone to talk to. Some callers simply needed reassurance, while others required urgent admission. Chancellor Padilla remembers a case where our volunteer monitored a patient who refused to be tested and eventually brought to the hospital. The call center was indeed a helpline. Chancellor Menchit Padilla is also an awardee of the Filipina Womens' Network Global FWN 100 Awardees in 2013 (https://filipinawomensnetwork.org/global-fwn100-2013).

March 21, 2020: Preparing the Frontliners

No one anticipated that PGH would be designated as a COVID-19 Referral Center until the Health Secretary of the Philippines announced it on March 19, 2020. We were never the chosen facility in past outbreaks, like SARS and H1N1 influenza; smaller, more organized hospitals were typically selected.

Preparing our hospital to function as a COVID-19 Referral Center in just 12 days was an immense challenge. We rapidly transformed our overcrowded ER and wards into isolation wards and ICUs. All current non-COVID patients had to be discharged or transferred to other hospitals, a task that seemed formidable, if not impossible. Surprisingly, it was not difficult. As soon as patients learned of our preparations to admit a large number of COVID cases, many volunteered to leave. Even diabetic patients recovering from amputations were eager to vacate the wards to make room for the 130 beds needed for COVID-19 patients.

We next created the COVID wards. The "**we**" here is in collaboration with hundreds of other healthcare workers, especially our male-dominated hospital administration, who provided the budget, funds, outsourcing, manual labor, carpentry, electricals, and similar needs.

But "***we, the women***," developed the policies, defined the needs, detailed the processes, listed the requirements, and gave the go-signals for almost every aspect of the transformation to the COVID-hospital. We had to fix the beds, windows, oxygen tanks, ventilators, giant electric fans, ventilation direction, traffic flow, everything! We had to buy individual thermometers, pulse oximeters, and BP cuffs; nothing could be shared nor recycled. We designed patient traffic flow that would not allow virus transmission: exactly where to walk, what to wear, what to do, and how to do the usual stuff. Hurriedly, the HICU developed numerous COVID policies, issued hospital memos, designed training modules, and re-oriented the staff. With limited information, we made COVID guidelines and created new pathways, algorithms, and people traffic flows. Most of us were on the frontlines and directly testing, preaching, and implementing our HICU policies

At this point of the pandemic, I worked closer with some extraordinary women of character! Meet Dr ***Joanne Carmela Sandejas (#6)***! Joanne was the Chief Fellow of the Infectious Diseases fellows in training when the pandemic broke loose. She was a workhorse! Guiding the fellows, guiding us too. She worked closely with us and communicated well with the other hundreds of doctors in the hospital. I also came to know more about ***Ysabella Veneice Ponce (#7)***, who was then a medical intern. We call her Ven. She is also my sister in our medical sorority. By then, the UP College of Medicine students were asked to go home. But Ven stayed on and actually approached me and asked how she could help us. I thought hard about getting her on board. We weren't seeing patients at the office then, and I thought it should be perfectly safe. I asked Ven to help us make videos of how to wear the Personal Protective Equipment correctly. She filmed our nurse experts and edited them and Ta-da! Her video product became a lifeline for most healthcare workers (HCWs). Personal Protective Equipment was at the core of our response. PGH was the first to have "Levels of PPE for COVID-19" or Levels 1,2,3.

In the meantime, HICU continued training and re-orienting the nurses and the doctors. There was still that cloud of fear and despair of worse things to come. Who could forget scenes of the series of never-ending face-to-face COVID meetings, demo and return demos to our HCWs, preparation of the specimen collection kits, swabbing patients, transporting specimens, releasing of results, approval of PPE, mask fit testing, staying in a hotel for two months, sharing the shuttle services, and covid contact tracing. And giving out the results, as bringer of Bad News. However, the most memorable was swabbing the first suspected COVID-19 patient admitted to our hospital. I remember how anxious I was while waiting for the result of this patient.

Usually, by the time I finished giving a COVID-19 lecture or when calling a healthcare worker to relay the results of the COVID test, the people at the other end would be bursting into tears, and most nurses who are mothers would be crying in empathy. Mothers were so afraid! The men tried to look brave. We all tried to be kind and patient.

I met Dr. *Nicole Marella G. Tan (#8)* in this setting. We call her *Alla,* and she was a second-year resident of Dermatology at that time. She was one of the first to volunteer for duty because she had no co-morbidities. The volunteers assisted and supported the frontliners and, in the process, became frontliners themselves. The task we assigned their group was to be trained observers, eventually called the "Safety Officers." This meant they would intently watch each frontline put on their PPEs and assist or correct them accordingly. It was a tough job and a big responsibility. The level of confidence of frontliners tremendously increased! When the Health Secretary visited our hospital weeks later, he thought having that layer of Trained Observers was an ingenious move. Additionally, our staff started to have free skincare consultations from Alla on how to look beautiful before and after their COVID duties!

If a PGH staff member missed the departmental webinars and town hall meetings, they attended the *Stop COVID Deaths: Clinical Management Updates Webinar Series* of the UP System's TVUP, in partnership with the UP Manila NIH National Telehealth Center. It featured engaging discussions by experts, clinicians, administrators, public health specialists, and researchers sharing the most relevant and up-to-date burning issues on COVID patient care. This would show live every Friday from 12 noon to about 2 pm . Eager audiences would come from PGH, all over the Philippines, and several other countries. The series became so popular as a prime source of reliable COVID information that it won the prestigious **2022 Gold Quill Award of Merit** by the International Association of Business Communicators (IABC). The award was given in New York City, USA, and received by then-UP President Danilo Concepcion, UP Vice President for Public Affairs Elena Pernia, and Chancellor Menchit Padilla.

March 28, 2020: Preparing the Backend Behind the Scenes

We had three doctors at the back-end of COVID-19 doing the thinking, organizing, and communicating for us.

Dr. Eva Cutiongco dela Paz (#9) is the executive director of the UP Manila National Institutes of Health (NIH). Through her and the efforts of the NIH team, UP was one of the first responders to the country's need for SARS COV 2 testing. She was at the helm of putting together laboratory components of the COVID test operations so that PGH healthcare workers would have access to a reliable COVID test. Upon passing the requirements at lightning speed, testing for COVID-19 was already possible by the time the PGH opened itself as a COVID Referral Center. Putting up the laboratory, however, was only half the battle. During its first eight weeks of operation, the NIH COVID-19 Testing Laboratory was run by about 30 volunteer staff - NIH research faculty and university researchers, faculty of UP Manila, and Research Assistants of DOST-funded molecular biology research projects. Because of the ECQ, everyone had to be provided meals and accommodations, and the UPM administration responded speedily by providing space on the 6th floor of the UP Manila dormitory. The PGH Dietary Department delivered meals for our volunteers every single day. By the 9th week, all the volunteers had to go back to their DOST-funded research projects. Fortunately, through the DOH Human Resource for Health Augmentation program, the NIH, through the PGH, was able to hire new staff – pathologists, medical technologists, molecular biologists, and encoders who are now the new COVID-19 Testing Team. It took a whole village to make testing available for the PGH patients and the UP community.

Dr. Scarlett Mia Tabuñar (#10) was responsible for managing donations from around the world. This special assignment required someone with high integrity and unwavering grit. Mia embodies these qualities: she is reliable, scrupulous, and incorruptible. She noted that one of the most significant challenges of this once-in-a-lifetime assignment was ensuring all donations, whether cash or in-kind, benefitted the entire hospital and reached their intended recipients. She admitted that the sheer volume and varied nature of the donations put her organizing skills to the test daily. The influx was so immense that a seemingly endless variety of materials filled entire buildings.

Dr. Alla Tan, who doubled as a Safety Officer, was also a lead in the behind-the-scenes of the very powerful UP-PGH COVID-19 IEC. This group made the world of difference between our hospital and the rest of the country. Through our daily IEC Committee meetings and the detailed discussions of each infographic, we likely reached every healthcare worker (HCW) within and outside PGH. One day, I unforgivably fell asleep and was unable to transmit the day's census, causing a slight delay in releasing the day's information that many were eagerly awaiting.

Alla recalls the early days of how the group started. Hand-picked by Dr. Eric Berberabe, the IEC group comprised the hospital's most creative, responsive, and down-to-earth individuals. They had the energy and perfect vibes to communicate accurate information, new knowledge, policies, trends, and complex but valuable concepts effectively and efficiently to a huge public audience. Their infographics were widely used, shared, and highly regarded. The end-product delivered practical instructions for all healthcare workers, including doctors, nurses, utility workers, security, and maintenance staff. The IEC team transformed DOH algorithms, testing advice, disinfection techniques, census data, and other essential information into easily consumable infographics. Exhausted and worried healthcare workers, at the end of their long shifts, needed vital information presented optimally for easy absorption.

Being residents themselves doubling as Safety Officers, the IEC team were effective and knowledgeable graphic designers. Alongside the IEC consultants, they meticulously selected the most critical pieces of information and optimized their presentation for the healthcare workers. In half a year, we created over 3,000+ infographics, posters, and tarpaulins, reflecting PGH's preparations for the pandemic. In hindsight, a staff member fondly described our infographics as "snackable, easy to digest, easy to share, and presented in a palatable form." The secret to the PGH COVID IEC Committee was its "magical" diversity and how each member contributed positively to the efforts. Regardless of age, we collaboratively refined and perfected each infographic. Alla felt this was one of the best examples of teamwork she had ever experienced. It truly is phenomenal what we can accomplish when we work together!

March 30, 2020: The Opening of the COVID-19 Referral Center

The day of reckoning came! At the break of dawn on March 30, 2020, Dr. Gap Legaspi, our PGH director, sent off our staff and opened our wards to COVID patients in the Philippines. Our staff in hazmat went onto the wards as if they were men in battle, prepared by our reliable "Trained Observers" with the rest of us staying behind and bidding them good luck!! There was an almost jubilant sense of camaraderie! Stronger than ever before was the ***Bayanihan*** spirit!

Joanne still remembers the very first COVID-confirmed patient we admitted a 68-year-old male, a balikbayan from the United States. He was oxygen-requiring in distress upon admission and diagnosed as COVID-19 severe. He had to stay in the hospital for almost a month but was able to be discharged and later was able to go back to his home. His family was so grateful to everyone, and they repeatedly would say that will never forget the care we did for her husband. After he was able to return to the US, they sent over a balikbayan box of donations of alcohol to the staff who took care of him.

April 15, 2020: Reducing the Loneliness of Dying Alone

Soon, the patients came and rapidly filled up our beds. Our huge COVID wards were setup so that beds were in four columns spaced out about 3 feet apart. So, patients were not really alone. They could see and talk to others around them. But they were not with their loved ones or family members. The companion or "bantay" was not allowed. They were with strangers, doctors, and nurses all totally covered from head to their shoes, wearing caps, goggles, N95 masks, hazmats, gloves, and shoe covers. They could also see when other patients become sicker or carried out from their beds because they didn't make it.

Kindness was overflowing at that time. While we were intensely afraid of contracting SARS COV2, behind all the faceless PPEs were compassionate hearts. The nurses started hanging their photos in front of their hazmat uniforms so that the patients got a glimpse of what their nurses looked like.

When I heard one of the nurses describing their genuine efforts to be more caring to the virus-stricken contagious patients, I felt partly guilty because my usual HICU instructions to all was to be quick and careful in providing the medical service the patients needed: medicines, fluids, oxygen. I completely forgot about being kind, being gentle, and being courteous. I didn't talk about assisting them to the bathroom, feeding them, and helping them change their soiled diapers. But fortunately, PGH nurses are naturally kind and as Filipinos are instinctively warm and caring.

Then there's SIBOL, who invented a way for a gadget to be wheeled to the COVID wards and be connected to the WIFI so the patients can talk to their family members. It was the early version of the Zoom meetings. UP SIBOL is short for University of the Philippines Surgical Innovations and Biotechnology Laboratories (https://www.facebook.com/watch/?v=7397839463574729).

This way of connecting the patient to his family waiting for him outside was experienced first-hand by Mr. B, a 42-year-old cab driver whose COVID was so critical he had to be intubated and on breathing machines for a long time. When he finally got better and could breathe on his own, he requested to have a video call with his wife and kids. For the first few minutes he was just sobbing in happiness proudly showing the absence of all the tubes and IV lines he used to have. He was eventually discharged to home. That was a happy ending.

But for every one happy ending, we probably heard three to five sad stories of devastating loss. We had admissions who would be part of a family where members are dying one after the other. No words could seem to console these patients, grieving alone and at the same time trying to survive the virus; we could only extend our hand in silence trying to comfort. And at the same no words could relieve the anxiety of the family left outside at a distance waiting day by day hoping for encouraging news.

Finally, and ultimately, there is something therapeutic when patients receive a blessing from a priest. Maybe it is a holy transformation or a restoration of faith or it is the forgiveness of sins; whatever the mechanism, I realized just how important it was for patients to have spiritual management during devastating illnesses such as the COVID-19. While I worried about the safety of our beloved priests led by our chaplain Fr. Marlito Ocon SJ., they made me realize that they, too, can be trained on how to keep themselves safe. And with their connections with the divine, who am I to even doubt for their safety? Much later, post-pandemic, I learned it was only at the PGH where the priests were allowed to minister to the COVID-19 patients. As we reviewed their religious protocols: i.e. what to do with excess holy water and holy oil in the COVID ward? How to safely put the sign of the cross on the forehead of the COVID patient?? I learned more practical ID stuff we often did not even think about. From a patient's perspective, the visit of the priest is probably as powerfully therapeutic as the antiviral medicines.

April 30, 2020: Forging the Bayanihan Spirit

The days passed quickly. In two weeks, we filled all the beds we prepared. Things became routine. Donning the PPE, which initially took over 20 minutes, now could be completed in 3 minutes. We became real pros at donning and doffing PPEs safely. Daily endorsement and duties with other residents, fellows, consultants, and nurses in charge became habits—we became more attuned to the needs of the COVID patients and what to watch out for.

We also became more and more attuned to our own needs and those of other healthcare workers. We realized we needed one another, each one and everyone. The boundaries that divided the departments and units were dissolved, and duties were split across all specialties. Even the dentists came to help with the swabbing of staff and patients. There was one goal and one task: to take care of the patients. Ven would remember that the hours in the COVID ward were long and tedious, but she didn't feel as tired because the friendliest and kindest nurses in the wards would surround her. Because of the cost of the PPEs, the staff were obliged to stay in their assigned areas for the entire duration of their duty. When there was downtime, sharing our stories about our backgrounds and families was always lovely.

And who could forget the weekly Crisis committee meetings every Tuesday from 10 am-12 noon? We became each other's strength and source of courage. Our relationships strengthened even more with the shared pandemic experience we had. We were all experiencing the same problems in various layers and wanting to reach the same goals. We learned to listen to each other, think of solutions, and learn from each other. Mam Germs kept repeating, "Just listen to the experts." Over time, we all became the experts

April 10, 2020: Good Friday of our first Pandemic Holy Week

And then it was Holy Week. The first Good Friday of the pandemic was the quietest we have ever experienced. We don't usually have to go to the hospital on Good Friday. But today, all ten of us found ourselves in the hospital. The PGH chapel was closed, and so were all the churches in the city. There were only virtual services for the whole of the Holy Week. It was odd to be working on this holy day. But then again- it was only fitting that we were working as we were that day. The Lord will understand if we were instead working and not praying.

What were we doing on Good Friday of 2020? Joanne was on duty that day. It was also her father's birthday, and she spent a few precious minutes video calling her family. That was as close as they could get. The day before was Maundy Thursday, ordinarily spent doing *Visita Iglesia*, and completed doing the Stations of the Cross virtually. Germs continued to monitor the wards. Eva and Mia carried on with their behind-the-scenes work silently. A lot of donors sent food of all sorts to frontliners working during the Holy Week.

As for me, I made rounds as if it was a regular workday. Some hospital workers tested COVID-positive a few days ago. One of them was Mam Merly Maat. During those early days, the PCR test was sent out and results would take several days to come back. Eventually, Mam Merly and her family members were admitted to PGH. Some hospital officials also tested positive. The combination of health workers and hospital officials testing positive was worrisome. In the afternoon, I met with the PGH Oncology team to work out what to do with their hundreds of cancer patients who needed to continue their chemotherapy sessions amidst the pandemic crises. I intentionally asked the Oncology group if we could finish before 3 pm. Reminding them it was Good Friday and that we should pause for a few minutes.

That day, Mary became busy as she had to perform swabs for SARS CoV2 on several contacts of our newly detected cases. During the early days, collecting samples for PCR test was a special skill and Mary was one of the first few who was skilled.

Hidden in the laboratories were Eva and her team who continually checked on the integrity of their laboratory facilities. By this time, expanding existing laboratories became the wisest thing to do. The abilities to test, trace, and treat are vital in curbing the spread of the pandemic. Aside from expanding the capabilities of existing laboratories and building new ones across the regions, proper training is required to equip all personnel handling COVID-19 testing.

July 7, 2020: The first 100 days as a COVID-19 Referral Center – Are we doing it right???

Three months into the pandemic, staff started to worry whether we were getting the virus at work then passing it to family or patients. We haven't been doing the routine mandatory testing of every two weeks- we didn't have the funds nor enough reagents to test everyone repeatedly. We only had enough for our patients. But near the first 100 days, we decided to have mass testing; to test our processes in PGH. HICU organized the first ever COVID-mass testing – and lo and behold- it was the biggest turnout of any HICU project of all time!!! And we didn't even have any incentive or gifts or extra points to entice staff to volunteer. Everybody, as in all of the 4871 frontliners and backend staff, came to the PGH Atrium during their assigned time to take the COVID swab test! It took us almost 3 weeks to finish everyone- and hundreds of manhours of 24/7 ultra-careful specimen collection and handling and emotion-filled post-test counselling. But it was all worth it! Our hospital processes were affirmed! Only 99 persons or 2% were stricken ill- and not from inside the hospital – but community exposures! We were indeed on the right path! And doing the swab and reassuring the 98% of our team put back the confidence and trust of our staff, realigning ourselves back to our commitment!

March 30, 2021: First Year as a COVID-19 Referral Center- About sending them home

Here are some candid notes from Ven, by then a first-year resident who was seeing COVID patients at the ICU. "I will not forget the day that I was able to send home my previously intubated patient. In the categorization of COVID patients, she belonged to the Critical Covid with survival rates of about 50%. When you see so many people die from a virus you know so little about, it gets so hard to keep on trying. I can still hear the beeping of the ventilator or the haziness of a hand trying to call my attention amidst the fog of my goggles. It was challenging to service a ward of "ICU" level patients. Being able to send even just one of them home is perhaps the best gift of a miracle anyone could ever experience."

Were we ever afraid? What were our greatest fears?

All of us were afraid to get COVID-19 and die because of it. Behind all the masks and the hazmats, we were trembling with fear of getting the virus from the patients in front of us. The possibility of dying was never more evident than how we felt during the earliest days – when patients were dying one by one... fast. We would see our patients in the morning, and they would be gone by the afternoon. As Mia most graphically put it, she feared the possibility that she would be the next sick patient. When Ven got accepted to the Medicine Residency program, her mom begged her not to pursue it as she feared for her daughter's life. Indeed, we were terrified but pretended to be brave.

But an even greater fear than losing one's life was the unforgivable possibility of our beloved families getting sick, dying because of us. And Joanne expressed the fear we hid in our hearts, that our family would get sick, and we would not be there for them or with them.

As for me, overseeing and securing everyone's safety, I was gripped with the constant worry that someone from the PGH frontliners would get so sick because we didn't prepare them enough or our system didn't protect them enough.

March 30, 2022: Second year as a COVID-19 Referral Center-What worked? What learning do we want to share?

After talking to everyone, what ultimately worked in navigating the very complex pandemic at our hospital was **TEAMWORK!** Recognizing that each one and everyone Is important. Every person, every idea, every effort, every donation, every act of kindness and love mattered. **Working on the frontlines like Joanne, Ven, Alla, Merly, Germs, Mary, and me, and supporting at the back end like Menchit, Mia and Eva- we all had our stuff to do!** A role to fill in!

As Alla said, "Everyone is important, from the hospital director to the janitor. HCWs of all kinds have given so much of themselves to battle this pandemic." Mia also said, "The whole COVID experience was a lesson in *HUMANITY*. It's taking care of all the people around you and not only thinking of yourself. You cannot just be mindful of your own safety but also the safety of other people and understand that there is a bigger picture in the fight against COVID. We all have to do our share to ensure the success of all the efforts in ending the battle. No matter how minuscule or high profile your role was in the COVID journey, knowing that you did your best to accomplish it, you can be proud that you were part of the victory against the COVID war."

There's a special ingredient to the teamwork we experienced at PGH during the COVID-19 pandemic. I think it is best captured by the word "Bayanihan" from the word "Bayani." BAYANIHAN is a unique Filipino value of working together. And at our worst and best moments, it was the Bayanihan spirit that pulled us through.

May 5, 2023: The End of the State of Public Health Emergency-What happened to the ten of us? What did we learn? How did we move on?

Here, we are survivors in our own ways. Ven has become a resident, finished IM residency, and is now applying for a fellowship. At some point during her residency we applauded so loudly when Ven was crowned as Miss PGH! Joanne graduated from the Infectious Disease fellowship and was hired by the hospital as a Medical Specialist. Alla, too, graduated from dermatology residency and received additional training in Singapore and the United States. Mam Merly and Mam Germs decided to retire. Chancellor Menchit too, after several extensions, decided to retire. Germs was not yet retirement age but felt that after overcoming two COVID infections, she had to spend more time with her family, who after all the challenges she faced, was her source of strength. She felt a calling, that "God still has a plan for me" and she is out to search for what "He wishes for her to find and do." The rest of us continue to work at our beloved institution.

Mary remembers the saying: "Difficult times forge strength." We all learned that we could hold our own if needed and had to constantly remind ourselves that all these difficult times, these, too, shall pass. Our faith in the Lord and our prayers go a long way to nourish our souls whenever we most need it, not just on Good Fridays. When we have to think about the whole pandemic experience again, we glow with pride and relief and still get that strange giant lump on our throats. When asked if we were willing to go through that experience all over again- we all say "Yes!" It was an honor and a privilege to have served so closely as each one of us did. And kept our sanity and strengthened our faith.

This is our pandemic story, one we could tell over and over again. Today, we can smile and confidently say, "We survived and made a difference in many people's lives." We can look back fondly on the intense and challenging times, as well as the joyful moments we shared together—not just for ourselves and our loved ones, but for the greater good. Just as Mam Germs continues to pray for PGH, we hope the legacy of **PGH— being Persons Giving Hope** will remain forever.

KRISTINE CUSTODIO SUERO, ACP

Vice Chair/Commissioner
San Diego County Commission on the Status of Women & Girls
Legal Professional and Educator
US FWN 100™ 2012, Global FWN 100™ 2022

Overcoming "JUST": Being Underestimated is a Superpower

A poignant reminder that love is central to the most significant social justice movements in our time, author Kristine Custodio Suero shares her journey to her most important work in diversity, equity, inclusion, and belonging. *Fearlessly and fiercely taking up space and holding space in her leadership roles while facing exclusion, othering, and flat-out denigration, this reflection on the precipice of her fifth decade of life provides hope for a world steeped in justice and equity and a return to Joie de vivre.*

Kristine and I met through our involvement with Silayan Filipina eight years ago after a conversation that lasted several hours wherein we began to find key parallels in our respective journeys in the legal field. Kristine's introspective article is raw, real, and relevant as to why Filipinas need to take up space *and share in each other's struggles to combat the feelings of disconnection. Her article takes us on an important journey of self-discovery and growth, which can only happen in real conversation with our Filipina sisters. Like Kristine, I also struggled with finding safe ways to engage in these "critical conversations" with my Filipina sisters especially those in the legal field where we lack representation. As an undergrad in the early 90s, Audre Lorde's quote from Sister Outsider, "...and that visibility which makes us most vulnerable is that which also is the source of our greatest strength," deeply resonated with me as I tried to be visible on my own terms while dealing with the vulnerability of doing this alone. Kristine's reflection gives us the path forward by addressing the isolation. Her words "I find myself in a constant battle to suppress the habit of masking to be the authentic leader that my students and peers deserve, and more importantly, I deserve to embrace my whole self without shame or fear" is a truly courageous statement. She is naming the pain of our isolated struggles in order to encourage us to share our experiences to move forward together and finally inhabit spaces as our full authentic selves."*

Anne S. Bautista, Esq.
Legal Support and Strategy Director, Casa Cornelia Law Center

Bopping along in my gray pinstripe slacks and canary yellow cardigan, I enter the faculty in-service training to a sea of white hair washing over in my direction. The stares penetrate through me like Superman on a mission seeking out crime. Cloaked in my cheerful outfit, I attempt to disappear in my chair amidst the scent of Old Spice and the seeming uniform of polos and khakis. Apparently, I did not receive the memo about the uniform. Being the youngest and the one other female instructor in the Paralegal Program housed under the Criminal Justice Department of our college in my early thirties both terrified and excited me. But for the leadership of our Department Chair, an African-American woman with a PhD and strong will, I wonder if my career and pathway into higher education would exist today.

The culmination of my experiences up to this point in my life catalyzed my areas of interest, research, and civic engagement. As a higher education instructor in law and an appointed Commissioner and Vice Chair for the County of San Diego Commission on the Status of Women and Girls, I understand the importance of advocacy and representation in my work. Opportunities to collaborate with other like-minded people on a global scale as a delegate to the United Nations Commission on the Status of Women (CSW68) in March of 2024 in New York City, indeed, stand as a defining moment.

Being in a space where I did not have to waste precious time and energy convincing others that gender equity is a problem and that it matters elevates the work that we are all doing in our respective regions. Hearing statistics about how women and girls are impacted by poverty and gender-based violence, particularly in conflict zones, layered another dimension on the focus of my Commission's body of work and priorities.

Awareness of Self and Others

The circuitous path of my nearly two-decade legal career foists me into a curious place, like the in-limbo state I feel when I reflect on my cultural self-identity. On one hand, I am an American because I was born in the United States of America. On the other hand, I am the daughter of Filipino immigrants who migrated to this land for opportunities like so many others seeking a better life. And like so many others in my situation, our chameleon-like tendencies to blend in and assimilate ourselves by masking any hint of a foreign accent, insisting on culinary choices for my meals at school to be consistent with what everyone else was having and attempting to mold myself into something that physically and genetically I would never be. I find myself in a constant battle to suppress the habit of masking and covering to be the authentic leader that my students and peers deserve and more importantly, that *I* deserve to embrace my whole self without shame or fear. However, the fear of loneliness and isolation is real and can rear its ugly head when seeking a way forward to reconcile competing self-identities. The internal struggle to fit in and the desire for acceptance balanced with the authenticity of one's whole self remains a constant reminder for me as I ascend in my leadership journey, especially when those spaces lack diversity.

Add another layer of being subjected to outright denigration and job shaming for your position in the perceived hierarchy of importance in professional roles. It's interesting how other's perceptions shape their behavior in initial encounters or interactions with me. When I am introduced as a paralegal, depending on the audience, that one word can have a loaded impact on how I am received and treated. In an audience of my paralegal peers, I am welcomed with warmth and respect. In audiences primarily composed of attorneys, I am often dismissed or overlooked. I imagine this experience must parallel what nurses endure, being relegated to "just the nurse" and not the doctor. The roles of paralegal and nurse are akin to the paralegal-lawyer and nurse-doctor dynamic. As an astute observer of the world and its inhabitants, I take note of these interactions and inquire with others about their experiences.

In fact, in my role as the Chair of the National Association of Legal Assistants (NALA) Diversity, Equity, and Inclusion Committee, I had the opportunity to lead a listening session on behalf of our committee at our last annual conference. The emerging theme that struck me is that my attorneys do not respect me. This theme started a litany of questions in my mind. What do you mean? Can you give me examples? Tell me more. What surfaced armed me with content for my teaching, coaching, and consulting practice: Being Underestimated is a Superpower.

Words matter, especially the internal dialogue that we have with ourselves. Being the target of preferential treatment, or lack thereof, based on my role or title smacks of typical classism. Additionally, the othering because of an immutable characteristic by one's peers is even more hurtful and is flat out dangerous and damaging. Ask any child who is the target of bullying or woman attempting to shatter the glass (or bamboo) ceiling. One of the worst feelings is to feel excluded and that one is not accepted as they are.

Isabel Wilkerson's book *Caste: The Origins of Our Discontents* examines hierarchy and class and its impacts on race in America. The author offers readers a framework to navigate these complex dimensions of identity and arms us with language to affirm and validate how so many of us feel about our lived experiences and the overall impacts on societal mental health and social justice in a purported "post-racial" America. The Black Lives Matter movement of 2013, the January 6, 2021 insurrection in our nation's capitol and a deeply polarized and divided America of today, the discontentment is at a boiling point threatening the very existence of our democracy. Hyperbole intentional.

In this introspection of intersectionality, as a Filipina-American I wonder: what is my place in all of this? How did this discontentment impact me in my formative years as an adolescent in the 1990s, eventually into adulthood and now into middle adulthood? In ways that many of us who are similarly situated are still attempting to find the words for and are in constant quest of being seen and understood, I still grapple to make sense of it all. Yet, even while in the throes of confusion and iteration, I, and so many of my peers, continue doing the equity work needed to ensure a fairer, just and equitable world for all of us, sometimes to the point of exhaustion and loneliness.

Presence: Holding and Taking Space

"If they don't give you a seat at the table, bring a folding chair."

- Shirley Chisholm

Our moral compasses point us toward being on the right side of history and being good humans. Yet the way forward often coerces, lambasts, and bamboozles us. Add to that the glossiness of social media, sometimes referred to as a fool's paradise, where purveyors are lulled into a trance of unrealistic and unrealizable images of what we should be. It's a vicious cycle of "shoulding" all over ourselves, sometimes to the point of existential crisis and mental health issues including social isolation. These impacts on our well-being can affect anyone at any stage in life and compounded with other life stressors in a specific season of life. Mental health and wellness rest at the forefront of societal woes especially for our youth and particularly the dangers of social media addiction. At the root of these issues lies abject disconnection.

When I became the primary caregiver for my parents in my mid-forties, the incessant scrolling on social media lead to major FOMO (fear of missing out). Faced with a demanding professional career in a law firm and teaching legal courses in the evening while trying to maintain a semblance of a personal life, I hit my breaking point. I felt alone. And hopeless with no end in sight. I never became a parent but I imagine that the pain, turmoil, worry and defeat emanating from every step and decision I made for my parents rivaled that of a mother for her child. The loneliness in this role as parent to my parents haunted me as if I were a lost soul roaming the plane of purgatory. Disconnected and alone.

Social disconnection is a prevalent affliction among older adults, with profound effects on mental health. (Necka, 2021). In 2023, the U.S. Surgeon General, Dr. Vivek H. Murthy, issued a report, *Our Epidemic of Loneliness and Isolation*. Dr. Murthy discusses the healing effects of social connection and community and offers The Six Pillars to Advance Social Connection including:

☐ Pillar 1: Strengthen Social Infrastructure in Local Communities

☐ Pillar 2: Enact Pro-Connection Public Policies

☐ Pillar 3: Mobilize the Health Sector

☐ Pillar 4: Reform Digital Environments

☐ Pillar 5: Deepen our Knowledge

☐ Pillar 6: Cultivate a Culture of Connection

Dr. Murthy suggests that Pillar 6 is necessary for our society to be successful in the other pillars. Murthy goes on to state:

> *Such a Culture of connection rests on core values of kindness, respect, service, and commitment to one another. Everyone contributes to the collective culture of social connection by regularly practicing these values. Advancing this culture requires individuals and leaders to seek opportunities to do so in public and private dialogue, schools, workplaces, and in the forces that shape our society, like media and entertainment, among others. Behaviors are both learned from and reinforced by the groups we participate in and the communities we are a part of. Thus, the more we observe others practicing these values, the more they will be reinforced in us.*

In other words, as the famed African proverb goes, "It takes a village to raise a child." It also takes a village to produce a healthy adult. However, as Murthy and Wilkerson suggest radical empathy and a reminder of shared humanity or connection are solutions that only scratch the surface of necessary healing and shifting all of us into a society that faces all of our parts, even the ugliest ones, so that we can unabashedly face what got us here to this inflection point where our well-being as individuals and collectively as a society are both at stake.

Being aware of such data points, as reported by the U.S. Surgeon General, feels daunting and hopeless at times. Further, in our leadership journeys, we all face moments of doubt and question our own abilities. Studies report that women are less likely to apply for jobs than their male counterparts because they need the requisite skills and competencies listed in the job description. And it's not news that pay equity remains an issue until the present day and that the number of female CEOs wanes abysmally compared to the number of male CEOs. The data shows us that improvements on all of these fronts are slow. There is still much work to be done.

Data, awareness, and education all matter in holding ourselves accountable and serve as reminders to celebrate even the smallest wins along the way as well as the biggest ones. In the 2024 self-titled Netflix biopic Shirley, the story of Shirley Chisholm, the first black woman elected to the United States Congress and the first woman and black candidate to run for the Democratic Party's nomination for President of the United States of America, reminds us that the extraordinary is often born out of the ordinary.

To my students, I proclaim: trust your power! If we count ourselves out from the beginning, we will count ourselves out of important connections, conversations, and opportunities. Our self-awareness of our inherent worth is mission critical to the genesis of movements that change the world. We must know our worth in order to exert and share our power.

SUPERPOWER: Solutionists and Activists

"Indeed, all the great movements for social justice in our society have strongly emphasized a love ethic."

-bell hooks

In October 2023, sitting amongst my FWN sisters in Lisbon, Portugal, during the global pitch session of our leadership summit and absorbing their passion for the projects, I was left refueled to continue carrying the heavy load of improving the conditions for other women and girls experiencing injustice, sexism, racism, and any form of discrimination. The status updates that followed stoked the fire in my belly to pick up the mantle once again and create support systems and solutions for my fellow sisters.

My original FWN global pitch project, initially titled CONNECT: Answering the Call to Serve (NextGen pipeline development for Filipina elected officials) evolved and shifted focus to a particular demographic. It's what I refer to as the deep void. The 25- to 30-year-old Filipinas with active social and cultural connections while in college find themselves searching for similar connections as they navigate their early professional careers and opportunities. Many of our young sisters find themselves yearning for those connections in the workplace. After all, the sage advice of seeking a mentor, or *fem*tor, practically screams from every article on career advancement for young professionals.

My friend, colleague, and attorney, Anne Bautista, sparked this shift in my CONNECT project, now called CONNECT: Crucial Conversations. Anne's legal work and representation helped women, primarily immigrants/asylees/refugees, seek justice under the Violence Against Women Act (VAWA). After decades of practice and representing hundreds of VAWA clients and cases, Anne found herself at a point in her career struggling to make sense of the injustices committed against her clients by law enforcement and other agencies, specifically overburdensome evidence needed to prove abuse in marital relationships where violence and emotional abuse claims re-victimized her clients. Anne decided to return to school but this time with the goal of enhancing her life's work with a master's degree in women's studies from San Diego State University. Anne invited me to witness her thesis defense in December of 2023. The through-line in Anne's research interviewing women experiencing these issues was evident. Without their support networks, their journey to healing would be nearly impossible.

A few months later, as part of a delegation from San Diego traveling to the United Nations CSW68 in New York City, the reporting of worldwide gender-based violence, discrimination, and inequities committed against women and girls shocked and appalled me. After spending a week hearing story after story of horrific violence and atrocities, I left knowing that all of our work must continue. Anne's research rang even more true than ever on a global scale. Our work is impossible without our support networks.

This support network is where women hold the key. When we bear witness to others suffering in our communities, these crucial support networks are activated and deployed. During some of the worst times of my life, my support network rallied and fed my body, heart and soul so that I could find my way to the path of healing, strength and power. Despite physical, emotional and legislative barriers undermining the work for gender equity, we must hold space for each other and show up. Even when it is hard and even when we are excluded.

Reflection: What Does the Future Hold?

On the precipice of five decades of life, the power of the pause is not lost on me. The projects that I commit to are strategic, intentional, and well-considered. In my constant quest for impact at critical mass and broad reach, the communities and causes where I expend my precious time, resources, and energy revolve around educating women and girls in business, law, and media. My support network includes other influential women who, like me, mean business.

Time is life. And in pondering the second half of my life, the clarity in my purpose guides my work. In my eyes, the future is female.

Knowledge of self, resilience, persistence, and grit are essential components of success and the drivers of change. In dismantling systems that promote caste discrimination, racism and sexism, policy and legislation are at the heart of this equity work. And this work is more needed now than ever. The origins of some of the most significant movements in our recent history were rooted in a love ethic and the sheer determination of ordinary people accomplishing extraordinary feats despite being underestimated.

Being underestimated is a superpower. Get out there and connect. Have crucial conversations. Problem-solve, ideate, innovate and activate. Imagine the collective power of all of us united towards a common goal of equity with shared policy and legislation resources to be used as blueprints across the globe. The world needs all of us now more than ever. We must hold space for one another and when we see our sisters carrying a crushing load, we must offer a helping hand. The importance of self-care to continually filling our cups is ever more crucial to sustaining the energy needed for this Herculean task. But remember my dear FWN sisters, in solidarity, we are unstoppable. The time is now.

> *"Never doubt that a small group of thoughtful, committed citizens can change the world. Indeed, it is the only thing that ever has."*
>
> *- Margaret Mead*

ELLEN SAMSON, CDP, CADDCT, CMDCP

Certified Dementia Practitioner, Certified Alzheimer's Disease and Dementia Care Trainer, Certified Montessori Dementia Care Professional Trainer President, American Geriatric Care Management

President, American Geriatric Care Management

President, My Own EVA

Founding Executive Board, Coalition of Filipino American Chambers of Commerce (COFACC)

Global FWN 100™ 2019

From Harried Child to Resilient Leader

S ome lead with quiet strength, resilience shaped by faith, and unwavering perseverance. Others transform that strength into a legacy, lighting the way for others. I am honored to know someone who does both: my friend, confidante, and soul sister. From the moment I met her, I knew she was extraordinary. Her journey of sacrifice, triumph, and unshakable faith has inspired me and stands as proof of what's possible when a woman rises above her challenges. As the eldest in her family, she bore heavy responsibilities early in life. Yet, she carried them with grace, shaped by cultural and gender expectations that would have crushed many. What makes her remarkable is not just the weight she bore but how she transformed it. When told to be silent and endure, she found her voice. When faced *with impossible circumstances, she chose to leave everything behind in search of peace. Her bold move from the Philippines to America was not a retreat—it was a declaration of self-worth. Starting from scratch in America, she rebuilt her life, humbling herself in jobs far removed from her former executive role. But she didn't just survive—she thrived. Her resilience and vision led her to create a successful business, redefining standards in an industry that often underestimates women like her.She didn't stop there. She turned her success into advocacy, becoming a fierce champion for dementia care and a leader among Filipino-American entrepreneurs. Her journey, from a girl who sacrificed her childhood to a woman at the forefront of business and advocacy, is nothing short of inspiring. Her legacy will be felt for generations, and I am proud to stand beside her as she continues to rise. To my dearest friend, this is only the beginning.*

Janice Jimenez

CEO, Regal Group of Companies and Ellen Samson's Ride or Die

Childhood: Defining Who I Am

From Playgrounds to Pressure Cookers: My Early Lessons in Adulting

Growing up as the eldest child in my family wasn't exactly a walk in the park—it was more like a crash course in adulting. I was the default second mom; it was about navigating a complex web of cultural expectations and gender roles. As a girl, I was expected to be nurturing, responsible, and self-sacrificing—qualities that were seen as inherent to my identity. I was responsible for things like ensuring my siblings didn't burn the house down while my parents were out working. This wasn't a choice; it was just the way things were. My father's sky-high expectations weren't just about me succeeding; it was about upholding the family's honor. In our culture, family wasn't just important—it was everything. Failure wasn't just personal; it was a stain on the family's reputation. I was constantly reminded that if I slipped up, the whole pack would follow suit. No pressure, right? These early responsibilities shaped me into someone who always had to be "on," but they also made me acutely aware of the different standards I was held to as a girl. I couldn't afford to be carefree because failure wasn't an option. Playtime? What's that? I watched other kids play while I was on duty—either literally or in my mind. And that nagging sense of duty followed me into adulthood. I had to constantly prove that I was capable and that I could handle the weight of the world on my young shoulders. I became the queen of overthinking, constantly analyzing every possible scenario to avoid even the slightest chance of failure. This fear wasn't just a little voice in my head; it was a full-on marching band. This intersection of gender and cultural expectations didn't just drive me; it defined me. The pressure to be perfect wasn't just about personal achievement; it was about fulfilling a role that had been predetermined by my gender and cultural background.

But the constant pressure to be perfect wasn't all bad—it made me resilient. However, it also made me feel guilty for taking breaks or simply enjoying life. Downtime felt like a luxury I couldn't afford. Even now, when I do manage to take a break, I'm haunted by that childhood guilt, wondering if I'm wasting precious time. But I'm learning— slowly—that it's okay to rest. It's okay to let go, even if just for a moment.

Giving Up Everything for Peace of Mind: Leaving the Philippines

Trading Turmoil for Tranquility: My Bold Escape to Freedom

Let me tell you, leaving the Philippines wasn't just about hopping on a plane and escaping a failed marriage—it was about challenging societal norms that women should endure, and should suffer in silence for the sake of family and community. It was about starting fresh—it was about saving my sanity. Staying felt like living in slow motion, watching myself fade away. Staying meant losing myself, and I couldn't let that happen—not for me, and not for my children. I had to break free from the expectations that were suffocating me. But leaving? That was terrifying. It meant uprooting everything, taking my kids along for the ride, and stepping into the great unknown. Leaving wasn't just terrifying because of the unknown; it was terrifying because of the judgment, and the whispers that would follow me.

I had this persecution complex, feeling like the universe had it out for me. But then, in my darkest moments, I turned to my faith. I made vow prayers, desperate promises to God in exchange for just a little bit of peace. And you know what? Those prayers worked, or maybe I just needed to believe they would.

My decision to leave was as much about reclaiming my identity as it was about finding peace. "Peace of mind" at that point meant escaping the constant chaos and fear that had become my life. It meant giving my children a stable environment where they could thrive. But leaving wasn't just scary—it was a monumental decision that shook me to my core. I knew I had to leave, but the moment I made that decision, I felt an overwhelming mix of relief and dread. Would I fail? Would I regret this? But in the end, I had to trust that this was the right path—for me and my kids.

Starting Over in America

From Boardrooms to Broomsticks: Reinventing Myself in the Land of Opportunity

Landing in America was like being dropped into a parallel universe. Everything was different—the language, the pace, even the way people looked at you. My first jobs were a far cry from my corporate life back in the Philippines. One day, I was a high-flying executive; the next, I was a karaoke master and saleslady in Downtown LA. Talk about a humbling experience.

But here's the thing—those odd jobs tested my resilience in ways I hadn't anticipated. I had to dig deep, real deep, to keep going. My kids were adjusting to a new life, and I was determined to support them, even if it meant swallowing my pride and doing whatever it took to put food on the table.

As an immigrant woman of color, I faced challenges that many of my colleagues didn't. I wasn't just starting over—I was starting from a position where I was seen as "less than." My qualifications and my experience—were all dismissed because of my accent, my skin color, and my gender. The intersection of these identities made my journey even more challenging, but it also made my victories all the sweeter. I wasn't just surviving; I was building something new despite the odds stacked against me.

The transition from corporate executive to caregiver was particularly jarring. Imagine going from making boardroom decisions to cleaning up after someone else. It was a hit to my self-image, no doubt about it. I felt like a loser, like I had fallen so far from where I was supposed to be. But in those moments of humility, I found a different kind of strength. I wasn't just surviving; I was building something more significant. And that's when the idea of starting my own caregiving business began to take shape.

Reaching Success in Business

Turning Trials into Triumphs: The Birth of American Geriatric

Founding American Geriatric was a leap of faith, and honestly, I wasn't sure if I'd land on solid ground or fall flat on my face. The early days were rough, starting a business in a foreign country, navigating the legal landscape, and building a client base from scratch was no small feat. But slowly, steadily, it grew.

At first, it was just me and a few clients—ten, to be exact. But word got around, and soon, we were up to 25 clients, then more. Scaling the business was a challenge, especially when it came to maintaining the quality of care. But I was relentless, always pushing for more while making sure we never compromised on our standards.

Of course, there were mistakes—plenty of them. Overextending ourselves, taking on too much, too fast. But every mistake was a lesson, and every lesson made us stronger. As a Filipina entrepreneur in a predominantly white industry, I faced barriers that others didn't. There were assumptions made about my capabilities, my knowledge, even my motivations. But every obstacle was also an opportunity—to prove myself, to show that I wasn't just a businesswoman, but a leader, an innovator. I started employing my siblings and other family members, turning the business into a family affair. This wasn't just about making money; it was about building something that could last, something that could give back.

Finding the Advocacy

From Business to Benevolence: My Journey into Dementia Care Advocacy

My work in caregiving naturally evolved into a personal advocacy, particularly around dementia care. I saw the struggles families went through, the heartbreak, the confusion, and I knew I had to do something more. That's how the Dementia Up Close and Personal Workshops were born.

Empowering Families on the Dementia JourneyWhat started as a business strategy quickly became something much more—a way to give back, to make a real difference.

Becoming a Certified Dementia Practitioner was a game-changer. It wasn't just about having another title; it was about solidifying my knowledge and expanding the reach of my workshops. The feedback I received was overwhelmingly positive, and it was clear that these workshops were changing lives. But I didn't want to stop there. My dream is to establish a foundation for seniors, a lasting legacy that will continue to serve the community long after I'm gone.

My advocacy work is deeply personal, shaped by my experiences as an immigrant, a woman, and a caregiver. I'm driven by the desire to ensure that the most vulnerable in our society—those with dementia and their families—have the support they need. It's not just about business; it's about justice, equity, and making sure that everyone, regardless of their background, has access to the care and dignity they deserve. See Table 1. Dementia Up Close and Personal (DUCP) for more information.

Table 1. Dementia Up Close and Personal (DUCP)
Empowering Families on the Dementia Journey

Introduction:

The Dementia Up Close and Personal (DUCP) workshops provide invaluable support to families and caregivers facing the challenges of dementia. These workshops focus on delivering practical guidance, helping participants better understand dementia while equipping them with the tools to provide compassionate care for their loved ones.

Mission and Vision:

DUCP is dedicated to empowering families with the knowledge and skills they need to manage dementia care with confidence and empathy. The program emphasizes the importance of understanding the right language and approach to dementia care, ensuring families can maintain a strong emotional bond with their loved ones while navigating this difficult journey.

Founding and Leadership:

As a respected Certified Dementia Practitioner, and Trainer through the International Council of Certified Dementia Practitioners and Trainers (ICCDPT), I founded DUCP in 2013. I have experience as a Geriatric Care Manager and Family Dynamics Coach, with deep expertise in guiding families through the complexities of elder care. Drawing from her personal experiences and professional knowledge. I started DUCP to offer much-needed support to families around the world. My workshops have reached communities globally, ranging from small, personal gatherings to large-scale events, each designed to offer practical and emotional help to caregivers.

What DUCP Offers:

DUCP workshops provide critical insights and hands-on strategies for caregivers. Key topics include:

- ☐ Understanding Dementia: An overview of dementia and its progression.
- ☐ Decoding Dementia Behaviors: Tools to interpret and respond to the behaviors of loved ones with dementia.
- ☐ Creating a Care Plan: Immediate steps after diagnosis to support both the family and the individual with dementia.
- ☐ Maintaining Caregiver Well-Being: Strategies to help caregivers balance their own needs with those of their loved ones.
- ☐ Finding Resources and Support: Access to local and national resources that ease the burden of caregiving.
- ☐ Planning for the Future: Guidance on preparing for the progression of dementia and its long-term impact on family life.

A Unique, Global Initiative:

What sets DUCP apart is its holistic and empathetic approach to dementia care. As the first global initiative of its kind, DUCP combines practical, real-world advice with emotional support, offering caregivers the tools they need to face both the medical and social challenges of dementia. Its success stems from this unique blend of compassionate guidance and actionable steps that empower families worldwide.

Impact and Reach:

Since its inception, DUCP has had a profound impact on families, helping caregivers feel more confident, prepared, and supported in their role. The workshops provide not only the practical knowledge necessary for caregiving but also emotional resilience, ensuring that participants can better cope with the complexities of dementia care.

Who Should Attend?

DUCP workshops are designed for anyone involved in caring for a loved one with dementia, including family members, friends, and professional caregivers. Participants come away with a deeper understanding of dementia and the skills to provide more compassionate care while preserving their well-being.

Looking to the Future:

As DUCP continues to grow, the organization plans to reach even more families worldwide by expanding its workshop offerings and forging partnerships with healthcare professionals and community leaders. By increasing awareness and accessibility, DUCP remains committed to making dementia care more manageable and less isolating for families everywhere.

Giving Back to the Community

Scribbles to Success: How a Napkin Sparked a Movement

My first Filipino event in America in 16 years was eye-opening. It was at this event that I realized I had been missing out on my community. That's when I got involved with the Filipino American Chamber of Commerce. I saw the potential to promote diversity, equity, and inclusion within the Chamber, and I knew I had to step up.

This led to the creation of the Coalition of Filipino American Chambers of Commerce (COFACC). What started as an idea scribbled on a napkin turned into a powerful organization that supports Filipino American entrepreneurs across the country. But I wanted to do more. That's how the MIHMUM Initiative—"Make It Happen, Make Us Matter"—came to be. It's about making sure our contributions as Filipinos are recognized and that we're seen and heard.

Table 2. Make It Happen, Make Us Matter.

MIHMUM is the battle cry and movement spearheaded by the Coalition of Filipino American Chambers of Commerce (COFACC).

What is MIHMUM?

MIHMUM represents a commitment to assert Filipino Americans' rightful place and recognition in the American landscape. It's a call for Filipino Americans to step out of the shadows and demand the recognition and resources they deserve, rather than being perceived as a "quiet model minority."

How is MIHMUM Related to COFACC?

MIHMUM is intrinsically tied to COFACC's mission and vision. It encapsulates COFACC's drive to:

☐ Empower: Encourage Filipino Americans to take active roles in their communities and beyond.

☐ Advocate: Push for equitable recognition and allocation of resources to Filipino Americans.

☐ Innovate: Foster an environment where Filipino American businesses and professionals can thrive.

COFACC, as the leading organization behind MIHMUM, uses this movement to galvanize its members and the broader Filipino American community towards achieving collective goals and breaking through barriers.

MIHMUM's Initiatives

1. Advocacy and Representation:

☐ Policy Influence: Work on advocacy to ensure that Filipino Americans receive fair representation and resources.

☐ Community Engagement: Mobilize community efforts to raise awareness about Filipino American contributions and issues.

2. Leadership Development:

☐ Training Programs: Offer training for emerging leaders and professionals to equip them with skills to excel and advocate effectively.

☐ Mentorship: Provide mentorship programs to support the growth of leaders within the community.

3. Strategic Partnerships:

☐ Collaborations: Forge partnerships with other organizations to amplify efforts and resources.

☐ Networking: Create opportunities for Filipino American businesses and professionals to connect and collaborate.

4. Community Support:

☐ Resource Allocation: Advocate for increased support and resources for Filipino American businesses and community projects.

☐ Program Development: Develop programs and initiatives that address the specific needs and aspirations of the community.

By embracing MIHMUM, COFACC aims to transform the landscape for Filipino Americans, ensuring they are not only seen and heard but also valued and respected in all spheres of American life.

This Girl Has Grown Into a Leader

From quiet strength to a legacy of empowerment

Inspiring future generations is at the heart of everything I do. I want my story to be a beacon for Filipina women and all women of color, a reminder that no matter where you begin, you can rise, you can lead, and you can create a legacy that truly matters. My journey is not mine alone—it's the shared story of countless women, immigrants, and those who have fought for every inch of their success. It's a story I hope will ignite the courage in others to chase their dreams, to break through the barriers they face, and to leave their own mark on the world.

Through every challenge, every sacrifice, and every moment of doubt, I've come to realize that true strength isn't in never falling—it's in rising, time and time again. It's about finding grace in the midst of struggle and uncovering purpose through pain.

But more than anything, this journey has taught me that success isn't solely about what we achieve for ourselves—it's about how we lift others as we rise. If my story inspires even one person to see that they are capable of more than they ever imagined, then every hardship, every sleepless night, and every doubt will have been worth it. We don't just survive—we evolve, and through that evolution, we don't just change our own lives; we transform the world around us.

Because when we rise, we rise together. And in that, we create a legacy that truly endures.

To God be all the Glory!

JUDGE ROHANEE ZAPANTA

San Diego Superior Court, State of California
Global FWN 100™ 2023

Identity, Law & Justice*

A piece of clothing.
An office gadget.
A kiss from Lola.

ometimes, the simplest things we overlook hold the most profound meaning, shaping how we see the world. There's a rare talent in recognizing their value—a quiet superpower that allows us to see beyond the surface and understand how they fit into the bigger picture. This is the nuanced work of those who serve in the justice system. Judge Rohanee Zapanta embodies this gift. Raised with the values of her heritage, she approaches social justice by seeking the true essence of each issue, looking beyond appearances to uncover the deeper story. Her perspective, rooted in her experience as the daughter of immigrants, a Filipina American, and a champion of the law, informs her work with a balance of fairness and compassion,

---

45   This chapter reflects the personal views of Judge Rohanee Zapanta. Her thoughts and comments neither endorse nor challenge viewpoints on social justice and the legal system or those proffered by other authors of this book.

understanding the ripple effects of every decision. Her cultural heritage enriches her ability to find meaning in the most minor, most ordinary things, turning them into reflections of identity and purpose. She asks, "Who do you see?" and examines how our roles—within family, community, and culture—intertwine to shape who we are. For Judge Zapanta, these seemingly simple moments become touchstones of her identity, grounding her professional commitment to upholding the U.S. Constitution.nReflecting on her journey to the bench, she reminds us that true strength comes from owning and embracing every aspect of who we are.

Lory Jarvina
Captain (Retired), Military Intelligence Officer, United States Army
Chief of Operations, Cyber Security, Department of Defense

Look In the Mirror

When you look into the mirror, who do you see? It's an easy enough question, but many say it's difficult to answer. Think about the image reflecting on you. Would your answer start with the familial roles you take on? Parent? Child? Sibling? Do you answer by explaining how you contribute to your community? Teacher? Mentor? Spiritual provider? Or do you answer by describing how your image presents to others? Filipina? Asian? White? Multi-racial? Do you factor in age? Young? Middle-aged? Senior? There are so many ways to answer the question, "*Who* do you see?" Of course, the legal mind would answer, "Well, it depends…"

Here's my take. As a judge, I review all the evidence before me, then apply the law to the facts, before rendering my decision. Keeping this same legal approach, I continuously process how I reflect upon my identity. It's always a work in progress, understanding who I see in the mirror and deciding how I choose to present myself to others.

My process begins with a deep passion and respect for our United States legal system. It has withstood centuries of government and social change. It is far from perfect, but it continues to grow and develop to serve all Americans from different lived experiences best. When I took an oath to uphold the United States Constitution, I realized that as a Filipina American, I should understand how that oath becomes part of my identity -

one with a narrative I control. It's an identity that strengthens the integrity of what it means to me to be a strong Pinay.

Blue Rubber Bands

"Lola, where are you going," I would ask my grandmother as she got ready for work. My earliest memories of my *Lola* (grandmother) are in bits and pieces. I may have been around four or five years old watching her put on some smock as she combed through her thick, long black hair and pulled it back into a bun. All my life, Lola had one hairstyle: the low bun, which was elegant, practical, and revealing. It showed off her striking features, high cheekbones, and deep-set penetrating eyes.

Lola had eyes that were windows to the soul. They were eyes that held the lived experiences of unimaginable strength and courage. Lola was the only grandparent I ever knew, my father's mother. She only spoke Tagalog, so I attribute my conversational command of the language to her. Lola never learned to read or write as she never completed formal schooling. I sadly remember how embarrassed I was as a child when she lived with us and could not converse with my friends or watch television shows without us interpreting. Little did I know, then, that her inability to learn English was the greatest gift she could give me – forcing me to learn our family's language.

She talked with me about being widowed at a young age, pregnant with her 13th child from her husband, whom she wed in 1937 at the young age of 15. She described to me the day she gave birth to her youngest child – alone and weeping, terrified about what the future would bring to her and her children, knowing she had no formal education to get a job that would support all her kids. Fortunately for her, she was beautiful, made friends quickly, and was an active church member. She always stressed the importance of presentability and engagement with the community. She would attend church services and functions with her hair pulled back, powdered face, and rouge lipstick. Her children would always be found well-groomed. One significant life rule she held and enforced with my mother was – *don't ever let your child look less presentable than you.* She believed children should always be clean and groomed, as should the mother – to reflect discipline, cleanliness, and love for self and family. Through her work at the church, the *"Pag-Ibig"* club sponsored my father's high school education. He was the third eldest child and the first to immigrate to the United States as a US Navy Steward, changing the trajectory of our family's future generations forever.

Tagalog opened a world of funnier jokes, juicier gossip, and, of course, my favorite stories from Lola of her years in the Philippines. She tried to describe the vegetable "*cigarillos*" when she taught me to sing "Bahay Kubo," a folk song describing different vegetables. I thought they were cigarettes for a while, and she would laugh. There were serious stories, too. I remember the somber look on her face when she talked of how afraid she was of walking alone on the streets at 13-14 years old. "Japanese soldiers would kidnap young girls off the streets and hold them hostage as comfort women." Lola described it as slavery. But her mood never dampened with me. She always ended our talks with affection through a hug or strong sniff-kiss on my cheek.

"*Lola, where are you going* I asked again, sitting at the edge of the bed. I watched her draw her long black hair into a tight bun at the nape of her neck. Then she carefully placed the hairnet on, turned to me, and said, "Banchan." She smiled and pulled me in to give me another sniff-kiss. My father was already waiting in our living room to drop Lola and my uncle off to the farms in Salinas. "Banchan." This was always Lola's answer when she went off to work. Or at least, that's how I interpreted her response. Throughout my childhood and into adulthood, it never occurred to me to ask exactly what Banchan was. I figured it was some vegetable.

In an immigrant household filled with Tagalog speakers and American-born grandkids, I accepted words for exactly how I heard them. Since I was learning both Tagalog and English, we never questioned pronunciation or grammar in my early years. We accepted words just as they were delivered, without judgment. Communication was open, comfortable, and loving in our household. To this day, as a judge, I do my best to create that open, comfortable, and supportive environment for communication, keeping in mind the diversity of litigants entering my courtroom.

It wasn't until decades later, years after my Lola's passing, that I had an epiphany. I was grocery shopping with my children when I caught a whiff of the green onions on display. Then, I noticed the tiny blue rubber bands that held them together. At that moment, a flood of memories came all at once – the dirt under Lola's fingernails, her smell after she'd come home from work, the hairnet. I whispered softly to myself, "Bunch onions," tears welled up in my eyes, and I choked up with emotion. Banchan was a bunch of onions. Lola would bunch the onions using these tiny blue rubber bands. All these years, it never mattered to me. But at that moment, I was a young mother, attorney, and wife, and I finally understood my Lola's "bunched onions." In that discovery, I learned a little more about myself. My head tilted a little higher, my posture straightened, and a sense of pride washed over me. I went home and took off the blue rubber bands from the green onions and saved them. It has become a habit of mine to save and reuse these rubber bands, keeping in mind the resilience and flexibility my Lola had to live out her life.

Justice is fair and free. It should be offered to everyone and shouldn't cost a thing. When I think of justice, I think of the blue rubber bands and all that they represent— flexibility and resilience. When I look in the mirror, I see my face being held lovingly between my Lola's two strong hands—hands that did so much for so many.

The "Sample" Blazer

I was about five or six when I recall waiting for my mother to come home from work. I sat on the couch, looking out the front window. A co-worker dropped her off that night when I watched her walk up our small path to our front porch. She was holding up a black garment bag. This was the first time I had ever seen something like it. Growing up, we didn't shop for clothes where one would need a garment bag. Clothes came from the discount store Kmart or from the donations sold at Goodwill. This garment bag had an emblem on it from my Mama's work. It was a gold cypress tree. Mama worked at a clothing factory, where she was part of the assembly team that sewed on sleeves to blazers.

What is that, Mama I asked. She excitedly opened the garment bag and showed me the items she brought home from work. One item was a blazer. It hung on a hanger that matched the garment bag, that matched the label and tag hanging from the sleeve – all adorned with the gold cypress tree. I had never seen such a fine piece of clothing. My fingers ran across the gold cypress tree emblem embossed on the tag. Then my fingers traveled along the blazer's sleeve, onto the embossed emblem on the neckline, and onward to the emblem of the thick black hanger. *"Oooooh Mama, this is fancy,"* I said, moving my hand along the blazer, the label, the hanger, and finally, the tag. I felt the embossed gold emblem under my fingers. *"This must be expensive,"* I whispered.

Mama smiled and said, "Oh no, *anak* (my child), this is a sample; it has no liner. I got it at a discount." I asked Mama the purpose of a liner in a blazer. She explained that it helps keep the blazer's actual shape when a person wears it and moves around. "Maybe when you graduate college, you can wear a blazer with a liner," she said with raised brows and a smile. I recall my mother wearing this blazer many times with pride on several special occasions over several years.

When I think about my younger self and how I struggled with my personal identity, I think of this blazer. I was that blazer – putting myself on display but feeling incredibly vulnerable. After years of enduring several micro and macroaggressions, I felt discounted. I didn't stop to think about what was on my hanger, or my label, or my price tag – what was my worth? In all my efforts pushing through college and law school to learn and achieve professional growth, I somehow lost my sense of self. Where was my gold emblem?

As my career developed, so did my personal life. I got married, had children, and created my own family. I found it more important to rediscover the roles I took on, traditions, and cultural core values. I understood the importance of that blazer. The emblem on my hanger began to match my label and my tag. I started to see and experience my worth both professionally and personally. The difference was that as I grew older, I needed a liner. My liner is made up of my core values, which always stayed the same as I collected personal and professional achievements. This liner helps me keep my shape when life brings me through twists and turns.

The blazer makes me think of equal access to justice. Seeing the garment bag, hanger, and blazer for the first time is a strong memory because it was one of my first encounters with designer clothing. Resources in my family were not used for designer clothing – ever. There was never a need to be fancy. Justice is the same way. There is never a need to be fancy. In my courtroom, I ask that you simply be. Not everyone can afford to pay for legal representation, present in court with flowery language, or wear professional attire. In my years as a judge, I've seen many litigants rush into their court hearings after sitting for hours on public transportation to make it to their 15-20-minute court appearance. They come into court still in work uniform, explaining their position as best they can with simple, straightforward vocabulary. These litigants deserve the same care and attention as any litigant who paid their attorney to appear on their behalf.

In my courtroom, everyone is valued, regardless of their role or status. Whether they have the fancy gold emblem or not or possess a prestigious title, each person involved in the court proceedings plays a crucial part in administering justice. Everyone includes the witness who recalls the make and model of the getaway car, the expert neurologist who provides insight into head and brain trauma, the file clerk who assembles and delivers the essential court files, and the court reporter who meticulously records every word spoken. Each of these participants contributes to the fair and thorough administration of justice. I made my Mama proud as she witnessed over my legal career as an attorney that I owned many designer blazers with liners. In 2018, my Mama watched in the front row as I humbly turned in those designer blazers for a black robe.

My Calculator

In 2002, I started as a junior associate attorney. Being a junior associate required me to crunch numbers and reach a suggested quota designated by my law firm. My calculator became my best friend. It had large numbers and big dark gray buttons for addition, subtraction, multiplication, and division. That calculator was always on top of the work area of my desk within arm's reach. I'd instinctively turn to it whenever any issue with numbers arose. I was so obsessed with no one stealing my beloved calculator that I wrote my initials on the top of the display screen with a thick black Sharpie pen. I grew to love my basic Texas Instruments computer-beige calculator. Over two decades, even when I could use other fancier devices or my computer to calculate figures, I always turned to my calculator for the final confirmation.

The practice of law requires constant calculation, both literally and figuratively. Attorneys literally must continuously crunch numbers in almost all areas of law. For example, in California, where I preside, family law requires calculating the division of assets, time spent with children, and, of course, child and spousal support. In criminal law, calculations are used to mandate minimum and maximum exposure of years in jail or prison. Or in civil law, where the obvious calculations quantify punitive damages and pain and suffering. In a large firm, attorneys continuously calculate their billable hours by adding time increments down to the minute, which is then multiplied by a dollar amount. The overall performance equals the value each attorney brings to their law firm and., thus, becomes one of the factors that ensure job security.

The figurative approach usually involves lawyers calculating risk. Each lawyer must sit down with their client and review the weight of risk involved in making decisions on moving forward with the case. Every step of litigation requires strategic calculation of risk attributed to legal options available. Clients must remain informed and consent to how a case moves forward in litigation. How do you calculate risk? Attorneys often find the quickest method through evidence-based assessment. They calculate based on bits and pieces of evidence that hold weight in the case. Sometimes, cases have evidence in an extensive collection of smaller bits that reveal the best legal option to pursue.

However, some cases only need a few pieces of evidence where their significant weight can dictate the entire perspective and become the most persuasive.

These calculations lead one to ask, is justice quantifiable? Justice can be the great equalizer and can compensate for loss with gain. I've witnessed justice administered in my courtrooms over the years, and my answer would be, as all those in law would say, "It depends." Some litigants will tell me they feel justice was served based on the percentage of relief and closure they gain from a major legal decision. Other litigants will argue that they do not believe justice was served because the punishment imposed upon the other litigant is limited based on statutory boundaries. My overall assessment is that justice is ingrained into the American culture. The United States was born out of a fight for justice. The Constitution has built-in unalienable rights" afforded to each American. However, this cultural analysis of justice would argue that it can be quantified by how "American" a person feels. This argument can easily be a slippery slope in this nation of immigrants. My final answer is that there is no answer. The conclusion on law-based justice in quantifiable terms must come from the person entrenched in the litigation of their case. It boils down to the lived experience of that person when the case is finally resolved. But timing can always change perspective as memory can be deceiving. In the end, calculations help maintain the integrity of justice.

I now realize my emotional connection to the calculator developed because it was reliable, familiar, simple, and yet precise. Throughout my profession, I've encountered so many overwhelming barriers to my development as a law practitioner. I struggled to maintain a sense of diligence and resilience. However, in those times of struggle, a tool as accessible as my calculator supported me during those hard times. It reminds me to turn to the reliable, that which has worked for me in the past. I know to look for my constant familiars, those core values that continue to define me underneath layers of external accomplishments and recognition. I remember to go back to what is simple in any web of complicated mental or emotional challenges. Finally, when facing any potential barrier, my approach is planned and intentional – precisely attacking the barrier.

I only gave the calculator any true significance last year when I attended a state judicial training. As an icebreaker, participants were asked to select an item from a box of random objects. I saw the same calculator in this box – old, dirty, neglected, and tossed into a box of random items for this icebreaker. I don't think it was a coincidence that

I found the same calculator to select as an icebreaker object when introducing myself and sharing a little about myself. The more I thought about what to share, the more I felt a firm conviction for what the calculator represented. My calculator still sits on my desk in my judge's chambers. It provides me with that same tried and accurate service. But it also reminds me that when I look in the mirror, I see a person who has all she needs and requires nothing more to serve her community with reliability, familiarity, simplicity, and precision.

The *Filipiniana*

After being appointed to the bench, I was invited to speak at many community events. These were opportunities to feature native Filipinx attire as part of my outfit. My first speaking event as a judge was scheduled just a few weeks after being appointed. I was asked to be one of the keynote speakers at a Pan Asian gala. I chose to wear my *Filipiniana* top paired with black slacks. The native top was silky sheer cream, embellished with black embroidered flowers. I wore it with a solid silk cream tank underneath, revealing my arms through the sheer butterfly-shaped sleeves that shimmered and fell to my elbows. I asked my husband for his opinion on my selection. Do you think this top represents Spanish colonialism and oppression? As a public figure, I was worried about appearing offensive or disrespectful to some community Fil-Am leaders who expressed their disdain for the native garb.

My husband responded without giving me a direct answer. He said, "I have always been told that the *barong* (men's version of the *Filipiniana* top) was made sheer to dissuade Philippine servants from having weapons when called to serve the elite Spanish colonizers at special events." Interesting, I thought. I knew attendees at the gala would inquire about my native top. I had to be prepared with an answer. I didn't feel comfortable having to explain my native garment through references to Spanish colonizers and their fear of an armed attack from their Philippine servants – not a great cocktail conversation.

The night began, and several community leaders attended wearing native garb or culturally referenced pieces to accent their outfits. Within moments of my arrival, before I could sit at the speakers' table, I was approached by a lovely colleague who said how much she admired my top. I thanked her and explained it was a native Philippine top influenced by the beauty of Spanish design and embroidery. It also honored the native material of *pina*, a fabric made of pineapple fibers, providing a sheer look. There,

I figured I had a neutral yet sufficient answer that paid homage to my culture. Did it really? I asked my inner self. Just like my husband, I couldn't give myself a direct answer.

Much like the *Filipiniana*, justice in the United States is transparent. The path to justice through law in the United States is never a secret. Lawyers, judges, and jurors write and apply the law consistently and uniformly. It is interpreted and delivered in varying ways, depending on lived experience and precedent. It is embellished and influenced by other cultures. Yet, its beauty is unique to the beholder. Americans protest it and revere it. After a significant court decision, the public can celebrate victory or scream in horror. Some believe there is no beauty and that having a transparent justice is an illusion. Others believe that, much like the Spanish elite and the *barong*, the transparency of justice hides the truth that people in power are afraid of. Yet others still believe the American justice system is an even more beautiful replica of different designs originating from other countries. Still, it was presented as visually stunning once it was worn proudly by the United States. Others believe and continuously hope American justice takes on a unique identity, inheriting only the visually stunning yet keeping the main fabric that holds it together, true to the native land.

Years later, I've learned to reconcile my personal conflict with the *Filipiniana*. When I wear it, I feel its beauty and power within me. I wear it as a personal reminder of a time when colonizers took over a nation of separate Philippine tribes and regions and unified them through servitude. The thought of it makes me sad, yet I still proudly wear the *Filipiniana*. I look in the mirror and see its honesty – its transparency. I am reminded of how, in forced servitude, my ancestors found ways to unite and foster *kapwa*, that sense of inner-self connected through the resilience and fortitude of their people. When I attend community events wearing *Filipiniana*, I celebrate diversity and *kapwa*. I can't help but lift my chin a little higher and revel in the beauty and transparency of the garment, reminding me that I have nothing to hide. I present my authentic self, someone who came from a bloodline spanning hundreds of years of a resilient, unified people.

The *Malong*

I was first introduced to the significance of this garment when planning for my wedding day. My husband and I both knew we wanted a *Filipiniana-themed* wedding, where our bridal party and guests wore *Filipiniana* attire. In our initial planning and vision of a crowd of cream-colored garments adorned with embroidery, we didn't realize something was missing. We agreed on most of the planning. However, my husband offered his opinion when I told him that my bridesmaids would also accentuate their gowns with large *Capiz* seawater shell medallions surrounded by a string of freshwater pearls. Since my bridesmaids were *bongga* (extravagant), he wanted his groomsmen to present more "swag." One groomsman proposed embellishing their *barongs* with a *malong*, a tribal piece.

He showed me the *malong*, a red woven tube garment adorned with colorful geometric tribal patterns. The groomsman wore it once to another wedding a few years back and said it added that pop of color during the ceremony. All the groomsmen were excited to adorn such a fabric of significance. My husband was more excited that visually, his groomsmen would present a tribal symbolism. Such a spectacle would likely be the fashion topic of conversation during the reception. The wedding was visually stunning and a memorable one, where guests, as expected, complimented my husband on his groomsmen's attire.

I was recently asked to be a keynote speaker for a Filipina lawyers' conference. That speaking event was an opportunity not only to personalize cultural representation rhetorically through my words but also visually through how I presented. I'd have the attention of hundreds of people. The audience was expected to look and listen. For the look part, I had a plan. The magnificence of the *malong* was that not only did it originate from indigenous Philippine tribes, but it was also intended to have many uses throughout one's life. From infancy to death, the *malong* could carry an infant, be worn throughout childhood and into adulthood as a skirt, headdress, or jacket, transport items in a sling in daily activity, and ultimately cover the person as they transition into the afterlife. No wonder a traditional Philippine dance was created to pay homage to its magnificence. The dance is performed as a solemn homage to the *malong* where performers maintain a flat affect – no expression, never smiling. The audience is meant to focus on the carefully calculated hand movements that manipulate the fabric into its various forms.

I adorned the top of my business suit with a malong as an add-on native accessory. The image I hoped to achieve was to exude its magnificence. I looked in the mirror and saw a serious Pinay on a mission. I intended to communicate a message with carefully calculated words. I carried a message of inspiration through rediscovering one's identity. The message was that we all could maintain our true selves, much like the *malong*, with the ability to take on many forms and serve many roles throughout life. My reflection in the mirror revealed well-thought methodical patterns of bright stitching lined up along the vast fabric folded across my suit. The fabric started at my left shoulder, then continued at a diagonal like a sash, and ended in a ruffled gathering pinned at my hip. The pale, silky fabric complimented the vivid geometric-shaped pattern.

Administering law and justice parallels the functionality and fashion of the *malong*. The fabric of law and justice is akin to the United States Constitution. It's what holds law and justice together, providing its shape. Much like the bright, colorful patterns woven into the fabric, each state has its own unique set of laws that more directly affect Americans. As a judge, I administer state laws that directly impact residents of my state of California. These laws are unique to the region, honoring the demographic of those who live here. It's important to understand that California has a unique set of bright and colorful laws, creating patterns of fairness and assurances that law and justice are free from prejudice and discrimination.

World views of American law and justice vary as much as the different types of *malongs*. Some countries see America as the idealistic law and justice – home of the free and the brave. This view is the shiny, silky *malong* with woven or stitched-in floral or latticed patterns that embellish the garment. It's meant to be admired for its beauty. Movies and national holidays celebrate this idealistic view that often identifies what it means to be American. This view is worn like a sash, one of royalty or high stature. American laws and justice have usually become the standard for other countries to emulate.

American law and justice ideals are as important as their ability to function and endure for centuries. What makes a *malong* magnificent is not only its beauty and tribal identity but also its functionality and dependability. Administering law and justice in the United States requires consistency and preservation of individual rights. Americans have come to depend on the idea that individual rights are protected and promised to everyone, regardless of lifestyle or status. The stitching on the functional fabric of American law and justice is strong and resilient. This fabric has endured through a civil war, terrorist attacks, and a global pandemic. However, repeated use and advocacy have worn and torn it. Thousands of legal issues strain the fabric of affected populations, including those impacted by environmental issues, communities of color, and people living in poverty. American law and justice serve multiple roles, offering support and protection during years, months, or even brief moments of struggle.

The *malong* was a big hit that day as many attendees approached me, complimenting me on the statement piece. A young mother approached and commented on how the *malong* was such a nice touch. She had her 6-month-old daughter strapped to her chest in a baby carrier. I explained how she could use this *malong* to carry her daughter, and in fact, I used a *malong* to carry my youngest child from infancy until about age three. Then we talked about its magnificence and ability to maintain its form and function while taking on many roles throughout a person's life. She and I hugged and shared a connection not only as mothers but in the symbolism of the *malong* as *Pinays* (Filipina women) in law.

The Gavel

I actually don't use a gavel on my desk in court or what we call "the bench." The object itself holds significant weight in its use and symbolism of American justice. When people see a gavel, many admit they think of a judge banging it on the bench and yelling, "Order in the court!" Some will share that they imagine the gavel going down with a bang after a monumental ruling. Those scenarios are pretty dramatic. Realistically, throughout my workday on the bench, I make so many rulings and orders that the loud bang of a gavel with every decision or case would likely interrupt the efficient flow in my courtroom. By the end of the day, I've made so many decisions that I really don't want to decide anything else. After the last case and legal decisions of the day, I warily walk back to my chambers, remove my black robe, and look in the mirror. I see a woman with decades of significant decisions in life, but one decision stands out – the decision to enter the legal profession. The journey to the bench started with the decision to become a lawyer.

Why law? There are countless reasons I can share why justice is so important to me. However, my decision to enter law stems from my experience as a child of immigrants. Thanks to Lola, I learned to speak Tagalog. As a teen and young adult, I was often sought to translate important documents and applications for many family members and friends. From job applications to forms for Social Security or Immigration services and medical paperwork, I helped clarify what was needed and often helped fill out the documents. I experienced and witnessed first-hand how important it was to understand the "rules of the road" for immigrants to navigate their way in this country and ultimately reach their destinations.

I think of the gavel and how it connects to my decision to enter the field of law. The gavel not only represents justice. The gavel is a tool used to command the court's attention. It demands respect and deference to a legal system designed to ensure fairness and freedom for everyone. Today, I look in the mirror and see a reflection of a Pinay wearing a black robe and holding a gavel. I feel its weight in my hands. I also pay homage to those whose shoulders I stand on to grasp and take hold of such an honor. Life has placed in my hands a gavel with its weight of responsibility to administer justice and command the court's attention. As I look at my reflection, I hear the voice announcing my presence,

> *"All rise, in the presence of our flag and the principles of the constitution for which it stands, the Honorable Rohanee Zapanta presiding, come to order…."*

And You?

I ask you once again, "When you look into the mirror, who do you see?" Perhaps there are personal items in your reflection, collected over the years, that hold deep significance. I invite you to gather these treasures and honor them. Seek out the pieces that resonate deeply, reminding you of your essence and values. I believe that when you recognize those items in your reflection, you will inevitably lift your head a little higher, stand up a little straighter, and smile at yourself in all your glory.

GLOCAL

"The concept of glocalization means the simultaneity—the co-presence—of both universalizing and particularizing tendencies."

— Roland Robertson

"... to cultivate global citizens that feel obligated to create innovative solutions for their communities and the World to achieve a prosperous and sustainable future in accordance with the United Nations Sustainable Development Goals framework."

— BAU Global

MYLA ARCENO, MCSP

Councilor Myla Arceno
Martins Wood Ward
Stevenage, Hertfordshire
Cardiac Rehab Specialist Physiotherapist
Team Manager
Hertfordshire Community National Health Service (NHS) Trust
Global FWN 100™ 2022

The King and I

G rowing up as a Filipina in the small town Pulupandan, Myla's journey was shaped by the rich tapestry of cultural heritage, gender expectations, and the immigrant experience. These intersecting identities became the foundation of her resilience and the lens through which she approached leadership. As a Filipina immigrant in the UK, she encountered both overt and subtle challenges in navigating a predominantly white, male-dominated sphere. Yet, these challenges have only strengthened her resolve to advocate for diversity and inclusion, ensuring that voices like hers are heard and valued. Myla's lived experience and intersectionality challenges resonate with my experience of being Mayor of Daly City, CA. As the first Filipina women elected public officials, we carry significant *responsibilities to be the best and to ensure the next generation is in the pipeline. Public service is my passion; Myla certainly has it in her heart.*

Mayor Juslyn Manalo
Daly City, California, U.S.A.

The story started with many years of preparation from my childhood that I was unaware of. Growing up in the small town of Pulupandan, Negros Occidental, Philippines, where everyone knows everyone was already the start of my journey to meeting the King someday. That phrase that I say jokingly with school friends, "*I will go to London to visit the Queen or the King,*" was a seed that grew into something more significant. I have indeed met the King! So, don't underestimate your wish or take that joke lightly; who knows where your journey or destiny will be?

I moved to Stevenage from the Philippines in 2003, accompanied by Joseph, my husband, and John, my son. My family expanded in 2005 with the birth of Mary, my daughter. What we thought would only be a few years turned into over twenty years, and we continue to reside in Stevenage, love, and be loved by our fellow community. I have been active in civic life over several years, co-founding the Stevenage Filipino-British Community, Philippine Theater UK, European Network of Filipino Diaspora (ENFID), One Philippines newsmagazine, United Kapiznon, Stevenage Philippine Dancers, the Hertfordshire-wide Barrio Festival, Chartered Society of Physiotherapy, Stevenage World Forum, *Barkada ni* Maria rosary group and other various diverse groups in Stevenage.

When I was elected in 2021, I became the first female elected Filipina councilor of the Constituency Labour Party (CLP) of the UK and, as councilor, was elected mayor in 2023-2024. I stand on the shoulders of two *Kababayans* who made their mark as political leaders in the U.K. Another FWN sister, Cynthia Alcantara-Barker, served as Mayor of Hertsmere from 2020 to 2021. Danilo Favor is the first Filipino to hold elective office in the U.K. He made history anew when proclaimed as town mayor of East Grinstead in Sussex following the 2019 local elections there.

Meeting King Charles in Stevenage was one of the highlights of my mayoral year. I will remember this and happily share it with others for many more years. After all, not everyone has had the chance to meet the King in person or have a conversation like I have.

When I met him during his visit to Stevenage, Hertfordshire, King Charles was newly crowned King of the United Kingdom. Stevenage is a town in England about 27 miles north of London, with a population of about 90,000 on the 2022 census. Stevenage is a town steeped in rich heritage and culture, with a long history from Saxon times.

In Stevenage, we take pride in our beautiful diversity, and our town motto is "The Heart of a Town lies in its People." We have MBDA (a military defense systems company), Airbus (home of Mars Rover), the Centre of Cell and Gene Therapy, Formula One driver Lewis Hamilton, the nearby Knebworth House, historical Roman barrows, a football stadium, churches, a cathedral, and many more, but above all, it's the Stevenage people who are the center and main focal point of the town.

As Stevenage Mayor from May 2023 to May 2024, it was the busiest year in my calendar duties. I kept my clinical work as a specialist physiotherapist in cardiac rehab but dropped my other clinical responsibilities in our local hospital to give way to my mayoral duties.

As a clinician and a cardiac rehab specialist physiotherapist, I greatly advocate the importance of physical activities and exercises. In the cardiac rehab clinic, with a multidisciplinary approach, I assess patients with cardiovascular diseases who had a heart attack or myocardial infarction, Stents, Coronary Artery Bypass Grafts, and Heart Failure. I facilitate the education of our service users, at times with their families, to prevent and minimize the risks of further cardiovascular issues. The exercise classes with the cardiac rehab team are for improving the level of fitness and confidence and achieving each specific goal while ensuring a safe and effective way of exercising. My role also includes being a clinical educator for University Physio Students on placement and for a learning shadowing experience for high school pupils with plans to take a physio degree.

As Mayor, I attended 366 official engagements with the support of my son John, the Mayor's consort. The engagements were very special to me, especially meeting so many groups and individuals who were inspirational and passionate about serving our community.

My role as the first Filipina Mayor in Stevenage is more than a personal achievement; it represents a breaking of barriers for other women of color. It sends a powerful message to the next generation that their dreams are achievable, and their identities are assets, not obstacles. About 1,000 people identified as Filipinos/Filipinas in Stevenage. They mostly work in the local National Health Service NHS hospitals and care homes.

The United Kingdom has a Parliamentary form of government. There are 13 wards/areas in Stevenage, with three councilors elected by the electoral residents on each ward with a 4-year term. Councilors represent their ward and the public interest. They are community leaders who are responsible for a wide range of duties, including representing their ward, dealing with residents' concerns, policy-making, strategic and corporate management, and regular contact with the public through council meetings, telephone calls, and surgeries or open sessions.

The 39 councilors elect the Stevenage Mayor for a one-year term. As the Mayor, I am honored to be known as the town's first citizen and represent the people of Stevenage in various civic and community events. I chaired the council meetings to discuss and debate the motions, which I really enjoyed during my term.

The 5th of December was the day of the King's visit to the Coptic Church, The Orthodox Cathedral in Stevenage. Buckingham Palace initiated the visit, which was not publicly announced. I learned about the visit three weeks before; I was told not to tell anyone. Imagine how challenging it was for me to be excited but at the same time not to share what I'm excited about! It must be a secret even to my husband and my son, the Mayor's consort--who unfortunately was not invited and was so disappointed, of course, when he knew afterward, but he got over it so quickly. The Mayor's office had sent my biography as required by the palace.

The important day came. I was wearing my fabulous Filipiniana with my hair fascinator, the fashion I subconsciously developed with a fusion of Filipino-British tradition. I looked beautiful and confident in representing the Stevenage people and my Filipino background. Most guests were from around the country, with dignitaries, diplomats, Orthodox Church members, and leaders of various Stevenage churches. I did what I always do best, welcoming them to our town as Stevenage Mayor.

The group that welcomed the King were the Lord Lieutenant and his wife, the High Sherriff of Hertfordshire, the Chairman of Hertfordshire, the CEO of Hertfordshire, Matt Partridge, the CEO of Stevenage, the Stevenage Mayor, and Bishop Angaelos, OBE.

The King took his time speaking to each of us, but he stayed longer talking to me; he had an impressive retention of information he knew about me. He talked to me about the Filipino nurses who visited Buckingham Palace a week before and asked about my National Health Service (NHS) clinical work, to which I replied, *"I took a day off because of you."* He laughed out loud, captured in a video that aired on The Royal Family Channel and then shared on other media channels.

That was a truly memorable experience, and I was humbled to meet King Charles. The King was gracious and spoke to me like I was the most important person at that moment. He studied my biography and knew about the individual people he was meeting that day. I couldn't help but notice his gardener's hands, so what was said about his working hands was true. The King was truly remarkable! He is a human being like anyone else and deserves courtesy. I went home that day, elated with my experience and grateful for the opportunity to meet the King.

On the 8th of May 2024, I showed up at Buckingham Palace at the Kings Garden Party with my Filipino-British fusion of fashion. This time, my invitation was with my son John as the Mayor's consort. It was a lovely day with thousands of guests enjoying the music, food, and drinks. The guests were carefully chosen for their contributions to our community and our country. The King, Queen, Duke, Duchess, and many royal family members were there, but this time, there was no personal conversation but a smile and a royal wave.

It reminded me again that my childhood girly imagination of meeting the royal family came true. I traveled across continents and oceans from the Philippines to the United Kingdom to become the Stevenage Mayor, serving my community and fulfilling my destiny of meeting King Charles.

Throughout my career, I've had to confront and challenge the stereotypes often associated with being a Filipina woman in leadership. By embodying both strength and compassion, I've worked to redefine these narratives, proving that leadership comes in many forms.

As someone who bridges two cultures—Filipino and British—I've learned to weave global perspectives into local leadership. This fusion allows me to create a more inclusive community in Stevenage, a community that values diversity and fosters global understanding.

And here's the reflection that summed up the many years.

Stevenage, here I come,
That was 2003.
The NHS brought my hubby,
To work in the wards of the elderly.
So, there I was with our little son, John,
Followed him dutifully.
From Pulupandan, where I was born,
To Roxas City to be with my hubby,
And Stevenage ultimately
Where Destiny dictated me to be.
Stevenage is now my community,
Where my heart is
And my home with my family.
2023- 2024, my name is Myla Arceno,
The Stevenage Mayor that you all know.
I have my passion, values, and wisdom,
That I carry with me,
All 366 official Mayoral engagements,
Since May 2023.
I am a reflection of my faith, my culture,
And the foundation of education
My parents and teachers
Instilled in me.
I wish and pray to bring peace, harmony, understanding and respect,
Wherever I will be.
I carry my smiles that come naturally,
May this bring people at ease
I've met along the way.
No man is an island,
I am not alone in any of my duties,
I have my family, friends, colleagues, and many other communities.
Together, we are all gathered here,
The FWN sisterhood is so dear
We women of today,

With courage, we have our voices heard
We continue; there is still more to be done.
With our Friendships, inspiring Inclusion and Togetherness we have a community
That is FIT.
F for Friendships for what I believe feeds my soul
Friendship and Faithfulness with each other, even with our differences,
In our community, we all belong.
I for Integration and Inclusion we all come to know,
We think, speak, and look in our unique way,
We all have our purpose and role,
In understanding, listening, and respect
We will achieve the success that we genuinely expect.
T for Togetherness is like a hand
With each finger with a different movement
-Opposition, adduction, abduction, flexion and extension.
With different sizes- small, big, tall, and short
But take one or hurt a part, and you will never get a firm grip and grasp.
Stevenage is like that, with our diversity, Faithfulness, integration, and
togetherness,
We are all one in making our community.
My Stevenage, My Destiny,
Where we met,
The King and I.

MARIA A. BEEBE, PH.D.

President, Kaisipan
Consultant, Asia Open RAN Academy
Portland State University, Department of Anthropology affiliate
US FWN 100™ 2011, Global FWN 100™ 2013
Continuing Influential FWN 100™ 2019

Fractals: Recursive, Non-linear, and Ever-changing.

D r. *Maria's life unfolds like a fractal, with each phase reflecting interconnected experiences that shape her identity and mission. As a Filipina, educator, and international development advisor, her journey spans diverse cultural and geographical landscapes—from the Philippines to Africa to Afghanistan—each adding depth to her understanding of herself and the world. The Kabul experience, with its moments of fear, resilience, and determination, echoes being born in Zamboanga and growing up in the Philippines, where the intersections of colonial history, gender, and ethnic identity influenced her path. Her narrative is not linear but a dynamic blend of past and present, personal and political, much like the fractal metaphor suggests. Her initiatives—the Afghan e-Quality Alliances, Asia Open RAN Academy, and Kaisipan's Digital Capabilities—demonstrate her commitment to education, digital literacy, and gender equity. These projects reflect how her work in international development builds on past efforts while adapting to new challenges. Each iteration of her experiences—whether in Kabul or her current life balancing remote work and caregiving—reflects the recurring and ever-changing intersectionality themes she navigates.*

Our lives first intersected in 2007 when I joined Dr. Maria's team in the Afghan e-Quality Alliances, a USAID project in Kabul. Her guidance helped me navigate project operations and stakeholder engagement, and she supported my decision to apply for the JICA scholarship, which launched my career as a diplomat. Through our shared work in Kabul, we formed a strong bond, united by our commitment to gender equity and community empowerment through education and development. When the Taliban took over in 2021, I became an exile while serving as Deputy Chief of Mission in Paris. Now, I find myself among refugees in the U.S., seeking a future in a political environment that is both welcoming and unwelcoming.

Parwana Paikan
Former Deputy Head of Mission
Afghanistan Embassy, Paris, France

"Fractals provide a language and visualization that represents the both/and of similarity and difference, where the repetition or recursive construction of patterned privilege/marginalization creates a unique image of repeated, intersectional experiences."

Jenna Abetz and Julia Moore (2018) p 36

I have walked this way before. There is a thin layer of asphalt, non-existent in some places. I must turn right at the next fork. It is eerily quiet. The familiar seems strange. I quicken my pace. I follow the curve of the road and then bedlam. I face tens, nay, hundreds of men doing what looked like war drills.

"Assalamalaykum."
"Dr. Maria, you are early."[46]

---

46   Fractals: Recursive, Non-linear, and Ever-Changing
Abetz, J. & Moore, J. (2018). Visualizing intersectionality through a fractal metaphor.

"What is she doing here?"[47]

"She should not be here."

"We asked her to come."

"Dr. Maria ..."

Guns, rifles, and swords. Oh my!

I drop to my knees, put my hands up, yet somehow hold on to my files.

2005-2013 - Afghanistan

In my right hand, I held my files and somehow managed to clutch my mobile. My coat was draped over my left arm, which hid a bottle of red wine – a gift from an embassy colleague. My breath, I was sure, smelled of pork. Pork, as I stifled a giggle, was a definite sin of commission in Afghanistan. I had just finished a meeting with my point of contact at USAID, located at the embassy compound. My colleague was going to Washington, DC, and needed a progress report about the various project activities from me as the Washington State University (WSU) Chief of Party. Seven Angel Centers functioning. One at Kabul University. Another at Kabul Medical University. Kabul Polytechnic. Two at Herat University and one at the Department of Education. Two at Balkh University in Mazar Sharif. Check. The new Minister of Education has been named. Check. Master's course in Development Economics ongoing. Check. Engineering Faculty members accepted by Ohio University have their visas. Check. Anything else? No – no Afghan who was studying in the US has absconded to Canada to ask for asylum. No, not from the latest cohort.

I lived off-campus with permission from WSU. However, I had to move from guesthouse to guesthouse for security reasons. For a time, I lived at the German guesthouse on the Ministry of Higher Education grounds. It was called the German guesthouse simply because the Germans funded it. There were ten guest rooms with en-suite bathrooms. Development and aid workers from Germany, Australia, India, and the U.S. called the guesthouse "home." At breakfast, we swapped *"Shelter in place. Stay away from windows and doors"* stories and the latest security alerts.

Routledge eBooks, 31–43. https://doi.org/10.4324/9781351209793-3

47   Dunn, J. C. & Jimmie, M. (2018). Transgressing Feminist Theory and Discourse. Routledge eBooks.

Kabul is at a dangerously high risk for militant attacks, including vehicle-borne improvised explosive devices (VBIEDs), direct and indirect fire, and suicide bombings. The same terrifying risks loom over other major cities in Afghanistan, such as Herat and Mazar-e-Sharif. Hostile acts are a constant and ominous threat throughout the country, striking fear into the hearts of U.S. and other foreign nationals, whether through targeted or random violence.

> *"Extremists associated with various Taliban networks and members of other armed opposition groups are active in every province of the country."*

> *"Travel to all areas of Afghanistan remains unsafe due to ongoing military combat operations, landmines, banditry, armed rivalry between political and tribal groups, and the possibility of insurgent attacks, including attacks using vehicle-borne or other improvised explosive devices (IED)."*

> *"At approximately 0800hrs, a suicide bomber detonated his explosives-filled Toyota Corolla close to a US convoy in the Qalai Khayat area, district nine of Kabul city. This is approximately 200 meters north of Masood Circle."*

> *"Advisors will go under Restricted Movement. (Movement restrictions are limited to mission essentials, which are work-related only. No social venues or shopping will be authorized during this time)."*

Lunch was generally at our various workplaces, partly to minimize road travel. Guests could sign up for dinner at the guesthouse or go to any approved restaurants considered safe.

This fateful night, I had a working dinner with my colleague while providing an update on the project—who was doing what, where, and when. Then, I headed for my guesthouse.

It was a short walk from the compound to where my driver could pick me up. While some official cars were allowed to exit to and from the compound, my university status did not merit a special license plate. Hence, the short walk. I made sure the driver knew the drill.

"Drop me off here."
"Pick me up in another spot."
"No, you cannot park in the same area."
"I will text you when I exit the compound."

However, I never got used to the security arrangements. A maze of barbed wires. Huge concrete barrier blocks. Guard towers. A more sinister version of Stalag 13. Hogan's Heroes without the fun part. American security was on the perimeter of the US compound. Then, at some mid-way point, Afghan guards.

That night, when I carried a bottle of red wine in my left arm hidden by a coat draped over my arm, an Afghan guard stopped me and asked seemingly innocuous questions:

"What are you doing here?" "I am a university professor."
"What is your work?" "Teaching English and computers."
"What is your name?" "Maria."
"Mariam."

Then he started to touch my head scarf. Onto to my arm, snaked down my back and onto my breast. I thought he was checking for weapons. It dawned on me that he was caressing my face, my arm, and my body with his right hand while he held his rifle with his left hand. I do not remember if it was pointed at me. I tried not to panic. Lucky for me, he had to open the barricade to let a car through and admonished me to stay quiet and stay put. I quickly called my driver and said, "On my way, please continue talking to me." I dared not look back, did not run, but walked normally, all the while fearing being shot.

How did I, a Filipina (sometimes mistakenly identified as Hazara), woman, 60plus, educator, international development advisor, IT expert, and naturalized American representing USAID, end up with dreams that mirrored reality in Kabul?

It was a distressing experience, but it paled in comparison to what Afghans endured daily. Those ten harrowing minutes were just a fraction of the countless moments when Afghan colleagues and strangers alike treated me with kindness and respect. This ordeal didn't deter me from my mission in Afghanistan: to lead the Afghan eQuality Alliances. This initiative focused on creating global development alliances to empower Afghan universities to harness the Internet for learning and teaching. This work was built on my previous efforts in Africa, where I established global development alliances with higher education institutions, fostered knowledge exchanges and learning partnerships, and built a network for telecommunications capacity building. Connecting African and US universities aligned perfectly with my lifelong purpose of making a difference and contributing to society.

When people asked why I chose Afghanistan, I answered: "Afghanistan called me." The timing was perfect. With a Ph.D. in education, I had the intellectual capital, thought leadership, and clout needed for international development. I have developed expertise in digital development capability. I gained extensive international experience as a Peace Corps Volunteer, a USAID contractor in Sudan, the Philippines, Liberia, and South Africa, and as a faculty member at Oregon State University and Washington State University. This journey was deeply rooted in the concept of *pakikipagkapwa*.

I dared to say "Yes" to the call and "No" only when I felt my work was complete, having trained and mentored enough Afghans to carry the torch forward.

2001- 2021 US and Afghanistan

Then, on August 15, 2021, Kabul fell to the Taliban, marking the end of nearly 20 years of war in Afghanistan that had begun with the US invasion. The withdrawal of US troops from Afghanistan commenced in April 2021, following President Biden's announcement to pull out all troops by September 2021. This announcement was followed by a shockingly swift takeover by the Taliban, the predominantly Pashtun Islamic fundamentalist group that had been ousted in 2001.

Was my time in Afghanistan all for nothing? I wrote about Harmonizing Global Teams in Afghanistan as a chapter in *DISRUPT. Filipina Women: Proud. Loud. Leading without a Doubt* when things looked optimistic in 2015. I believed then, as I do now, that the Islamic leadership model requires the leader to:

> Inspire the vision (to serve Islam)
> Strengthen the Heart (with Imam [faith in God] and
> Taqwa [inner consciousness toward Allah])
> Lead the way (with the Quran and the Sunnah)
> Assess actions (accountability of actions)
> Mobilize the community (to develop an Islamic civilization)

When I first met Afghan President Ashraf Ghani, he was then the Chancellor of Kabul University in 2005. He declared that he did not want Afghanistan to be balkanized or become like the Philippines, where the conflict between the Philippine government and the Moro National Liberation Front (MNLF) was affecting the lives of ordinary citizens.

What went wrong? What led to the US and Western failure in Afghanistan? Mudassar Ahmed (2022) argued that a significant blind spot in the Western foreign policy approach is an insufficient understanding of religious texts, practices, and traditions intertwined with sociocultural and political realities. Hence, Ahmed suggested that religious diplomacy should be considered when the West reengages with the current Afghanistan leadership.

In hindsight, we can better understand Afghanistan's complex identities and power dynamics through an intersectional lens, which may have led to more effective, context-specific policies. By ignoring the country's rich ethno-religious tapestry, the US's goal of transforming Afghanistan into a democratic state was destined to face challenges and, ultimately, failure. Here are some key points:

Cultural and Gendered Assumptions: Afghanistan's intricate tribal, ethnic, and cultural dynamics were at odds with Western ideas about democracy, governance, and human rights, especially gender rights. Beginning in 2002, the U.S. urged Afghan women and girls to enter the classroom, parliament, private enterprise, and military. Since August 2021, women have been excluded from the judiciary and public office; girls are banned from attending secondary and tertiary education, wiping gains made in gender rights. The Taliban's stance on women's rights stems from a strict interpretation of Islamic law or Sharia.

Ethnic and Tribal Complexities: Interpretation of Islamic Law is compounded by a diverse mix of ethnic groups, such as Pashtuns, Tajiks, Hazaras, and Uzbeks, each with unique cultural norms, historical grievances, and traditions of decentralized power.

Economic Disparities and Aid Distribution: Ethnic and tribal identities intersected with economic class and aid distribution, deepening economic divides. Steve Hanke (2021) indicated that "the bribes that flowed up the hierarchy formed the tribute, the protection money, or the informal taxes that were a necessary part of obtaining employment and conducting business in Afghanistan," making the Afghan elite richer while sowing resentment against them.

Power Dynamics and Local Governance: The push for a centralized governance model in a country that has been highly atomized in reality needed a balance that avoided extremes of centralization and decentralization. Local power holders favored greater autonomy, whereas some ethnic groups favored a strong central government based in Kabul. The US and NATO's interactions with local Afghan leaders often exacerbated conflicts and undermined traditional governance structures.

Impacts on Local Populations: Men and women, various ethnic groups, and urban and rural communities experienced the conflict and the presence of foreign troops differently; some gaining, some losing.

Was I complicit?

Are international development experts and workers to blame? Should they heed the "calling" or reject the call for service when intersectional considerations are lacking?

Must human rights groups, nongovernmental organizations, academics, and other civil society actors from outside continue to work to improve Afghans' lives? Some will say, "Yes," but simultaneously, an intersectional lens must accommodate the Afghan people's ethno-religious sentiments. Thus, Ahmed's 2022 call for religious diplomacy.

1898 – 1948 – US and the Philippines

What happened in Afghanistan mirrors what happened in the Philippines when it was annexed by the United States following the Spanish-American War in 1898. The resulting Treaty of Paris allowed the United States to buy the Philippines for $20 million from Spain. This American expansion did not consider diverse ethnoreligious realities that shape Philippine society, social identity, and power relations. What prevailed was the US vision of American efforts to encourage Christian immigration to Muslim Mindanao, which was motivated in large part by the intention to "civilize" Muslims in the Philippines by contagion.

> *"The problem of civilization of Mindanao and Sulu according to modern standards, or as it may be termed, 'the Philippinization' of the Mohammedan and pagan regions which comprise almost the entire territory of Mindanao-Sulu, has its most expeditious and positive solution in the movement under Government direction to that territory of sufficient numbers of the Christian inhabitants of Visayas and Luzon" (Carpenter quoted in Gowing 1983, 294).*

Among those outraged at a perceived overreach of power were Mark Twain and other anti-imperialists who opposed American expansion for varying reasons. The anti-imperialists were referred to as "Aunties," an effeminate derogatory.

> *"It [the Philippines] was not to be a government according to our ideas, but a government that represented the feeling of the majority of the Filipinos, a government according to Filipino ideas. That would have been a worthy mission for the United States."* —Twain

A significant shift began in 1935 when the islands of Mindanao and Sulu were brought under the Philippines' Commonwealth territory (Gutierrez and Borras, 2004) and started boosting opportunities and offering substantial assistance to settlers from the North. This policy, however, led to the marginalization of the local Muslim population. Many Muslims did not apply for the newly available lands created by road construction, nor did they claim their existing lands (Thomas, 1971). In contrast, Christian settlers quickly snapped up the best new lands, received crop loans, and enjoyed other government support. As a result, these new Christian communities flourished, becoming tightly connected with trade centers and each other through an extensive road network. Meanwhile, Muslim communities remained relatively isolated, missing out on the wave of development and integration.

My father, Faustino Africa, was one of those settlers who moved to Zamboanga to start a rubber plantation after WWII. That is why I was born in Zamboanga in 1948. That is where my story begins. Father: Ilokano. Mother: Kapampangan

My Mom, Estela dela Rosa Africa, is a quintessential mestiza Filipina woman of mixed native Filipino and Spanish ancestry. Her father's grandfather was, first off, the ship carrying a silver cross. She was so beautiful; people did not expect her to have brains. I have yet to meet someone who could finish a New York Times crossword puzzle in one sitting as she could.

When I was five and ready to go to school, my ordinarily quiet mom, who acquiesced to my father's decisions, decided frontier life was not for her children. She issued an ultimatum: "I will return to Luzon so the kids can attend school. Seek your fortune here in Zamboanga or follow us back in Luzon." She boarded a ship with three kids and was pregnant with a fourth. Despite the fear of what lay ahead, she took control. She was, after all, the daughter of a *katipunero* and a *kumander*. A potent mix of courage. Her father, my Lolo, Juan Dela Rosa, was a runner for the Katipunan (secret 19th-century

Philippine revolution society) as a young boy who delivered messages between troops. Her mother, my Lola Inda Candida Turla Dela Rosa, told my husband, James, that she was known as Kumander Dayang-Dayang and was a formidable presence, even pounding the table during meetings with the Huks. Lola Inda was 75 when she shared these memories with James in Kapampangan, and I was the translator. She believed James resembled William Pomeroy, a legendary fighter for Filipino independence and a committed member of the Communist Party, which sparked her storytelling.

I regret not following her stories more closely. Now, I know a historical figure, Kumander Dayang-Dayang, existed. Her name is Felipa Culala, and she is from Mandili, Candaba, my Lola's birthplace. I'm curious if my Lola Inda was part of her squad or if there was a deeper connection. I wonder if my Lola Inda misremembered her role with the Huks.

Regardless, these memories have been my touchstone, symbolizing perseverance and fortitude. They inspire me to challenge myself and others, speak up for what is right even in the face of opposition, act on my convictions even when they are unpopular, and take actions that require courage.

2013-2019 – Spokane, Portland, Hawaii

My time in Afghanistan (2013) was followed by self-reflection, reading papers at international conferences, reconnecting with my Philippine roots, and finding my tribe with the Filipina Women's Network. I decided to give back by contributing my editing skills. I ended up editing four books about the leadership of global Filipina women: *DISRUPT1.0. Filipina Women: Proud. Loud. Leading without a Doubt* (2014); *DISRUPT2.0. Filipina Women: Daring to Lead* (2016); *DISRUPT 3.0. Filipina Women: Rising* (2018). *DISRUPT 4.0. Filipina Women. Being* (2022). And now, *DISRUPT 5.0. Filipina Women Leading with Intersectionality.*

I also wrote chapters for two books:

☐ The Leadership Repertoire of Select Filipina Women in the Diaspora and Implications for Theorizing Leadership. In J. Storberg-Walker & P. Haber-Curran (Eds.), 2017. Theorizing women & leadership: New insights & contributions from multiple perspectives. Charlotte, NC: Information Age Publishing.

☐ Passion, risk, and adventure in developing my international development leadership repertoire. In R. J. Thompson & J. Storberg-Walker (Eds.), 2018. Leadership and power in international development. UK: Emerald Publishing.

In 2017, I received a short-term specialist Fulbright grant to teach about using critical discourse analysis to understand women's leadership at the Asian Institute of Management in the Philippines, and in 2023, to teach about digital capabilities at Benguet State University in La Trinidad in 2023.

2020-present – Back to the Philippines, Virtually

When I said goodbye to Afghanistan in 2013, I thought my international development days were over. I was wrong.

In December 2019, Boying Lallana, Toni Torres, and I were shocked to learn that the Philippines scored lowest in reading and second lowest in math and science in the Program for International Student Assessment (PISA) PISA in 2018. We asked why. What can we do? Do we have the courage to act to make a difference? All of us have been committed to the use of information communication technologies (ICTs) for development. All of us have experience with e-learning, i-schools, and digital solutions. So, we decided to go for it. We thought we had a year to plan and locate funds. Then COVID-19 happened. We fast-tracked our thinking. Amidst challenges, we adapted, pivoted, and launched Kaisipan to transform learning and teaching through digital learning solutions. Funding came from private donations, and the Beebe retirement fund, although insufficient to cover our ambition. We persevered.

Our mission is digital literacy for all Filipino educators. We define digital literacy as a set of cognitive, technical, and humanizing capabilities for using ICTS to iLearn, iCreate, and iShare. Our vision and mission would help Sulong Edukalidad achieve quality education for Filipino students and contribute to the UN Sustainable Development Goal 4 to ensure quality and inclusive education by 2030.

Our Kaisipan Board of Directors, Experts, Fellows, *DalubGuros*, *Kapwa* Teachers, and our partnerships with schools, colleges, universities, the private sector, and other players have enabled us to do the following activities, albeit via live remote:

1. Co-created 15 Blended courses for Professional development for K-12 teachers.

2. Conducted training workshops and deep dive into Open Education Resources (OER) for K-12 teachers in different subject matters.

3. Provided on-demand webinars and lightning talks on digital capabilities and literacy.

4. Implemented enrichment programs for students on coding, financial literacy, youth leadership, social-emotional learning, and digital On-the-job training (OJT).

5. Developed a learning management system app for online/offline use.

As I write this, we are in final testing mode for the Isip app. The app includes resources for teachers in the Philippines participating in Kaisipan-supported courses. Users can download content for offline use. The app is the brainchild of Mike Dawson, a colleague during my Afghanistan years.

It's amazing how technology has become the most important thing I own. I am an early technology adopter. From the rotary phone to Motorola to Nokia-the start of mobile gaming to Sharp- the first camera phone to Nokia 9000 that gave access to the Internet to the iPhone, described by Jobs as a "revolutionary and magical product" to the T-mobile, the first android smartphone to the modern smartphone to smartphones with augmented reality, real-time language translation, and increased 5G-enabled connectivity. The future is now. I am sure I have owned all these generations of phones. As an adopter, I never bothered to "look under the hood." Until I received a call about developing a curriculum for open RAN. The RAN (Radio access network) is the cell tower that links cell phones or remotely controlled user devices to other network parts through a radio link. I said "Yes" and seized the opportunity to lead, explore, and innovate, opening the RAN to bridge the digital divide.

Hence, the Asia Open RAN Academy was co-created as remote work from Naples, Florida, in collaboration with academic, private sector, and government institutions in the Philippines, Japan, and the United States. USAID funds were channeled through its implementing partner, International Development Group, as part of the Biden administration's Indo-Pacific economic framework.

Asia Open RAN Academy (AORA) aims to benefit stakeholders invested in digital access, equity, and inclusion for nation-building. Its mission is to advance an open, interoperable, reliable, and secure internet and foster a vibrant digital economy through increased cooperation, competition, and choice.

Incorporated as a nonprofit corporation in March 2023, AORA is built on Partnerships, Open Education Resources, Curriculum Standards, and Community principles.

AORA supports human and institutional capacity development by upskilling the telecommunications workforce to test and deploy open network architectures. Launched in the Philippines in mid-2022, with plans for regional expansion, the academy provides learners with access to course content, technical experts, an interoperability lab, certification, and opportunities to participate in research and development, use cases, and capstone projects, enhancing their employment and salary prospects.

Remote work has been a lifeline, preserving my sanity in ways I hadn't anticipated. About six years ago, my husband James received the diagnosis that turned our world upside down: Alzheimer's, more delicately termed "mild cognitive disorder." The signs were subtle at first, just small lapses in memory. But the reality struck hard when he struggled to assemble a crib for our soon-to-arrive grandchild. This man had always thrived on the hands-on challenges of our old homes in Washington, DC, Spokane, and Portland, relishing the immediate satisfaction of fixing an attic or basement and meticulously measuring twice before cutting.

In a rare moment of clarity, James confessed, "This is not how I planned our retirement years." So, we made the tough decision to move from Hawaii to Florida, settling in Arbor Trace Tower, a 55+ retirement community. Our new home, advertised as "the perfect place to call home," boasts on-site amenities and a supportive community, making it a haven during this challenging time. As early as our fifties, James and I had our difficult conversations about life and death matters, living will, advance directives, and do not resuscitate (DNR) orders—all ran contrary to Filipino/a cultural tradition, norms, and beliefs about caring. A transgression. For a Filipina. Woman.

As James's short-term memory deteriorated and his physical health began to decline, the aftermath of Hurricane Ian made it clear that I could no longer care for him alone. The adjacent assisted care living facility within our community, just a five-minute walk away, offered the round-the-clock care he needed. The staff there adores him, and he recognizes me on good days, depending on how his neurons are misfiring.

Meaningful remote work has allowed me to balance my professional responsibilities while being close enough to ensure James receives the best care possible, providing a semblance of stability in what is euphemistically called "the long goodbye."

To truly succeed in remote work, it's essential to get it right. Success in this environment often hinges on a few essential practices: creating a dedicated workspace, dressing for the job, structuring your days, developing a routine, allowing time for deep work, overcommunicating, clarifying expectations, and knowing when to unplug.

However, remote work shouldn't mean total isolation. Balancing it with occasional face-to-face interactions is crucial, even if it's just once a year. Meeting up with the team from the Philippines in 2023 was a perfect example. That year, I celebrated my 75th birthday on July 1, a Saturday. The Board of Directors, undeterred by the weekend, scheduled an in-person meeting. I made it clear I had a hard stop for lunch with my FWN sister, Marivic Lualhati. Maricor Akol, a Board Member, offered to give me a ride, ensuring I made it to the surprise birthday celebration they had orchestrated. My three networks—FWN, Kaisipan, and the Asia Open RAN Academy—were there. It was the best way to turn 75.

Navigating this so-called "retirement" has reminded me that we have the power to design our journeys, even in the face of unexpected changes and curveballs that life throws our way. These sudden and unforeseen challenges can knock us off balance, but it's in these moments that we discover our resilience. We pause, recover, and find ways to cope. We uncover hope in the depths of despair. We draw strength from our lived intersectional experiences. Recognizing this ability to adapt and thrive is incredibly empowering!

> **(Hay) Naku**
> *Fractals*
> *Intersectional Experiences*
> *Recursive. Non-linear. Ever-changing*[48]

DENISE VIARDO KOH, BSC, MD, CCFP, MPH, FRCPC, ACBOM

Public Health and Occupational Medicine Specialist, Hypnotherapist, Life Coach, Author
Assistant Professor, University of Manitoba
President, Federation of Medical Women of Canada-Manitoba Branch
Founder, MedResRx
Creator, the MedResRx Hypnotherapy App
Global FWN 100™ 2023

Finding Filipina, Embodying Intsik: -Isms of Intersectionality

"So, what kind of Asian are you, anyway?" "But where are you really from?" "You don't look Filipino."

These are questions I find myself answering almost daily, navigating the need to explain my Chinese last name while asserting my Filipino identity. Growing up, I even considered changing my surname to my mother's more regal-sounding Spanish maiden name. I recently considered adopting my fiancé's more traditional last name. As humans, we crave a sense of belonging, a desire to be accepted by our communities. But even when we feel we are part of something meaningful, we are often reminded that we're still being "othered." We're not Canadian enough, yet we're also not seen as 'true' Filipinos. This constant questioning of our identity leads us to internalize our lack of belonging, becoming defensive in the process. In my own life, I find myself explaining, "My name is Katrina Leong. Even though my last name is Chinese, I am Filipino," especially when encountering fellow Filipinos. It wasn't until I read Dr. Koh's story that I began to reflect on the weight of shame I've carried for years—not because I'm mistaken for another ethnicity, but because my very sense of self is questioned.

In this chapter, Dr. Koh shares the experience of being a Chinese Filipina as a second-generation Canadian and how this identity has shaped her journey to becoming a physician—for better or for worse. She recounts her candid path from trying to assimilate to eventually embracing and celebrating her Chinese Filipino heritage. Dr. Koh's story serves as a powerful reminder of the richness of Filipino history and culture and how these roots make our community so unique. Ultimately, no matter what society dictates, it is up to us to define who we are, where we're headed, and how we'll navigate our way forward.

Dr. Katrina Leong
Lecturer, Department of Family Medicine
University of Manitoba

Peripheral Pinay

As I inspect my face in the mirror, my fingers sweep over the skin, asking, *"Who Am I?"* I see tired *pingkit* eyes, dark tinted circles under them, the fine laugh lines at the corners, then the deep glabellar crease between the eyebrows that won't go away no matter how much I try to smile it out. My instinct is to fret about this flaw. Asians don't raisin, right? But this crack divides my face; it's an exclamation point screaming to the world. I have seen pain, suffering, discontent. Anger. Rage. Grief. I've felt these, pondered long about them, much longer than it would take my face to reflect I'm over it. *Who am I?*

I hear the triumphant chant 'I. Am. Canadian,' echoing over a stadium crowd. A rush of goose pimples erupts in my arms. I feel a twinge in my chest as I picture the tortured movements of our *kababayan* struggling to wave our flag, passionately reenacting the fight to uphold it. I hear a deep alto, proud and mournful, '*Ako Ay Pilipina...*' Faces flash before me--my kids, Kris, Mom, Dad, sisters, family, friends, loved ones over the years. Dad, wordlessly pushing his last thoughts into me through unblinking eyes, as he lay in the hospital bed, gasping for air. I am Tsinay, '*a Chinese.*' I am a mom, daughter, sister, homegirl, soulmate. I feel reflexive fear, a noisy pager in my hands as I power-walk down dark hospital tunnels. I watch my fingers place the stethoscope diaphragm on skin as I close my eyes to block out the noises of a busy hospital, quieting my mind to listen. I am teaching, presenting, reviewing, analyzing, convincing, typing a response hunched over a keyboard or into a phone. I am holding someone's pain in my hands—*my heart!*-- and doing what I can desperately to relieve it with medications, treatments, touch, energy. Words: policies, guidelines, loud from a podium, soft, hushed in prayer, on paper, in text/email/D.M.s, recorded, therapy, pep talks, kiss-whispered into my child's sweaty sobbing head, love. I am a doctor; I am a healer.

But there's a tug—I am connected to something, the Filipina diaspora, and I see my thread join bright threads that have followed along thousands of Pinay lives, dreams, hopes, pain—immeasurable pain—weaving into a fabric that binds such disparate even foreign lives over time and space. Finding Filipina is plugging into this weave--identifying one's self in an aspect of the intricate design, the vibrant colours, how the cloth gets used, the roughness of an edge, its feel in your hand, even the opposite pattern on the flip side of the piece. It is every Pinay's struggle to find herself, to find home, to belong.

This connectedness seems harder to find these days; digital transformation and the pandemic have only exacerbated isolation and chronic loneliness. Worsening problems and recent socio-political events have polarized us as a society and kept us divided: the climate crisis, the rise of intolerance/hate speech and acts, the pandemic, narcissistic, paranoid, sociopathic men we've allowed to make decisions for the rest of us, war. Feelings of not belonging have concentrated in immigrants, refugees, and anyone who is not the dominant majority. "Diaspora" connotes a broad range, diversity within a group, not homogeneous. An identity based on moving away from home.

Feeling "othered" is particularly problematic in the Filipino diaspora and undeniable in our collective Filipina identity. Several work-related trends that Filipinos in Canada (compared to other racialized Canadians) experience reflect the complex issues that lead to this (Canada, 2021)[49]: top employment rates, employed at older ages, highest

---

49   Canada, S. (April 2021). A labour market snapshot of South Asian, Chinese

employment rate among all female visible minority groups, over-representation in COVID-19 cases, riskier front-line industries (health care/social assistance, manufacturing, accommodation, food services), under-representation in professional, scientific, technical services, financial, insurance, real estate industries, a significant gender imbalance with ~100K more Filipino women than men in Canada. We *rely* on the work and care of Filipinas as a society, yet they are more likely to be overlooked, undervalued, abused, and first to get sick.

For Chinese Filipinos within the Filipino community in North America, the othering is even more concentrated and yet more casually accepted by both Filipinos and Chinese. At first glance, it doesn't seem to come from a place of malice; I can't keep in my happy-*kapwa* surprise when I've realized a fellow Asian with a Chinese name is Filipino. What is telling is their response, much like my own, I admit, almost apologizing for not having a Spanish-sounding name. This reminds me that the concept of harm should be rooted in perspective—it's not about intent, but how others receive those words/actions.

While second- and higher-generation immigrants may not be migrating anywhere, they still connect with the diasporic identity and the different levels of cross-cultural adaptation and acculturation. That has certainly been my personal experience, reinforced by my research and work not only as a public health and occupational medicine specialist, but also in my various roles as a wife, mother, and community advocate. When I look back at my life as a 2nd generation Chinese Filipina born and raised in the Canadian prairies in the 70s and then upon my journey through academia, Medicine, and the workplace, most of it is tinged with an inescapable feeling of not really belonging anywhere. I'm too brown for the white community yet not even considered brown in the Filipino community--nobody ever thinks I'm Filipino. But there's another layer. When I try to connect, I always get that shock reaction, like Filipina didn't even make the top 5 list of potential heritages. "Oh! I thought you were a Chinese." It's as if "Filipino" is purebred instead of mutt; one can't be Filipino *and* Chinese. Not looking Filipino, not speaking Pilipino, no accent—I don't have that home-country-birthright swagger or even an FOB (Fresh Off the Boat) aura. I don't belong, shoved onto the other side of the line. I'm a peripheral Pinay with intruding *intsik* vibes.

---

and Filipino Canadians during the pandemic. https://www150.statcan.gc.ca/n1/en/daily-quotidien/210521/dq210521b-eng.pdf?st=n9jsxF4T

Why is there still a massive blind spot for the estimated 22.8 million Filipinos who have some Chinese ancestry in the Philippines, making up as much as 25% (Aspinwall, 2019)[50] of the Philippine population? And why do Filipinos--and the world—hate China so much? Given these significant biases and hits against me, how do I overcome them, succeed in life, and then lead in this world? You can't conquer a world you don't belong to. Well, you can, but no one's going to like you much.

2nd Gen, Canadian-born—we jokingly call ourselves "coconuts"/"bananas"/"Oreos" –brown/yellow/black on the outside, white on the inside. This incongruence between inside and outside colour accurately describes the conflict and actively promotes it. I guess I'm more of a marble cake with buttercream icing, aka a Pokemon cake. The irony is that in Canada, I'm technically on home soil, and those I'm trying to convince I'm one of them to advocate for are arguably the "foreigners." Regardless, my kind of dessert tastes like shame. And that taste makes me angry.

Cheesed Off Tsekwa

I come from a family of Hotheads. Mom, Dad, and us -- four daughters, 2 Philippine-born, 2 Canadian-born. I can't remember a time when all 6 of us were not pissed off about something, at the same time. Even celebrations and family reunions—all smiles, high fives, and heartfelt, inspiring speeches, but there's always an awareness of something negative, something not right, something that could definitely be better. Should be better. This discontent was usually some festering wound that would kill anything we celebrated.

Cases in point—Christmases--emotionally laden minefields—
Sisters home from university, *Oh how I missed you!*
It's always good until it isn't.
Festivities turn into frustrations, tears.
Laughter filled with hope and heart
turn to yelling filled with hatred and hurt
Suitcases hastily packed, and threats to leave and never come back.
Strong words--points rage-screamed into cases, ready to break us for good.

---

50   Aspinwall, N. (June 2019). We are Filipinos, and we hate China': China's influence in the Philippines, and backlash against Tsinoys. The China Project. https://thechinaproject.com/2019/06/06/we-are-filipinos-and-we-hate-china-backlash-against-tsinoys/

There were words, narrative words, code words between Mom and Dad, hushed....*oy ano ba? ...umiiyak siya...ang hirap hirap na naman...susmariyosep...putang ina...hm! bastos...ang dami dami...bakit... aalis na siya...*

I want to say we pulled it together for one time, Dad's funeral in September 2022, but he left 5 Pissed Off Pinays, and some of us are still not talking to each other.

I wonder if Dad started it. Dad was a brilliant mathematician who always focused on the 2% instead of the 98s on my exams. Granted, this strategy does work. It led to 99s and sometimes 100s—instrumental in academia and the hoops one needs to jump through in Medicine. But then, the 99 fades out of view, and the 1 is this looming gaping hole we fall into and can't seem to get out of.

Lola, the Concubine

Dad's Dad, Lolo Koh, was a wealthy Chinese lawyer in Manila who died when Dad was 4, keeping my Lola Felisa and her five kids in poverty since she was the 4th wife. These are not serial wives, as in, one after the other, but #4 to the mix of wives concurrently wifing—ie. sister wives. However, nothing here is equal; there's a hierarchy with concubines. Being the #4 widow meant she got nothing, as everything went to Wives 1 & 2.

So, Dad got to see and want a better life but not taste any of it. I think this was the seed of anger #1--being dirt poor. Being Chinese was seed #2--the other chink in Dad's armor. As the neighborhood brainiac, the kids would go to him for school help. Still, he was overlooked for all the top accolades/positions that always went to the "Filipino-blooded" students from grade school into university.

Despite or perhaps because of the anti-Chinese sentiment Dad faced, he was driven, getting degrees and his PhD in math and engineering at UP/Birmingham/Purdue University and marrying his childhood sweetheart, Donelita Viardo. After 2 of my sisters were born, they immigrated to the U.S. and then to Canada. We were one of the early Saskatchewan Filipino families, and Dad was the co-founder and first president of the Philippine Association of Saskatchewan. It was all about assimilating in the 60s and 70s, so I got a whitewashed name and only heard Tagalog when my parents talked to each other or other Filipinos.

We lived one year in Germany and three years in Saudi Arabia during Dad's U of R professorship. Between these experiences and our lives in Canada, we experienced plenty of racism, including store staff accusing us of stealing, ignoring us on purpose, and much worse. Dad often indignantly stood up for our family, to strangers and others who wronged or mistreated us. Mom's approach was based on fear, knowing the hardships that come to hotheads. She always warned us to play it safe, be quiet, smile, accommodate, and kowtow to the whites or anyone else who challenged us, even— especially--obvious racists clearly wrong in their assumptions.

I only met Lola Felisa once as a child. I had no Chinese culture growing up and only learned she was a Chinese concubine well into my adult years. There were no nuances; our Chinese heritage was a dark cloud. I could sense Dad's shame and occasionally felt it from Filipinos around me. I recall a *kaibigan* joking about going for "chink food," which I tried to laugh off. Chinese food was my family's go-to when we celebrated or ate with friends, yet Dad didn't feel at home with Chinese people like he did with Filipinos. When I dug deeper, he said that Chinese Filipinos were often Fukien, but he couldn't speak it. I never knew whether he was referring to us or generally, and I still don't know if he ever spoke/understood Chinese as a child or whether he may have just learned phrases as an adult to connect with others, as was his way.

Model Minority Math Nerd

In the early 80s, about 10 of us original Regina Mayflower Festival performers from the 70s reinvented ourselves into the Filipinas Youth Group. We were brown, Flips, coconuts, *barkadas,* and I belonged. During our Mosaic cultural celebration, we became fast friends and penpals with the incredible visiting Winnipeg *Magdaragat* dance troupe we billeted. Backstage, I excitedly asked if they were about to perform the *singkil* --my favourite dance--"you know, the one with the bamboo shoots." And they just laughed, finally explaining that the bamboo poles used in *tinikling* and *singkil* differ from the bamboo shoots you see in a stir fry. My whiteness, particularly around "real Filipinos" stuck out like a sore thumb.

At school, I was the only coconut. Schoolwork was easy for me, especially math, so I started to excel in my report cards, much to Dad's delight. Other Asian kids were FOBs and exchange students who stuck together, likely because of the language barrier.

Filipinos already know English, so should have an easier time fitting in. While I was friendly with all sorts of schoolmates, my inner circle friends were down-to-earth white girls. Hence, I was pretty white by association, right?

Near the end of grade 6, a group of white grade 5 boys cornered me by the high school and reminded me that I was not. They taught me this lifelong lesson, and that day's homework is called a Facewash. Darcy H grabbed a handful of snow and proceeded to "wash the ugly chink" off my face while Jason W and the others jeered and laughed. My two white girlfriends tried to chase the boys away, but I couldn't feel anything except the hot humiliation tears streaming down my cold but still yellow face. If I could have peeled my not-coconut-but-shit not-banana-but-piss skin off, I would have. That was the day I started to hate who I was.

I was already painfully self-conscious at that age, but that incident tipped me over the edge. I became obsessed with the popular white girls, the rich preppy ones I hated but secretly wanted to become. I studied their faces and bodies, hating my monolid eyes with their epicanthal folds, my too small nose with zero bridge, wide face, thick lips. Every aspect of me that was not like the perfect standard was magnified in my mind. I was the opposite of magazine beauty, so much self-loathing occurred then. These were the years I learned if I grief-cried for several hours, my puffy eyes 'grew lids,' so there's the white at the end of that tunnel. I learned to smile in a way that thins my lips. Anything that wasn't the white Barbie norm had to be corrected or hidden. This urge to fix myself was reinforced by the Filipino obsession with beauty that permeated what being a Filipina was all about--where Mom's brain and botany degree were rarely mentioned compared to her status as a UP sorority sweetheart and beauty queen, with plenty of suitors whom the brilliant-but-ugly Chinese guy beat out. The ideal Filipina was pious (virginal), "petite" (skinny), "fair" (colonizer-white) mestiza/Spaniard, even if one had to resort to toxic mercolizing creams to whiten the skin. In a household with 5 females, beauty was the standard against which we all were measured.

I saw school kids make fun of a shy, awkward FOB Chinese girl and made a mental note to be more outwardly confident, gregarious, and loud, like the popular girls. To avoid looking like a geeky brown-noser, I had to balance my perfect grades with popularity, so I got involved with a lot of school clubs and focused on my social life.

Oriental Mystique

My efforts paid off as I started getting positive attention. What a relief to be liked and accepted for a change! But it felt hollow. I found people and the concept of beauty fickle—one day, I'm this ogre that had to get the ugly scraped off with ice. Not even a year later, with the help of makeup and miniskirts, these same boys would whistle and try to flirt with me.

In the later 80s, my look was exotic, *"Oriental,"* being different was now a good thing. In grade 11, we used fake I.D. to get into nightclubs, which automatically catapulted our girl posse's status into uber-cool party girls, commencing our *barstar* years. But then I started to notice another ceiling--this disgusting Love-You-Long-Time hooker fantasy that men projected onto me, which was no one like me. Creepy *dewds* would try lame pick up lines—I'd get the Asian greeting I didn't understand, the "where are you *really* from" exchange, followed by his uninteresting history teaching English in Asia and some version of how I should be happy he's here to colonize me. He'd throw in a martial arts move. Yawn. *He's more connected to Asia than I am.* 2+ Asian ex-girlfriends in a prospective date's past would trigger a "Yellow Fever" alert. There were boyfriends I thought really cared about me, but after breaking up, I'd hear they were magnifying my exoticism and exaggerating—even rating--my sexual performance to others; I suppose they got bragging rights by making me look like a bigger conquest. It became very difficult to trust men, but also very easy to manipulate them while simultaneously hating the power and privilege they didn't deserve. I relished pointing out their idiocy, follies, and weaknesses to my homegals. We'd nickname these vacuous meatheads who filled the air with their self-fellating inane comments and mansplanations, which were just desperate attempts to get in our pants.

The Weight of White Work Spaces

The North American higher education system and associated institutions--particularly the field of Medicine--are traditionally hierarchical and rigid; I see now how blatantly sexist and racist it all was during the 90s. Medicine breeds Imposter Syndrome, worse for those outside of the mainstream—so I got my share. In clinical settings, female doctors constantly get mistaken for anyone else—nurses, allied health care workers, or even cleaning staff; the high Filipino nurse/care worker population in Canada also sets up an expectation that Asian females in a health care setting are nurses, not doctors. It's no surprise I felt foreign as a medical trainee and practicing doctor, regardless of who I was interacting with.

Early in Med School, I attended an Asian Medical Society gathering, where I realized there was another kind of Asian, and I was the wrong kind. These were East Indian Asians. I asked my East Indian classmate at the function what was up, and he looked at me and said, "Oh no! This is for *Brown Asians*. You're a *Yellow Asian*."

I was annoyed, never even thinking there was another brown, "No! We're brown! We've always been brown!"

He looked at me, then put his arm up against mine and said, "Who's brown? *I'm* brown. You're *yellow*."

As a budding doctor trying to be clinically objective, I had to concede, "Okay, yeah, well, I'm sort of beige. But I'm not *yellow!*" Yellow says weak, sickly, scared, betrayal— not the look I'm going for.

Reviewing my overall work experience to tease out the specific anti-Chinese racist experiences is challenging. My life-long response to macro- and micro-aggressions was to over-analyze what about me contributed to the situation so I could fix it. I've always struggled with inner conflict, angst, and mental load in figuring out my response to "-ist" incidents—my reflex was to smile and joke it off; *"I'm an all-Canadian prairie girl; I can handle this."* Racialized workers commonly code-switch which increases the risk for burnout (Johnson, 2021)[51]. Adjusting to majority spaces and negotiating white people's comfort is work the majority don't see (Nguyen, 2024)[52]. Time spent trying to minimize the angry BIPOC woman trope is also time not advancing one's career, writing grants, networking with peers, and conducting research with students.

---

51   Johnson, D. G. (2021). Social-Cognitive and Affective Antecedents of Code Switching and the Consequences of Linguistic Racism for Black People and People of Color. Affective science, 3(1), 5–13.

52   Nguyen, B. (2024, 07 24). The Chair Is a Pretty Accurate Portrayal of What It's Like to Be a Woman Professor of Color: That's Why It Can Be Painful to Watch. Time. https://time.com/6092072/the-chair-netflix-academia/

Navigating our reactions to -ist incidents is just the tip of the iceberg. Apparent aggressions female scientists commonly experience include unwanted sexual attention, coercion, and assault, while underneath the water are the less apparent ones: subtle exclusions, being left off an email, not being invited to collaborate, being passed over for promotions, sabotaging of equipment/workspace (Cheney & Shattuck, 2020)[53]. The ones that occur at the power tables behind closed doors are often more dangerous, even career-limiting, because we can't do anything to prevent them or protect ourselves. How many times have we assumed what we were given in the workplace was standard, only to find out, usually years to decades after the fact, that we have been given the shitstick so often it's engraved with our names? As I age in the era of wokeness from #MeToo #StopAsianHate and cancel culture, it has become much easier to see these incidents with clarity and work to revise my ingrained responses that center on white males' comfort.

On the wards, an older white patient asked me where I'm from, and I said, "Regina" in perfect Canadian English. He asked me to repeat myself, which I did. Then came the predictable, "No, where are you *really* from?" So, I said, "I was born in Regina, Saskatchewan," knowing I couldn't be clearer in diction.

"Oh," he said, finally okay with my answer, which had nothing to do with why he needed to see a doctor, "Red China. That makes sense." He couldn't hear anything past my Chinese face.

Male patients have tried to flirt with me, wheedle me into kissing them during physical exam, make up symptoms to prolong the appointment, and gotten irate when I've refused their advances or gotten male colleagues to take over care. After I'd explained to an articulate psychotic patient that I had to keep him in hospital against his will, he spent some time arguing with me before realizing I'd given him the best alternative— his voluntary stay. We were leaving the small discussion room with only one doorway, and I let him go first. He was over a foot taller than me and had a cane. He suddenly stopped in the doorway, blocking my exit, and looked over his shoulder at me with a

---

53   Cheney, I., & Shattuck, S. (2020). Picture a Scientist. https://www.pictureascientist.com/

menacing look. I was right behind him and almost ran into him. I looked up at him, clutching his chart to my chest, and quickly realized my blunder. *Fuck—he's got me.* He could have easily killed me, and I could tell he needed me to know right then that, regardless of his compliance to my physician's order, he had all the power. In that split second, I could only plead with my eyes. Satisfied, he left the room, and I left in-hospital psych service shortly after.

Nurses are more willing to serve and defer to male doctors, while they tend to approach female doctors on a more egalitarian basis and are more comfortable communicating with them, yet more hostile to them (Zelek & Phillips, 2003)[54]. As female interns, we quickly noticed the disrespect, frequent sleep-disrupting calls, outright mean behaviour, sabotage, and complaints about us—a 180 from the male intern experience: flirtation, coffee treats, jokey good times at the nursing station, quiet, restful nights on call. I have witnessed, personally experienced, and heard countless incidents of female physicians being bullied and "written up" by nurses in response to the exact same—usually nicer—behaviour exhibited by male doctors with impunity. On evaluations, male colleagues get praised for their leadership qualities, while female M.D.s get "not a team player" and "unprofessional" for similar behavior (Brucker, et al., 2019)[55].

My negative experiences were always with white nurses rather than Asian nurses (they may have also been conditioned to accommodate). Still, I couldn't tell if I suffered more than my white colleagues until I started to look for it much later. While some female docs (Bruker, et al., 2019)[56] recommend a "bitchy" response, such as insisting on the "Dr." title and loud snide retorts to shoot down haters, I found my informal collaborative approach worked and got better patient outcomes. I showed my extreme appreciation for nurses, profusely communicated my rationale for clinical decisions, and always asked if they were okay with my proposed action plan. I brought treats for the team and made attempts to connect.

---

54   Zelek, B., & Phillips, S. (2003). Gender and power: Nurses and doctors in Canada. International journal for equity in health, 2 (1). https://doi.org/10.1186/1475-9276-2-1

55   Brucker, K., Whitaker, N., Morgan, Z. S., Pettit, K., Thinnes, E., Banta, A. M., & Palmer, M. (2019). Exploring Gender Bias in Nursing Evaluations of Emergency Medicine Residents. Academic Emergency Medicine

56   Brucker, K., Whitaker, N., Morgan, Z. S., Pettit, K., Thinnes, E., Banta, A. M., & Palmer, M. (2019). Exploring Gender Bias in Nursing Evaluations of Emergency Medicine Residents. Academic Emergency Medicine

In government work, however, it is not uncommon for those with a nursing or allied health care background, such as occupational therapy, to climb up the ladder and get manager positions to whom the physicians typically report. I have experienced severe bullying by 2 of these white female managers and one white female executive admin staff who I've noticed have bullied/poorly treated/disparaged other staff who were racialized and female. I believe all of them derived some pleasure from bullying a female physician and now realize the bitch approach would have been best for these small power-hungry individuals.

The doctor dynamic requires a different set of rules. In the 3rd year our med class was divided into groups for afternoon teaching sessions. My group consisted of 5 male classmates and me. Our clinical preceptor for the day was Dr. H, an older white male radiologist known for having authored a history of Medicine book. We arrived at the designated meeting spot—this tiny room--and crowded around where he was seated beside a lightbox looking at a pile of radiographs. As we introduced ourselves, Dr. H. noticed me and stopped the discussion for his first and "most important" teaching point that day.

"Denise is a lady; she is a rose." I found it weird he'd used my name specifically. "You must ALWAYS treat her like a lady. Always hold the door for her and let her go first." He chastised my classmates for not letting me enter the room first. I was flummoxed, thinking, *"Is this guy for real? Is this some kind of joke?"* I could think of a million different circumstances that would be logical reasons NOT to let me go first, NOT to hold the door for me. I mean, we're doctors, right? Aren't we supposed to be saving lives here? I felt the glare of a harsh spotlight, wondering what I wore and how I presented myself that warranted being singled out like this. My classmates nodded and chuckled uncomfortably while I tried to send apologizing looks to them. He ended with, *"Remember—always treat Denise like a rose,"* and motioned for us to leave the room and head to the next spot. Instinctively, the ones closest to the door exited, and because I wasn't the first out of the room, Dr. H. stopped the group with, *"What did I just tell you? This is the most important thing you need to learn as future doctors."* It felt like a sentence—they were being punished for being associated with me, seemingly by a strange rule, and I did not know how to make it go away. Awkwardly, my classmates who exited scrambled back inside the tiny room, and everyone turned to me to go first. I could feel the heat rise in my face in horror as I scrambled to ease this tense moment and jostled past my colleagues to leave the room first. This charade continued throughout the rest of the afternoon with Dr. H. through countless rooms,

spots, and doorways in the hospital, including several painfully cumbersome elevator rides. Being the first into a crowded space, generally means you'll be the last to exit. So now I had the added burden of being responsible for any delays and minimizing the team's inconvenience every time we entered a new space. Obviously equating one member of an intelligent team to a flower negates any potential valuable contribution from her brain. I had now been pegged as someone who was getting in the way of efficient team function based solely on my sex. I couldn't focus on actual learning, because my job that day was ensuring my preceptor had a good impression of me and minimizing the hate and frustration my colleagues would have about me. By the end of it, I was exhausted physically and mentally. I hated my loud clip cloppy dress shoes, which slowed me down, and any attempts I'd previously made to look professional now seemed frivolous and "asking for it."

After that session concluded, I angrily shared the experience with some white female classmates. There were some raised eyebrows, but not many comments, let alone any indignant solidarity; perhaps they thought I was faking being offended, because roses are beautiful, right? I went to the college office to complain formally but was patronizingly told nothing could be done about it. That was when I learned a) beauty and standing out can make you lose in the workplace, b) be careful to whom you express your true feelings, and c) don't assume your female colleagues will support you. I assessed what I wore, my makeup, and my hair. I had to find that Medicine sweet spot -- attractive, but not too attractive, indeed not sexy, but of course not frumpy— men are still watching, and they hold the keys! Definitely, no more painful high heels, in case elderly attendings decide to be "chivalracist" and make you pay for their magnanimity—by doing laps. I started to minimize makeup, dampen my personality. Interestingly, was a name given by Allied troops in the South Pacific during WWII to all female English-speaking radio broadcasters of Japanese propaganda, which became a symbol of Japanese villainy for the U.S. Iva Toguri, the real Tokyo Rose[57] was vilified and indicted for treason; it took over 20 years to receive a pardon. *"Mekong Rose," "Saigon Rose,"* and *"Vietnam Rose"* have been slang terms used during the Vietnam War for both syphilis and gonorrhea--sexually transmitted infections that imply that Asian prostitutes were responsible for these epidemics rather than the soldiers and colonizers who brought these diseases with them.

57   Tokyo, R. (June 2024). Tokyo Rose. Wikipedia. https://en.wikipedia.org/wiki/Tokyo_Rose

Too frequently, I've been tone-policed to varying degrees by male colleagues who've assumed they are senior to me in training. As a patient who challenged my white male physicians' treatment plans, I have been labeled as *"difficult"* and threatened that if I were *"too anxious,"* I might not meet the criteria to be offered IVF. My worst workplace experiences ended with stealth sabotage at the hands of 2 white male colleagues, upheld by their bully groups, in a position of power over me—both leading to implosions of my medical career.

As the only female in my first residency, I spent a lot of energy trying to fit into the *"old boys' club"*: 3 white egomaniacs brimming with God-complexes, privilege, and cockiness who took themselves a little too seriously. A-hole #1 was my senior resident and the Ringleader—a small, sexually-repressed, shockingly ugly narcissist who relied on his biting sense of humour to make up for his looks. You could tell these guys were losers in high school, suddenly drunk from all that nurse adoration upon becoming interns, perhaps trying to recreate their lurid House of God fantasies. They filled the space with their crude, disgusting, misogynistic, racist, hurtful remarks and jokes. Nothing was off the table, and no one was spared, including all staff, female classmates, and my friends they wanted to have sex with. They were cruel to the staff behind their backs implying an older male attending was demented, and another colleague was a lesbian. They would imitate an East Indian female attending's accent and mannerisms in the residents' room and made it well known whenever she spoke that they did not respect anything about her, complete with childish eye-rolling, knowing glances to each other, and hateful body postures.

Unbeknownst to me, Ringleader was spreading lies about my performance to all my rotations before my arrival—my friend overhead him telling other residents and staff that I was lying about attending our specialty's protected Academic Half Days to get out of rotation duties and going to neither—not one iota true. In hindsight, these core rotations were particularly challenging and wreaked havoc on my self-confidence; the male residents and staff were extremely cold and cutting to me, insinuating I was a bad resident shirking my work. I took a much-needed medical stress leave. I'd started to challenge Ringleader's comments with zingers of my own and not laugh at his cruel jokes. I wonder if he, like many, harbors a deep subconscious hatred for Asian women. Perhaps his reaction to not getting idolized by an Asian female was so strong because the expectation of cheap Asian female love is so steeped in mainstream society.

Conversely, I also wonder whether the power differential that white male physicians experience from their privilege and fragility is so great they are blind to the potentially disastrous consequences their prejudice and small-to-them spite comments can have on the racialized women around them.

On my return, Ringleader graduated to become my program director, while his reinforcer-turned-bully became the Department Head. Together, they proposed changing policy and the evaluation forms so that I could get removed from the program—their rationale being my stress leave gave them the right to question my mental state and, thus, my ability to complete the training program. Prior to the end of my 3rd year, they told me that none of them would sign my Final In-Training Evaluation Report (FITER)—which is based solely on the 4th year and required for any resident to be able to sit the fellowship exam. Not only was this clear evidence of their prejudice, it was also clear direction to me not to bother continuing the program any further. My union fully supported my grievance to challenge this abuse of Human Rights and to request my remaining funding to complete the training elsewhere. My parents went into significant debt to pay my legal fees; however, upon my lawyer's direct questioning, Ringleader didn't deny any of what he did but just said, "I don't recall" to each question. Strange, such a brilliant, lauded man could quickly memorize tiny details about everyone to bully them, yet he couldn't recall whether he did and said these specific things to end my career. Perhaps it shouldn't have been *my* mental capacity to complete the program that they challenged. I'd recorded one male Asian preceptor's admission and apology for initially lying about Ringleader's rotation interference, while another rotation preceptor shadily avoided my direct questions. In the end, it was determined that while how I was treated was *"unfair,"* it didn't constitute *"harassment,"* even though it would today. The College of Medicine immediately terminated my residency program, which it had wanted to do from the beginning.

I occasionally wonder how Ringleader sleeps at night, particularly since he left the province shortly after and made a name for himself in Canadian Medical Ethics (on paper). I guess it's okay to play dirty, as long as one *"doesn't recall it"* and others—aka Bully Outsiders--are too scared to protest.

Devastated, I moved to Alberta. I worked in Ethics and Pediatrics before entering the 2nd CaRMS match in 2003 to vie for the remaining residency programs from that year's graduating medical classes. It was incredibly tough. Despite being a Canadian graduate with over 2½ years of successful postgraduate training, my one preceptor I considered fair and removed from the situation refused to provide a reference. Albeit racialized, he was affiliated with this boys' club—a close-knit group in a small specialty. Consequently, most programs I interviewed with assumed I was the problem, except for the Community Medicine (Public Health) program at the University of Manitoba. Here, I reinvented myself by reconnecting with my roots. I studied the challenges faced by Filipino care workers—nurses, caregivers, and doctors—in Canada, earned my MPH, and learned to use my voice to advocate for Filipino and ethnocultural communities in Manitoba.

The story of my second saboteur and bully group is fresh, still mired in the legal system, and will be the focus of my next book. It covers the reprisal from my voicing concerns in 2016 to protect Manitoba's workers, up to all my successes during the pandemic and to date despite the chronic severe bullying at the hands of Middle Management bent on keeping my angry truth-telling mouth shut. It also clearly supports what we already know: the world hates China (Wilson, 2024)[58].

Fu Manchu, Dragon Lady, and Chinese Supervillainy

Anti-Asian hate in Canada is not new, with many examples dating back from the late 1800s to today: the Chinese head tax, the Chinese Exclusion Act, the Komegata Maru incident, the Japanese Canadian internment. This has been reinforced by the consistent narratives in North American movies and books that slot Asian characters into tired, entrenched stereotypes: the demon/villain (Decome, 2016)[59] or the bumbling book-smart-but-dangerously-dumb idiot. Check out Yellowstone's recent portrayal of an Asian tourist group to see how easy it is to deride Asians. These roles portray Asians as having low to no worth, easily bought, with questionable morals, and thus easy to dehumanize, despise, and dispose of, like garbage.

During an Air Canada flight, I was seated among a group of Southeast Asians who were not fluent in English. The white flight attendant was collecting the trash from the drink service. The couple beside me tried to hand their not-completely empty cups

58   Wilson, B. (June 2024). World Hates China, Poll Finds. The Washington Free Beacon. https://freebeacon.com/latest-news/world-hates-china-poll-finds/

59   Decome, M. (2016). The Rise of the Chinese Villain: Demonic Representation of the Asian Character in Popular Literature (1880–1950). M. Decome, Intercultural Masquerade, 119-133. Springer.
decome

204 | DENISE VIARDO KOH, BSC, MD, CCFP, MPH, FRCPC, ACBOM

back to her. She angrily flicked her fingers up, signaling them to drink as she would not accept their cups until they emptied them. Confused, they kept the drinks as she went on, as I silently seethed with rage. When she returned, I angrily called her out on her racism; her job was to clear their garbage and she needed to apologize to the couple. Flustered, she tried to apologize to me before I redirected her to apologize to the couple. I still don't know whether they understood what happened, as they seemed to shrink away from my anger.

In Manila, during my MPH work in 2007, I could tell I was treated differently based on looking Chinese. The cab drivers evidently tried to cheat me, driving me much longer than necessary, and one even stopped to fill the gas tank *while the cab was running*. I jumped out of the cab, refusing to get back in. I asked my Filipina massage therapists about anti-Chinese sentiment. I was told it had to do with a history of the Chinese taking advantage of the Filipinos, income inequity, and land. Almost two decades later, there are similar reports that cite reasons many Filipinos distrust China: events that have triggered a renewal of old stereotypes claiming Chinese Filipinos control a disproportionate amount of the nation's wealth (Aspinwall, 2019)[60], threats to Philippine sovereignty related to the contested South China Sea land claims, China's increasing dominance, unkept promises to the Philippines, an estimated influx of 100-250K mainland China workers alleged to have come as tourists but working illegally, not playing by Philippine rules, and associated with a growing list of controversies, including online gambling, driving real estate prices up, love scams, kidnapping, and smuggling. One writer (Collas-Monsod, 2018)[61] suggested brainwashing against China since the communist takeover and took aim squarely at Chinese-Filipinos, questioning their allegiance, alleging most billionaires had Chinese heritage, saying Tsinoys were the most hated employers, purporting they treated Filipino fishermen poorly, and suggesting male Chinese-Filipinos preferred not to marry Filipina women—not the case with my Dad, who said he did everything he could to prove his love to my Mom's parents after they eloped. This hate-mongering drivel supports that a few racialized

---

60   Aspinwall, N. (June 2019). We are Filipinos, and we hate China': China's influence in the Philippines, and backlash against Tsinoys. The China Project. https://thechinaproject.com/2019/06/06/we-are-filipinos-and-we-hate-china-backlash-against-tsinoys/

61   Collas-Monsod, S. (November 2018). Why Filipinos distrust China. Inquirer.net. https://opinion.inquirer.net/117681/why-filipinos-distrust-china

minorities' bad behaviors constantly get judged to reflect negatively on the whole group, whereas the opposite isn't true with good behavior (Pratt, 2021)[62].

Chinese immigration to the Philippines occurred during the 16th to 19th century during Spanish colonization. Many were displaced, expelled from communities, and victims of numerous massacres during that time (Aspinwall, 2019)[63]. Apparently, Tsinoys were known for holding prominent roles in politics and business and establishing schools and charitable foundations. Many families with monosyllabic names tracing back to Chinese ancestors have become fully Filipino, losing their ability to speak Mandarin and Hokkien throughout the generations. Tsinoys harbor strong resentment toward mainland Chinese immigrants. It's not far for the hate to jump to those who shouldn't have to prove their allegiance as was suggested in some media; I can understand the resentment of being asked to prove one's family's generations-long loyalty after being lumped in with shady-seeming newcomers.

Not only does the world hate China, but the world also loves to hate China. And I'm learning that the world loves to hate Chinese women, which includes females who look Chinese. The 2021 Atlanta spa shootings, where the sex-addicted shooter targeted Asian women at three massage parlors he viewed as temptation, made this evident to me. The event fueled a surge in AAPI hate crimes, with women reporting incidents 2.3 times more than men. As early as the 19th century, the U.S. government superficially profiled Asian women as unclean prostitutes and effectively emasculated Asian American men through its legislation. Asian women were reduced to objects of desire yet representing a "moral contagion" dangerous to American society. This was reinforced by a military presence in the Asia Pacific that enslaved 100s of 1000s of comfort women deployed to provide sexual services to troops. Large numbers of American men were going abroad where they could blow off steam via recreation sites with Asian women providing sexual gratification. "White men have been trained, peer pressured, and hazed by the U.S. military to release their anxiety, self-loathing, and hatred of the enemy onto Asian

---

62   Pratt, T. N. (2021, August 27). Netflix's 'The Chair' is a needed yet unrealistic depiction of academia. National Catholic Reporter. https://www.ncronline.org/news/opinion/netflixs-chair-needed-yet-unrealistic-depiction-academia

63   Aspinwall, N. (June 2019). We are Filipinos, and we hate China': China's influence in the Philippines, and backlash against Tsinoys. The China Project. https://thechinaproject.com/2019/06/06/we-are-filipinos-and-we-hate-china-backlash-against-tsinoys/

women's bodies" (Jabola-Carolus, 2021)[64]. The fetishization of Asian women in popular culture is often expressed through highly sexualized stereotypes, such as the submissive and sexually compliant Lotus Flower/China Doll, the desperate and hypersexualized Me-So-Horny prostitute, or the cold and manipulative Dragon Lady who uses her sexuality for power. These damaging portrayals are exacerbated by the limited representation of Asian women in mainstream movies, contrasting with their over-representation as victims in violent pornography. The mail-order bride industry also perpetuates this harmful perception. Additionally, the model minority myth—the false narrative that Asian Americans are inherently more successful than other ethnic minorities—contributes to a paradoxical situation where Asian women are simultaneously both fetishized and despised, highly visible as subjects to be dehumanized and deemed disposable (Lang & Cachero, 2021)[65].

At the end of med school, a group of us classmates with mixed ethnicities went to Cuba together. I was not the only Asian in the group but the only "yellow Asian." We went to a crowded local town square--no whites, no tourists other than us--to look around. Then a local man started whistling loudly and motioning to his friends. They all started whistling, and the whistling spread. We were nervously looking around trying to figure out what caused the whistling. We realized the men were motioning to me, whistling, and saying "Cheena! Cheena!" My friends were surprised and laughing, but I freaked out. I didn't feel safe. We left quickly. We concluded that they didn't see too many yellow Asians there, but I knew there was something else. Why were the other women in our group, who were foreign, even non-yellow Asian, not pointed out? And why was there extreme othering of just me in the group? One has to look at why they picked me to be the butt of this display, but also how quickly they went from a level of normal social decorum to that level of disruption where my whole group felt unsafe. It felt like they didn't even see me as human.

64

65   Lang, C., & Cachero, P. (2021, April 7). How a Long History of Intertwined Racism and Misogyny Leaves Asian Women in America Vulnerable to Violence. Time. https://time.com/5952819/history-anti-asian-racism-misogyny/

Nakakahiya

"You're Not Filipino," repeats this smug white dude who was dating my sister, in front of my family, while sitting at the grand opening of Winnipeg's first Jollibee. I was excited about this big event, regaling my Jollibee experiences in my trips to the Philippines and how important this restaurant was to our Filipino community in Manitoba. I thought his first statement was a joke, and sort of half-laughed it off. He was dead serious, smirking as he repeated himself. I have never wanted to punch anyone in the throat as much as I did this asshole at that moment. I look at my sister, who is bent on impressing this loser and apparently, in some weird other dimension, is completely fine with this. I then look at my parents who not only aren't correcting his dumb ass, they're *agreeing* with him. This moron, who is nowhere near a genealogist or even a data entry clerk at 23andMe--on OUR turf, with OUR family, has the balls to make a summary statement about who we are and worse, who we're not—something even he in all his generations-long white male privilege can't even comprehend the nuances of or pretend to know in the time it's taken to bone my sister and have her fall in love with him?! What was worse was the betrayal from my family. I thought, *"So, Mom, if you remove the zero drops of Chinese blood you have in your body, that somehow makes you…nothing?"* Have we collectively stooped so low as to put up with this fucked up dystopian ruse just so this man will not be put out by his wrongness and stay with my sister? Is this what we're okay saying now? Is this who we are now??

I still feel rage when I think about this incident, which did not include a throat punch, nor any effort to set him straight. As the *bunso*, anything other than nodding in agreement would have led to sharp disapproving looks from my parents and sister. I didn't even discuss my dismay at their betrayal with them afterwards. But I also hate that I mentally measured my Chinese-ness, as if the answer made me any less Filipina. Maybe the real question I need to ask is this: Why do *I* hate China?

My prejudice against China has been shaped by my ignorance of world politics and history, my medical and public health knowledge, and the news headlines and articles I've been able to follow: Chinese superpowers in *Hongcouver,* buying up real estate, money laundering, a flagrant disregard for human rights and basic health, the kidney and organ black market supplied by China's Falun Gong practitioners, cheap labor and cheap lead toys that have made their way into Canada and made our kids sick, the use of melamine to increase perceived protein content falsely, the concern with Chinese interference involving Canada's politicians, bigwig scientists at NML, the suggestions of a Chinese origin of COVID-19. The pandemic was not a time to be Chinese-proud. For me, there has *never* been a time to be Chinese-proud.

The common denominator that I've noted in all of these interactions in my various roles in various settings over the years is this: East/Southeast Asian females are at the lowest of the power differential, with such an economic disparity and driving force between Asian countries and the rest of the world that has allowed East/Southeast Asia's women to be equated to the cheap plastic toys that come out of China. Asian women can and will be bought and sold as commodities; even our own countries take advantage of this. Our world is so used to using them as a commodity, cheap labour, and treating them as disposable that the level of hatred for them is inherently attached to this power dynamic. When you dehumanize someone and believe she is lower than you, even at a subconscious level, and she then tries to exert power over you, you and all people get enraged. This dehumanization is why male patients couldn't look past their projections of me as a submissive Asian female and had a difficult time accepting me in my physician's role and authority. They could be exceedingly nice to me, assuming they could use their power over me to get what they wanted. The distrusting hate is why my bullies could so easily overlook my accomplishments and value and why the sheeple—including racialized friends and loved ones who had their own internalized isms--could jump on the false narratives put forward by my bullies. It wasn't until I challenged them and didn't do what they wanted or expected me to do that they then could get quickly mean, abusive, and violent.

It is hard not to internalize this level of lifelong hate that surrounds my Chinese ancestry, particularly when I know so little about it, and I have had so little positive reinforcement in celebrating my Chinese heritage.

Wu Nai to Why Not

Wu Nai, a sense of hopelessness or helplessness, was a predominant feeling associated with Asian Canadians who'd experienced Anti-Asian Racism and hate (Sakamoto, et al., 2023). Part of this was tied to repeated traumas and the strong urge to keep silent and carry that level of fear.

I have a vivid memory of talking to Dad about how lucky I was to receive the WXN Top 100 award. After he'd had time to reconcile the idea—evaluating whether I truly deserved it with his brilliant mathematical mind—he responded angrily, "Why Not?!" It was a moment of realization. Of course I deserved the award. I deserve the recognition, to be seen and celebrated. We deserve the best life, not just the one we are permitted to have, confined to small doses of privileged guilt doled out like apologies by those with power—be it white, male, or other majority privilege—whose work doesn't always merit their status.

We must overcome this "Tiara Syndrome," where we wait forever for these packets of recognition to be handed out to us for our hard work. We can create a different pathway and crown our own glorious heads. Dad's words come to me when I hesitate to pursue a bold idea, questioning whether I'm too insignificant or audacious to tackle something massive. We've been trained to heed to these blocks to power for our survival and comfort. But accommodating doesn't move us forward. Who am I not to be the one to challenge a system that has consistently held me and my people back? Why not us to do the work and make change happen? It's time to shift our paradigm from *Wu Nai* to *Why Not* and let the necessary changes unfold.

With all the -ist hate directed at us, we must be realistic and strategic about our responses. When we are angry, it means that a boundary that we have set for ourselves has been crossed, and we need to deal with this—not necessarily by changing that boundary. The worst thing to do here is nothing, because giving up our sense of agency damages our self-worth. Constantly changing our boundaries to accept wrongs against us sets ourselves up for illness, unhealthy coping mechanisms that prolong the injury against us, our people, and potentially intergenerational trauma. It's okay to review the boundary and make revisions that are situation-dependent, as long as they come from a principled stance and a place of integrity. We don't mess with the core beliefs that make us who we are. There are an infinite number of ways to respond to hate that do not decrease our self-worth, and don't necessarily require standing up to the aggressors. Choose a response that makes even a tiny improvement in minimizing the risk of those standards being broken again, whether it means modifying our behavior to lessen exposure to hateful people, self-defense, improving awareness about power dynamics and levers in the workplace, connecting with other victims to be strong, documenting hate, and speaking out. Channel anger into a passion for healing. I've found that the best way to heal is to actively take a part in dismantling the structures that led to our original injury. How badass would it be for the perpetually beaten dog to take the bully's stick, or better yet, break the stick and change the rules so that bullies can't access those sticks as easily?

From Patients to Powerhouses: What, Why, How

My story is my blueprint for success because I persisted, grew stronger with each successive attempt to hold me back, and now use those strengths to help myself and others and change the playing field to put healing back into health care. My termination forced me out of the relative comforts of my "safe" doctor life--albeit in a soul-sucking toxic environment filled with bullies and saboteurs--and into survival mode. I had no choice but to urgently come up with ways to sustain my family, which then became a catalyst for incredible personal growth and positioned me to make a significant impact in my life and the lives of others. My most satisfying moments as a life coach have been turning my doctor-patient relationships into coach-client ones, where I've helped transform patients controlled by their illnesses and situations into the powerhouses who take that control back.

To win, we need a crystal-clear vision of what we want our lives to look and feel like— our "*What*." As Stephen Covey suggests, "Begin with the end in mind." While it's easy to focus on what's wrong in our lives, dwelling on these issues keeps us in a mindset of lack, not possibility. Instead, our goals should be SMART: specific, measurable, achievable, relevant, and time-bound. It's crucial to stretch ourselves with "achievable." Why aim for millionaire status when we can aim for billionaire? Don't let your mind limit your potential. This is your vision, so don't be afraid to be bold and unapologetic with your goals. Even if you don't reach them, you'll achieve more than you initially thought possible. It's important to have a clear picture of your goals and a visceral sense of achieving them.

Next comes our "*Why*." It should be strong, connected to who we are as people, and felt in our bones. Our *what* should be tied to this foundational *why*, because our principled and integrated identity will drive us to accomplish our *what* more easily. For example, wanting millions of dollars just for an easy life isn't compelling. However, if these financial goals align with a desire to heal this world and make a positive impact—i.e., becoming a *badass enlightened billionaire* the journey becomes more meaningful, and you are using your persona—i.e.--your best you--to drive your success. The abundance mentality and connecting our *what* to the good we can contribute to the world are vital to our success, and the universe will assist us in achieving this when we embrace this mindset. With a strong enough "**Why**," we can overcome any issues with our "**How**."

Our "**How**" is our massive action plan, which should be broken down into tiny steps so that we always progress towards our "**What**." My "**How**" involves hypnotherapy, which I discovered as a client around 2008 while preparing for my fellowship exam. By facilitating relaxation to access the powerful subconscious mind, I'm able to reprogram limiting beliefs into empowering ones. This method is extremely fast, effective, and time-efficient--a game-changer that I've used to smash every challenge since manifesting everything in my beautiful life today, helping my patients achieve incredible results, and training myself to be relentless in transforming setbacks into unbelievable outcomes. Additionally, my "**How**" includes embracing my unique skills and challenges, opening to and jumping on the connections and opportunities the universe sends my way, incorporating my learnings and technology to level up, reframing thoughts and feelings to serve me best, relaxing into a flow state, and following my intuition in a flexible, joyful manner.

If you want to join me on this mission of healing, please connect through my website, drdenisekoh.com. Love and healing to you all!

DONNA AVELLANA KÜNZLER

Head of Procurement Process Excellence & Digital Transformation Robotics & Discrete
Automation, ABB Switzerland; Board Member, Limbic Life AG;
Board Member, BSM Global Association
Global FWN 100™ 2023

Being an Overseas Fabulous Pinay

D*onna explores her unexpected journey of moving abroad despite initially being skeptical of living overseas. What began as a curiosity-driven decision evolved into a thriving life as a global Filipina, now known as an "Overseas Fabulous Pinay." Through her leadership journey, Donna shares six key learnings that have shaped her identity and success: Making unconventional choices led her to a profession that became her key to global mobility; Embracing the teacher mindset, pushing herself to acquire and effectively impart knowledge, ultimately establishing herself as a subject matter expert; Learning how to pivot and bring value, even in challenging or tricky situations; Finding the courage to ask questions, even when it seems daunting or unconventional; Using the power of self-reflection, which has allowed her to make necessary changes in their life; and Discovering her purpose and gaining clarity on how to be of service for the greater good. Through these experiences, Donna has embraced life abroad and thrived, embodying the essence of* *an empowered and globally-minded Filipina. Donna illustrates a path of empowerment, resilience, and purposeful living, making this chapter a valuable guide for anyone seeking to thrive internationally.*

Pamela Gotangco

CEO and Founder of PamPinay

The Unwilling OFW

"Why would I want to live abroad? Ayoko nga magpakahirap! I don't want to be a second-class citizen or work two jobs. And I especially don't want my life showcased in a Maala-ala Mo Kaya episode, OFW drama special."

That was my 22-year-old self responding to a friend when asked if I ever wanted to move overseas. I was pretty comfortable where I was: a stable job at a multinational company, a serious relationship, family, and friends all around. All seemed peachy.

A few months after that, in March 2001, I ate my words and ironically found myself en route to Singapore after accepting a job offer with one of the biggest accounting firms in the world. I got curious, and somehow, the offer was served to me on a platter, waiting to be devoured. I decided at the time that since I would still be in Asia, I had an existing network in Singapore, and I just planned to stay for two years; it was worth the shot. And, of course, I will earn four times my current salary.

Fast-forward to 2024, and I'm still overseas. After Singapore, I also lived in sunny San Jose, California, vibrant London, England, and quaint but international Basel, Switzerland. Zurich, Switzerland, is now my home.

My international relocations were primarily motivated by love, but they were always made possible through my employment. I take pride in knowing that each move was facilitated by my professional qualifications, with my employers consistently providing sponsorship.

Thanks to my competence in information systems (IS) auditing and consulting, specializing in the SAP system (the biggest enterprise resource system in the world), I have always been considered highly skilled, so there was very little challenge in getting work permits.

I have accumulated leadership learning experiences over my twenty-six years of professional experience, twenty-three of which were spent living abroad. This chapter will take you on my leadership journey through the key six learnings that definitely contributed to who I am as a global Filipina and, more importantly, an Overseas Fabulous Pinay.

Dare to be Different

For as long as I can remember, I have never followed conventions and have always chosen a different path than most.

For instance, when we were still reviewing for the Philippine Certified Public Accountant (CPA) licensure exams in 1998, most of my batch mates preferred to join SGV & Co. (then an Arthur Andersen affiliate) and only accepted a job offer after securing the CPA license. Not me, though. I deliberately joined Joaquin Cunanan & Co. (then an affiliate of PriceWaterhouse) and accepted the job offer before knowing if I passed the CPA licensure exam. My thought process at the time was, how could I gain exposure to top companies if I joined an already crowded and competitive firm? By accepting the job offer ahead of everyone else, I reasoned that I would still have a job even if I didn't pass the exams (though I was confident I would). It would be much more challenging to secure employment without a CPA license.

Becoming an Information Systems (IS) auditor was a serendipitous decision for me. Typically, those with an Accountancy degree are encouraged to join one of the Big Four accounting firms and pursue a career as a financial auditor. At that time, financial auditing was not a sexy profession and was not particularly appealing (and perception hasn't changed much). Financial auditors often had to manually schlep and manage large volumes of client paper files and were paid relatively low salaries.

I was immediately interested when I discovered the more attractive option of becoming an IS auditor, a sexier way. This position offered a higher salary, more tech-savvy work, and the perk of having a laptop. The only requirement was passing an entrance exam, which I approached with confidence and determination.

Little did I know that my unusual choice would be my key to global exposure and mobility.

Be a Teacher, Be an Expert

I come from a family of teachers. My mother was a Chemistry instructor at Cavite State University for 40 years until her retirement. My father, a CPA, taught Accounting subjects part-time at his alma mater, Baguio Colleges Foundation, early in his career. Both of my sisters also taught part-time at universities at some point in their lives. I had the same path and more.

Fresh out of university in the Philippines, I taught part-time for two semesters at the University of Perpetual Help in Cavite. My students were junior and senior Accountancy majors, often the same age as me or just a year or two younger. It was both fun and intimidating, but ultimately a rewarding learning experience. I learned how to present the material effectively and anticipate challenging questions. More importantly, I enjoyed being in the spotlight, imparting knowledge, and hoping to make a meaningful difference in my students' lives.

Training became one of my core competencies as I advanced in my professional career. In most of my roles, I provided training as a natural consequence (or perk) of being a subject matter expert.

Interestingly, I became a technical expert without obtaining any of the sought-after technical credentials. How did I achieve this? By adopting a teacher's mindset and leveraging creativity and resourcefulness like any Filipina.

When I joined Singapore Airlines (SIA) as an IS Auditor in the early 2000s, SIA had one of the world's largest SAP ERP system implementations. My projects involved conducting pre- or post-implementation SAP system audits across nearly all SAP system modules. Despite the lack of extensive audit work programs to guide me, the expectation was that I already knew how to perform these reviews. The challenge, of course, was that I needed to learn more, yet I still needed to deliver and prove my worth in the role.

One significant advantage of moving from an accounting firm to a corporate setting was the extended timeline for audits. Instead of having just two weeks to complete an audit, I had at least a month. This was a major adjustment for me, and although I eventually grew bored with the longer timeframe, leading me to return to accounting firms, those extra weeks were invaluable. They provided the learning time necessary to deepen my technical knowledge.

To enhance my skills, I frequently turned to the SAP Help Library and SAP community boards for research. Adopting a teacher's mindset, I always aimed to answer two key questions: 1) How can I teach someone to audit, understand, or implement this topic? and 2) What questions might arise when I teach this topic?

My 1.5 years with SIA proved to be worth the time investment. Those years launched me towards my specialization and gave me the confidence to venture even further.

After SIA, I joined PricewaterhouseCoopers' (PwC) SAP Advisory practice in San Jose, California. Joining the advisory arm of a Big Four accounting firm is a major step, as advisory consultants were perceived and expected to be more technically competent compared to auditors. And this could not be truer. Clients do expect more from consultants, i.e., value for money, extensive client experience, recommendations for practical implementation, and so on.

A pivotal moment for me was when I was handpicked to join the firm's first-ever SAP Lockdown event and was officially recognized as a Global SAP Subject Matter Expert (SME). A lockdown event is a gathering of around 30 global SAP SMEs for two weeks to develop the firm's standard audit programs, practice aids, and training materials for global deployment. It felt great to be recognized as a Global SAP SME for a Big Four accounting firm with around 150k employees at the time. Of the 30 SMEs, only 3 of us were of Asian origin. For better context, an accounting firm's audit programs, practice aids and training materials are their main intellectual property, as they guide how a topic is audited or reviewed. They are what sets their service apart and how they can control service quality and consistency, as delivered by their auditors and consultants.

My stay in Silicon Valley was short but definitely sweet. I received recognition as a Global SAP Subject Matter Expert and had exposure to Fortune 500 companies, such as, Microsoft and Amgen.

When I moved to PwC London, I retained my Global SAP SME title. I was privileged to be a core trainer on SAP Business Process Audit and Controls for two seasons and worked on various internal projects to further advance the firm's global SAP practice.

As I mentioned earlier, training has been a core component of my career and a significant enabler for me. Beyond advancing my technical competencies, it elevated my profile within every organization I joined. Most importantly, it instilled in me a confident "I can learn it" attitude.

In the past three years, I have advanced from internal trainer to public speaker, being invited to conferences, talks, and symposiums relevant to my field of process improvement and digital transformation.

Bring your own *Baon* and Don't Come Empty handed

What do you bring to the table? What is your value-added in any situation?

Moving to the PwC London Embankment office was a totally overwhelming experience compared to PwC Silicon Valley. It was more diverse and much bigger--the Embankment office building has around 4,000 employees, and for the Risk Assurance London Top-tier (clients) practice where I was, we had about 700 employees. So, my question then was, "How can I stand out?"

During one of my early engagements at PwC London, I was assigned to a special project in Bavaria, Germany, collaborating with PwC Germany colleagues for a global leader in agricultural machinery and equipment. The project involved an SAP system pre-implementation review to ensure the client's implementation project considered relevant application system internal controls. Given the implementation team's tight schedule, they needed more time to engage with us.

Recognizing this constraint, I deviated from the conventional approach of starting with a blank slate and gathering information from the client before providing recommendations. Instead, I prepared a list of expected controls and engaged the client in a productive dialogue to validate them. My German colleagues were initially unimpressed by this unconventional approach, possibly thinking, "Who is this Asian lady (who speaks excellent English compared to us) to think she has a better way?" Well, sometimes, you need to be flexible (this is hard for most Germans) and insist that there are many ways to skin a cat...and accept that you just cannot please everyone.

Fortunately, my approach earned me brownie points with the client. First, I was sensitive to their situation; second, I introduced a more efficient method; and third, I was able to showcase my technical expertise by providing practical advice and examples from other companies. As a result, we completed the task without disrupting the client's project, and I delivered my work on time. My German colleagues were surprised, and the client requested that my approach be adopted across the board.

Following this successful engagement, I was assigned to one of PwC's top global accounts, Royal Dutch Shell. It became my primary client for most of my time with PwC London, for about four years, where I progressed from audit assistant manager to global audit account delivery leadership roles.

Several years later, when I decided to leave the IS audit and consulting field, my next role was as a Program Manager of the exciting field (for the data nerd me, at least!) of master data management (MDM) for a Swiss industrial engineering and manufacturing firm. Everything was going well - the CIO, CFO, and CEO were all behind the program. The program was very strategic and will enable critical projects within the main company-wide transformation program. Less than a year into my role and promising area of discipline, a new CEO shook things up.

This is expected when a change in top management occurs. However, it led to the transformation program's scope to dwindle to the point where my MDM program no longer had any key projects to enable.

As a result, my MDM activities were significantly limited, and my role became uncertain. Fortunately, my strong audit background and credibility came to my aid. Having been with the company for six years, including a tenure in Internal Audit before my MDM role, I was appointed as the IT Due Diligence Lead. This opportunity arose due to the surge in mergers and acquisitions (M&A) projects following the top management change.

At a time when I could have regretted my bold decision to leave the audit field for a completely new role, when it also seemed premature to apply for the same role elsewhere, and when the additional role given to me was primarily because of my audit background; I chose instead to embrace the challenge. I thought about what value I could bring to this area. With the six months that I spent in the IT Due Diligence Lead role, I managed to change it from an ad-hoc, informal, and unstructured delivery to a systematic, formalized, and structured delivery by enhancing the company's IT Due Diligence Review methodology and applying it to my reviews. This increased the profile of the IT function as a vital member of the overall due diligence team by highlighting key IT risks in potential M&A target companies and providing realistic integration budgets.

There is a chance to shine in every situation-- believe that you have something good to offer, and you will get something out of what you put in.

Just ask…Even if it Seems Out of the Question

It's always better to ask then you'll know the answer, rather than not asking and wondering what the answer would have been.

I know it is not always easy, and one must be a bit brave (and thick-skinned) to ask questions, but I found it to be very liberating in the end. If the outcome is favorable, then definitely it is a win. If not, then at least I know and can move on.

When I left the Big Four professional services domain and joined a Swiss industrial engineering and manufacturing firm, where I stayed for nine years in various roles, my first role was to be the first and only SAP system auditor, reporting to the Head of Internal Audit. I was in charge of auditing the company's IT organization, strategy, and processes. For a 3-billion-dollar company, this can be huge and complex.

One significant difference I noticed when transitioning from a Big Four firm to a corporate environment was the responsibility for my own learning and development. Unlike the structured talent development paths at Big Four firms, this company did not offer clear career progression plans. Despite this, I took the initiative to advance my skills while also contributing to my colleagues' growth. I provided training on conducting SAP audits and on effectively utilizing data in our reviews, helping to enhance their capabilities as part of their upskilling process.

During that time, I aspired to be a Chief Information Officer (CIO). So, when I was reflecting on my learning and development plan, I aligned my career aspirations and actual work. I found a CIO development program that fits my needs. The only challenge was getting it approved since it was a costly external training. I prepared my business case to my boss. My pitch was, "How can I effectively audit the CIO (and the IT function) if I don't know how or what it's like to be one?" My boss agreed and I attended the training. Most of the participants were either new CIOs or CIO direct reports. When each participant had to do an introduction, I introduced myself proudly as an Internal Auditor. Everyone was surprised and became curious. It was certainly a conversation starter and elevated my profile with the cohort.

After spending sixteen years in the IS audit and consulting field, I decided to move on to a different area for a change and to grow. By this time, I have already been with the 3-billion Swiss industrial engineering and manufacturing company's Internal Audit division for four years. As you can imagine, the majority of my internal network was within the IT function, making it a logical move for me to join the IT organization. So, one day, I summoned the courage to ask the CIO for a job. To my surprise, her reply was, "We have three, take your pick!" This was definitely one of the most memorable moments of my career when my network, profile, and credibility have all come together to my advantage. I'm so glad I asked.

In all aspects of our lives, we can face possibilities and opportunities that seem unreachable as we have our insecurities and biases. Because we are not the final decisionmakers, we may be discouraged to even take the first step of asking the question. As a leader, I constantly challenge myself to take this first step to gain clarity. Hence, I know if I can push through or work towards the development of making such an opportunity possible.

Talk to the (Wo)man in the mirror

With the number of geographic and career moves that I have made in the last 25 years, I realized that taking a step back and reflecting on my life is essential and something that I have done quite regularly.

I may have moved several times, but I definitely did not take those decisions lightly. After all, it is general knowledge that moving is considered one of the most stressful events in life.

It is also part of self-care to periodically assess my well-being - both in the professional and personal aspects of my life.

Back in 2014, I was in my late 30s and in a stable relationship, albeit not yet married. However, career-wise, progression was unclear. I was doing audits like clockwork and was traveling for business almost every 2-3 weeks. I needed a change as both aspects of my life were satisfactory but not great. I decided it was time to say goodbye to audit and find a new challenge. I managed to get a new role in the IT function, and funnily enough, all the stars aligned in my life shortly after: my husband (then boyfriend) and I moved in together, got engaged, and got married nine months later.

I have always dreamed of earning a degree from one of the top universities: Cambridge, Harvard, and Oxford. I have put off earning an advanced degree for the longest time since I did not have the resources, and I only wanted to do so if I would study in one of my three dream schools. In 2018, I partially realized this dream as I managed to get into a one-week executive program called Women Transforming Leadership at Oxford's Säid Business School. The program focused on self-reflection: where I was and where I wanted to be. As an outcome of the program, I had never been more convinced that I needed an advanced degree to advance in my career and life in general. I was feeling stuck in my career, feeling that something was blocking me from advancing. I realized that even if I was a high performer, management did not seem to see me as senior leader potential. It was like no matter how good I was at my job; I was still someone who had a third world education. It was high time that I showed them I am world class.

So firmly clinging to my dream, I researched potential postgraduate degree programs that suit my interests and career aspirations. I was quite lucky as I was part of the Finance Mentorship program at my company during this time. My mentor then was a woman who was one of the division CFOs. I brainstormed with her my potential selections and with her guidance, I zoomed in on one program that resonated well with my personal and work life. I checked the requirements of the master's program, but I felt a bit insecure, especially about the academic requirements. Before proceeding with my application, I needed to know if I even stood a chance. Application for the program entailed getting two references and providing two essays, so I wanted to ensure acceptance before I went through all the trouble. I contacted the program contact and checked. I was asked to submit my curriculum vitae for review and shortly got the response that my credentials are exemplary. With that cleared, I then went ahead and sent in my formal application. I was accepted to the Postgraduate Degree in Strategy & Innovation program of Säid Business School, Oxford, and officially completed my degree in 2022. It was tough, especially doing it part-time. In my case, I did this mostly when taking care of our baby daughter, job hunting, and then transitioning to a new job in a new company. Reflecting on how I did it, I realize that it really takes a village for a mother to pursue further studies and a career. I was very lucky that I had my husband's support, as well as my friends, neighbors, study group mates, and line manager.

Be Fabulous Have a Purpose

Getting married at almost 40 years old was a huge milestone for me. I remember sitting in bed and thinking, "Wow, that was it. All my years as a single woman, that chapter of my life has finally come to an end."

But I was not ready to let it go.

Something was prodding me to do something, something BIG and impactful. Leave a legacy? Preserve my experience? Share my stories?

So I decided to write a book. I figured I could hit two birds in one stone: share my story as a global Filipina in the hopes that my book will help others aspiring to live abroad, and, at the same time, I can leave a legacy.

There was just one challenge: I have never written a book. All the writing I have ever done was journalling, producing audit reports and PowerPoint presentations, and developing training materials.

Still, I tried. I was aiming to write a chic lit novel akin to Helen Fielding's Bridget Jones's Diary or Sophie Kinsella's Shopaholic series. Still, at some point, all that came out were how-to's, recommendations, and guide questions. Who am I kidding, right? My essence has always been about telling people (and companies) what they can do to make themselves better.

So then I shifted to writing a self-help book. Before I continued, I researched to check if such a book exists and to check my target market. When I read the 2015 CFO Statistics on Philippine International Migration (https://cfo.gov.ph/wp-content/uploads/pdf/2017/2015compendiumstats-insidepages-2017-06-29.pdf), it moved me to learn about the increasing number of Filipinos that go abroad (more out of necessity than by choice), and that majority are women. Brave women who probably have not experienced living on their own, who will for the first time be on a plane, in a foreign country, and who have not had the chance to interact with people who are not from the Philippines. I need to help them with all the knowledge and experience I have accumulated over years of living abroad. It then became clear that my book would have a more profound purpose.

I casually continued writing my book using my iPhone Notes app during my daily commute, which is around 20 minutes one-way by train, and also during weekends and holidays.

In late January 2019, my husband and I received the best news ever: we were pregnant with our daughter. I was excited and anxious at the same time, knowing that I was a geriatric pregnancy case; I was 41! Thinking that I might not get a chance to finish my book after our daughter arrived, I hired an editor to push me to complete my

224 | DONNA AVELLANA KÜNZLER

manuscript. The edited manuscript was finished on August 30, and I gave birth to our daughter on September 4, 2019.

While adjusting to motherhood and family life, in parallel, I worked on producing my book with the help of my friend's boutique creative agency in the Philippines--book cover design, layout, review of proofs, branding, website, etc.

The book production was completed in December 2019, my website went live in January 2020, and my book, "The Overseas Fabulous Pinay: A Modern Filipina's Handbook on How to Thrive Abroad" was officially published on March 8, 2020.

I specifically chose Women's Day as my publishing date as my book is primarily for Filipino women. When I was thinking of my book's title, I wanted it to be close to OFW, though mine resulted in OFP. Close enough! And when people ask, "Why fabulous?" It's because I want to project a positive feeling or image for Filipino women. We are extraordinary, we are fabulous.

It was exhilarating to see and feel my books, hardbound and paperback, and to have them on sites such as Amazon and Apple Books.

Before I became an author, I was quite a private person. Transitioning to a public persona was daunting as I really did not know what to expect. I was a nobody and I did not know how people will react to me and my book. I had to step out of my comfort zone and learn. My corporate training and presentation skills definitely came in handy.

When things get scary and intimidating, I remind myself why I'm doing this. I want to contribute to changing the narrative of Filipino women abroad by:

1. Empowering Filipinas with my book so they can plan and integrate to life overseas more effectively;

2. Uplifting the image of Filipinas in the diaspora, to let the world know that we are a diverse set of women and, yes, some of us are successfully thriving overseas;

3. Promoting self-love, by teaching my readers that they must always prioritize self-care as everything stems from the state of our well-being, and,

4. Increasing the awareness of the Filipino people. We are our own people; we are everywhere; let us be known and acknowledged.

There is still a lot to do, but I am hopeful that my purpose will resonate with many people and we can make it happen.

In the meantime, I'll continue being fabulous!

MARLA DE CASTRO RAUSCH

Animation Vertigo and Kampilan Productions, Founder and CEO

Global FWN 100™ 2021

Navigating Dual Worlds: A Filipina leader's Journey of Resilience and Creativity

Marla De Castro-Rausch is unassuming, but underneath that exterior is a socially skilled introvert who yields effective influence in the animation and gaming multiverse. She exemplifies the transformative power of embracing dual identities, not in the likes of shapeshifters, but turning dueling worlds into negotiated worlds. Growing up in the Philippines, Marla never envisioned leaving her homeland, content with the life and career path that awaited her in Manila. Surrounded by traditional values and modern thinking, she was deeply rooted in her family's customs and her city's vibrant culture. However, her journey took an unexpected turn when she met and married an American and moved to the United States. In this unanticipated transition, Marla navigated two distinct worlds. The familiar traditions and communal support of Manila were starkly contrasted with the independence and individualism of American life. The challenges she faced—adapting to a new culture, understanding the intricacies of daily life in a foreign land, and finding her professional *footing—were daunting. Yet, Marla's resilience and creativity shone through as she carved out a new life for herself and her family. These qualities that she leans on continue to give her strength. Marla's journey is marked by key learnings highlighting her sensible ability to blend, take risks, and transcend cultural boundaries: embracing unconventional choices, building a new foundation, balancing cultural identities, finding confidence in leadership, integrating Western and Filipino values, and redefining success. As a Global FWN 100™ awardee, Marla continues to inspire others by showing that a self-proclaimed introvert can defy stereotypes because of their astute ability to observe, embrace, and transcend challenges. My friend is a force and her story is a testament that success is not confined by geography, it is by balancing the two cultures within her harmoniously.*

Carmina Aldana
Founder and Executive Director, The Neurosurgery Outreach Foundation, Inc.

"I learned very quickly that when you emigrate, you lose the crutches that have been your support.; you must begin from zero, because the past is erased with a single stroke and no one cares where you're from or what you did before."

Isabel Allende, Paula.

Growing up

I never really thought I would leave the Philippines. I didn't think it was necessary, possible, or particularly desired. I knew many Filipinos had dreams of working abroad, with promises of a better life, but it wasn't my dream. Not that I didn't want to travel or see the world, but it never really occurred to me to leave and live somewhere else. Most of my family stayed in the Philippines and held various government, private sector, and non-profit positions, and I was content to follow the same.

My childhood was a blend of tradition and modern thinking. I remember being told to go to my *Lolas* and *Lolos* rooms at 6 pm and being told to bless, taking their hand to our forehead to receive their blessing. It was a chance for us to see how they were doing and catch up with them. Sometimes, it interrupted my childhood play and annoyed me, but looking back at it now, I see that it is a memory that speaks of respect for elders and care. Sunday masses were done early in the morning, and if we were late, we repeated the Mass until the point where we came in - just like a movie. I always thought that was funny. Our family also took part in the annual Lenten parade. They even had their own float that carried the statue of the crucified Jesus. During the non-Lenten season, it was quite surprising to find the carving of the life-sized Jesus resting on top of a table in one of the guest bedrooms. I still remember jumping when I once walked in and saw it there.

Traditionally, gender roles were very important; women and girls were to help with the kitchen planning and serving food, and the men and boys were tasked with more menial tasks - carrying things into the house, moving furniture if needed, and manly chores. I was not always happy with this, as, often, during a family reunion where all cousins were gathered in the room watching TV, some adult would call the girls to go to the kitchen while the boys were allowed to stay and watch. I had called it out once and was told in no uncertain terms that they didn't help in the kitchen because they were boys. It still annoys me to this day.

Rituals And Traditions Were Well-Ensconced in Our Way of Life.

On the other hand, while strong practices were deep in tradition, our families were also open-minded regarding ideas and education. There was a strong emphasis on studying and trusting us to choose what we would do in life. The options were all open to us, and I learned there were no limitations on what I could do.

As much as we had to follow what our parents and grandparents told us and instilled in me a sense of order and obligation, it allowed me to decide on my own what I wanted to study and ultimately do. At the time, I didn't think of art or animation as a university course because it wasn't available for the general population yet, and I didn't really think of myself as that kind of artist. Writing was my medium of creativity and one of the reasons why I took up journalism as a major in college. Perhaps not the most lucrative career choice, but my parents never said anything about that. Their only thought was that I pursue what I wanted and be a contributing member of society.

I studied elementary and high school in one of the private girls' schools in Manila and then went to college at the University of the Philippines in Diliman; the opportunity wasn't something I felt I would lack. In my mind, I was either going to be a journalist, a lawyer, or a diplomat, but all of that was happening in the Philippines, in Manila.

Manila, for all the chaos and uncertainty, possessed a sense of order and familiarity that those born into it can figure out how to navigate the paths of disorganization. Despite its size, there is a sense of community, but this community can be selective. Available for certain privileged groups of people, to the detriment of a large part of the population. This is the Manila that I knew and one I learned to navigate and journey through. Building relationships and friendships that were precious and at the same time helpful, intentionally or unintentionally.

Manila is a big city with small-town networks. It seemed everyone was connected to everyone else in less than the six degrees that Kevin Bacon had indicated. Because of that, while life was full of red tape, bureaucracy, and various inefficiencies; if you knew someone, there was always a shortcut available to speed up the process if you were in the know or tapped into the intricate pulse of the city.

Living in Manila, I was surrounded by a rich tapestry of culture, family, and community. Little did I know, my journey would take me beyond what I knew and was familiar with to the hugeness and seemingly vast opportunity-filled world of the United States. Even more unexpected, being in the technology and creative industries, I couldn't imagine anything more surprising.

Most of my family stayed and lived in Manila and still do. The few who did immigrate left when I was younger, and I've often just thought of them as living abroad, but I didn't really connect the idea that they chose to leave. So, the thought of leaving the Philippines was not something I entertained.

But all that changed when I met my then fiancé, an American who had been hired in the Philippines to train up a team of 3D animation artists.

Admittedly, even when I was dating him, I didn't think about the possibility of moving to the US. I knew he wasn't going to stay in the Philippines, but the closest to a discussion about the future for us was that we would try for a long-distance relationship and "see where it goes." That changed when I flew to meet his family, and he proposed to me at the airport.

That was the first time I even considered what it would be like to live in another country. At the time, I remember just feeling excited about a new place, new people, and new adventures. I lived in Geneva for three months in my 20s and loved the whole experience. I imagined that would also be how it would be moving to the U.S.

I Couldn't Have Been More Wrong

There is a big difference between living in another country temporarily and actually moving to another country. As a temporary visitor, you don't build roots or need to figure out how to navigate the day-to-day routine. Being a visitor, it's easy to think of trying out new things, visiting places and sights, and generally being a tourist. Living in another country, you start thinking about the daily activities - groceries, pharmacies, doctors, driving - all the things I've taken for granted living in Manila.

Adjusting after the first few months was easy enough. I spoke what people called "American English" with no accent. My general attitude and perspective were pretty Western, even when I was in Manila, and everything was so new. I was happy to explore it with my fiancé.

After getting married and settling down, the change was more palpable and evident. The most minor things were a challenge. How do I find a doctor/dentist/eye doctor? What is the difference between an HMO and a PPO in health insurance? The dollar's value was also tricky. I kept converting it to pesos, which made me look at the cost of a tube of toothpaste, making it seemingly expensive; I couldn't figure out if it was too much or cheap. The cultural differences also started to show up - in the Philippines, social interactions were far more common. Seeing friends for lunch or dinner, after work, etc., was expected. I found it less so in the US, as social interactions happened more at work, and everyone went home.

I didn't start feeling homesick until about my eighth month. I just wanted to feel something familiar and experience something I knew. At that time, I was already pregnant, so there was definitely a lot more that I was feeling because I didn't have that community support that I would have had in the Philippines. Luckily, I had a chance to visit home in my second trimester and splurged on the full Manila experience.

I was out with family and friends almost daily, eating Filipino food and seeing sights. It was perfect because it was exactly what I needed to boost my spirit, and when I got back to the US, I was ready to face things again.

I needed to find things that would make me feel at home even when I was not home. I needed to find a way to make the new country my new home. Disconnecting was the first thing that I had to do. My mindset had to change so that I didn't need to feel I needed to go back to Manila to be able to function. I needed to find things that I had in Manila and accept that even if they weren't exactly the same, they would be enough.

Also, I needed to be open to seeing what my new home country offers that I can embrace.

What made that transition easier for me was getting into the workforce. Once I had my employment clearance done, because being married and applying for my immigration status change didn't automatically mean I could work immediately, I started to get familiar with how things worked in the US.

Learning things in the Philippines comes naturally because you have friends and family around you to show you the ropes. When you go to a different country, even with friends, it is like trying to discover things on your own. You understand where to go to get your driver's license, but I didn't know what to expect. And that's something that I need to prepare for things properly. Getting my driver's license in the Philippines was simple enough. I had so many friends who did it before me; they gave me step-by-step instructions on what to do and told me what to expect, as well as tips when about bringing something to drink as you'll be in for a wait.

I didn't have much guidance in the US beyond *"Make an appointment at a DMV and read the book."* Luckily, once at the DMV, it's pretty straightforward and easy to process with clear signs and instructions. That was how I needed to manage in the US. While I generally needed step-by-step guidelines on the processes in the Philippines, it was more straightforward in the US.

Finding my bearings has become easier as time passes. That includes finding places, restaurants, parks, malls, etc., that I now regularly visit. It was also easier to make friends once I started working. But getting familiar with how things work is one thing; acclimating to this new world is another.

Integration is an interesting aspect of migration. On the one hand, you feel the necessity of embracing where you live now and start accepting how things are done; on the other hand, you also realize that the person that you are was built through the years of experience that you've gained from family and friends, as well as the culture you've imbibed from the time of your birth. Changing mindsets and behaviors to adjust to the norms of the new environment sometimes becomes challenging. Sometimes, it is an easy transition because it fits my personality and my usual practice. Other times, it felt like I was betraying who I was and what I was taught because it was so alien to what I was brought up to do; for example, the treatment of older people in the US is very different from how I was raised to give respect to the elderly automatically.

Identity was also an interesting aspect, especially during the tricky times of Asian hate. Because of the lack of a Filipino accent and my "Western" attitude, most people thought that I was born and raised in the US. In fact, it always surprised people when they found out that I moved to the US only in my late 20s. Talking to several Filipinos living in the States, they said that would have given me an advantage just because it seemed that I was "from there."

I've been asked if I've ever experienced discrimination while living in the United States. Since I lived mostly in Southern California, I know it's a privilege that I haven't really experienced that - although, I should mention that the closest I had ever gotten to experiencing discrimination was while shopping in San Diego, in Seafood City, one of the Asian supermarkets where a lot of Filipinos shopped for their favorite hometown goodies. Mostly, when I shop with my Caucasian husband, I would get stares from fellow Filipinos almost in an attempt to judge how or why we got together. But that's a whole different story altogether - and an aspect of migrants' stories that seems to be universally talked about.

> *"They have no idea what it is like to lose home at the risk of never finding home again, have your entire life split between two lands and become the bridge between two countries."*
>
> **Rupi Kaur, Milk & Honey**

We moved our family to San Diego when I was pregnant with my first child, where I spent my first ten years in the US. My biggest challenge in migrating was figuring out what I wanted to be in this new country. In Manila, I had my sights set on goals. It changed as I grew up from journalist to lawyer to diplomat, but the common thread to all that, aside from my interest, was the ability to give back to my community. How would that be in this new environment and culture? I focused on what I was interested in and started there.

In the first three years since my move to the US, I learned how to do motion capture cleanup because of my husband. I learned this while waiting for him to finish work, and I was bored and pregnant. I figured out how to apply for jobs in a new city and worked in areas I had no interest in nor idea how they worked, like gap insurance, before finding something that interested me.

Having a young family and being an immigrant, I wanted to contribute by understanding how to manage finances in the US. My husband was working then, and I was raising our daughter. So, while she napped, I would read up/watch/research on how to save, invest, and manage finances. During this research, I clicked on "I want to learn more..." on a financial planning and literacy website from American Express. This led to a phone call and a meeting, and what was supposed to be a financial planning call turned into an invitation to join them. I studied to be a stockbroker and insurance agent and took on the position of a financial advisor.

It was nice to study again, which was required to become a stockbroker and insurance agent. It was nice to go to the office and meet with people I had fun with and challenged me. The financial industry, especially stock brokerage, was mostly a male-dominated industry, and I found my group of friends there. I was finding my routine: I would bring my daughter to daycare, go to the office, and sometimes help during crunch time at my husband's studio when they needed extra hands.

When I got pregnant with my second child, it threw me into a loop initially as I felt I was just getting used to my routine, and now there was a new thing thrown in. I decided to take on the role of a paraplanner for two reasons: 1) it allowed me to be flexible with my schedule while taking care of my son; 2) I wanted to learn more from seasoned financial advisors without taking on the additional hours that it would have taken if it was just me. This new role allowed me to gain more insight into how the American culture was structured and the expectations and general practices as I managed the office and clients and conducted interviews for new assistants and paraplanners. I realized that I had learned enough about how things worked that during an office move, my senior advisor was talking to me and had asked me when the internet, office network, and phones were going to be installed, and I had replied it was all connected and we were ready to go on the first day of our move.

I remember how proud I was when he looked at me with surprise. This efficiency and system building was something I wasn't equipped to do when I was in the Philippines with its "who-you-know" and shortcuts. In a world where things are convenient and customer service is important, getting what you need is more effortless. This skill was born out of living in my new country, and I was good at it. It gave me more confidence that I was adjusting and finally getting used to my place here in this new country.

But life isn't about staying put. It isn't about being comfortable and staying there. Sometimes, it's seeing what opportunities are available and taking a leap. Such an opportunity presented itself and opened the door to returning to the Philippines and giving back. This thinking was something other than what I had before moving to the US. This isn't to say it wouldn't have been something I learned if I had stayed in the Philippines, but moving allowed me to see things from a different perspective.

A book I had read before called "Quiet: The Power of Introverts in a World that Can't Stop Talking," spoke about the perceived differences between Western and Asian perceptions of being an introvert. In the West, introverts tend to lose out on opportunities because they tend to be quieter, listen more, and not be as aggressive or loud in social settings. They can be seen as timid, too risk averse, and therefore not a good leader. In Asia, respect is given to introverts because they are seen as more thoughtful, strategic, and able to command a room without resorting to antics. However, the book recognized the advantages of both perceptions and how each can contribute to the success of an organization depending on the need.

I have always been an introvert and sitting in a room full of men discussing stocks and portfolios, I find it easy to be silent amidst boisterous arguments and jokes. In a motion capture stage, it is easy to sit and watch as men joke around and discuss the technology and what challenges they're finding trying to capture motions that might be too fast for the camera to catch, for example. As an Asian, I found myself often confronted with stereotypes that were all too common and easy to come by. I still remember sitting with my team in financial advising as we were trying to compute for something, and one of my friends turned to me and said, *"You're good at math; can you figure this out?"* I laughed so hard. I majored in Journalism and threw a party when I finally finished my final math class in college. Now, because I am Asian, people assumed I would be good at math.

In a room full of men, it would have been easy to be intimidated and quietly correct that false assumption, a fairly typical response by Filipinos. But by this time, I had been acclimated to the casual and easy joking with colleagues. I immediately asked him if he had just applied an Asian stereotype to me, and we all had a good laugh. The joke was even more effective because I was quieter and more reserved than the rest of them.

Finding my voice to give my opinion was also difficult, again because I was usually with men. I don't have a loud voice to begin with, and interrupting wasn't something that Filipinos do in a professional setting because we feel it is disrespectful. But the benefit of speaking softly and being the only woman meant that when I did speak, they had to stop talking to hear me. And a suddenly silent room is so compelling to delivering your message. I didn't come off as disrespectful and always presented myself in a way that allowed them to feel comfortable talking to me.

I learned from being in Manila amidst the Titas and Titos and other older generations. Being loud, disrespectful, and giving opinions that might be contrary to theirs is not acceptable. Even if you might be right. It is delivering the message the "right" way that would be heard. Growing up in Manila, I learned to position myself this way. Doing so in the US required a bit of tweaking, but the process is the same.

During my stint in financial planning, I learned this term called the shit sandwich. When delivering criticism, it would be better received if you said a positive, a negative, and then ended with a positive. The shit sandwich allows the avoidance of hurt feelings and ensures that you are heard in the process. I thought in a strange way, this is like giving criticism in the office in the Philippines - not quite a shit sandwich but rather a positive hurricane with the bad news smack in the middle like the eye of the storm. Most Western friends call it beating around the bush, which can get frustrating when trying to convey what is needed, but it is necessary if you want to make sure that things go your way.

Finding common ground between two seemingly different cultures was a constant challenge. It never came easily or naturally. At times, I would deliberately speak English in a way that masked my Manila upbringing, simply to blend in with those around me. It always felt strange and wrong, but I convinced myself it made navigating social situations smoother. Conversely, when I spoke with a Filipino accent, I felt a pang of guilt whenever people expressed surprise, assuming I was a Filipino born in America. In those moments, I felt disconnected from my heritage, as if I was betraying a part of myself.

But in the end, I have realized this is all part of the journey. Discovering who I am amidst the two dueling worlds I seem to belong to has been a journey. Being able to navigate personalities, situations, and events was made simple because that's the kind of thing I learned living in the Philippines. At the same time, seeing the benefit of being straightforward, voicing an opinion, and realizing my own value in this competitive and challenging world gave me the confidence to try new things and put myself in an uncomfortable situation.

When the opportunity arose to start a business—something I never imagined doing in a million years—I took the time to carefully consider it before founding Animation Vertigo. It was serendipitous, I thought. I was very familiar with how things were run in the Philippines, had the network to get things done, and got me closer to fulfilling a previous goal of serving the country. I was also knowledgeable enough to make a business plan and understand the nature of the business I was starting. I was confident about trying to make the necessary connections to get the company off the ground.

When I became a citizen of the United States, I took the oath, and my husband and very young kids were with me; then I went back to work. I remember when I was at the oath-taking and seeing all the families there who were so proud and happy about this event, and I wondered if I had underestimated what this event meant. All the families planned celebrations for this momentous occasion. I was proud that I became an American. However, at the same time, it felt very weird and almost seemed like a betrayal to swear allegiance to a different country and to sing a different national anthem.

At this time, I felt a certain level of permission the change of citizenship gave me. In a strange way, it felt like it made sense to accept this part of my personality that I had gotten used to—the more Western side of me. The journey to who I was took on another facet that freed me to take on more opportunities and challenges.

Freed is an appropriate term because citizenship allowed me to take on the person that I was, and it didn't feel like I was pretending to be something I was not. It had always been inside of me, but because of the expectations of my Filipino culture and what I was "supposed" to do, I didn't really express that side as quickly as I could have.

I took time to explore this side of me a bit more. Integration isn't just putting things together but making sure they are really who you are. What I've found is that there were already a lot of things about me that were "Western," and it was just the "permission" I needed to be myself.

Animation Vertigo has been in operation for 20 years now, and I am constantly surprised when I think about that. In that time, I've gone from operating in the basement of our house in Manila to an office in the business district in Mandaluyong, from 6 people to 50, from 10 clients to over 50 with game titles and film work spanning years and genres. I've gone from working only within the Animation Vertigo internal team to meeting up with international clients by myself, going to conventions and summits, giving talks, and participating in panels.

It was an honor for me to be nominated for the Filipina Women's Network Most Influential Filipina Woman of the World Award and to win under the Founder & Pioneer category. It was another tangible reminder for me that the work, effort, and energy I put into doing what I do was worth it and worthy. It was also an acknowledgment for me that the integration of two different cultural influences was successful.

Being outside the bubble of a single culture allows us to see things from a different perspective. We can envision ideas and possibilities that were difficult to see in one culture. And this goes both ways. I saw possibilities in America that were distinctly Filipino. Through interactions with Fil-Ams and others from different diasporas, I realized that much can be gained when collaborating and listening to each other.

Home remains where my children are, where my family is. And that means that things continue to grow, change, and develop. From a foundation of family and community in the Philippines to the strength of individuality and independence found in the United States and the gains from interactions with different cultures and people, there's so much to gain by being open-minded, curious, and willing to try.

When I was younger, just after deciding to become a lawyer and taking the Ateneo Law Exam, I remember my Journalism professor asking me why I wasted his time teaching me how to write well when I was going to ruin it by becoming a lawyer and writing legalese. I joked with him and said that his teachings would remain with me and that I might be the one who changed how to write legal jurisprudence. We both laughed. As I look back, it is interesting to see all the skills and things I've learned as I changed career paths. From journalist to lawyer to diplomat to financial advisor to business owner. I was adapting and refocusing my energies to the new end goal.

In the same way, we can accumulate skills and adapt to new priorities; the same goes for the cultural influences we grow up with and are brought into. It's not about adapting to fit but about finding who you are amid all the changes and differences. That's how I expressed myself best - because I found who I was throughout all the changes and adapting. Some things I discarded immediately, some things I tried but ultimately figured out it wasn't who I was. Some were already part of my personality, but I haven't allowed them to be because of my biases and perceptions.

Animation Vertigo, and now my new venture, Kampilan Productions, thrive because I empower my team to experiment, innovate, and explore new possibilities. My ventures reflect the dynamic spirit within me—constantly adapting, finding its niche, and contributing meaningfully to the world. Animation Vertigo and Kampilan Productions are testaments to the transformative power of embracing and merging diverse cultures. By blending Filipino values with American experiences, I have crafted a distinctive leadership style that drives the success of both a US and Philippine company, showcasing the powerful synergy of cultural integration.

LEGACIES

"If your actions create a legacy that inspires others to dream more, learn more, do more and become more, then, you are an excellent leader."

—Dolly Parton

"Legacy is not what I did for myself. It's what I'm doing for the next generation."

—Vitor Belfort

MARY JOY CANON ABAQUIN, ED.D.

Foundress, Multiple Intelligence International School (MIIS).
Global FWN 100™ 2021

Leading with Purpose:
Shaping a More Just and Equitable Future

Mary Joy Canon Abaquin's journey exemplifies purposeful leadership shaped by the intersection of faith, gender, culture, and education. As the Foundress of the Multiple Intelligence International School (MIIS) in the Philippines, her narrative reflects her identity as a woman, educator, and changemaker. In a patriarchal society where fields like law and medicine were considered prestigious, Mary Joy pursued her passion for education—a field often undervalued in Filipino culture. The pressures of gender and cultural expectations shaped her decision to follow a path many saw as less rewarding. Her journey also highlights her experience as a Filipino in the U.S., navigating the challenges of being a woman of color in foreign academia while holding onto her dream of returning home to serve Filipino children. Her faith has been central to overcoming personal and professional barriers, grounding her resilience. At the core of her leadership is the belief that education is a tool for equity, empowering marginalized communities. By introducing the Multiple Intelligences framework to the Philippines and advocating *for inclusive, student-centered learning, Mary Joy has demonstrated her commitment to a more just and equitable world, inspiring future generations of educators and leaders.*

My life story intersects with Mary Joy's story in many similar ways.

1. *Both cultures -Filipinos in the Philippines and Filipino Americans in the United States – undervalue careers in education.*

2. *Mary Joy' and I both majored in sciences that were to lead to perceived prestigious positions (Mary Joy majored in Psychology/I majored in Biology), but we found ourselves wanting to give more to society, which eventually led us to the career path in education.*

3. *As an educator and educational leader, we:*

a. *Find fulfillment by giving back and paying forward.*

b. *Believe that educating others opens doors of opportunity.*

c. *Believe in making this world a better place by serving and educating our future generation; and*

d. *Believe in giving education access to all and not just to the privileged.*

Cynthia Rapaido, Ed.D.
K-12 Educational Leader and Educator, Educational Leadership Consultant

We are all created for a purpose and called to find the courage to live it. My journey is fueled by the dream of a sustainable future for the Filipino child. As an educator, I want to live a life that matters and I know this is possible only if I matter in the life of a child. The legacy I want to leave behind is a generation that would create a kinder and more equitable world to live in. I know that this is a legacy worth living for.

All journeys start with a destination. Fueled by a pioneering spirit, I have chosen to take the road less traveled when standing at the crossroads. Inspired by the greatest teacher whose teachings reformed the world, I aspired to teach like Jesus. God led me to open closed doors, but I had to trust that every step I took would bring me to my ultimate destination.

Beginning of A Dream: A Journey of Hope

Our choices define us. Every time we say no to a path, we say yes to another.

My journey started as a young Psychology student at the University of the Philippines, Diliman. I came from a private all-girls Catholic high school, and for the first time, I was confronted with a very diverse reality. I was among very bright scholars, but their lives differed from mine, like night and day. The realities of poverty stared me in the face as some of my classmates struggled with finding their daily allowance to eat a meal. This was the first spark that ignited my heart as an educator. I realized that **education is a great equalizer.**

I always knew that I wanted my life to be a life of purpose, but I did not think I would be an educator. My father was a lawyer, and my mother was a psychologist. After high school, respectable careers for intelligent girls were to pursue law, medicine, or business. I knew I would be good in all three, but somehow, I knew it was not enough to be good at something, as I wanted to find what I was most passionate about. I pursued psychology, thinking it would allow me to discern which path to take. Sadly, being a teacher, at that time and to this day, is a vocation that is not perceived as prestigious as being a successful lawyer, doctor, or businessman.

To serve was a choice I made. This led me a step further in my journey. I volunteered in a children's orphanage and saw babies and toddlers banging their heads in their cribs due to lack of stimulation. My heart broke, and I had to apply the theories I had learned in child psychology to solve the problem I had seen. Again, inequity stared me in my face. Education, became a tool I used, as I rallied to fundraise and convert an old conference room into an early childhood center for these children. Armed with a vision for a playspace for children to do free play since there was a scarcity of adults to supervise them, I would spend weekends painting the walls with murals and filling the shelves with toys. I found genuine joy in seeing the children play and enjoy the space, a far cry from banging their heads against their cribs. I realized that **I wanted to live a life that would make a difference in the lives of children.**

As my sense of purpose unfolded in my life, God propelled me to my destiny. There is a saying that goes, "*When God shuts a window, He opens a door.*" As for me, it was more like, "*When a blackout happens, God opens the light.*" On Graduation Day, I was given the privilege to deliver the Valedictory Address for the College of Social Science and Philosophy. I was about to speak when a blackout happened, and the whole auditorium went pitch black with no microphones. The Dean looked at me and said, "I don't think you can continue." However, I saw my mother in the audience, who at that time suffered a sprain and went up in crutches on the many steps of the building to hear me speak. I wanted to do it for her and honor the hard work my parents have given me for my education. I told the Dean that I would continue despite the blackout. To my amazement, I mustered up the courage to speak in the most commanding voice in the dark to an audience that went silent, allowing me to be heard throughout the hall. My message about our responsibility as the Scholar ng Bayan of the University of the Philippines to make a difference and help the underprivileged using the education received resounded to all. Because of this, I got noticed by the Dean, who offered me a job as part of the Psychology department right after graduation. At 21 years old, I became the youngest member of the department.

Eleanor Roosevelt said, *"The future belongs to those who believe in the beauty of their dreams."* I was extremely blessed to be a young instructor at the university, yet I felt that there was a greater purpose waiting for me to discover. I was teaching psychology, but the pull towards teaching young children kept tugging at my heartstrings. Fellow academicians felt that I was crazy to give up the opportunity to teach at such a prestigious university to pursue another path. A dream to teach young children and open my own school was born.

> *I stood at the crossroads. I had to choose whether to stay on a well-laid-out academic path or pursue an uncertain future chasing an elusive dream. I chose the road less traveled.*

Without much resources, I applied to universities in the United States to pursue a master's degree in Early Childhood Education. I prayed for God to put me in the right place and provide the needed resources to make this dream happen. To my surprise, I received numerous acceptance letters even from Ivy League schools, but only one university gave me a 50% tuition waiver. I knew I could not afford it even with the tuition waiver, but my father believed in me. He was about to retire and said, *"I will bet my last money on you."*

With my Papa's blessing, I set out to Boston University and began my journey of hope. With my suitcase, I took my father's hope in me and my mother's hope for the fulfillment of my dream. My compass was to lead me to my dream of creating a school for young children. Stamped in my passport were the faces of children I encountered in the orphanage who needed early childhood education. Etched in my heart was my profound hope that education would be the great weapon for change, that my beloved country, the Philippines, direly needed.

The American Dream or the Dream for the Philippines

I landed in Boston, a beautiful city that became my second home. I have never been away from my family, nor have I ever been to Boston. I only knew of Boston, from the picture book, Make Way for the Ducklings. I would read that to the children in the Philippines, and I never imagined that I would be walking its pages. Every day, I would wake up deeply conscious of the privilege of the education I was receiving. I said YES to every opportunity given to me. I soaked in all the ideas and stored all the tools I knew I would need for my journey when it was time to go home.

My years in Boston were instrumental in my growth as a person and a professional. Boston opened my eyes to what was possible in education. These were to form the foundational thinking for educational reform that I dreamt of for the Philippines. I knew that I would need to create the change that I wanted to see in education.

Intelligence for All. Growing up in the Philippines, my experience as a student made me acutely aware that in every class there were students who were considered intelligent, and there were those who the teacher thought were not so bright or even "stupid." When I worked with children in the slums as a volunteer tutor, I was surprised to observe that they thought they were stupid because they were poor. Poverty has disempowered them as learners.

I was first introduced to the cognitive theory of multiple intelligences, which changed me as a person and educator through a book I picked up by chance in the bookstore. It was entitled 7 Kinds of Smart by Thomas Armstrong. I read it and did not put it down because of the compelling argument it made. All individuals had seven intelligences, which differs from a traditional IQ-based model wherein some kids were intelligent and others were not. It was a revolutionary thought. As a teacher, the book resounded with my core belief that all kids who entered my classroom had their own unique intelligences, and it was my job to develop these innate intelligences.

My research led me to Howard Gardner, the Harvard-based psychologist who was the proponent of the Multiple Intelligence Theory. By the time I met him, he was proposing not just seven, but eight intelligences. I wanted to bring this educational reform idea back to the Philippines so that every Filipino child could be empowered to believe that they are intelligent in different ways and can learn and contribute to the world, regardless of socioeconomic status. Intelligence is for ALL, not just for a FEW.

To Reach and Teach All Students. My personal experience as a learner in the Philippines was juxtaposed with the American ideals of equity in education. Schools in the United States were advocating for No Child Left Behind. Coming from a traditional school system that was teacher-centered instead of student-centered, I wanted to bring this educational reform element back to include all students. As a student in the Philippines, whenever a teacher taught a lesson and a student did not understand it, this was the problem of the student for being a weak student and not the problem of the teacher for not teaching it well enough to be understood by all. I believed otherwise. Teachers have the equal responsibility to reach and teach all students. I was challenged to learn how to give teachers the necessary tools and pedagogy to make learning accessible for all students.

I knew that education was a powerful tool to create a better future for Filipino children. However, as I became more comfortable with life in the United States, the realities of the Philippines seemed more distant. I started teaching in a private preschool in Boston that sponsored me with a work visa. I was advised that if I stayed for a few more years, I would qualify for a green card. To everyone I knew, this was the ticket to the American dream. I had to search myself to find my true purpose and passion for where my journey should take me.

> *I found myself at the crossroads of my journey. I had to choose whether to stay on a well-laid-out path or pursue an uncertain future chasing an elusive dream. I chose the road less traveled.*

Everyone thought I was throwing out the once-in-a-lifetime opportunity to live the American Dream. I was told it was futile to go home to the Philippines, beset with problems that had no solutions, and to a poorly paid career as a teacher. Some even made the argument that I was wasting my hard-earned American education to go back home. But my dream for the country and my love for family burned stronger and brighter than the American dream. Equipped with hope and new tools, I journeyed back home.

Leading with Purpose - Pioneering Change

Coming home, I was full of hope and excited to be a changemaker.

Reality set in when I realized the truth of the adage, "No one is a prophet in their own land." I wanted to share my ideas by returning to my university to teach, but that door was closed. I was advised to change departments since I was now in Early Childhood Education rather than Psychology. I then decided to do consultancy, but again, I faced obstacles and closed doors. Many schools thought my proposed ideas were too difficult to implement in the Philippines. It became clear that any changes I recommended in education would be met with resistance.

Why change when many believed there was nothing wrong with how schools operated? I would enter preschools to see children as young as three years old sit for hours and do workbooks instead of playing and doing developmentally appropriate activities. Parents would enroll in preschools to prepare children for the "big schools" and were equally unaware of what good early childhood practice looks like. The Philippine education system is predominantly rooted in the traditional system of education. Teacher-focused direct instruction, rote learning, memorization, traditional quantitative pen-paper measures, and an emphasis on the 3Rs - Reading, Writing, and Arithmetic- were the key learning areas that comprised the predominant Philippine landscape. The definition of intelligence was mainly I.Q. based and students perceived their abilities based on where they would fall in that ranking. I could not seem to push for change, so I decided that it would be best if I created a model for change.

> *I found myself at the crossroads of my journey again. I had to choose whether to stay in my comfort zone or start my own school. I chose the road less traveled.*

I made the most significant decision in my life, which has made all the difference. I believed in myself and in my dream, to decide to create the change I wanted to see in the world. I stopped asking myself, what I was going to do, and started to ask myself, what I wanted to be. I knew that I wanted my 8-hour day to make a difference in someone's life. I knew that I wanted my life to lead others to dream of a kinder and better world. I knew that I wanted to live out my purpose as a vocation. I knew that I had to be vision-driven and purposeful in the school I was going to create because I wanted it to make a difference.

The Multiple Intelligence International School (MIIS). In 1996, I opened our school doors to introduce pioneering ideas. I established Child's Place Preschool to be a progressive school embodying the best child-centered learning. In 2000, MIIS opened its doors to first-graders, which eventually grew into an entire pre-K-12 school catering to students from 1 ½ years old to 18. MIIS aimed to pioneer progressive global education with the theory of Multiple Intelligences (MI) at the heart of its practice. MI is used as a powerful lens to view and value every child. MIIS led the way in raising awareness among Filipino parents and educators that "Every Child Is Smart." Through a national school reform convention attracting 2500 educators throughout the Philippines, together with Dr. Gardner, the school reform agenda was rolled out. The school reform agenda proposed an alternative paradigm to view intelligences, which empowered every child to discover and develop their unique intelligences. This opened doors for the inclusion of all learners, to work together in a culture of respect. Long before Inclusion, Diversity, Equity, and Anti-discrimination (I.D.E.A) became buzzwords, MIIS advocated for embracing diversity and celebrating different ways of teaching and learning. Beyond academics, students were given opportunities to hone their interests and strengths to discover their purpose and passion.

Multiple Intelligences Does Good Work. Along with my decision to return to the Philippines was the intention to raise the next generation of children who would choose to use their intelligences to make a difference. Unlike other multiple intelligence schools in other parts of the world that focused on honing student intelligences to be excellent, I knew that the Philippines did not need more smart crooks, but rather individuals who would care about creating a better and just world. Since the Philippines is a developing country, I recognized the powerful role that education plays in forming the next generation of leaders who would be positive changemakers. Because of this vision, MIIS is recognized by Dr. Howard Gardner for its pioneering effort to bring together Multiple Intelligences and Good Work. Good work is defined as excellent, engaging, and ethical by the Good Work Project. The advocacy to use one's intelligences to make a difference has become my biggest contribution to the body of work on the application of MI to education.

Smart Start School Reform. I have always believed in the old African proverb, *"It takes a Village to raise a child."* Raising the next generation of leaders should be everybody's concern. I opened the classroom doors to the world, forging partnerships with business, socio-civic organizations, and experts in various fields, becoming part of the Village that will share wisdom and mentor students to problem solve prevalent problems and care about the common good. In turn, we have also shared our resources to help underprivileged communities improve the educational experiences of young children to have a Smart Start.

With a clear purpose and vision to create positive change through education, I wanted to respond to a fast-changing world and the changing paradigm of education, triggered by the pandemic and technological change. I knew there was a need to put together almost three decades of work to make the Filipino child globally competitive and a key player in creating a sustainable future.

Making A Difference for A Sustainable Future - Leaving A Legacy

The COVID-19 pandemic has forced individuals and industries to re-envision the future ahead. For almost three decades, I have led a community of students, teachers, and families to respond to shared concerns and pursue the common good by using their intelligences to make a difference. Our Kids Can: For Kids, By Kids movement has led students to address issues of poverty and social justice, lead reforestation and environmental projects, and create social enterprises through youth entrepreneurship to address economic inequalities.

We challenged every child to use their intelligences to make a difference through the Kids Can! Movement. We wanted the school to be a reflection of what society could be if every citizen was invested in doing good and creating solutions for prevalent problems. I did not believe that children could only contribute when they were old enough or when they were adults. We wanted each student to be empowered and grow up knowing that they could already create that change, no matter how old they were. In a world filled with apathy, selfishness, and individualism, we needed all children to care about making the world better. I did not want to raise a ME generation, instead, I wanted them to be a WE generation.

At MIIS, we open doors for students, create opportunities, and provide mentors for numerous student-initiated make-a-difference projects. Preschoolers use their spatial intelligence to create artwork and auction it to help children with cancer. First-grade students campaign and sustain a reforestation project through a Rainforest Cafe. Students empathize with underprivileged Indigenous People who have no access to books by organizing toy and book libraries. Musically inclined students organize Harana concerts to raise funds for scholarships. Even boys who enjoy e-games channel their passion for Smash Bros to a Smash That Movement to Smash Trash in the Pasig River. Every student at MIIS is challenged to think of problems that they want to solve through their intelligences.

I knew that our journey in the three realms of sustainability - economic, social, and environmental- would lead us to a final destination of educational reform in the Philippines. I wanted to leave a legacy for the next generation to be leaders for sustainable development.

> *I find myself at the final crossroads of my journey. Do I choose to end the journey and celebrate all that has been achieved, or do I embark on a new journey to once more reach new heights of an elusive dream? I choose the road less traveled.*

My journey has brought me to many crossroads. I have always chosen the road less traveled and pioneered ideas that could create positive change. My journey has been fueled by my desire to make a difference in the life of a child. However, like all paths, my journey has also had its share of difficulties. I have experienced the hardship of treading on unbroken ground, the rejection of new ideas, and even the outright attacks on the concept of the school, breaking ground in the community it seeks to serve. I have always dreamed of building a master-planned school, but all these plans did not come to fruition as the doors were shut. In hindsight, He had a masterplan that would best allow us to make the dream a reality. In all the ups and downs of the journey, I have always asked myself, what would the Greatest Teacher do? I continue to choose faith over fear and I step with courage to finish the race to a sustainable future.

I am leading our journey forward, by responding to the call of the present times. The Philippines continues to be beset by problems in all aspects of sustainability - social, economic, and environmental. The Philippine educational system faces many challenges and is in dire need of reform. Raising the next generation to use their multiple intelligences to make a difference and create a sustainable future has become even more critical. I know that *"We cannot do all the good the world needs, but the world needs all the good we can do."*

I have chosen to open a new chapter in our institution's life by building a Leadership School for Sustainable Development in the first green urban estate in the Philippines. This school will serve as a laboratory for innovative ideas and new approaches to creating a more sustainable future for all. My hope is to raise the next generation of changemakers—individuals with the minds to innovate solutions to shared problems, the hearts to care about equity and social justice, and the hands to work toward global sustainability.

Growing up, my mama would always remind me that *"Who I am is God's gift to me, but who I become is my gift to God."* As an educator, I know that the generation I leave behind will be my greatest legacy. May this be my gift to God at the end of my journey!

RHODORA PALOMAR-FRESNEDI

Founder, Sunshine Farm Philippines
Chairperson, Best Buddies Philippines
Global FWN100™ 2019

What Will My Mother Say?

"To be beautiful is to have experienced life."

- Rhodora

I have told Rhodora that she should trademark her words. It is a profound yet simple statement that we can internalize. In this chapter, she connects with readers in a warm, personal way without sacrificing the integrity of her message. There's more to savor between the words of this poetic author. Her collection of wisdom on leadership from distinct women in her life, especially her late mother, is greater than the sum of their stories, which she gladly shares with the next generation. Like the good friend that she is, Rhodora's chapter is a joyful, intelligent, thoughtful, and inspiring read.

Carmina Aldana
Founder and Executive Director, The Neurosurgery Outreach Foundation, Inc.

Inay

"They were in an accident…"

I haven't heard five words that immediately triggered 50 other questions. *"Who's "they"? What happened? Where? When? How?"*

My husband sat me down in my office in Manila to tell me about the tragic news. The van traveling from Las Vegas to San Francisco turned turtle in the scorching summer heat, instantly killing 6 of its ten passengers. Five of them were my very close relatives in California, with whom I spent Thanksgiving and Christmas. The sixth one was my mother. Together with two other teenage girls, my father survived. He, who had a double bypass operation seven months earlier, survived. A twist of fate. The mother of the two young girls, a nurse, age 51, did not.

That was 25 years ago, and I still feel a hundred little pricks inside me as I write these words. I thought time heals all wounds.

I remember our flight to San Francisco that same night. I ruminated on my mother: *Inay,* the teacher, the counselor, the *babaylan.* I thought about our last phone conversation the weekend before, both of us squeezing the value of every minute of the prepaid phone card as we rushed through story after story. We laughed together at our naughty sharing, enjoying the no-filter perks of adult conversation. She was no longer talking with the voice of the experienced mother who knew what was best, and I was no longer the naïve, young daughter who should always do as she was told. I was in my 30s, old enough to be naughty with a little gossip.

With every conversation, though, came nuggets of wisdom. *Inay* always found ways to insert life lessons into the conversation. She was always teaching - even when she wasn't. She asked about my work, as she often did. She reminded me frequently about what our priorities should be: our kids. That was when I became the youngest and the first Filipina board member in the 70 years of Unilever in the Philippines, and my husband became one of the youngest corporate officers in San Miguel Corporation's history. Her perspective was good grounding and the reminder that my husband and I both needed. Another thing she and my father would often say was to live with integrity. They both said that we should live our lives so that we would not be afraid to read about it in the following day's newspaper. It was the front-page test before the age of social media.

Her voice in my head echoed above the hum of the engine 30,000 feet high. Occasionally burdened with distant relatives who have often asked for help and support, she admonished: *"Mas mabuti na ang nagbibigay, kaysa nanghihingi."* (It is better to be the one giving, than the one asking for help.) Or when one felt victim to inequity, unfairness, or injustice, a version of the same message came in the form of *"Mas mabuti na hindi ikaw ang nagkulang"* ('Tis better if it isn't YOU who failed the other.)

She lives in me.

I often think of my mother. Sometimes I talk to her. I thought about how much fun she was to be with. One morning, I found myself writing the following:

> *I know she is in another dimension, and I can feel her presence. This is a different kind of feeling. I miss her, but it is a peaceful kind of missing, the acceptance that her energy will always be with me.*
>
> *My sister Ophie describes the struggles she had when my mother died together with five other loved ones. We both felt the deep chasm created by that loss inside our bodies. There was an emptiness that seemed impossible to fill. My mother's presence in that void is still missed a quarter of a century later. I realized she could never be replaced.*
>
> *That void used to be raw, flesh burning, not unlike that carved earth scorched by a meteorite. It is a sensation that makes one throw up with the memory of that impact, that time when the news hits you: Your mother passed away in a tragic accident that killed five others of your loved ones".*
>
> *That scorched flesh healed slowly through the years, but the void remains. Moments of celebration bring poignancy, the reminder that someone is not physically there. Our milestones and those of our children's bring back silent tears and a wish: "I wish Inay could see this."*
>
> *One lives with the pain. In my case, I moved with the pain, pushing myself to be productive with her loving memory.*

She was the epitome of loving-kindness. She made us, all 9 children, feel loved in every way, unconditionally, giving us enough always to remember that we are in her heart. And yet, she had more love to give. Our home became a sanctuary for the misunderstood teenager fighting with his parents, the lost soul who did not know where to go for help, the nephew who yearned for motherly love, the young teacher who made her first mistake at work, the woman who married someone younger and who was learning to live with someone, the doctor's grandchild with undiagnosed symptoms. And many more! She listened to all of them, giving every person who came to see her what she had in abundance: unconditional love.

She was fair and just. She knew how to balance views and show someone the perspective of another. Thus, she settled many disagreements. She was never one to take sides, always protecting the ones not present to defend their views.

She worked tirelessly to instill in us, her children, a deep love and respect for one another. Her greatest wish was for us to get along and support each other throughout our lives. This lesson has stayed with us, and we remember it well. We enacted it.

While these serious causes and accomplishments define much of who she was, it would be a disservice not to highlight the playful, fun-loving side that made Inay such a joy. Inay had a trickster's spirit that brought laughter and surprises. Twice in my life, she wrapped presents containing items I thought were lost. One memorable Christmas, she handed me a beautifully wrapped small box. "Big things come in small packages," I thought as I eagerly opened it. To my delight, and with a hearty laugh, I found the watch I had thought was lost. Her girly giggle still echoes in my memory. She pulled the same trick again when we lived in San Francisco. After I misplaced my watch (yes, again!), she waited until Christmas to place it under the tree, nicely gift-wrapped.

Oh, how I miss her laughter! She had the funniest stories and the wittiest side remarks. She was never beyond poking fun at her children, often reminding Ophie to always look nice so she wouldn't "look like a yaya" (nanny) to her beautiful Fil-Am baby daughter, Shiloh. But she set boundaries. She could make those remarks, but no one else could. Inay was the first to come to the defense of any of her children. NO ONE would dare look down on them or treat them unfairly.

On one occasion, without my knowledge, she confronted one of my teachers when she heard that he had been unfairly judging my capabilities. I wondered back then why the teacher's attitude towards me changed.

Inay was both intelligent and street-smart. She rose from the hardship of World War II in her teenage years and took pride in her professional journey. She became a teacher, took her Master's degree while raising kids, and rose to the public school ranks to become a district guidance counselor. She upheld the nobility of the teaching profession and admonished younger teachers to maintain decorum and dignity. The choice of some local teachers to become domestic staff abroad always saddened her. For her, the financial merits of a job abroad should be evaluated against the loss of psychic income measured in a teacher's stature, impact on young minds, and contribution to the country.

She always dressed nicely but within budget, with colors matching head-to-toe, including a ubiquitous umbrella that matched her outfit. She had all the umbrella colors, which was always a welcome gift. She also always smelled nice, leaving a scent in the clothes she wore.

Inay's unfulfilled ambition was to be a lawyer. Well, maybe not in her lifetime. She did get more than one Atty. Palomar down the family line.

Inay believed in karma and thus, ensured that she kept doing good --- so that the next generation of her bloodline would have the blessing of her faithful work.

Doing good, working through my pain of losing her 25 years ago was my way of honoring her and filling in the vacuum that she left.

The wounds of loss are no longer threadbare. At 2 a.m. this morning, I remembered her vividly: her smile, her laughter, her wise counsel, her stories, her scent, her joy. Unlike previous moments, I remembered her with calm and peace: no grief, no painful memories, no tears.

I wanted her to hug me and talk to me in my dreams. I got what I wanted. She hugged me in my dreams. I felt her love for me and for all those she cared about. I felt the good that she did and her wishes for continuance.

And I feel it still as I awoke. As I write this, I noticed I was switching from past to present tense. Somehow, Inay seems to talk to me in the present tense. She IS with me and she continues to do things through me.

Did her passing wound me? Deeply! However, today's memory showed me how that scorching wound healed through the years and how the void from her absence filled.

It was love—love filled the void. The mother's love she left with us to see us through the most difficult times saw me through. The love she left with those she touched came back to us a thousandfold, in many little ways – hosting a visit, telling us how she made them feel, what difference she made in their lives.

Maya Angelou was right. We do not know our legacy. Our legacy is embedded in every person we have touched. Inay showed me that.

My sister Ophie, in her infinite wisdom, is right. It's not time that heals all wounds. It's love. Love heals all wounds.

Inay Tanda of Tiaong, Quezon

Ninety-five kilometers south of Manila, Tiaong, a first-class municipality of 100,000 people, sits at the edge of three provinces: Batangas, Laguna, and Quezon. I was born in Tiaong.

I have always wondered how much geography influences the kind of person someone becomes. There must be something about growing up as a female in a melting pot of three provincial cultures.

Ten kilometers north of Tiaong lies San Pablo City, Laguna. The same distance west is Lipa City, Batangas. The neighboring town east is Dolores, Quezon, sitting at the foot of Mount Banahaw, an active volcano. Southwest leads to the beaches of San Juan Batangas and Sariaya, Quezon. The cities offer sophistication. Batangas province is famous for its assertive locals who will not run away from a fight. Mt. Banahaw is well-known for its mystical and healing powers. Quezon offers an environment for ladies to grow up able to skillfully navigate the fine line between being prim and proper and having a drink of *lambanog*, a local gin made from coconut, with men. With all the geographic and cultural influences, a woman from Tiaong embodies the spirit of three provinces. My great-grandmother, Inay Tanda was a testament to that.

Tomasa Apolinar Locso was Inay Tanda to us, her family, and Nanay Asay to many. When her husband died during World War I, she became a young widow with four kids to raise on her own. She found ways to support herself. She operated a bakery and managed the crop yield from her modest land holdings planted with coconuts, *lanzones,* cacao, mango and other fruit-bearing trees.

She prayed faithfully and worked diligently. She lived the adage, *"Nasa Diyos ang awa, nasa tao ang gawa"* (Mercy is with God, work is with man.). She kept an altar of various saints enshrined in her room. It was an altar we knew too well. Young boys and, occasionally, girls gone astray knelt in repentance before the many saints, sometimes on mongo beans.

Her bakery was well-renowned, with lines forming during the morning and afternoon baking hours. Long before the business concepts of just-in-time production, supply chain and working capital management became business standards, she knew and practiced them well.

She was generous to a fault. She made sure that every member of the extended family had their meals for the day, sending a ration of bread baskets for breakfast. She supported grandchildren going to school but admonished everyone to watch every penny, literally. *"Ang piso ay hindi magiging piso kung kulang ng isang pera,"* she often said as an argument to support her lesson. (You will not complete one peso if you are missing a centavo.)

Inay Tanda's big ambition was for her children to live post-war lives better than she had. She believed it was possible through education.

"Palawakin mo ang iyong harapan", she would often say. (Expand your horizon.) For someone who lived most of her life in Tiaong, Quezon, she encouraged her descendants

to attend the best schools they could afford outside of the small town. She also said it is good to marry outside of one's hometown to have a wider view of the world and experience another culture.

Inay Tanda's small business and modest land holdings supported generations of her descendants through college. While she did not finish college, she nurtured a family of professionals: teachers, engineers, architects, lawyers, nurses, public servants, and a doctor.

She was a disciplinarian. She was home most of the time when I was growing up. The mere thought of her presence kept us on our best behavior - even when outside the house. *"Naku, lagot ka sa Inay Tanda!"* (Oh dear, better watch out for Inay Tanda!) was a phrase we were all scared to hear.

As a widowed matriarch, Inay Tanda did it all. And she had it all, as a businesswoman and head of the family, loved and respected by many.

Shanghai, China, 2010

There are people we meet whose stories are immediately imprinted in our being almost as soon as we hear them. Fourteen years ago, I had the privilege of being part of the transformative Dell Women's Entrepreneur Network Conference in Shanghai. We were a small group of women who shared our triumphs and challenges as women leaders and entrepreneurs. Two narratives stood out to me as epitomes of determination; two women who defied what society predetermined for them.

Debra Ruh

The first one showed me how to look at disability through the eyes of a mother and her unwavering belief in the power of self-determination. Her name was Debra Ruh, and she has a daughter, Sara, who was born with Down's Syndrome. Consistent with the average prognosis for children with developmental disabilities, Sara's doctors declared that she would not be able to communicate well and her future would be severely limited. Debra heard that Sara would not be good for anything. Debra was warned she should prepare for the eventuality of Sara's lifelong dependency on her and inability to add value to the workforce. Debra refused to accept the medical experts' declaration of Sara's future.

Debra's next steps went beyond the adage, turning a lemon into a lemonade. She didn't settle for a drink; she built a lemonade stand and made it global. She established TecAccess, a company that provided accessibility to persons with disabilities. She worked alongside her daughter, defying the odds against them. Sara learned to communicate well enough to connect with employees at TecAccess and thereafter, well enough to share her story publicly, in different forums worldwide. She eventually held the position of CIO – Chief Inspiration Officer.

Sung-Joo Kim

She was born a girl and could not inherit all or any of her father's business holdings. So, she built her own.

Sung-Joo Kim sat in the panel of accomplished women with grace and gratitude. There was not a hint of bitterness in her voice for not having the same opportunities as male heirs in the East Asian culture. She shared her story for what it was: just a given, a platform from where she could start building. She has always wanted to be in business and knew she would not get it through inheritance. After all, she's a woman. The sons get the father's company.

Sung-Joo Kim, like Debra Ruh with her daughter, refused fate as defined by societal norms or as dictated by her gender. In her mid-thirties, she founded her own company and brought fashion brands like Gucci, Yves Saint Laurent, and Marks & Spencer to Asia. From there, she grew her business and established Sungjoo Group. Fifteen years later, Sung-Joo Kim grew the company big enough to acquire MCM, a German luxury fashion brand founded in Munich in 1976. By the time I met her in 2010, she was already the Chairman and CEO of a multi-million-dollar business and had already been named one of the most powerful women in business worldwide by several organizations.

Sung-Joo Kim's journey is a testament to the power of self-belief, resilience, and commitment to a vision. Her story is a fitting exemplar of what happens when one decides to carve out one's path, regardless of what society dictates, including what gender roles permit.

Debra Ruh and Sung-Joo Kim showed me what possibilities can be created, in the words of the young poet, Amanda Gorman, "If only we're brave enough to see it, if only we're brave enough to be it".

Mountain Province, Philippines, 2024

"Are you ready for this?" I asked Jesse the night before her appointment to have an indigenous figure tattooed on her back.

"I am, Mum. Are YOU ready for this?"

I was not sure I was. There we were in Buscalan, Tinglayan, Kalinga, 6,500 feet above sea level, with the Butbut tribe famous around the world for Apo Whang-Od, the oldest traditional Kalinga tattoo artist in the Philippines.

Buscalan is a village nestled in the mountains of Kalinga province, 448 kilometers from Alabang, Metro Manila from where we came. It is home to about a thousand people and a cultural tourist destination for at least another thousand people daily on weekends.

London, 2012

My daughter Jesse was in her final year at Central Saint Martins, the highly competitive, prestigious college of the University of the Arts London. It has a six percent acceptance rate and has produced some of the world's most renowned artists from Lucian Freud to Pierce Brosnan to Stella McCartney. From 8th Grade, Jesse aimed to be there. Thus, when the admission representative who saw her high school exhibit offered her admission on the spot, she was beyond thrilled. For Jesse, it was *the* school, forsaking all others.

My husband and I thought that she was better suited for a career in international relations, political science, or business. After all, she was the activist in the family. She was the one who blurted when she was only five, "I'd like to give speeches that inspire people". She also sold her handwritten poems for five pesos. However, we adhered to our parental philosophy: there are things we could teach, but there are many more that she would have to learn independently. Whether Communication Arts and Design was for her was something she needed to experience and then decide for herself.

I was a block off Oxford Street, Central London's shopping mecca. Jesse's graduating cohort installed a pop-up shop showcasing their products. The business plan and execution were part of their finals. What a practical aspect of the curriculum! That was an actual test of art and design that sells. Jesse seemed to enjoy the setting up and managing their pop-up shop. She was thrilled with every sale. Her product was a temporary tattoo with letters in a font she designed on purpose. The font felt like a timeless hug, like a softer, warmer gothic. Classy. And classic.

The words of the temporary tattoo said: *What Would My Mother Say?*

Buscalan, 2024

Our kids managed to get through their teenage years without any ink marks on any part of their bodies. They sensed my trepidation when the subject came up. There were pressures from around them. After all, tattoos for their generation no longer carried the same level of stigma and stereotypes that my generation used to have. Often, the desire for self-expression outweighed the practical implications of the choice to have a tattoo.

I exercised my right as a mother to remind them to think carefully before they get a tattoo. Be clear why. Be sure you want it, and for the right reasons, because it IS permanent. Test for skin reactions. If you are clear and want to act, choose a reputable tattoo artist, and make sure you have evaluated the health risks. I cannot forget the story of a friend. Someone he knew had an unusual allergic reaction to the ink. The ink seemed to have poisoned her blood and the person became unwell for the rest of his life.

The subject of tattoos occasionally came up again as our children reached their twenties. By that time, we surrendered to whatever their decisions were. Their bodies, their choice. Their lives, their decisions. We gave our opinions when consulted, but for the most part, we let them be who they needed to be at every stage.

What then were we doing in Buscalan?

One of Jesse's classmates at Montessori became the photographer who took recent photos of Apo Whang-Od, the oldest *mambabatok* (master tattooist) in the Philippines. The photo landed on Vogue Philippines when Whang-Od turned 106 years old, the oldest model to grace the beauty magazine's cover.

Jesse expressed a desire to see the Apo, and maybe consider getting the Kalinga signature three dots. As an artist, Jesse was drawn into the intricate patterns of the traditional tattoo, and as a feminist activist, drawn into the life story of Whang-Od. She infected me with her curiosity.

I arranged for the 13-hour trip up north to see Whang-Od's tribe, and yes, to meet a national treasure of the Philippines. Winding through the mountain province, the van ride was interrupted only by short stops for gas, a little stretch, and quick meals. We arrived at Kalinga before sunrise, took an hour's nap, and then prepared to hike down the valley and up to Buscalan.

It was a 45-minute trek for the hale and hearty. But the trek became two hours for my husband and me, fresh out of holiday overeating and surrendering to the art of doing nothing.

We arrived at the house of our host, Joyce. She would host us for the night. Breakfast, a quick wash, and change we explored the tiny village and got oriented with its history and culture. We watched Apo Whang-Od in action. She with her rose-colored glasses and bright red lipstick, served 75 people a day. In a few weeks, she would turn 107. Note to self: I should make sure I age similarly.

I soaked in her story.

Apo Whang-Od

Whang-od gained international recognition for her traditional hand-tap tattooing technique, which is deeply rooted in Kalinga culture and has been passed down through generations. People from various parts of the world travel to Buscalan to see her and to experience the rich cultural heritage of her tribe. She has appeared in a feature on Discovery Channel, been written about in hundreds of articles, and been honored with the Presidential Medal of Merit. She is currently in the final stages of being granted the National Living Treasure Award in the Philippines.

A celebrated centenarian. Yet there she was, squatting on her house's untiled, parched ground, pounded and packed daily by thousands of footsteps that came to visit. The spartan space was filled with people eager to take a picture with her or in line from early morning for her signature three-dot tattoo. She was wearing a green top, her head partially wrapped in a red bandana, round spectacles reminiscent of John Lennon, albeit with rose-colored lenses, and bright red lipstick on her lips. She has tattoos in all the visible parts of her body, save for her face. She's every inch what the online site, Rappler quoted, "the badass grandmother we always wanted."

One can read and watch everything about her and still not soak in the equivalent of being in her presence or feel what it is like to be in a community life made possible by one woman who has lived through five generations.

The locals are eager to pass on the oral history of Whang-Od. Repeated through many voices is the narrative that becoming a *mambabatok* is pre-ordained, a gift and skill passed to the male heirs of a master tattooist. Until Whang Od at age 15. Her talent and potential broke the patrimonial tradition when her father, a master tattooist, trained her to succeed him.

The Kalinga community embraced Whang-Od as a trusted master of the hand-tapped tattooing process. She, in turn, embraced other women, transferring her skills to women in the community. She never married or had children. Thus, she chose two grandnieces, Grace and Ilyang, to be her chosen genetic successors. In addition, she has trained at least twenty other women in her tribe to be skilled in traditional art. All of them are now practitioners. She trained many more in the other communities.

Every anecdote filled me with soaring inspiration. Here is one woman, barely five feet tall, less than a hundred pounds, breathing life into a community in the mountains. By herself, she is fueling big, life-sustaining activities.

First, she makes economic empowerment possible. The cultural tourism she generates supports the tribal village and the surrounding areas. Residences are homestay havens, local meals are served 24-7, the Kalinga rice and coffee are packed for take home, and souvenir items from magnets to t-shirts are peddled. Her significant economic impact is visible through the changing face of the landscape. There is a zipline that transports luggage from one end of the mountain to the other. A bridge is under construction to connect one end of the valley to another, expected to cut the hike through an up-and-down zigzag trail by 30 minutes.

Second, Whang-Od preserves and promotes the traditional art of Kalinga: hand-tap tattooing or "batok." This ancient tradition has been passed orally from generation to generation. It is believed to have been practiced in the Philippines for thousands of years, dating back to pre-colonial times. That fact makes me want to run back to the history books I read as a student and remove everything that says, "The Philippines was discovered by Ferdinand Magellan in 1521."

We were not discovered. Long before 1521, there was a Philippines with tattooed communities rich in their own culture and traditions—yes, including the ancestors of Whang-Od.

Third, Whang-Od, in being who she is, challenges all of us to revisit and revitalize indigenous cultures and traditions, honor our history and ancestry, and take pride in what we have, wherever we come from in the world.

Whang-Od is the epitome of authenticity, a beacon of resilience and empowerment, and a cultural hero.

Indigenous Tattoo

I watched Whang-Od's grandniece Grace inscribe her art on the arms of someone who booked the session with her the year before. The customer came from Australia. Tap, tap, tap. The sound of every mark echoed as the lady looked out into the valley in the seventh hour of her session.

Outside in the foyer, a film crew from the United States captured the scenic mountain range, the long lines of vans forming on the other side. A Filipina anthropologist from Alaska was with them. In a corner of the balcony sat a woman, her right arm beautifully marked by indigenous art. I struck up a conversation with her, inquiring about the stories behind the tattoos. She spoke eloquently and passionately about her affinity with the Butbut tribe. She shared the trips she had taken and how many *batok* sessions she had. She returned to get her left arm tattoo, complementing her right. She was expecting at least a 10-hour session. She spoke softly but firmly as she told her story. I felt her every word radiated a connection to something bigger than herself and her commitment to a cause. She did not say who she was and what she did for a living, but I later found out she was a university professor, an advocate for women, a champion for indigenous weavers, and a political scientist.

I learned that in the indigenous community, a woman without a tattoo is not yet considered beautiful. In the strictest of traditions, one earns a tattoo. Indigenous tattoos represent a connection to one's culture and ancestors. Each mark carries both symbolism for the community and a personal milestone. Receiving a tattoo is a rite of passage, a visible representation of personal growth and achievement. To be beautiful is to have experienced life, to have learned, to have contributed to the community, to have earned respect. To be allowed to receive a tattoo is to be beautiful. Thus, the more tattoos given to you, the more beautiful you are to the community.

Dot-Dot-Dot

Whang-Od has expanded the influence of the *mambabatok*. The traditional tattoo is no longer bound by the prerequisites and ancient rituals of the Butbut tribe or exclusive to the community members. Today, everybody who wants to receive a tattoo can get one. There is also a master list of the symbols one can get. There are several tattoo artists in Buscalan; most can give a person any of the designs chosen. Except for one specific tattoo: the signature three dots.

The signature three dots are the only tattoos of the Butbut tribe that can be given only by Whang-Od or her descendants, Grace and Ilyang. It is exactly what it says: three dots arranged one after the other in a straight line, vertically or horizontally. The three dots represent Whang-od herself and her two grandnieces, the only apprentices related to her by blood.

● ● ●

The ellipsis

Infinity. ● ● ●

A pause. ● ● ●

An unfinished ● ● ●

A signal to fill in the next thought ● ● ●

An omission. ● ● ●

A connection to shorten the space between two ends with missing details. Like "12 3 ● ● ● *100". An invitation* ● ● ●

Complete me.

Connect me to your thoughts.

Replace me with your reflection.

Make me your own.

● ● ●

"Are you ready for this?"

"I am, Mum. Are YOU ready for this?"

Jesse is in line to see Ilyang Wigan, the youngest of the "three dots". She decided to sit for the three dots under symbols for traveler, courage, and protection, placed at her back, just below her nape. She had her name listed from the day before. We checked to see when her turn would be.

In the two hours of waiting in the morning, I watched the rituals of those ahead of her. Dot Dot Dot. Eight minutes on average for the three signature dots. Artist and pen fashioned from a bamboo-like plant called the *lana*, takes 8 minutes to become one, connecting with the person on the seat who ends up indelibly marked by an indigenous tattoo.

I heard Jesse's voice in my head and recalled the moment she declared, *"I have come all the way here. I am getting an indigenous tattoo."*

I understood her. Buscalan beckons. From the balcony of our homestay location, I feasted on the place, my senses alert, my mind open. The mountains of Kalinga stood magnificently around it, the native trees stood erect, reaching out to the vast blue dome above it. Straight ahead, the sun's rays made the short rice blades glisten on the terraces as natural light and water collided. The zigzagged paths of the valley below, some parts rough and others easy, revealed the journey of the day before, the road that led us to the moment.

I bathed in the rays of the January sun and understood the source of the sun-kissed glow on the faces of Whang-Od, Grace, and Ilyang. I inhaled deeply, absorbing the purity of the mountain air. I closed my eyes and images of the tribe thousands of years before me appeared like a fast-moving silent movie. Whang-Od and his father. Whang-Od traverses across mountains to give a warrior his victory tattoo. Whang-Od taking a vow not to marry. Whang-Od and her devotion to the preservation of their cultural heritage. Images of locals going up and down the steep steps of mountains as easily as I walked through the flat, concrete road from where I came. Stories of survival and resilience, of reinvention and transformation.

"Mountain juice. That's our drink," a voice echoed. He was making a pun of Mountain Dew.

My thoughts were interrupted by the explanation of a local where they get their drinking water. I thought about the local grains and diet that keep everyone fit. They were all in harmony with what was outside of them and what was inside their bodies.

Ilyang

Jesse's turn with Ilyang came.

I stood close to her, her back to me, Ilyang next to me. I turned on my phone camera and started to record the moment.

Tap tap tap. My camera captured every dot that pierced my daughter's pale, smooth skin. Every tap opened a pore, releasing a tiny drop of blood, which the black ink immediately replaced.

I felt bits of me breaking with each tap. I have protected every inch of my daughter's skin against the threats of any potential scar from her childhood. There I was, releasing her to her choice of what to carry as a permanent mark on her body.

Tap tap tap. I wondered whether Jesse was in pain as droplets of red oozed out of her back. Ilyang wiped each spot clean fast, but not before I could imagine how each tap felt. My maternal instinct wanted to protect Jesse from suffering.

Tap tap tap. I was breaking, indeed. But I realized I was not breaking down. I was breaking open.

Tap tap tap. I opened my imagined tight hold on my daughter, releasing her to her concept of beauty, to her decision of how to memorialize a long trek to this place, to acknowledge her Philippine roots, and to honor her people.

Tap tap tap. I was opening myself to a deeper affinity with these women, my connection to this place, and my recognition of this tradition.

Tap tap tap. I was opening myself to my beliefs. In my mind's eye, I saw my thoughts wash away boundaries and dissolve previous notions about body art.

I felt each tap brought me a greater understanding of indigenous art and culture and the need to stay rooted in the same. Each tap allowed me to have a deeper appreciation of the challenges of upholding, preserving, and promoting our cultural heritage. Each tap made me identify more closely with this tribe, with these women, and with this ritual.

Sixteen minutes and 46 seconds in my thoughts, I watched Ilyang clean up the tattoo she gave Jesse. Ilyang touched up the signature three dots. Jesse's back was visibly red from the tapping. As Ilyang wiped off the rest of the bloody residue in the area, the space revealed a beautiful piece of indigenous art on Jesse's back.

I stopped filming, and before anyone could say a word, I heard myself say, *"Me! I'm next."*

My words startled Jesse, and she let out an audibly mixed *"Whoa!"* I confused her. Me, the mother who kept saying no to tattoos when they were growing up.

> *The ellipsis.*
>
> *Three dots.*
>
> *Complete me.*
>
> *Connect me to your thoughts.*
>
> *Replace me with your reflection.*
>
> *Make me your own.*
>
> *Our three kids*
>
> *Jesse, Juliene, Jason.*
>
> *My grandmother, my mother, me.*
>
> *Passion. Purpose. Possibility.*

I sat next to Ilyang and offered my hand for her signature dots. I felt Whang-Od and Grace with her, as she tapped three equidistant dots, in line with my right thumb, just above my wrist.

"Are YOU ready for this, Mum?" Jesse's words from the day before echoed.

As I sat and watched through the 8 minutes it took to get the signature indigenous tattoo, my thoughts ran through as follows.

> *Yes, I am ready for this. I acknowledge and honor my Philippine roots. With pride, I say I belong to a tribe of women from the Philippines who go out into the world, who may acquire other citizenship but would stay rooted and connected to who we will always be: proudly Filipina. With humility, I say, this is the mark that will keep me constantly focused on what is truly, deeply important to me: my husband and our three children. It is also the mark for what I believe is the true measure of inclusion, a community, a world where every person can say: "I am valued. I belong. I make a difference."*

Epilogue

What Would My Mother Say? Or rather, what would I say to her now?

Well, this: thank you, mother and all women in my life.

I am the product of the intersectionality of generations, geography, and gender. I am grateful for the influences of many women in my life who lived in systems that survived generations. I am the sum of all the people I have met, the places I have been, and the women in my life.

Inay, my mother, passed away in the manner of her choosing. On the day she passed, she was returning home from the funeral of an aging uncle who had a lingering illness. The sad event was capped by an extended family reunion marked by the retelling of happy memories of younger days with cousins. The reunion in Las Vegas followed an earlier reunion in Canada the month before, another happy occasion. My mother spent the six months before she died connecting and reconnecting with those she loved. In a way, that was her saying goodbye. She has always said that she would not want to be under long-term care and that she would never want to be a burden to any of her nine children. She got her wish. Sudden. No pain. No long-term burden to anyone she loved.

My great-grandmother, with her meticulous hygiene practice, took a final bath one day, went to sleep, and never woke up. She was 97. The bakery that she started shortly after World War 1 is still standing. It is now managed by a fifth-generation great-great-granddaughter. Her legacy bakery remains famous for the heritage *pan de aleman* and *biscocho*. The former is a packed dinner roll that comes out of the old-fashioned brick oven, brown, but not toasted like a sourdough, soft but firmer than a dinner roll. It is a heavenly treat with melted butter. The *biscocho* is the next-generation *pan de aleman*. The *pan de aleman* is sliced thinly into nearly paper-thin pieces and baked again, resulting in this crisp *biscocho* that goes well with coffee, tea, or ice-cold Coke.

The *pan de aleman* and the *biscocho* are now brought to different parts of the world by locals of Tiaong as *pasalubong*.

Debra Ruh has expanded her influence in the accessibility arena, with her voice reaching as far as the United Nations. Sung-Joo Kim continues to make waves globally as a businesswoman. Her international recognitions include an award from the late Queen Elizabeth as Honorary Officer of Order of the British Empire (OBE). MCM Group where she sits as Chief Visionary Officer is now over 1 billion dollars.

Apo Whang-Od turned 107.

My daughter Jesse's tattoo healed beautifully. I know my other daughter, Juliene, may like one too. And so would our third dot, our son, Jason.

I see my tattoo every day, a fitting reminder of what was, what is, and what is yet to come.

And what we, Filipinas around the world together, can make happen . . .

● ● ●

ATTY. LORNA PATAJO-KAPUNAN

Senior Partner
Kapunan & Castillo Law Offices
Global FWN 100™ 2016

"Been There – Done That!"

I 've known Lorna for over 40 years, our friendship beginning in 1989 as charter members of Zonta Club of Makati-Ayala. She was a pregnant lawyer, and I, a new widow. Her mastery of parliamentary procedures, particularly Robert's Rules of Order, impressed our senior Zontians, and she often saved the day at meetings. Lorna even held a workshop for us on parliamentary basics, which was a huge help. As we became more active in the club, our bond deepened. We worked on many projects, including "Adopt-a-Cop," which fostered strong ties between residents and police, decreasing crime in Barangay Pio del Pilar. Lorna also proposed the first women's desk in the precinct, and JICA later sent the precinct commander to Japan for training.

Our personal lives were intertwined. I became the godmother to her youngest son, King, and she was a sponsor at my wedding. We supported each other through losses—her husband and son, my battle with cancer, and my husband's passing. Lorna's resilience during those times was inspiring. She channeled her grief into her work, and Zonta became a form of therapy. We traveled together to international conferences, *where she won a hotly contested Area Director race by a single vote. She became a go-to person for women's issues and offered support for personal problems, marital or otherwise.*

In 2006, Lorna and I orchestrated secret meetings between presidential candidates Raul Roco and Bro. Eddie Villanueva, hoping they would unite. Although the plan fell through, it was our bold, cloak-and-dagger effort. Later, Lorna ran for Senate in 2010 under Grace Poe's ticket. Though unsuccessful, her popularity soared. Wherever we went, she was asked for photos, always obliging, much to my frustration as I ended up being the photographer.

Lorna's work as a consummate lawyer to a sterling list of corporate clients is well known. She is a tough, fearless litigator and legal practitioner, unwavering in her pursuit of truth and fairness. But to me, she's also a fun, loving, down-to-earth friend and ally—a true woman for others.

Marily Orosa
Founder/President of Studio 5

After 46 years of law practice (yes, I graduated from the University of the Philippines (UP) College of Law in 1978), I thought I could say *"Been There, Done That!"*

As a lawyer, I have practiced in Courtrooms, sat in Board Rooms, and been in C-Suites. I have handled mergers and acquisitions, restructuring and bankruptcies, sent people to jail or get them out, annulled marriages or reconciled spouses, settled family estates, tax issues, and labor problems. Dealt with celebrities and their matching egos. Done property deals- consortiums and joint ventures, securities, franchising, land acquisitions. Protected intellectual property rights over patents, trademarks, and copyrights.

Been There, Done That!

All the above in a *"Grand Manner"* as we were taught at the UP College of Law. My various awards and recognitions through my years in the legal profession speak for themselves- the Order of the Purple Feather, Phi Kappa Phi Honors Society, UP Outstanding Women Award, UP Women Lawyer's Circle (WILOCI) Defender of Women and Children Award, Awards for Litigation Practice, Best Corporate Law

Firm, Certified ISQ (Institutional Spirituality Quotient) given by the Bishops Business Conference, Top 100 Lawyers for 3 consecutive years, The Outstanding Women In The Nation's Service (TOWNS) Award for Corporate Law, Filipina Women's Network (FWN) Outstanding Women Global Leaders Award, Linguistic Intelligence Award, Asia's Iconic Award For Law, among others. Do I need more awards? No!

Been there, Done That!

But the journey to where I am now was not without any challenges. To name a few--

My Pedigree

I had the genes of both my illustrious father, former Supreme Court Justice and Commission on Elections (COMELEC) Commissioner, Lino Mejia Patajo and remarkable mother, Dean Cristeta Taaca Patajo of Manila Doctor School of Nursing, Vice President for Academic Affairs United Doctors Medical Center, and Professional Regulations Board for Nursing.

While the genes were a definite plus, I started my law career as my father's daughter-- and making a name for myself and by myself was a challenge. Even in Law School, my professors compared me to my father. I was not deterred. I wanted to be a "Chip of the old Block." My father gave me the best accolade by saying I had become the "Block of the old Chip"! (Disrupt 4, 2023 Ed., Chapter 3.1 at pp. 465-476).

Gender Bias

Significantly few lawyers were women, and even fewer were women litigation lawyers. I was among the few. In the days when the male lawyers came in suits, I too went to Court in suits—albeit miniskirts with matching high heels, bags, briefcases, and yes, overpowering perfume. I had to overcome the condescending glares, the cynical smiles, and the patriarchal attitude. And my way was to prove that not only was I equal, but I was better. And by winning case after case and beating up my opponents to a pulp, I gained the respect I enjoy now. Not because "I have balls," as the men would say, but because "I have a vagina – I am a woman and proud of it!"

Work Home Balance

I married my classmate in UP Class '78--Eduardo Roden (Bong) Eco Kapunan. We have five sons (yes, no daughters!) Like me, he was a practicing lawyer but later was appointed Judge of the Regional Trial Court (RTC) of Guagua Pampanga and then promoted to RTC Manila. Bong had colon cancer diagnosed when it was already at its critical stage. After six months of both Western and Eastern medical treatments, he succumbed to the cancer. He transitioned in 2001. How was I to raise five young boys, all in exclusive boys' schools? I raised them well by God's grace and with the full support of my parents and siblings--a sister and two brothers. Being both mother and father to growing boys was tough. But I was ever-present for "Father and Son Night," "Camping," and "Inuman" with the Dads, as well as my sons' football, wrestling, and swimming activities. Balancing home and career, juggling family time and office hours, the kid's homework, and my client's demands was a challenging ordeal. But I survived!

Transcending Grief

On top of this, I lost my youngest son, King, to leukemia in 2003, 2 years after I lost my husband. He was a perfect 8-year old boy. My world collapsed. I turned away from God, friends, and family—and retreated to my own sorrowful world. But—I transcended my self-pity and became involved in socio-civic professional organizations. I was invited, elected, appointed or "voluntold" to many organizations. To name a few: Philippine Red Cross (PRC), World Wildlife Fund (WWF), Cultural Center of the Philippines (CCP), Rotary International, Zonta Foundation, UNIFEM (now UN Women), The Outstanding Women in the Nations Service (TOWNS), Ballet Philippines, People for the Ethical Treatment of Animals (PETA), Kilusang Makabansang Ekonomiya (KME), Management Association of the Philippines (MAP), SharePhil, Womens Business Council (WBC), Intellectual Property Association of the Philippines (IPAP), Asean Patent Attorneys Association (APAA), UP Women Lawyers Circle (WILOCI), Integrated Bar of the Philippines (IBP), Philippine Bar Association (PBA), Licensing Executive Society of the Philippines (LESP), and Filipina Women's Network (FWN). In these organizations, I played a key role as founder, president, chairman, governor, trustee, adviser, and counsel.

Been there, Done that!

Quo Vadis

Despite my achievements as a lawyer and various involvements in socio-civic-professional groups, I had to do more. Not for the awards or the recognition. Service beyond self was a mantra that kept calling to me.

In 2016, I was asked to run for public office. Politics, I knew, was not my ballpark. But I also accepted that this was my opportunity to serve beyond myself. Pay back, pay forward. I ran for the Senate--but without guns, goons, or gold, the outcome was predictable. I lost--but the experience of going around the country and meeting real people from all walks of life--the marginalized, poor, downtrodden, hopeless, homeless, and hungry, was life-changing. All these people were abandoned and invisible--except during election time when their votes were being courted. I knew then my calling--to be an advocate and agent for change. I visualized myself as a whirlwind and tsunami combined, a David ready to combat the Goliaths of the world. The opportunity came when Ambassador Cabangun Chua (owner of DWIZ) invited me to host a Saturday weekly *teleradyo*, *"Laban Para Sa Karapatan."* This was my chance to delve into real issues affecting real lives. In the show, I interviewed guests on issues such as poverty, unemployment, hunger and malnutrition, OFWs, lack of housing, inadequate funding for health, mental wellness, and education, wastage of public funds through corruption, pork barrel, lack of accountability of public officers, combinations in restraint of trade and monopolies, disparity in the distribution of wealth, greed of big businesses, political dynasties, gender discrimination, collapse of the Justice System, breakdown of the whole moral order.

But I Felt I Could Do More

The *"He for She,"* *"Me Too,"* *"Black Lives Matter,"* *"No to Asian Hate,"* and *"Say Her Name"* movements were then raging worldwide post-pandemic.

I wanted to be involved in all of these movements. However, I knew I needed to educate myself to understand that they weren't just fads or "trends" but significant movements impacting real lives. Was it just my FOMO (fear of missing out) that motivated me to speak up and be counted?

Intersectionality

When I was asked in 2022 to be one of the keynote speakers at the Filipina Womens' Network (FWN) Annual Meeting in Prague on the issue of Intersectionality – I asked myself, "What's that?" Thus began my quest to learn more.

From my readings, I have learned that Intersectionality is the acknowledgment that everyone has unique experiences of discrimination and oppression. We must consider everything and anything that can marginalize people--racial identity, sexuality, gender, disability, nationality, religion, economic, social status, and education.

First coined by Professor and lawyer Kimberle Crenshaw in 1989 and added to the Oxford Dictionary in 2015, its importance is increasingly recognized in women's rights. Kimberle Crenshaw tells about an experience that led to her coining "intersectionality." As the story goes, a US judge dismissed the claim of an African-American woman named Emma De Graffeneid, a working wife and a mother. Emma applied for a job with a local car manufacturing plant. She was not hired, and she believed that she was not hired because she was a black woman.

The judge dismissed Emma's case, arguing that the employer hired both African-Americans and women. However, the judge failed to acknowledge Emma's real point: African-Americans typically hired for industrial and maintenance jobs were all men. In contrast, women who were usually hired for secretarial or front office positions were all white. This revealed the double discrimination Emma faced. The Court, however, refused to let Emma combine these two issues in her case, believing it would grant her preferential treatment. Instead of broadening the perspective to include African American women, the judge dismissed the case entirely.

To Kimberle Crenshaw, this was an apparent injustice. She realized that a simple analogy to an intersection might help judges better understand Emma's dilemma. Because Emma was both Black and female, she was positioned exactly where these roads overlapped, experiencing the simultaneous impact of the company's gender and race biases. In this analogy, the law is like an ambulance that arrives only if it can be shown that Emma was harmed on either the race road or the gender road, but not where those roads intersected.

Hence, the term and concept of Intersectionality was born. We credit Kimberle Crenshaw for this.

Face 2 Face

With my newfound knowledge of Intersectionality, I got out of my "**Been There Done That**" mode and decided to do something about Intersectional Injustice. I wanted to be a "Crenshaw--Philippine Style". That opportunity presented itself when I was invited in 2023 to participate in the show" Face 2 Face" on a major TV/media station TV5. The program "Face2Face" is the first and only Barangay settlement on air. The Barangay is the primary local government in every City or Municipality. According to the latest survey, there are 42,029 barangays in the Philippines. The law mandates that residents of the same barangay must attempt to settle disputes among themselves amicably. This step is necessary and must be exhausted before filing any case in Court.

In "Face 2 Face," a team of researchers from TV5 go to the many Barangays and inquire if there are residents who, failing to get a settlement from their Barangay, are willing to go on TV to air their disputes and claims. Real people, real problems. Mundane and minor issues, perhaps, to the more privileged of us but very real to the disputants. The show airs daily, Monday to Friday, with national and international broadcasts through YouTube and Facebook. Notwithstanding the minimal talent fee (vis-à-vis my hourly billing rate) and despite knowing that this would take a toll on my already hectic schedule, I said YES to the invitation to become one of the three panelists composed of a spiritual adviser Brother June "Dr. Love" Banaag, a resident psychiatrist Dr. Camille Garcia, and myself as legal adviser.

In "Face2Face," the concept of Intersectional Justice becomes a living reality. Daily, Monday through Friday (10:15 am—11:15 am and a repeat telecast at 8:00 pm—9:00 pm), we hear stories of systemic injustice and social inequality at the Barangay level. Attempting to untangle the lines that create the complex web of inequalities and giving proper legal, spiritual, and psychological advice is a continuing challenge.

The show's reach extends to various socio-economic classes from A to F--the poorest of the poor. We have an educated, uneducated, mal-educated, or illiterate live and virtual audience on television and all social media platforms. We talk to kids, adults, millennials, Gen X", "Y," "Z, and "A" (the IPad babies), parents, grandparents, and senior citizens. Our studio guests include people from all walks of life. The housewife, mistress, house helper, husband, father, single parent, teacher, farmer, fisherfolk, barangay official, tricycle driver, motorcyclist, office clerk, vendor, garbage collector, squatter, homeless, drug addict, alcoholic, street sweeper, the employed/unemployed, loan shark, OFW, seafarer, LGBT. These people come on the air seeking advice, solutions, and help with their problems.

The premise of "Face2Face" show's vision is that IF we reach the people at the most significant structural disadvantage, THEN we reach everybody.

The show enables me to use my legal skills, knowledge of the law, and wisdom gained from years of experience.

Some typical problems and advice:

> Problem: Live-in couples for more than five years, comprising about 90% of our studio guests, say that they cannot afford even a simple wedding because of their poverty.

> Advice: You don't need a marriage license if you have cohabited as husband and wife for five years or more. It is a simple and inexpensive civil ceremony before a Judge, Mayor or local official authorized to solemnize marriage. A church wedding is not necessary to give the union legal effect.

> Problem: Single parents with minor children.

> Advice: Single Parent benefits are available under the law. With the Barangay for a Single Parent ID they can apply and receive a monthly P1,000.00 allowance, free public education for the children, free medical benefits and free vocational or technical training at the Technical Education and Skills Development Authority (TESDA) for the single parent who wants to learn a skill to be gainfully employed.

> Problem: Senior Citizens (60 years old and above)

> Advice: Studio guests and viewers are reminded about the benefits under the Senior Citizens Law including retirement benefits from Social Security System (SSS) Government Service Insurance System (GSIS), Pag-Ibig (for housing), PhilHealth (free/discounted rates

for medical, mental health, hospitalization, medicine); 20% Senior Citizen deduction and 12% VAT exemption; 20% discount for all public transportation, restaurants, groceries; priority lanes for Seniors, among others. Senior citizens, often neglected by their own families, feel less despondent after knowing their rights

Problem: Addiction to drugs, alcoholism, gambling, school absenteeism and dropouts, early child pregnancy, date rape, "barkadas", and cyber and real-life bullying have become increasingly rampant at the Barangay level.

Advice: This is a reminder to parents, guardians, and teachers as substitute parents that the root causes of these problems are parental abandonment or neglect, lack of guidance and supervision, absentee parents, parents giving bad examples to their children, no values education, and no spirituality in the family.

Problem: Victims of violence, which may be physical, psychological, verbal, emotional, mental, and/or economic violence (i.e. failure to give support).

Advice: Leave their abusers and file for a Protection Order with their barangays. Barangay officials are reminded of their obligation under RA 9262 (Domestic Violence Law) to give adequate protection for the victim spouse/partner/children and refer them to the Department of Social Welfare (DSWD) for financial assistance or to the Free Legal Aid Clinics/Advocates for free legal assistance in filing the appropriate criminal/civil case in Court.

In "Face2Face," as studio hosts, we inculcate respect for the dignity of work, reminding our studio guests and viewers: There is no shame in being a garbage collector, street sweeper, waitress, tricycle driver, grab delivery driver, market vendor, house helper, "tubero", "labandera," night club entertainer/hostess. These are decent jobs that bring food to the table, pay for the rent of their shanties, enable children to go to their schools with "baon" and notebooks, and provide gasoline, jeep/bus/tricycle fare, and clothing on their backs.

The studio hosts read the riot act on penalties of imprisonment and fines for the following offenses: *Jueteng*, illegal MERALCO/NAWASA connections, garbage dumping on others' property, drug pushing, loan sharking, smoke pollution, unkind treatment of animals, gossip-mongering that has become commonplace at the Barangay level.

The studio hosts have severely reprimanded "LGBTQI" studio guests and viewers who resort to pulling each other's hair at the show, throwing insults at each other, yelling, screaming, and kicking. The advice to them is to show respect and dignity for each other to gain the respect of the public.

The families who appear in the show tell us on air that their home is under the bridge, their toilet is the Pasig River, they eat from leftovers found in the garbage, they have no jobs, their children are forced to beg in the streets, and they fall prey to loan sharks. They are invisible to the Barangay because they are not registered voters but squatters with no permanent address. Their lives don't matter. They can't vote. The studio hosts call out the Barangay and local officials for their apathy, lack of social responsibility, and neglect of duty.

These are a few of the many problems we try to solve at "Face2Face". Some heed our advice—kiss and makeup. Some remain bitter, angry, and unmoved. Most feel repentant of their wrongdoings, enlightened of their legal rights, and determined to move on and aim for a better future. And that makes it all worthwhile.

Not Enough

"Face2Face" celebrated its first anniversary on air in May 2024. Over the past year, I have interacted with the poorest of the poor, the marginalized, the downtrodden, and the invisible, and given proper legal advice. Have I done my part? Not enough!

According to the latest Social Weather Station (SWS) survey in March 2024, 46% of families said they were poor, 33% said they were on the borderline, and only 23% said they were not poor. The 46% translates to around 12.9 million families. SWS found that 33% of families in the country considered themselves food-poor. Thirty-six percent said they were borderline food-poor, and 41% said they were not. The Philippines was ranked 69th out of 121 countries in the Global Hunger Index 2022. The country ranked number 74 as the poorest of 190 countries (SOURCE: International Monetary Fund, World Economic Outlook April 2024).

Various studies cite the many causes of poverty in the Philippines, including bad governance, corruption, a political system dominated by political dynasties, vulnerabilities to environmental disasters, lack of available jobs, income inequality, subpar educational outcomes, health care access issues, inability or unwillingness to work, high rates of disruptive or disorderly behavior and improvidence.

Scarcity and inadequate government support systems affect living conditions in densely populated areas of the Philippines. Access to basic necessities like electricity, safe drinking water, and quality education remains uneven. Scarcity not only limits the country's potential for development but also perpetuates inequality. As a result, impoverished communities face daily struggles, making it even more challenging to break free from the cycle of poverty.

Amid these stark realities, how can anyone even say, "I have done enough--Been There, Done That!."

I have seen, heard, felt, and experienced poverty daily vicariously from the people who were our guests in "Face2Face." I have given legal advice when needed. But this is not enough. More is needed.

At 72 years of age and 46 years of law practice, I aim to live longer and do more. Enough is not enough! I cannot eradicate poverty, hunger, discrimination, inequality, social evils, and intersectional injustice. I do not see these problems being solved in my lifetime or even in generations after me. But certainly, I can live a purposeful life with a passion for change and the combined fury of a whirlwind and tsunami.

And when my end finally comes, I want my epitaph to read:

BEEN THERE, DONE THAT!

ROSEMARIE P. RAFAEL

Chairperson and President
AIC Group of Companies Holding Corp.
Global FWN 100™ 2023

Lead Like the Bamboo

L ike the bamboo that spends years developing its roots before growing rapidly, Rosemarie's success in leadership has required a significant investment of time and effort. She has worked hard to make it happen, consistently developing her skills, building relationships, and refining strategies to achieve long-term success. She is also adaptable and flexible, adjusting her strategies in response to changing circumstances. She has focused on nurturing her team and creating an environment that supports growth and development. Ut (Rosemarie's nickname) excels not only with her team but also in the friendships she cultivates. Though she is often the busiest person in the world, with a mere 24 hours in a day never enough for her work, she consistently makes time to nurture our friendship. Whether it's early morning exercise walks or brief visits to my house on her way home from work, she always tries to find time. Ut has a knack for sharing little delights with me, whether it's food or something she picked up from her day. Whenever possible, we seize the opportunity to travel together, cherishing every moment we can. This is the essence of

*who Ut is—she dedicates every minute to productivity, whether it's for
her professional pursuits or for fostering meaningful friendships.*

Ida Manalo Joseph
Co-owner, Ralph's Wine and Spirits

I have just been appointed as a Member Representing the Labor Sector in the Philippine Commission on Women (PCW), formerly known as the National Commission on the Role of Filipino Women (NCRFW). This appointment is particularly meaningful to me as it connects with the rich history of Philippine feminism, women's movements, and gender mainstreaming—areas that have long been central to my work and advocacy. The Commission, as the primary policymaking and coordinating body on women and gender equality concerns, continues to build upon past efforts to advance the status of women in our society. It acts as a catalyst for gender mainstreaming, an authority on women's issues, and a powerful advocate for women's empowerment, gender equity, and equality. Receiving this appointment is a pleasant surprise, but it also feels like a natural progression in my journey, as it aligns with the recognition I've received from both local and international award-giving bodies, including the Asia CEO Awards, ASEAN Business Awards, ASEAN Women Entrepreneurs Network, and Global FWN100 Awards.

In line with this commitment, I recently had the honor of speaking at the Asia CEO Forum, where I addressed the importance of breaking the bamboo ceiling—an analogy for the invisible barriers that women, particularly in Asia, face in climbing to leadership positions. Despite the challenges and hurdles that come with being a woman in leadership, I emphasized the significance of the 6Cs principle—character, commitment, connectedness, communication, culture, and courage—as vital elements that ensure success in any organization. This principle is something I carry into all aspects of my work, including my new role with the Philippine Commission on Women, where I will continue to advocate for these values as part of our efforts to promote gender equality and empower women across the nation.

Asia CEO Forum is the largest regular business event in the Philippines and is considered one of the most important in the Asia Pacific region. Events are organized by an alliance of Filipino and international businesspeople with a mission to promote the Philippines as a premier business destination for global decision-makers. Asia CEO Forum functions as an activist to promote the activities of local and multinational organizations across Southeast Asia. Held in Manila, presenters are leaders in their industries and engaged in pursuits of significance to the entire region.

I am also a leader in the Women's Business Council Philippines (WomenBizPH), which is composed of the Philippines' top female business leaders and entrepreneurs. WomenBizpH is the leading voice of women in commerce, inspiring and empowering women in the country. Serving as the platform to discuss issues for women in business and possible government policies and solutions, WomenbizPH is the lead private sector partner of the government, particularly the Department of Trade and Industry and the Philippine Commission on Women and represents the Philippines in APEC and ASEAN events.

Bend like the bamboo

When I started my career, I did not envision myself in sales, particularly because the industry was predominantly male, and women were often seen as less capable in such roles. However, I quickly realized that to reach my career goals, I needed to overcome these barriers and embrace a sales career. It was initially challenging, especially as I had to adjust my mindset and adapt to an environment that wasn't always welcoming. But I persisted by reframing my role—not as someone who was merely selling, but as someone who was providing solutions to clients' problems. This approach, rooted in genuine care and a desire to help, allowed me to navigate the complexities of being a woman in a male-dominated industry. Discipline was key; I had to push myself initially, but over time, it became ingrained in me, shaping my work ethic and approach to business.

I studied AB International Studies at Maryknoll College. I pursued this course because I dreamed of becoming a diplomat. My degree provided a foundation, but it was not sufficient for running and managing a business, especially in an industry where I would be constantly underestimated. I chose this course because it lacked the accounting and number-focused major subjects that had always intimidated me. However, it gave me the discipline and work ethic that has been crucial throughout my career. To supplement my education, I took short courses in finance and management, including the Management Development Program (MDP) at AIM, where I was among the top ten percent of the class. This education helped me overcome the financial literacy barriers that often limit women in business, giving me the tools to understand better and grow my company.

After college, I entered the airline industry as a passenger sales agent. As a woman, I had to work harder to prove myself, learning every aspect of the travel industry. One morning, while on a call with a client who was sending overseas workers to the Middle East, I was summoned to a sales meeting. I asked for a few more minutes to finish my call, but when I knocked on the meeting room door it was locked. My boss told me I was no longer needed in the room, and I could leave. Based on a small delay, this exclusion was a stark reminder of the additional hurdles women face in the workplace, often judged more harshly than their male counterparts. Feeling deeply hurt, I returned to my desk in tears, only to receive a call inviting me to interview with the largest airfreight company in the Philippines at the time. In that moment of vulnerability, I said yes. I was hired as a sales executive and later promoted to sales manager within a year, a testament to my resilience and capability despite the gender biases I encountered.

I was comfortable in my role but circumstances I did not anticipate pushed me out of my comfort zone. I believe that God places us in positions to prepare us for greater things, even when those positions challenge the status quo, such as when I decided to open my own business during a time of national upheaval.

When I opened my air freight business in the same year Ninoy Aquino was assassinated, the country was in economic turmoil. There is no ideal time to start a business, especially as a woman in a male-dominated field. However, I believed in God's timing and felt a deep alignment with my values, which no longer matched those of the company I was working for. When I informed my British boss of my decision to leave and start my own company, he questioned, "Why be a small fish in a big pond?" I answered, "Being a small fish in a big pond offered more room for growth." This response reflects my belief in my potential and my determination to carve out a space for myself despite the systemic barriers in place.

At that time, the company I worked for was the number one IATA agent, a position it had held for many years. Five years after I left, they dropped to number two, while the company I founded, Airspeed, became the number one IATA agent. This success speaks to the power of perseverance and the importance of aligning one's work with one's values.

Grow like the bamboo

Airspeed is an end-to-end logistics solutions and express courier company that has been in the industry for over 30 years. It offers multi-modal solutions that combine air and sea freight and land transportation. We employ the right people, manage an updated system, and uphold the following values:

- ☐ Loyalty – being faithful in little things leads to being trusted,

- ☐ Integrity – doing what you say you will do

- ☐ Value of honor and respect – honoring and respecting everyone

- ☐ Excellence – doing the best so it becomes part of our DNA

- ☐ Stewardship – optimizing and maximizing our God given talents.

At Airspeed, we value our people and stakeholders. We believe that having happy employees leads to satisfied customers. This principle has guided us through various challenges, including those exacerbated by the intersections of gender, economic instability, and industry norms.

As a company, our team fulfills all of our clients' logistics needs and helps them grow their businesses. We customize our services based on their logistics requirements because we make it happen at Airspeed. I invested in the best facilities and technologies to ensure that Airspeed's cargo is handled and monitored efficiently. For example, its warehouses have CCTV cameras and alarm systems to ensure safe storage. It provides nationwide distribution, door-to-door delivery, and inter-island delivery services.

In an industry as complex as logistics, especially in a country like the Philippines with its 7,100 islands, we have faced numerous challenges, but our commitment to innovation and service has allowed us to overcome them. For instance, when many retail stores closed during the pandemic, we adapted quickly by shifting our focus to essentials and health-related products. We also expanded our services to cater to individual customers, many of whom were women managing households and businesses, navigating the same economic pressures and societal expectations I once faced.

We launched PUDO (Pick Up and Drop Off) services in collaboration with M Lhuillier and SM Markets, creating accessible service points across the country. This initiative reflects our commitment to understanding and addressing the needs of all our customers, regardless of their gender, economic status, or location.

In addition to our core logistics services, we have started working on projects like APDEC (Amazing Philippines Digital Economy Corporation) and platforms such as Speedgifts and KH-PH.com, which aim to support MSMEs and provide market access to products from various regions in the Philippines. These projects are particularly important for women entrepreneurs who often struggle to access markets due to systemic barriers.

Through these efforts, we are future-proofing not only our business but also contributing to the broader economy by addressing the needs of diverse communities, including those often marginalized in traditional business models. Our ability to adapt and innovate, driven by a deep understanding of intersectional challenges, ensures that we remain relevant and resilient in an ever-changing world.

Intersectionality Lessons

In leading Airspeed for the past 33 years, I have learned several valuable lessons that are deeply informed by my experiences as a woman in a male-dominated industry and as a leader who navigates various intersecting challenges. I first shared these lessons in a July 15, 2019 article in Manila Bulletin entitled "This logistics industry stalwart is a lady" by Bernie Cahiles-Magkilat.

First, it's crucial to continuously question whether we are doing the right things—not just for the business but for the diverse communities we serve. We must ask if our strategies and focus areas are inclusive and equitable, and whether they consider the different needs and experiences of our stakeholders. It's easy to get distracted by short-term goals, but we must stay focused on what truly matters: creating an inclusive and supportive environment where everyone can thrive.

Second, simplicity in operations and processes is key to moving things forward, but simplicity should not come at the expense of inclusivity. Streamlining processes should also make them more accessible and equitable for all employees, regardless of their background or position within the company.

Third, consulting and seeking advice from those who excel in areas where we may lack expertise is essential. As a woman in leadership, I've found that having mentors—especially other women and marginalized leaders—has been incredibly empowering. I maintain relationships with two to three business leaders who serve as my mentors. I actively pursue their guidance and listen to their experiences, which often include navigating challenges related to gender, race, and other intersectional factors. These interactions encourage me to push beyond what I thought possible and advocate for others facing similar challenges.

Fourth, I believe in fostering a culture of continuous learning that values diverse perspectives. As a voracious reader, I seek literature and resources that broaden my understanding of gender equity, racial justice, and inclusive leadership. As a hands-on manager, I ensure that my approach to seasonal logistics operations prioritizes inclusivity and equity, both for my team and our clients. I plan and pace myself, ensuring that my actions contribute to broader equity and social impact goals.

Fifth, it's also important to know when to take a break. I travel with my family, which gives me the opportunity to learn from the people and cultures of different countries. These experiences deepen my understanding of the diverse backgrounds of our clients and employees. Spending quality time with my children and husband is also essential; it reminds me of the importance of work-life balance, not just for myself but for all the women and caregivers within our organization.

Over time, I envision Airspeed becoming the preferred logistics provider in the country, highly respected by its peers and clients, and a brand synonymous with reliability, integrity, and inclusivity. I want Airspeed to be known not just as a company of integrity, but as a company that champions equity at every level.

I want my team to realize that our company's reputation is built on the people we keep. If we foster an environment of integrity, inclusivity, and excellence, these values will become habits ingrained in our corporate culture. We must focus on what matters most: adding value not only to our customers' businesses but also to their communities and lives. By building an inclusive and equitable business, we contribute to the growth and empowerment of all the communities we touch and serve.

The COVID-19 pandemic accelerated our transition from an offline traditional freight forwarder to a digitalized online service provider. The internet made this transition possible. In December 2021, I shared a YouTube video *called ICON 2021—Leveraging*

From Offline to Online, based on my experience with Airspeed. I am re-sharing these tips for transitioning from an offline to an online business. These tips cover various aspects of a digital transition, emphasizing strategic thinking, digital tools, customer engagement, and marketing.

Strategic Mindset

1. Think Outside the Box: Don't limit yourself to traditional approaches; embrace innovation and creativity. Better still, get rid of the box.

2. Engage with Your People: Prioritize the well-being of your team to build a strong internal culture. At the same time, engage with relevant external stakeholders. During COVID-19, our team prioritized helping front liners.

3. Reposition Your Brand: Adjust your business positioning to capitalize on current trends and market needs. Turn adversity into opportunity.

4. Identify a Niche: Focus on specific areas, as we did by combining food delivery with grocery services, to stand out in a crowded market.

5. Adapt to Changes: To remain competitive, stay flexible, and anticipate market shifts. Be agile to make quick decisions and plan how to execute once the decision is made. Listen to customers who need solutions for their problems.

6. Align with Values: Ensure that changes are consistent with your company's core values and culture.

Digital Transition, Tools, and Technology

7. Embrace Digital Platforms: Utilize platforms like SpeedFoodX for efficient B2C delivery a

8. Digital Solutions: Invest in digital tools, solutions, and apps to streamline operations and enhance customer experience.

9. Technology to Scale: Invest in technology that supports scaling your business operations.

10. Use a Fulfillment Platform: Implement an e-fulfillment platform for efficient order management.

11. Create an App for Resellers: Develop tools like, Pinaspeed, to help online sellers for a reliable and secure delivery.

12. Community Groups: Use platforms like Viber and create viral giveaways to build and engage with tribes or community groups.

13. Chatbox and chatbots: Use chatbox and chatbots to monitor and respond to customer inquiries in real-time.

14. Shipping Aggregators: Offer multiple shipping options through aggregators for customer convenience.

Customer-Centric Approach

15. Help Your Customers: Offer solutions that genuinely address customer pain points. Give your customers not just a product but a quality experience.

16. Transparency: Be clear about shipping charges, taxes, and any upfront costs. Provide a tracking mechanism to build trust in the product's delivery.

17. Payment Gateway Options: Provide multiple payment options to cater to different customer preferences.

18. Positive Perspective: Maintain a positive outlook, taking control of the situation with a thorough market analysis.

19. Customer Reviews: Leverage reviews to build credibility and trust in your products or services.

Marketing and Engagement

20. Content Marketing & SEO: Create relevant content that ranks well in search engines to drive organic traffic.

21. Brand Promise: Consistently deliver on your brand's quality promise to build loyalty.

22. Focus on Social Media: Engage with your audience on platforms like Facebook and Instagram to build a strong online presence.

23. Build an Email List: Cultivate a list of customers for targeted marketing and communication.

24. Upsell and Cross-sell: Increase sales by offering additional products or services to existing ones.

As I begin my appointment term with the Philippine Women's Commission, I urge you to support initiatives that build businesses, empower lives, and develop communities as a champion of women's empowerment.

MAKE IT HAPPEN!

NORA KAKILALA TERRADO

Board Member/Advisor to Boards

Global FWN 100™ 2014 & 2016

Fifty Years of Pivots and Synergies

N
ora Kakilala Terrado (or 'Noya' as she is fondly called and well known) is a Global FWN 100 honoree in 2014 and 2016. She spent five decades navigating corporate, government, and nonprofit leadership roles. Her journey is a tapestry of accomplishments woven from the character, values, talents, and skills that have shaped her from her early years up to the present. Noya has a deep understanding of how to drive positive change and excellence. She is an out-of-the-box thinker and refuses to maintain the status quo. She is driven to break stereotypes and overcome the biases that tend to marginalize. Instead, she embraces diversity and intersectionality, fostering collaboration, inclusivity, and synergy to consistently bring people and organizations to higher and higher levels of success. Framing all these qualities is her clear sense of meaning and purpose, which have allowed her to focus and prioritize her mission during different seasons of her life.

In her inspiring narrative, Noya invites us to reminisce with her as she shares parts of her life and career. I am fortunate to have been part of her life, having worked with her in the software association and *collaborated in women's initiatives during her time in government. But I am most blessed to be her friend, sharing meaningful experiences with our group of software industry lady friends, who we call the Wopees.*

Noya's generosity is evident in her narrative and we can all learn much from what she has shared. I hope our lives will not stop intersecting for many more years to come and that she will continue to inspire the next generations of leaders.

Ito Gruet
IT Entrepreneur and Co-Founder, Computer Professionals Inc.

Early Curiosity

As a child, I loved asking questions, often starting with "why." Not all my teachers had the patience to answer, but those who did quickly became my favorites. One day, my arithmetic teacher, perhaps having a bad day, dismissed my curiosity. When I got home, I told my father what had happened and asked him the unanswered question: "Why does 10 + 20 equal 30 and not more?" He replied, "Remember that it is OK to be inquisitive and to ask the right questions. In life, there are boundless possibilities; just dream, believe, and make 10 + 20 greater than 30." This response was unexpected, but it struck a deep chord with me.

Back in public primary school, most of my teachers relied heavily on memorization and repetition. While this approach did help build a foundational knowledge base for future learning, I often wished for more opportunities to understand concepts deeply. Not everyone in class had the same aptitude and abilities for memorizing multiplication tables. Those who struggled with memorization received lower grades and were unfairly regarded as slow learners by some teachers. I recall that some of my classmates, once considered slow learners, eventually became successful engineers, programmers, and business leaders. Reflecting on this, I realize that the teacher-centric culture at the time discouraged a supportive classroom environment where mistakes were valued as learning opportunities. Such an environment could have reduced anxiety and fostered confidence in pupils who struggled with memorization.

Case in Point. Empowering Intersectional Learning

My young brother faced significant challenges when he moved from the province to Manila to continue his elementary schooling. For him, it was a wake-up call that he was not on par with his classmates. He had to learn Filipino, the predominant language in Manila, and catch up with his arithmetic. Without the benefit of kindergarten and with a weak learning foundation from his primary school in the province, he struggled. He was grouped with the slow learners, but one teacher saw beyond this label. She recognized that he was at an intersectional disadvantage due to his previous lower educational standards, the new language he had to learn, and the need to integrate into a new community.

This teacher collaborated with our family to provide differentiated instruction tailored to my brother's learning style. She encouraged him to be inquisitive and coached me to tutor him using visual aids and sticks. My mother would use errands for my brother as practical, hands-on activities that integrated arithmetic lessons into real-life situations, like shopping (calculating discounts and change) and playing games that involved numbers. These methods helped my brother catch up in class and accelerate his learning. Today, my brother is thriving both at home and at work, where he heads a mission-critical function in an airline company.

Lessons Learned. My childhood experience with diverse abilities and aptitudes, dialects and regionalism, and learning structures in school have given me the perspective that unrecognized biases and the disadvantages they cause are a crucial step towards fostering empathy and inclusivity in education. Biases can perpetuate inequality. Unmasking them requires empathy—the ability to see beyond labels and recognize humanity.

Professional Foundation

As a young professional. a fresh graduate from the province, I embarked on my career journey in finance in the hallowed halls of the Philippines' top public accounting firm. There, I received the best training in auditing intricacies. But it was not just about numbers; it was about excellence woven into our D.N.A. I honed my technical skills, learned professionalism and better interaction with clients and colleagues.

In the audit trenches, I formed my opinion based on substantive evidence, and I was able to determine what were best practices or those that might be shadowed by malfeasance or misconduct. In the bigger picture, I realized that the best organizations I audited had robust compliance programs, sustained rigorous controls, and fostered a culture of ethics.

Case in Point: First Encounter on Intersectionality

Barely three years into my auditing career, I found myself navigating uncharted waters as a first-time team leader. With newfound confidence, I began formulating client recommendations based on my team's observations. These recommendations focused on continuous process improvement, strengthening checks and balances, and harnessing the power of data analytics. Our goal was twofold: to prevent fraud and address any errors or unethical behavior.

However, my supervisor tasked me with presenting these recommendations to a long-standing client. I presented to the Chief Accountant, who posed a significant challenge—not because of the content but due to my youth and relative lack of business experience. Even more troubling, she unnecessarily remarked that "corruption is, after all, an insurmountable issue in the country," which I thought was

entirely inappropriate.

My supervisor recognized the potential value of our team's insights. He encouraged me to deliver the presentation, understanding that fresh perspectives could drive positive change, even if he might have an inkling that the Chief Accountant, a seasoned professional, might be resistant.

And indeed, she was. Having been with the company for years, she knew the company well and held a position of authority. Unfortunately, her attitude during my presentation reflected complacency. She dismissed our ideas, citing our age and inexperience. When my supervisor intervened, I realized she was just concerned about the perception it would cause if our recommendations reached the client's headquarters. Things turned around when my supervisor intervened and cleared the air. I had his backing.

Lessons Learned. As a young professional, I faced the challenge of navigating differences in multiple identities, such as age and experience. This experience taught me that biases can influence interactions and perceptions. Consequently, I realized the importance of thorough preparation when interacting with clients, as resistance is common. Handling such situations diplomatically and empathetically was key, as demonstrated by my supervisor.

The chief accountant's behavior could have led me to form a negative perception of the client as an organization. Leaders set the tone for fostering a culture of diversity and inclusivity in the workplace. Demonstrating respect and openness to diverse perspectives encourages others to do the same, creating a more inclusive environment.

Age should not be a barrier to contributing valuable insights. Young professionals bring innovative solutions, and experienced individuals should recognize their potential.

Building a culture of compliance requires overcoming resistance. Leaders must actively support initiatives and challenge prevailing notions.

Negative perceptions caused by complacency can harm an organization's image. Through proactive actions and a commitment to positive change, trust can be rebuilt.

Balancing Act: Navigating Work, Family, and Shared Goals

As C.P.A.s, my husband and I knew the balance sheet at heart.

My journey as a young wife unfolded in the delicate balancing act of work and life. I made a deliberate choice to step away from professional practice and spend sixteen years within the same organization—not for the corner office or the prestige, but for something more elusive: predictability. This schedule allowed me to fulfill my roles at home while still savoring the flavors of building my career in financial management.

During this time, my husband transitioned from corporate career to entrepreneurship. Together, we wove our ambitions into the fabric of our lives in our resolve for integration--not as a cold fusion of separate spheres but as a harmonious blend where work, family, and dreams coexisted.

I chose to stay for a time on the predictable path, where the organization's clock ticked steadily. Predictability allowed me to wear the hats of wife, mother, daughter and professional without tripping over the hemlines. My husband, too, charted his course—a business owner navigating uncharted waters. Work from Home or WFH was his operating model when that was not yet commonplace. Our paths diverged, yet they intersected at shared dinners and whispered dreams.

There is value in time fusion. We realized that value wasn't a zero-sum game. It multiplied when we combined our hours judiciously. Work didn't steal from family; it enriched it. And vice versa. Our children witnessed parents who juggled workbooks and bedtime stories with equal grace. We immensely enjoyed the basketball games of our two growing sons.

Distant clan elders whispered ancient norms: "Husband, breadwinner. Wife, caregiver." But their script didn't bind us. We broke the traditional molds. We shared our financial spreadsheets and childcare duties. The lead role? It shifted like the seasons. What mattered was our shared script—the one we penned together.

Our home had a quilt of support -- grandparents, siblings, a few close friends, neighbors, and trusted domestic helpers – all stitched together. Routine tasks? Delegated. Stress? Shared. Our well-being? A collective responsibility.

We were not just husband and wife. We were co-pilots navigating storms, welcoming the sunrise, and being grateful as we watched the sunset.

Our intersectionality? A blend of ambition, love, and pragmatism. The threads of our roles wove a tapestry that whispered, "This is us."

The compass pointed toward shared goals. Not just financial milestones, but moments—first steps, late-night talks, kite-flying with the kids,

Who led? It didn't matter. We danced, sometimes tripping, but always moving forward.

Business Leadership and Organizational Change

Over time, I assumed the role of Regional Chief Financial Officer at a global I.T. consulting company headquartered in the U.S. Following the Y2K era, our company faced a significant downturn in its I.T. consulting business across Asia. I was entrusted with leading the restructuring efforts for our Asian operations—a crisis that demanded profound change and a fresh perspective on how we operated, generated revenue, created value, and conducted ourselves.

In the Philippines, I stepped into the leadership void as a necessity. With only 125 team members remaining and a handful of viable contracts, I convened our key leaders to confront the realities and explore possibilities. Fueled by an unwavering determination to succeed, our Philippine team crafted an actionable Get-Well Strategy, which we presented to our Board. Our proposal? To shift away from I.T. consulting and fully embrace the I.T. outsourcing business model. The Philippines transformed into our offshore Global Delivery Center (GDC), supporting our onshore offices, primarily in the U.S.

Ultimately, the company made a turnaround. A private equity partner injected capital to fuel our growth. The success story of our Philippine operations hinged on our ability to pivot our business model, align around a shared purpose of value creation, foster mutual trust, and tenaciously overcome challenges.

Case in Point. The Power of Inclusion: How Women Transformed Our Tech Project

In the bustling world of technology, our team embarked on a high-profile application development project. The goal? To create a system that would serve train commuters from diverse backgrounds. But there was a hitch: client approval for our solution design remained elusive, causing frustrating delays.

As we delved into the project, something caught our attention: our design team was a sea of men. It struck us like a lightning bolt—we needed diverse perspectives. So, we invited women technologists to join the fray. Among them, Mary Rose emerged as a beacon of leadership, entrusted with heading the solution design group.

Our newly balanced team thrived on candid discussions, open communication, and genuine collaboration. The women brought fresh approaches and unique viewpoints to the table. Their presence sparked creativity and ensured we understood the intricate needs of our diverse commuters. Suddenly, our project felt more alive and more attuned to the real world.

Armed with collective design thinking and software engineering brilliance, we presented our solution and technical designs to the client. The result? Their approval! In 2003, we rolled out a system that not only met the immediate needs of commuters but also addressed broader societal challenges.

Lessons Learned: From that pivotal experience, our company adopted a new mantra: assemble diverse teams. Because when women play a central role in technology, everyone wins.

304 | NORA KAKILALA TERRADO

By 2003, our company stood at a crossroads. The business needed more than just financial injections—it craved growth, people development, and an expanded market reach. However, our sales and marketing machinery resembled a bicycle trying to compete in a Formula 1 race. Meanwhile, our Philippine operations across the Pacific grappled with the same challenges. Yet, amidst the struggle, it clung to a high Net Promoter Score—a testament to our commitment to quality service.

And then, the equity partners made their move—a merger—not a mere financial transaction but an intricate weaving of strengths.

Picture it: a US-based team with Centers of Excellence in India, wielding technological prowess and boasting an investment banking client base. On the other side, a US-based team with a Global Delivery Center in the Philippines—a strong process orientation and quality assurance discipline serving clients across retail banking, healthcare, and technology sectors.

The threads of expertise, cultural nuances, and shared vision came together, stitching a more vital organization.

Case in Point. Navigating Cross-Cultural Waters: Insights from a Merger

As I stepped into the newly merged company, the Chairman greeted me warmly. I found myself as the sole woman on the Senior Management Board (S.M.B.), surrounded by a whirlwind of vibrant conversations. Most of the S.M.B. members spoke at lightning speed, and understanding them initially posed a real challenge.

The Chairman took me aside (and the others as well), generously sharing insights on cultural nuances. Filipinos and Indians—two distinct worlds—were colliding, yet their potential synergy was undeniable. He emphasized empathetic communications, providing a crash course in cross-cultural navigation.

The S.M.B. crafted a threefold mission for the integration:

1. Core Business Focus: Ensure operational stability. Keep the customer happy. Avoid disruptions forbidden.

2. Clear Vision and Strategy: Like cartographers, we meticulously mapped out our path. A vision emerged—a North Star guiding us through the merger fog.

3. Retention and Engagement: Balancing the old and the new, we retained existing talent while welcoming fresh leadership. It was a delicate dance, ensuring continuity without stifling innovation.

The Filipino team radiated *"malasakit"*—deep care and empathy. They held each other's hearts, creating a supportive ecosystem. Meanwhile, the Indian team embodied *"jugaad"*—a magical blend of innovation and resourcefulness. They could turn a paperclip into a spaceship.

We gathered for sensitivity training—not to tiptoe around landmines, but to construct sturdy bridges to make our differences our strengths—the fiery curry and the comforting adobo. Yet, beyond the flavors, we rallied around shared values: Teamwork, Respect, Integrity, and Openness. These principles guided us like compass points. By promoting these shared values, they harmonized our diverse notes.

Lessons Learned. Integration is not about erasing differences; it is about celebrating them. While there were cultural nuances, addressing any implicit biases or stereotypes that arose during cross-cultural interactions was essential. For instance, assumptions about communication styles based on nationality can perpetuate stereotypes. Not all Filipinos communicate empathetically, nor do all Indians exhibit the same problem-solving approach.

The integration phase was not easy, but we completed it. Over time, the strategic collaboration between our centers in the Philippines and India significantly enhanced service delivery, operational efficiency, and innovation. Strong change management, a growth mindset, and intentionality in account management drove this success.

Case in Point: Building One Global Team

Our tenured account with one of the largest U.S. investment banks spanned key markets worldwide. To grow the account, we strategically combined the business development expertise of our New York office with the technical and operational capabilities of our teams in India and the Philippines.

We assembled a dynamic team with diverse backgrounds, comprising solution architects, technologists, and support specialists from the Philippines and India. Gayatri, based in New York, assumed the role of lead account manager. Supporting her were Joel and Anuraj, who led the Manila and Bangalore contingents, respectively. With team members in different time zones, work can continue around the clock. This significantly speeded up project timelines and improved responsiveness to clients and stakeholders.

The combined team made a follow-the-sun operation for the mission-critical programs possible. Our footprint in the account expanded, and so did our business.

Our client appreciated that our global team mirrored their own stakeholder base. Our team members represented diverse genders, ethnicities, ages, and cultural backgrounds. This rich diversity brought a wide range of viewpoints and ideas to the table.

Our global team for this account practiced an inclusive problem-solving and decision-making process. Every voice was heard and valued. As a result, employee satisfaction and engagement soared, directly impacting overall team productivity.

Lessons Learned. Diversity and an inclusive work environment for the global team created a synergy that improved overall performance. Mirroring the client's diverse stakeholder base with our global team helped build stronger relationships and trust, contributing to our business growth.

Overall, I spent 17 fruitful years at this company going through four major pivots. Each change was challenging, but our goal was always to create value. It wasn't until our last pivot that we indeed found our stride by focusing on our strengths in the capital markets. This focus paid off when the company was acquired, thanks to our high-growth business, talented leaders, and a potent mix of onshore and offshore teams. This journey is a story of resilience, adaptability, and the power of a united global team.

My journey in this company taught me the importance of humility, openness to learning, and the power of collaboration. It reinforced that with intentionality in a diverse and inclusive work environment aligned to a shared purpose, even the most daunting challenges can be overcome.

Government Service and Advocacy

I initially thought I was ready to retire, but destiny had other plans. I was called to serve as the Undersecretary of the Department of Trade and Industry (D.T.I.), an opportunity to give back and make a lasting impact on nation-building.

My initial assignment involved supervising the D.T.I.'s management services group. Later, I had the privilege of overseeing the agency's trade and investment promotion arm. As the D.T.I. champion for Gender and Development (G.A.D.), Ease of Doing Business (E.O.D.B.), and the startup ecosystem program, I played a lead role in events during the APEC 2015 hosting year and the ASEAN 50 hosting year in 2017.

I became particularly interested in Womenomics, a strategic approach popularized in Japan that aims to harness women's untapped potential to drive economic growth and achieve gender equality.

Between 2015 and 2017, the participation of women in the Philippine economy had both positive and concerning aspects. Studies indicated significant progress pointed to these areas:

- ☐ The Philippines ranked 17th globally in closing the gender gap, with 78.4% of the overall gap closed.

- ☐ 39% of businesses had women in senior management roles.

- ☐ Approximately 58% of micro, small, and medium-sized enterprises (M.S.M.E.s) were women-led.

- ☐ Women's representation in elected positions varied: 28.57% in the House of Representatives and 25% in the Senate.

- ☐ Female public prosecutors constituted 41% of the total.

- ☐ Women held 47.09% of C.E.S. Officers (Third Level C.E.S. Positions) and 46.34% of C.E.S. Eligibles (C.E.S.E.s).

- ☐ In second-level government positions, women accounted for 66.3%.

- ☐ Third-level government positions (C.E.S.) had 42.8% women representation.

However, despite these achievements, female labor force participation remained low at 49%, compared to 76% for Filipino men. The gap has seen minimal progress since 1990, with only a 0.3 percentage point reduction since 2015. This low participation represented a missed economic growth opportunity.

Accelerating progress and addressing the barriers to women's economic empowerment is crucial. By tackling the barriers, the goal is to create a more inclusive and equitable economic environment where everyone (especially marginalized women) has the chance to thrive.

Researchers identified numerous barriers to women's economic participation in the Philippines, including financial inclusion, access to education and skills training, social norms and stereotypes, the gendered division of childcare, discrimination and bias, mobility issues (especially for rural women), and the digital divide. These barriers may stem from systemic inequalities that intersect, overlap, and exacerbate each other. For women embodying different marginalized identities—such as gender, race, social class, sexual orientation, religion, ability, and age—these challenges create unique and compounded experiences of discrimination for each person. This challenge is immense and overwhelming.

I am reminded of a quote by South African bishop and theologian Desmond Tutu, a Nobel Peace Prize recipient: "*There is only one way to eat an elephant: a bite at a time.*" With limited resources, focusing on the few but the most impactful initiatives that would solve these formidable challenges made sense. By adopting a mindset of collective effort, akin to the Filipino concept of Bayanihan, we aim to ensure that when the work is done, and the goals are achieved, everyone can proudly say, "We did it together."

Case Study 1: Digitalization through the Digital eWallet System

The D.T.I. collaborated with the private sector (specifically GCash) to promote and push for adopting a digital eWallet system aimed at the unbanked population. The adoption was slow, especially for the micropreneurs and in areas with poor internet connectivity.

By providing an eWallet option into the D.T.I.'s Business Name Registration System, the initiative served as a catalyst for adopting eWallet payment processes, particularly among micro and small entrepreneurs.

The adoption of the eWallet improved slightly, but this initiative marked a significant step towards enhancing financial inclusion and simplifying the ease of doing business.

Integrating digital payment systems into existing business processes was a catalyst for change to kickstart and drive greater adoption. Targeting the unbanked populations helped bridge the financial inclusion gap. And as I look back from my rearview mirror, the system would have caused more of a digital divide for the unbanked sector had it not been put in place before the pandemic.

Digitalization simplified the payment processes and benefited the micro and small entrepreneurs, most of whom were women.

Case Study 2: Building Community Alliances

The D.T.I. formed a strong alliance with the Go Negosyo movement, spearheaded by the Philippine Center of Entrepreneurship. Through this partnership, D.T.I.'s regional offices launched the Kapatid Mentor Me (K.M.M.E.) program, an 11-module mentorship initiative designed for business owners from the micro, small, and medium enterprises (M.S.M.E.s). The K.M.M.E. program was implemented across 101 provinces and cities, benefiting over 26,500 MSMEs. A total of 802 volunteers from the private sector through the Go Negosyo community got certified as mentors and coaches. As a result, 12,176 mentee graduates were empowered to scale up their businesses.

Deliberately structured mentoring significantly enhanced the capabilities of M.S.M.E.s that participated in the K.M.M.E. The scope had a wide reach, and the implementation across multiple regions had a broader impact. Community Support demonstrated by the mentors' volunteerism fostered a supportive entrepreneurial ecosystem.

Case Study 3: ASEAN50 2017 - Empowering M.S.M.E.s, Women, and Youth

In 2017, the Philippines hosted the 50th founding anniversary of ASEAN, marking a golden year to promote trade and investments to help generate opportunities that develop businesses and create jobs for the people. The year-long program brought together not only high-level government officials, regulators, development partners, and sectoral leaders from ASEAN and other economies for policy-related dialogues but also industry and business leaders, investors, and private equity funders.

As the Chair for the Committed for Business and Investment Promotion (C.B.I.P.), I led in organizing various conferences and events that aligned with the ASEAN Economic Pillar on the promotion of inclusive and innovation-led growth. The goal, among a few others, was to elevate the business and investment dialogues to devise deliberate actions that will accelerate the internationalization of M.S.M.E.s, mainstreaming women's economic empowerment, promoting youth entrepreneurship, and developing a dynamic ecosystem for innovation and startups.

The ASEAN50 2017 hosting year was the best platform for developing a high-profile initiative that, in the long run, could address key intersectionality issues of the marginalized groups among M.S.M.E.s and the disadvantaged women and youth. Here are some notable outcomes from the various conferences and event:

1. Empowering Women: Programs like the S.T.E.A.M. Ahead Forum and the ASEAN Women's Business Conference provided women-led startups access to support services, market access, finance, and innovative business models, directly addressing barriers to women's economic participation.

2. Supporting M.S.M.E.s: The 7Ms framework and initiatives like Go Lokal! ensured that M.S.M.E.s had access to necessary resources and support, promoting their growth and integration into the global market.

3. Youth Entrepreneurship: The ASEAN Young Entrepreneurs Carnival and ASEAN Slingshot Summit focused on fostering a dynamic ecosystem for young entrepreneurs, providing them opportunities to learn, network, and access funding.

4. Inclusive Business Practices: The Inclusive Business Summit highlighted models and government interventions that benefit women entrepreneurs, promoting gender-inclusive practices across various sectors.

5. Creative Economy: The ASEAN Creative Cities initiative aimed to make culture and creativity a driving force for sustainable development, generating employment in the creative economy and promoting urban regeneration.

In hindsight, the approach to interweave the pursuit of womenomics within the approved D.T.I. mandate and programs, projects, and activities (P.A.P.s) proved to be a reasonable way to operate within the public sector domain. By leveraging already available platforms, including viable partnerships and collaborations, the ripple effects for continuity extended even after completing the P.A.P.s and even my stint in government.

As of today, inputs gathered from the 2017 ASEAN50 helped in shaping relevant policies now enacted into law, i.e., Philippine Innovation Act (Republic Act No. 11293), Innovative Startup Act (Republic Act No. 11337), the Ease of Doing Business and Efficient Government Service Delivery Act (Republic Act No. 11032), Corporate Recovery and Tax Incentives for Enterprises (CREATE) Act (Republic Act No. 11534) and the Philippine Creative Industries Development Act (Republic Act No. 11904).

Building a New Company

Just after I retired from government, I found myself on a new mission that was time-bound and ambitious. My task was to build a company of 2,000 associates in two years across two locations. As the Founder and Country Head of a newly established healthcare IT BPM company, I assembled a key leadership team. Together, we ramped up the workforce and built the workplaces from the ground up. Our higher purpose is to create employment and people development opportunities, especially in the countryside.

Ramon and I were the first associates in this company, a fully owned subsidiary of a U.S. health benefits insurance company. In 2019, we incubated the company with a shared mission: to improve lives and communities and simplify healthcare.

Our commitment extended beyond business goals. We were determined to maintain a workforce that truly reflected our customer base—the healthcare providers and health card members. Our H.R. team worked deliberately to recruit, retain, and develop associates from diverse backgrounds in terms of gender, sexual orientation, religion, age, skills, origin, school, and abilities.

Gender-inclusive and responsive corporate policies played a pivotal role in shaping Legato's highly valued culture of diversity and inclusion. This commitment to fostering empathy and genuine care—what we call "*malasakit*"—became a defining feature of our service.

The first year was tough, but the next three years, marked by the pandemic, were even more phenomenally challenging. We faced severe supply chain issues and disruptions in workways and working arrangements. Despite these hurdles, our company grew eightfold, completing four sites across Metro Manila and Iloilo, not in two years, but five.

We were certified twice as a Great Place to Work, listed among the top Best Employers in the Philippines, and certified as a HiTrust company.

But our hypergrowth brought mixed emotions—fear and confidence, weariness and energy, burnout and vigor. It was only through collective dedication and high team performance that we achieved these unimaginable outcomes during such a difficult time.

Planning ahead, I made sure to have a leadership succession plan in place as soon as I completed my mission. After all had been done, I was turning over to my successor a ~10,000-strong workforce, not just the 2,000 we initially planned for. The organization was ready for the next stage of its growth and maturation.

Leading with Purpose: Embracing Diversity and Building Synergy

Recently, I was honored to be admitted to the Society of Fellows at the Institute of Corporate Directors, where I aim to contribute to building better boards and fostering good corporate governance. I continue to mentor startup entrepreneurs and aspiring women business leaders, finding immense joy in learning from my mentees as they, in turn, help me grow. Shaping the next generation of leaders is a privilege, and I want to equip them with the confidence, tools, and knowledge to succeed.

Reflecting on my journey, I recognize that my many failures and shortcomings have made me stronger and more resilient. Along the way, I've gained invaluable friends and supporters, teaching me that creating value through synergies is about leading with purpose and heart. My awareness of intersectionality—the overlapping and intersecting identities and social positions—has deepened my understanding of collaboration and leadership. It has influenced my approach to creating value by fostering authentic partnerships and recognizing the unique strengths that diverse perspectives bring to a team.

People learn the most from their experiences, particularly through difficulties and failures, and achieve success through tenacity, courage, and focus. Synergy is about more than just working together; it's about embracing diversity, building genuine connections, and making teams succeed by leveraging everyone's strengths. Essential life skills like empathy, collaboration, communication, critical thinking, and creativity are essential competencies that define effective leadership.

My family's love, support, and understanding have been precious and inspiring constants in my life.

I believe that my purpose in life is to create a lasting positive impact in my mission field. As a Christian and Bible reader, I am blessed with God's grace and guidance in stewarding my life. I am profoundly grateful and assured that "surely goodness and mercy shall follow me all the days of my life, and I will dwell in the house of the Lord forever" (Psalm 23:6). To God be the glory.

These days, I fully appreciate the wisdom in my father's words—**10 + 20 can indeed be greater than 30.**

MARIA BENEL CORAZON G. SE, CPA

Managing Partner
JBC Group, LLC
US FWN100™ 2011 and Global FWN100™ 2022

Life Unnoticed: Legacy Built

W*hat a beautiful tribute to the author's mother! I enjoyed the theme of the "unsung" heroine and extracting the extraordinary out of an untold story. Stories such as these honor women who have paved the path for so many of us to trailblaze, pioneer, and kick down doors previously slammed in our faces and who center women who persevered during times when equal rights were still a pipedream for so many. Indeed, we are in changing times when equity is demanded by an ever-increasing chorus of justice-centered voices.*

Kristine Custodio Suero
Vice Chair/Commissioner, County of San Diego Commission
on the Status of Women and Girls

There comes a time when life-changing moments in history happen unnoticed. Many moments in women's history have never been told, often by design, especially in a society where male dominance is the norm. Women's achievements, leadership, courage, and strength are as vital as men's.

Times have changed. We now often hear of women's success stories in many outlets. Doors have opened for us, and across the planet, we often hear of women breaking the bamboo ceiling. And yes, for us Asian women, in my opinion, it is a harder barrier to break as we have the double disadvantage of being a woman minority.

Many stories of success come at a price, especially for women. To begin with, we are at a disadvantage. Saddled with stereotypes of weakness, there is often an expectation that we cannot achieve as good as men can. Many of us are expected to bear the child-rearing obligations while our partners work. Many of us are not expected to speak up. Many of us are not expected to succeed, period.

Put this in context of 1932, in a far way American colony called the Philippines. Put this further in a rural community where women are expected to be able to only do certain things, only hold certain jobs, and only compete with men *at their own risk*.

There was no social media to self-promote. There was no television to watch. There was only the newspaper or radio, and at best, often word of mouth as the only opportunity to hear about women's stories of success.

Finally, before this last generation, women-centric recognitions were few and far between. Trailblazers were limited to those whose life experiences were highlighted by stories important to advance media goals and profitability.

I am describing a time when a woman's personal struggle was limited to discussions among their circle of friends. It was a time when, despite an emerging class of newly liberated women in the West, those in the East were still struggling.

There comes a time when one story emerges as a surrogate for the multitude of disparate stories—a story that weaves through how we as women could be. For example, to get inspired by a person choosing to be unknown, their legacy is nevertheless built.

This is the story of Commissioner Josefina Garcia Se, a woman who toiled in the background and, while doing so, achieved success through those she helped and worked for while achieving her own success. This story is extraordinary because it is the story of a woman who was a pioneer and excelled in a male-dominated world.

Driven by her faith to make a difference in not only the lives of her immediate family but, more importantly, the lives of the people who helped her raise her children and the people who worked for her, she positively impacted the lives of millions of the underprivileged and vulnerable Filipinos, especially farmers, through serendipity, grit, and determination.

Commissioner Josefina Garcia Se's story is not a Hollywood story, but it is a made-for-life story worth emulating, and God guided her along the way!

Unexpected News

It was November 1997. I was about to return home to Los Angeles after a relaxing European pilgrimage. The day we were to part, my parents expressed concern about not having someone special in my life. When my mom was my age, she was already raising three of my siblings. And there I was, still looking. Nothing was wrong with that, but was I concentrating too much on one aspect of my life?

But fate had it that our trip to Fatima and Lourdes and Mom's weekly prayers in Baclaran Church in the Philippines led me to meet my future husband the day after I arrived in Los Angeles. Cris and I got married in December 1998. Twenty-five years later, my mom had something to look forward to--and rightfully so! Only 35 percent of American couples reach their silver wedding anniversaries.

Mom was not able to travel long distances anymore. To prepare, we thought it appropriate in thanksgiving to Mother Mary and God that my family—JP, Cris, and I—retrace our journey through the 1997 pilgrimage sites. Using technology, I brought Mom back to Fatima and Lourdes during Holy Week 2023. Our goal was to be with her and the rest of our family for our 25th Wedding anniversary later in the year. December 2023 was a little over a year after Mom's 90th milestone birthday.

The news on Easter Eve came so suddenly. We were talking to mom the night before. She was about to leave the hospital that morning from a short non-emergency confinement. Then I got a call from my siblings. *"Mom is gone. Mom has joined Dad in heaven."*

I succumbed to a fetal position, remembering those moments when I last saw her to celebrate her birthday just six months earlier. I wasn't sure if it was the last time. And it was.

Crying my heart out, I remembered fond memories of Mom sitting by me after her long day's work in the office. I remembered the trips with Mom throughout the Philippines when she was a Commissioner to meet with farmers. I remembered her as a great listener. I remembered my talks with her during breakfast and how she reminisced about her childhood in Guinobatan, Albay. I remembered her struggles while growing up and her moments of personal and professional triumph despite those challenges. As those moments flashed in my mind, I felt that I was the one who passed away. My life flashed quickly before me, but my mom was also with me.

By then, I realized that my mom was not just my hero but an unsung heroine to many. I realized that her unique story of a woman who could do it all in the circumstances that she went through needed to be told.

Mom may be physically gone, but her spirit lives on.

My Mom Rocks as an Empowered Career Woman

My mom, a devout Catholic, lived her purpose. She embodied St Agnes Academy, her Alma Mater's motto *"Ora Et Labora!"* Living a balanced life dominated by neither work nor prayer, my mom found an insatiable gratification in being of service to others. Because of her burning passion to be a *"**Man for Others**,"* she broke the barriers in a male-dominated society with her courage, fierceness & tenacity. She served as a public servant for almost four decades, relentlessly championing the cause of the poor and disadvantaged Filipinos, especially farmers.

Here's a little more about her amazing career. After passing the bar in 1958, she was appointed an Agricultural Tenancy Mediator at the Tenancy Mediation Commission. She served in that capacity until 1963. The first woman appointed to that position from 1963 to 1964, she then served as Special Attorney of the Office of the Agrarian Council from 1964 to 1968. Soon after, she was promoted to Senior Special Attorney of the Office of the Agrarian Council.

In 1968, she was the youngest District Judge of the Court of Agrarian Relations ever appointed. Then, in 1982, President Ferdinand Marcos, Sr. handpicked her as the Commissioner Chairman with the rank of Court of Appeals Justice, Commission on Land Settlement of Land Problems (COSLAP). In this position, she was also honored by President Fidel Ramos. With several satellite offices nationwide, she oversaw the resolution of land issues across the Philippines for 11 years before her retirement.

For the years she was at COSLAP, she would listen intently to all the workers who toiled the land and whose fruits benefited only the landowner. She would pause at those moments and think that nothing could be wrong with that, right? But then again, in a feudal country like the Philippines, what rights do farmers have other than the opportunity to share the richness of the soil they till equitably?

I knew all of this because I was there. I sat through many of those consultations as a witness to life-changing moments of historic significance. In the eyes of many, these events may not be grand in scale, but in the eyes of a farmer who has nothing, this was everything.

My Mom led with compassion, not with an iron fist. She earned her staff's respect, loyalty, commitment, and love, thereby creating a positive, caring, and productive work culture. She was a Mother Hen, more than a Boss, who always looked after her staff's best interests. Long after she retired, she went to great lengths to prevent her staff's displacement by personally seeking agency openings that could absorb them when COSLAP was finally abolished.

My Mom: The Empowered Daughter

My Mom was the eldest among all her siblings. With a blind father and a homemaker mother, she became a parent to her four siblings at a very young age. She became her father's eyes, constantly accompanying him to meet influential people in government. He endorsed her to work for these people who she also met in his practice as a lawyer before glaucoma totally impaired his vision. While working for then-Senator Quintin Paredes, my mom was able to pursue law as a working student until she passed the Philippine Bar.

Maybe this is why she is so keen to see other people succeed. Blessed by the professional opportunities she experienced, she turned around and became an instrument of opportunity for others.

My Mom mustered all her strength to achieve the most significant outcomes. Powered by a new career, she created a life of financial modesty and fiscally supported her siblings.

This sliver of her story reminds me of our overseas Filipino workers. They toil long and hard to support those they left in their barrios. Through the sacrifices they endure every day, they provide a better life for their own families. My mom was the "Bagong Bayani" of her time. A term coined only in 1988, "Bagong Bayani" was my mom's reality when she was a young professional.

She successfully shepherded her siblings to success, who also became successful professionals. One became an accountant, and another worked in the Philippine government. Two became lawyers, with one of them topping the Philippine Bar.

But my mom was not a one-trick pony. Later in life, I learned that she was also a track and field athlete while she was in school. Knowing this, I realized that her athletic skills helped her master time management and strategic skills. She was able to juggle her multiple professional and personal responsibilities while maximizing the results that she wanted to see.

Working, competing, and learning. My mom was able to masterfully and seamlessly achieve success.

My Mom: The Empowered Wife

We are all human beings. While some can live alone, others fall in love—and fall in love in a big way. I looked at my Mom and Dad's more than 50 years of marriage and tried very hard to understand and dissect how that relationship clicked. Through that search, I realized that three things really mattered between them: respect, empowerment, and, above all, God-centered love.

My dad was already a successful lawyer when he met my mom. My mom was already set in her career when she met my dad. But that did not get in the way of their relationship. They just respected that, as a couple, they could capitalize on their histories and work together to rear a happy, cohesive, and God-fearing family. There was that respect to not compete. It was fine whether my mom earned more than my dad. It was fine whether my mom had more recognition and opportunities than my dad. It was fine that my mom was very close to at least two Philippine Presidents.

What mattered to my mom and dad was that they were life partners. What mattered to my mom was a happy family. What mattered to my mom was to see my dad succeed and everyone else.

As the famous adage goes, *"Behind every successful man is a strong woman."* This holds true for my parents. My mom was a driving force behind my dad, Judge Benito Se's notable political and judicial career. She would always be supportive and respectful of his decisions. A case in point was when Dad decided to enter the dangerous world of Philippine politics. Mom tirelessly campaigned for Dad and represented him in campaign events, especially when conflicting schedules for Dad to personally show up were unavoidable. Their teamwork paid off, catapulting Dad as Vice-Mayor of Legazpi City, Albay, in 1971.

After his political career, my mom helped my dad seek Supreme Court appointment opportunities and transition back to his calling as a member of the Philippine judiciary. My dad was eventually appointed as a Regional Trial Court Judge in three major cities of Metro Manila: Pasay, Manila, and Quezon City. For Mom, no mountain is high enough to conquer through drive, perseverance, determination, passion, and faith in one's worth and capabilities.

My Mom: The Empowered Mom and Grandmother

Mom defied the traditional societal role of women in her generation. Back then, women were only mainly expected to manage the household, primarily as wives and mothers. She was a career woman throughout her life. However, she was able to keep a healthy balance between family and career.

Admittedly, she was not the typical mom you would find in the kitchen, busy cooking a sumptuous meal for her family. She fulfilled her wife and motherly responsibilities with the full support of our *kasambahays* (household helps) who we treated as family. She supported many of them to pursue their own education and careers. She paid for their education while helping Mom care for us all. With Mom's support, many of them finished high school, and many of them finished college and went on to build their own careers. One of them, Nellie Buzar, even became a successful accountant in the US.

We all felt her role as an empowered Mom as she juggled the demands of motherhood. She found time to be excitingly present in all of our scholastic and extra-curricular events. Despite her unimaginable schedule, she found time to sit with _each_ one of my siblings and me after a grueling time at work. She kept going until we mastered each one of those day's lessons. She actively participated in our growth, supporting, inspiring, and guiding us to shape our lives. She succeeded in all of this while making successful strides in her judicial career.

As a career woman, she contributed substantially to our household income. My parents sent us to the best Philippine schools to pursue professional studies after college and live comfortably. She deeply inculcated in us the value of education and the value of dreaming big. Our life lesson was beyond inspiration!

Her conscious effort to guide us on the career path was not in vain. All her children became successful professionals. Two of her daughters became lawyers; one was also a topnotcher in the Philippine Bar. Her older son finished law and eventually became a high-ranking Philippine Immigration Officer. Her youngest son earned a prestigious American MBA degree. I became a California Certified Public Accountant and am now enjoying the fruits of innovative entrepreneurship.

Mom's influence has transcended how we have raised our children and even her great-grandchildren. All 13 of her grandchildren and great-grandchildren are now on their way to successful careers in law, medicine and public health, advertising and marketing, entrepreneurship, engineering, and supply chain and logistics. Our son, JP, is the engineer!

Mom's relationship with JP was very endearing and special because we lived across the Pacific Ocean from each other. Though the distance was far, she made it a special point to ensure he felt her love when we visited. Even though 12 of the 13 grandchildren were in the Philippines, she made it known that JP was the *"not-so-secret"* favorite by putting up many of his photos in the living room for everyone to see. That gesture is only a tiny glimpse into the attention and care she put into her grandchildren.

The Sign

It was time to bid farewell. We were gathered around Mom's casket to see her for the last time. We must be strong.

I share the last notes I wrote for her:

> *Dear Mom, now that you have passed, your life has led me to become the best person that I am today. As a woman of color in a foreign land, I draw inspiration from what I have witnessed during my lifetime with*

you. I was not able to imagine then how powerful those life experiences were in shaping my womanhood. While life has taken me to start a new life in a distant land, I am able to live a life of simplicity, start a wonderful family, and become a community advocate using the lessons I learned from you. I will miss your hugs, your kisses, and most especially that smile. That wonderful smile! I love you!

After Mom's cremation, we went back to the crematorium and were greeted with a surprise. The Crematorium Director showed us Mom's remains and pointed to a large piece of my mom's unburned and intact green bone. I was personally confused about what that meant.

Green bones after cremation are believed to be a symbol of good luck. In our culture, green bones are also thought to be found in individuals who were good people during their lifetime and carried no nastiness in their hearts. We welcomed Mama Nel's last gift to us, and this sign confirmed everything I knew about my mom.

There are countless unknown outcomes of Mom's lifelong work. We will never be able to measure the full effect of those impacts on her family, her children, and the rest of society. However, if the stories we heard from everyone during her wake are any indication, those impacts are deeply rooted. They will continue to make a difference in Philippine society for generations to come.

Her life, until now, went unnoticed. Hers is a surrogate of millions of other women's stories, untold but their legacy built.

Mom, rest in peace knowing your life's story lives. Forever!

SYNTHESIS

Synthesis: Leading with Intersectionality – Crucibles, Champions, Glocal Leadership, and Legacies

L eading with intersectionality involves navigating complex layers of identity—such as race, gender, and culture—and leveraging personal and professional experiences to drive inclusive, transformative leadership. The themes of crucibles, champions, glocal leadership, and legacies collectively form a powerful framework for understanding how intersectionality shapes leadership and influences long-term impact.

Marily Mondejar's *In Filipina Women Leaders: Disrupting Stereotypes* examines how Filipina women, both in the Philippines and across the global diaspora, challenge deeply ingrained stereotypes through intersectional leadership. She ends her narrative with a challenge:

> *Our work is about individual achievement and lifting our global community. By embracing our intersectional identities and experiences, we're not just changing our lives – we're reshaping the world's understanding of leadership and creating more inclusive, equitable societies.*

Crucibles: Transformation Through Adversity

Crucible experiences are transformative challenges that shape a leader's character and approach:

- ☐ Deepened Empathy: Leaders who have faced significant challenges often develop a deeper understanding of the complex realities others face, particularly those with intersecting marginalized identities. This empathy fosters inclusivity.

- ☐ Catalyst for Change: These experiences can serve as turning points, inspiring leaders to advocate for intersectional inclusivity and address systemic inequalities within their organizations.

Like metals refined by extreme heat, crucible experiences forge stronger and more resilient leaders. Like a vessel that withstands extreme heat to refine metals, these transformative moments shape leaders' identities and leadership styles. Their experiences brought forth "gold." Instead of melting into insignificance and breaking under pressure, Filipina women leaders have extracted strength and wisdom from their most trying moments. These experiences compel leaders to question societal norms, reshape their leadership identity, and advocate for systemic change. Intersectional leaders emerge from these trials with deeper empathy and clearer purpose, better equipped to challenge injustices.

Intersectionality and crucibles define the journeys of remarkable women who have navigated challenges shaped by race, gender, culture, and personal adversity. Their stories reveal how they overcame their own crucibles—moments that tested and redefined their leadership and sense of purpose

Charina Amunategui's narrative explores her struggle with self-doubt and anxiety, illustrating the intersection of her identity as a Filipina in the high-stakes world of finance. Her internal battles became crucibles that forged her confidence and leadership journey.

Similarly, Sofia Aragon's experience in public policy and nursing reflects the intersection of race and gender as she navigated leadership roles in predominantly white spaces. Her crucible was the constant confrontation with racial and gender bias, which fueled her resolve to advocate for inclusion and diversity.

Maria Santos-Greaves explores the mental health crucible, reflecting on the impact of clinical depression and the importance of mental fortitude in navigating life's challenges, especially as a Filipina navigating cultural transitions.

Grace Gorospe Jamon's narrative, "By Grace, Through Grace," embodies a spiritual crucible. Her capacity for compassion and leadership in diverse spaces comes from her deep connection to her Kapampangan identity and unshakable grace.

Isabelita Manalastas-Watanabe's journey through the labyrinth of race and gender in Japan highlights the intersection of her identity as a Filipina and a woman in a foreign land, where her crucible moments in both personal and professional spheres shaped her into a triumphant leader.

These women's stories showcase how intersectionality informs their crucible experiences, forging their resilience and leadership in ways that allow them to transcend personal challenges and leave a lasting impact on their communities.

Champions: Advocating for Equity and Inclusion

To lead with intersectionality, leaders must actively champion the inclusion and advancement of marginalized groups:

- ☐ Active Advocacy: Leaders can leverage their influence to highlight and address the unique challenges faced by those with intersecting identities. This could involve pushing for policy changes, promoting inclusive practices, and ensuring representation.

- ☐ Mentorship and Support: By mentoring individuals from diverse backgrounds and advocating for their opportunities, leaders help dismantle barriers and create pathways for success, demonstrating a commitment to intersectional equity.

Intersectionality is pivotal in creating champions—leaders who use their platforms to advocate for marginalized communities. These champions confront social and systemic inequalities by leveraging their intersecting identities and using their leadership roles to foster equity and inclusion. They actively mentor and uplift others, creating pathways for future leaders to thrive.

Intersectionality and the role of champions are key themes that emerge in these compelling narratives of leadership, resilience, and advocacy. Each individual's journey highlights the powerful impact of intersecting identities—be it race, gender, profession, or socio-economic background—on their capacity to lead and champion change, the way they treat people, and the values they impart in their communities and beyond.

Dr. Regina Berba's story of leadership during the COVID-19 pandemic underscores how women at the Philippine General Hospital became champions of hope and healing. Navigating the intersection of gender, cultural expectations, and professional demands, these women united to combat an unprecedented global crisis, embodying resilience and compassion.

Kristine Custodio Suero's reflection on overcoming being underestimated demonstrates the power of intersectionality in leadership. As a Filipina in the legal field, her journey showcases the need for solidarity among women to break through isolation and take up space.

Ellen Samson's quiet strength as a leader in dementia care advocacy and entrepreneurship highlights how intersectionality can fuel transformation. Starting from a position of sacrifice, shaped by cultural and gender expectations, she emerged as a champion for her community, turning personal struggles into a legacy of service. Ellen Samson's work in dementia care advocacy and entrepreneurship demonstrates how personal struggles and cultural expectations can fuel leadership driven by compassion.

Finally, Judge Rohanee Zapanta's approach to justice is shaped by her Filipino heritage and immigrant background, allowing her to see beyond surface-level issues and champion fairness and compassion in her legal work.

These stories illustrate how champions are forged through the complex layers of identity and experience. By navigating and embracing their intersectionality, these women have become powerful advocates for equity, justice, and inclusion, leaving a lasting impact on their communities and fields.

Glocal Leadership: Navigating Global and Local Contexts

Glocal leadership integrates global perspectives with local realities, an essential skill for leaders operating across diverse cultural landscapes:

☐ Contextual Awareness: Intersectionality must be understood and applied differently in various cultural and local contexts. Glocal leadership involves adapting global principles of diversity and inclusion to fit the specific needs and dynamics of local environments.

☐ Cultural Sensitivity: Leaders must recognize how intersectional issues manifest differently in various settings and ensure their strategies are culturally sensitive and locally appropriate. This might mean addressing specific local challenges while drawing on global best practices.

Glocal leadership is about integrating cultural sensitivity with global best practices. Glocal leaders navigate the intersectionality of race, gender, and nationality, adapting their strategies to fit the specific needs of local communities while drawing on their global experiences. This leadership approach ensures that their work remains relevant and impactful across both local and international contexts.

Intersectionality and glocal leadership are central themes in the narratives of these remarkable women, whose lives reflect the blending of personal identity with global experiences. As Filipinas navigating diverse cultural landscapes and intersecting identities, they each embody resilience, adaptability, and a commitment to leadership that transcends geographic and societal boundaries.

Myla Arceno, for example, balances her Filipino heritage and immigrant experience in the UK, where she faces the dual challenges of gender and race in a predominantly white, male-dominated environment. Her journey reflects the importance of advocating for diversity and inclusion while holding onto the roots that shape her leadership style.

Similarly, Dr. Maria Africa Beebe's career as an international development advisor showcases how cultural and gendered intersections influence her work across various global settings. Her leadership, grounded in her Filipino identity, embraces the complexities of working across diverse socio-political environments, exemplifying glocal leadership in action.

Dr. Denise Viardo Koh's narrative explores the intersecting layers of racial, ethnic, and cultural identity as a Chinese Filipina in Canada, navigating the complexities of belonging and identity in both professional and personal spheres.

Donna Avellana Künzler and Marla De Castro-Rausch further illustrate how Filipinas abroad can thrive by embracing their dual identities, blending their Filipino heritage with the global cultures they inhabit.

These narratives highlight that glocal leadership is more than succeeding in international contexts. It's about embracing one's unique intersections—be it race, gender, or cultural background—and using them to lead with empathy, inclusivity, and a deep understanding of diverse perspectives. As these women demonstrate, intersectionality informs their personal identities and leadership, enabling them to create meaningful impact both locally and globally.

Legacies: Building a Future of Inclusivity and Justice

Legacy building in intersectional leadership is about creating enduring, positive change:

- ☐ Long-Term Impact: Leaders should focus on embedding intersectional values into the fabric of their organizations, ensuring that these principles endure long after their tenure.

- ☐ Institutionalizing Change: Building a legacy involves making intersectional inclusion a core aspect of organizational culture, policies, and practices so that the organization continues to advance these values in the future.

- ☐ Inspiring Future Leaders: By modeling intersectional leadership, current leaders can inspire and mentor the next generation of leaders to continue this work, ensuring that the commitment to intersectionality remains strong.

Intersectionality also plays a vital role in shaping legacies. Leaders leave behind legacies grounded in equity and social justice, shaped by their experiences of navigating systemic barriers. Their work builds lasting systems that empower future generations. Leaders who focus on legacy building institutionalize intersectional values, embedding them into the fabric of their organizations and communities. This ensures that the work of creating more inclusive, just, and equitable spaces continues long after they've passed the torch.

Intersectionality and legacies are woven deeply into the stories of individuals whose lives reflect the complex interplay of gender, race, class, and cultural heritage. In narratives like those of Mary Joy Canon Abaquin and Rhodora Fresnedi, we see how personal and professional paths are shaped by the challenges of navigating societal norms, systemic inequities, and generational expectations. These women demonstrate how their intersecting identities—be it as educators, leaders, or advocates—have informed their commitment to social change, empowerment, and building a more inclusive future. Their legacies, often born out of adversity, show the transformative power of resilience and the importance of creating spaces for equity and justice.

Similarly, the stories of Lorna Patajo-Kapunan, Rosemarie Rafael, and Nora Kakilala Terrado highlight the intersectionality of gender, race, and professional ambition. These women, from diverse sectors, have broken barriers in their fields, addressing the deep-rooted challenges of inequality while advocating for systemic change. Whether through law, humanitarian work, entrepreneurship, or public service, their narratives underscore the importance of empathetic, inclusive leadership grounded in marginalized communities' lived experiences.

Lastly, Benel Se-Liban's tribute to her mother, Josefina Garcia Se, reminds us of the often-unseen legacies women leave behind. In a male-dominated society, Josefina's quiet yet impactful work as a public servant is a testament to the enduring influence of women who lead with purpose and compassion, even when history fails to recognize them. Across all these narratives, intersectionality not only shapes individual experiences but also fosters legacies that champion justice, inclusion, and hope for future generations.

Integrating Crucibles, Champions, Glocal Leadership, and Legacy Building

Intersectional leaders create a sustainable leadership model by integrating crucible experiences, championing intersectional causes, practicing glocal leadership, and focusing on legacy building. These elements reinforce each other, enabling leaders to address immediate inequalities while creating lasting systems of change. Such leaders are empathetic, culturally aware, and committed to advocating for marginalized communities, focusing on building a legacy of equity, justice, and inclusion for future generations.

By drawing on their crucible experiences, championing intersectional causes, applying glocal leadership, and focusing on legacy building, leaders develop a holistic and enduring approach to leadership. This ensures that intersectionality remains a central part of organizational operations, responsive to both global trends and local needs.

Ultimately, **DISRUPT 5.0: Filipina Women Leading with Intersectionality** is a testament to the transformative power of intersectional leadership. Through the crucibles they endure, the champions they become, the glocal leadership they practice, and the legacies they build, these leaders embody resilience and purpose. Their stories inspire future generations to embrace intersectionality, challenge the status quo, and lead with empathy and inclusivity in a globalized world.

ACKNOWLEDGEMENTS

This book required a *bayanihan*, collaborative effort made possible by the following:

☐ Marily Mondejar, Founder, and CEO of the Foundation of Filipina Women's Network, provided executive oversight.

☐ Twenty contributing authors share their life experiences, emphasizing the importance of understanding how race, gender, class, and other identities influence leadership styles, access to leadership opportunities, and their challenges as leaders.

☐ FWN Lifetime members Adela "Delle" Sering, Angelica Berrie, Fe Punzalan, Loida Nicolas-Lewis, Maria Benel Corazon G. Se, Shirley Raguindin, Sonia Delen, and Susie Quesada provided updates on their leadership journeys since becoming lifetime members.

☐ For book cover design, Lucille Lozada Tenazas, Global FWN100™ 2013, and Henry Wolf Professor of Communication Design & Associate Dean of Art, Media and Technology, Parsons The New School for Design, and her associate, Yu Fu.

☐ Franklin M. Ricarte (Draft Orange), Social Media and Tech Guru, updated the Filipina Leadership website http://www.filipinaleadership.org/ and provided various media communications support.

☐ Georgitta "Beng" Puyat for underwriting the limited edition printing for DISRUPT 2.0, 3,.0, and 4.0.

☐ Carol Enriquez, MD, for printing the FWN magazine from 2018 till now.

☐ Our FWN and external peer reviewers who did a blind review and provided comments, recommendations for improvement, suggestions for edits, and previews – Edith Winterhalter, Velma Veloria, Thelma Boac, Leith Casel-Schut, Liberty Fajutrao, MD MSCE, Anne S. Bautista, Esq., Janice Jimenez, Lory Jarvina, Mayor Juslyn Manalo, Parwana Paikan, Dr. Katrina Leong, Pamela Gotangco, Carmina Aldana, Cynthia Rapaido, Ed.D., Marily Orosa, Ida Manalo Joseph, Kristine Custodio Suero.

☐ Our uber FWN Senior Fellow Isabelle Santiago.

Other *kapwa* global Filipinas are too numerous to mention here who gave us support in spirit and cheer us on.

Maraming salamat!

APPENDIX A

REFERENCES

Abetz, J. & Moore, J. (2018). Visualizing intersectionality through a fractal metaphor. *Routledge eBooks*, 31–43. https://doi.org/10.4324/9781351209793-3

Abrera-Mangahas, M.A. (1998). *Violence against women migrant workers: The Philippine experience.* International Labor Organization. https://pssc.org.ph/wp-content/pssc-archives/Philippine%20Migration%20Research%20Network/Filipino%20Workers%20on%20the%20Move_Trends,%20Dilemmas%20and%20Policy%20Options/04_Violence%20Against%20Women%20Migrant%20Workers_The%20Phil.%20Experience.pdf

Aguila, A.N. (2015). The Filipino, Diaspora and a Continuing Quest for Identity. *University of the Philippine Diliman, 11*(2). https://journals.upd.edu.ph/index.php/socialsciencediliman/article/view/4798

Asis, R. (2006). *The Impact of Overseas Filipino Workers on the Philippine Economy.* https://www.dfat.gov.au/sites/default/files/philippines_study.pdf

Aspinwall, N. (June 2019). *We are Filipinos, and we hate China': China's influence in the Philippines, and backlash against Tsinoys.* The China Project. https://thechinaproject.com/2019/06/06/we-are-filipinos-and-we-hate-china-backlash-against-tsinoys/

Aquino, K. (2017). *Racism and resistance among the Filipino diaspora: Everyday anti-racism in Australia*. Routledge. https://www.routledge.com/Racism-and-Resistance-among-the-Filipino-Diaspora-Everyday-Anti-racism-in-Australia/Aquino/p/book/9780367787219?srsltid=AfmBOopbop7ltXxILu-E37b_2JeofUuktqh8wyGBeDScu9J-wxHnqFrO

BAU Global. (2015). *…to cultivate global citizens that feel obligated to create innovative solutions for their communities and the World to achieve a prosperous and sustainable future.* United Nations Sustainable Development Goals framework.

Beebe, M. (2017). DISRUPT 1.0. Filipina Women: Proud. Loud. Leading without a Doubt. Filipino Women's Network. *CreateSpace Independent Publishing Platform.* ISBN 1505658446.

Bennis, W., & Thomas, R. J. (September 2022). Extraordinary leaders find meaning in—and learn from—the most negative events. Like phoenixes rising from the ashes, they emerge from adversity stronger, more confident in themselves and their purpose, and more committed to their work. Such transformative events are called crucibles—a severe test or trial. Crucibles are intense, often traumatic—and always unplanned. Harvard Business Review. https://hbr.org/2002/09/crucibles-of-leadership

Brucker, K., Whitaker, N., Morgan, Z. S., Pettit, K., Thinnes, E., Banta, A. M., & Palmer, M. (2019). Exploring Gender Bias in Nursing Evaluations of Emergency Medicine Residents. *Academic Emergency Medicine.*

Buchanan, C. (2018). *I truly believe that it's all of the hard times that make you step up to the next level, and that's what makes you a champion.* BrainyQuote. https://www.brainyquote.com/quotes/caroline_buchanan_754467

Bustos-Choy, F. (2009). Narratives on the impact of colonialism on the lives of modern-day Filipino American women in the workplace. *California Institute of Integral Studies.* http://rizalls.lib.admu.edu.ph:8080/proquestfil/3354490.pdf

Cagaitan, M.S. (2013). Behind the veils of industry: Contesting the victim discourse surrounding Filipino mail-order brides. *The McNair Scholars Journal of the University of Washington, 15.*

Canada, S. (April 2021). *A labour market snapshot of South Asian, Chinese and Filipino Canadians during the pandemic.* https://www150.statcan.gc.ca/n1/en/daily-quotidien/210521/dq210521b-eng.pdf?st=n9jsxF4T

Center for Creative Leadership (CCL). (2015). *Benchmarks by design.* https://www.ccl.org/leadership-solutions/leadership-development-tools/leadership-assessments/benchmarks-360-assessments/

Cheney, I., & Shattuck, S. (2020). *Picture a Scientist.* https://www.pictureascientist.com/

Chico, S.S. (2022). *Breaking Barriers: The Rise of Filipina Founders with Unshakeable Confidence.* PhilDev. https://www.phildev.org/news/breaking-barriers-the-rise-of-filipina-founders-with-unshakeable-confidence/

Chinese Filipinos (April 2024). Wikipedia. https://en.wikipedia.org/wiki/Chinese_Filipinos

Choy, C.C. (2003). Empire of care: Nursing and migration in Filipino American history. *Duke University Press*, 272. https://doi.org/10.2307/j.ctv11hpnv7

Collas-Monsod, S. (November 2018). *Why Filipinos distrust China.* Inquirer.net. https://opinion.inquirer.net/117681/why-filipinos-distrust-china

Commission on Filipinos Overseas. (2023). *Number of Overseas Filipinos.* https://cfo.gov.ph/

Crenshaw, K. (2013). Mapping the margins: Intersectionality, identity politics, and violence against women of color. The public nature of private violence. *Routledge*, 93-118. https://www.jstor.org/stable/1229039

Crenshaw, K. (2019). "Reach everyone on the planet....": Kimberlé Crenshaw and intersectionality. *Gunda Werner Institute in the Heinrich Böll Foundation and the Center for Intersectional Justice (CJI).* https://doi.org/10.25530/03552.11

Decome, M. (2016). The Rise of the Chinese Villain: Demonic Representation of the Asian Character in Popular Literature (1880–1950). M. Decome, *Intercultural Masquerade*, 119-133. Springer.

De Guzman, L.E.P. (May 2017). *Female powerhouses sound off on what it's really like to be a woman*. Business World. https://www.bworldonline.com/ sparkup/2017/05/30/143807/female-powerhouses-sound-off-on-what-its-really-like-to-be-a-woman/#google_vignette

De Jesus, M.L. (2005). Pinay power, peminist critical theory: theorizing the Filipina/ American experience. *Psychology Press.* https://catalogue.nla.gov.au/ catalog/3562448

Dominguez, M. (2022). *The Positive and Negative Impacts of Migration on the Philippines.* https://www.oecd-ilibrary.org/migration-and-education-in-the-philippines_5jfvqfvmdd24.pdf?itemId=%2Fcontent%2Fcomponent% 2F9789264272286-10-en#:~:text=Migration%20and%20remittances%20 have%20the%20potential%20to%20play%20an%20important,take%20 up%20unskilled%20jobs%20abroad.

Dunn, J. C. & Jimmie, M. (2018). Transgressing Feminist Theory and Discourse. *Routledge eBooks.* https://doi.org/10.4324/9781351209793

Ensler. E. (July 2005). *What security means to me.* TED Talks. https://www.ted.com/ talks/eve_ensler_what_security_means_to_me

Garcia, T.M.R. (2020). Violence against women in the Philippines. *Norwegian University of Life Sciences.* https://hdl.handle.net/11250/2678663

Graham, C. (2011). The Impact of Migration on the Philippines. Retrieved from https://www.ncbi.nlm.nih.gov/pmc/articles/PMC3229683/

Grothe, T. (April 2024). *Identity and Migration.* Social Science Libre Text. https:// socialsci.libretexts.org/Courses/Butte_College/Exploring_Intercultural_ Communication_(Grothe)/03%3A_Identity_and_Intercultural_ Communication/3.03%3A_Identity_and_Migration

Halagao, P.E. (201). Liberating Filipino Americans through decolonizing curriculum. *Race Ethnicity and Education*, 13(4), 495-512. h ttps://doi.org/10.1080/1361 3324.2010.492132

Hankivsky, O. (Ed.). (2012). *An intersectionality-based policy analysis framework. Institute for Intersectionality Research and Policy.* Simon Fraser University.

Hunter, C., & Hunter, J. (2018). Global leadership: A guide to developing your global mindset, skills, and knowledge. *Beaver's Pond Press.* https://www.amazon.com.au/Developing-Your-Global-Mindset-Successful/dp/1592989977

Johnson, D. G. (2021). Social-Cognitive and Affective Antecedents of Code Switching and the Consequences of Linguistic Racism for Black People and People of Color. *Affective science, 3*(1), 5–13.

Khanlou, N., Ssawe, A., Vazquez, L., Pashang, S., Connolly, J., Bohr, Y., Alamdar, N. (November 2020). *COVID-19 pandemic guidelines for mental health support of racialized women at risk of gender-based violence: Knowledge synthesis report.* https://cihr-irsc.gc.ca/e/52062.html

Kouzes, J. M., & Posner, B. Z. (2023.). *The leadership challenge: How to give and take extraordinary leadership.* Jossey-Bass. ISBN: 978-1-119-73612-7

Lang, C., & Cachero, P. (2021, April 7). *How a Long History of Intertwined Racism and Misogyny Leaves Asian Women in America Vulnerable to Violence.* Time. https://time.com/5952819/history-anti-asian-racism-misogyny/

Limpangog, C.P. (2013). Racialised and gendered workplace discrimination: The case of skilled Filipina immigrants in Melbourne, Australia. *Journal of Workplace Rights, 17*(2). http://dx.doi.org/10.2190/WR.17.2.e

Lubetzky, D. (2015). *Do the KIND Thing: Think Boundlessly, Work Purposefully, Live Passionately.* Crown Business. ISBN 9780553393248.

Lumayag, L. (2005) A lonely journey: Struggles of Filipino domestic worker in Malaysia. *University Putra Malaysia: Institute for Community and Peace Studies and Women's Studies Unit.* http://www.malrep.uum.edu.my/rep/Record/my.upm.eprints.30875

Martinez, J. (October 2020). *When Words Create Worlds - Celebrating Intersectionality In Filipino American History Month.* Forbes. https://www.forbes.com/sites/civicnation/2020/10/26/when-words-create-worldscelebrating-intersectionality-in-filipino-american-history-month

McFarling, U. (April 2020). *Nursing ranks are filled with Filipino Americans. The pandemic is taking an outsized toll on them.* STAT News. https://www.

statnews.com/2020/04/28/coronavirus-taking-outsized-toll-on-filipino-american-nurses/

Middle, H. (2020). *Mail Order Brides: Choice or Constraint? Critical Reflections: A Student Journal on Contemporary Sociological Issues.* Leeds Becket University. https://ojs.leedsbeckett.ac.uk/index.php/SOC/article/view/4602

Migration Policy Institute. (2023). *Filipinos Abroad.* Retrieved from https://www.migrationpolicy.org/

Nadal, K.L. (2020). Filipino American psychology: A handbook of theory, research, and clinical practice. *John Wiley & Sons.* https://doi.org/10.1002/9781118094747

Newsweek. (August 2023). *Speaking Up Became a Threat to My Survival.* Newsweek. https://www.newsweek.com/speaking-became-threat-my-survival-activist-philippines-1819167

Nguyen, B. (2024, 07 24). *The Chair Is a Pretty Accurate Portrayal of What It's Like to Be a Woman Professor of Color: That's Why It Can Be Painful to Watch.* Time. https://time.com/6092072/the-chair-netflix-academia/

Parreñas, R.S. (2008). The force of domesticity: Filipina migrants and globalization. *NYU Press.* https://www.jstor.org/stable/j.ctt9qghg8

Patterson, C. E., & Seligman, M. E. P. (2004). *Character strengths and virtues: A handbook.* http://www.ldysinger.com/@books1/Peterson_Character_Strengths/character-strengths-and-virtues.pdf

Philippines Statistics Authority. (2024). *Population of the Philippines.* Retrieved from https://psa.gov.ph/

Power, J. (2021). *Everyday racism is real, and the research says it makes people unhappy and sick.* Sydney Morning Hub. https://www.smh.com.au/national/everyday-racism-is-real-and-the-research-says-it-makes-people-unhappy-and-sick-20210624-p583y4.html

Pratt, T. N. (2021, August 27). *Netflix's 'The Chair' is a needed yet unrealistic depiction of academia.* National Catholic Reporter. https://www.ncronline.org/news/opinion/netflixs-chair-needed-yet-unrealistic-depiction-academia

Robertson, R. (1992). Globalization: Social theory and global culture. Sage Publications.

Rodriguez, R.M. (2017). Domestic insecurities: Female migration from the Philippines, development and national subject-status. *University of California*. https://ccis. ucsd.edu/_files/wp114.pdf

Romagosa, N. (2023). *Care, action, change: fashion professionals' journey to engaging with sustainability*. Stockholm University. https://su.diva-portal. org/smash/record.jsf?aq2=%5B%5B%5D%5D&c=6&af=%5B%5D&searchType=LIST_LATEST&sortOrder2=title_sort_asc&query=&language=sv&pid=diva2%3A1832888&aq=%5B%5B%5D%5D&sf=all&aqe=%5B%5D&sortOrder=author_sort_asc&onlyFullText=false&noOfRows=50&dswid=-5207

Ruiz, N. (March 2018). *I Am a Survivor of Human Trafficking: Nena's Story*. The Atlantic. https://www.theatlantic.com/business/archive/2018/03/human-trafficking-nena/554846/

Sakamoto, I., Tang, J., Lam, H., Yeung, B., Nhkum, A., Cheung, E., Lin, K. (2023). 2020 in Hindsight: Intergenerational Conversations on Anti-Asian Racism During the COVID-19 Pandemic Community Research Report. *University of Toronto*. https://socialwork.utoronto.ca/wp-content/uploads/2023/03/2020-in-Hindsight-English.pdf

Saleh, Z. (March 2022). *The Satwa Diaries: Dubai's Filipino Domestic Workers*. Artefact Magazine. https://www.artefactmagazine.com/2022/03/18/the-satwa-diaries-dubais-filipino-domestic-workers

Sarza, B. (2021). Babae on Bikes: Intersectional Feminism and Public Policy in the Philippines. *DLSU Research Congress*. https://www.scribd.com/document/695026779/Babae-on-Bikes-Intersectional-Feminism-and-Public-Policy-in-the-Philippines

Statista. (2024). *Annual value of incoming personal remittances in Philippines 2000-2023*. https://www.statista.com/statistics/880780/philippines-value-of-remittances/

Su,Y. (July 2020). *Meet the Filipino Women Activists of GABRIELA*. Mochi Magazine. https://www.mochimag.com/activism/meet-the-filipino-women-activists-of-gabriela/

Tokyo, R. (June 2024). *Tokyo Rose*. Wikipedia. https://en.wikipedia.org/wiki/Tokyo_Rose

United Nations Philippines (December 2023). *UN agencies, Senator Pia partner for experiential exhibit raising awareness, action vs. violence against women.* United Nations Philippines Press. https://philippines.un.org/en/254688-un-agencies-senator-pia-partner-experiential-exhibit-raising-awareness-action-vs-violence

Villalba, Maria Angela Mayan C. *Philippines: Good practices for the protection of Filipino women migrant workers in vulnerable jobs.* No. 993662193402676. International Labour Organization, 2002

Wilson, B. (June 2024). *World Hates China, Poll Finds.* The Washington Free Beacon. https://freebeacon.com/latest-news/world-hates-china-poll-finds/

World Economic Forum. (2024). *Global Gender Gap Report 2024.* Retrieved from https://www.weforum.org/publications/global-gender-gap-report-2024/in-full/benchmarking-gender-gaps-2024-2e5f5cd886/

Zelek, B., & Phillips, S. (2003). Gender and power: Nurses and doctors in Canada. *International journal for equity in health, 2* (1). https://doi.org/10.1186/1475-9276-2-1

APPENDIX B

ADDITIONAL WEB-BASED RESOURCES

Filipina Women's Network. (2007-2022). *Interviews with FWN100™ awardees.* The Filipina Women's Network interviews its Top 100 Most Influential Filipina Women awardees as part of its time capsule project intending to document the contributions of Filipina women to society to inspire future generations. https://filipinawomensnetwork.org/

Filipina Women's Network. (2007-2022). *FWN Global 100: The 100 Most Influential Filipina Women in the World.* Filipina Women's Network has published the Filipina Leadership Summit magazine from 2005-present. The magazine serves as a program and resource for attendees. The 2013-2018 issues showcase the Global FWN100™ Most Influential Women in the World. https://filipinawomensnetwork.org/

AAUW. *Barriers and Bias: The Status of Women in Leadership. This report examines the causes of women's underrepresentation in leadership roles in business, politics, and education and suggests what we can do to change the status quo.* https://www.aauw.org/research/barriers-and-bias/

Comprehensive Assessment of Leadership for Learning (CALL) Assessment. *CALL measures key practices across the district that impact school leadership. Download various papers that CALL researchers have written.* https://www.leadershipforlearning.org/research.

Hart Leadership Assessment. *This is a short questionnaire created to measure where your leadership strengths lie and where there is room for improvement.* https://www. smu.edu/Lyle/Centers-and-Institutes/Hart/Leadership-Development/Hart-Leadership-Assessment

Institute for Intercultural Communication. (2014). *Provides a list of selected intercultural training and assessment tool.* https://www.tripartners.com/Downloads/ Session1/TrainingAssessmentTools.pdf /

Kozai Group. *The global competencies inventory (GCI). Global Competencies Inventory measures three facets of intercultural adaptability in identifying personal characteristics related to successful performance in contexts where cultural norms and behaviors vary from one's own.* This tool is generally used for professional development, team building, and succession planning. http://www. kozaigroup.com/global-competencies-inventory-gci/

Leadership Assessment Tool Inventory - Assess Your Skills. *These exercises assess ability to apply critical management skills to identify and solve key organizational problems.* http://www.kellogg.northwestern.edu/faculty/uzzi/htm/teaching-leadership.htm

Leadership and Management Development Strategy. *Developed to endorse learning and development opportunities to strengthen the leadership and management capacity of the Newfoundland and Labrador Public Service.* http://www.exec.gov.nl.ca/ exec/hrs/forms/Peer_Assessment_Form2_Forms_and_Applications.pdf

Najafi Global Mindset Institute. *Global mindset inventory's three capitals. The Global Mindset Inventory is an assessment tool for identifying one's capacity to lead and influence individuals and companies in a global context, particularly those who are from a different culture.* https://thunderbird.asu.edu/faculty-and-research/ global-mindset-inventory

Northouse Authentic Leadership Self-Assessment Questionnaire. *This questionnaire contains items about different dimensions of authentic leadership.* http://people. uncw.edu/nottinghamj/documents/slides6/Northouse6e%20Ch11%20 Authentic%20Survey.pdf

Office of Personnel Management Assessment & Evaluation LEADERSHIP ASSESSMENTS . *A suite of leadership tools enhances self-awareness by measuring leadership effectiveness from multiple approaches.* https://www.opm.gov/services-for-agencies/assessment-evaluation/leadership-assessments/

Pew Research Center. (2015). Women and Leadership: *Public Says Women are Equally Qualified, but Barriers Persist.* http://www.pewsocialtrends.org/2015/01/14/women-and-leadership/

Via Institute on Character. Do you know your 24 character strengths? *The VIA survey was created to help individuals identify the make-up of their character strengths that are classified under six virtue categories. The survey can be taken online and is free of charge.* http://www.viacharacter.org/www/the-survey

Vincent on Leadership: Leadership Assessments. *The Vincentian Leadership Assessment (VLA) offers participants the opportunity to evaluate and grow in their leadership competencies in relation to the five orientations of the Vincentian Leadership Model 2.0.* https://resources.depaul.edu/vincent-on-leadership/training/Pages/assessments.aspx

APPENDIX C

Suggestions for Workshop Activities to Enrich the Book Reading Experience as Stand-Alone Activities or as Part of a Leadership Course

Target Audience: Corporate Employee Resource Groups, Human Resources Professionals including DEI (Diversity, Equity, and Inclusion), Staffing, and HR Business Partners (HRBPs). To book a workshop, please email fwn100@ ffwn.org

1.   Activity: FWN Disrupt Leadership Workshop

Objectives: To stimulate ideas to complement or enhance DEI initiatives in your organization. To raise awareness around hiring, recruiting, and developing diverse leaders through stories of Filipina women. To bring back new insights to your organization. To discuss what it means to belong in addition to being in a diverse, equitable, and inclusive environment.

Activity Description: Two-hour workshop to help HR and DEI professionals learn more about hiring, recruiting, retaining, and developing people of color, specifically Filipina women, using stories of their leadership journeys as data.

The book series project aims to fill the gap in the leadership literature that highlights the unique qualities of Filipina women whose culture, values, and faith make them influential leaders and managers. The leadership book series chronicles Filipina women's leadership skill sets and how Filipina women contribute as active participants in the global workplace.

2. Activity: Leaders you admire.

Objective: To seek leadership characteristics through personal experience

Activity Description: Divide the group into small groups. Ask participants to share a story about the best or most influential leader they have read about in the book. After each story, identify leadership characteristics by asking the question: "What was it that made this person such an effective leader?" Then as a group, identify the traits that all the leaders seemed to share. <http://www.workshopexercises.com>

3. Activity: Stand by your quote.

Objective: To introduce leadership discussion and awareness

Activity Description: Place thoughtful leadership quotes from the women authors on the walls, making sure the print is readable. Ask the participants to walk around the room reading each of the quotes. Then have them stand by one quote that resonates well with their personal views on what makes a good leader (there can be more than one person standing by a quote). When all participants have selected a quote, have each explain to the group why her chosen quote is important to them--share a leadership insight.

Check out: http://www.workshopexercises.com

4. Activity: Character strengths.

Objective: To learn your character strengths

Activity Description: Great leaders have identified and clarified their core working values. They understand how each of their core values translates into leadership behavior. Take the VIA survey to know your character strengths. Which character strengths do you share with any of the 3 or 4 women leaders? Are these character strengths unique to Filipino culture? Or to American culture?

Check out: https://www.viacharacter.org/survey/account/register

5. Activity: Leadership tips.

Objective: To find ways to strengthen leadership ability

Activity Description: Choose 2-3 chapters from the book. Compare and contrast the leadership story and the leadership tips and their implications for your own leadership experience. Make a list of intentional simple, on-the-job self-improvement strategies. For example, list ways of building meaningful work relationships. List ways of motivating others.

6. Activity: This I Believe Essay.

Objective: To describe the core values that guide your daily lives.

Activity Description: Follow the instructions for submitting an essay to 'This I Believe.' Write and submit your own statement of personal belief. Reflect how you approach new challenges through your interpretation of the individual chapter readings.

Check out: http://thisibelieve.org/guidelines/

Variation: Choose one of the women leaders and write a "This I Believe" essay from the woman's perspective--pretend you are that woman writing the essay. You may interview the author if possible.

7. Activity: Leadership theory and practice.

Objective: To define your own leadership theory and practice

Activity Description: From two or more of the chapters, share which leadership theory or practice you found most valid to your work-life and explain why. If none of the theories or explanations spoke to your personal experience, feel free to challenge the theory and propose your own explanation.

8. **Activity: Reflected best self.**

Objective: To compose a portrait of you when you are at your best.

Activity Description: (1) Solicit feedback about your best-self from others—classmates, work or community service colleagues, clients, personal friends, mentors, family members. Give them at least 2 weeks to respond. (2) While waiting for their responses, you should engage in a deep personal reflection about the times when you were at your best, write three short stories that stand out as times when you were at your best, then identify patterns or commonalities that arise across those stories. (3) Review your best-self feedback from others and look for themes. (4) Revise the portrait of who you are at your best, incorporating feedback from others with your own reflections. Your revised portrait should be a written description of the essence of your best-self. What are your key insights? What are the action implications for you, as you think about a) being at your best more often, and b) making your best-self even better? Which of the women authors is most like your best self?

Checkout: http://positiveorgs.bus.umich.edu/?s=reflected+best+self Or <http://faculty.som.yale.edu/amywrzesniewski/documents/ReflectedBestSelfExerciseIntroduction-2014Careers_000.pdf>

APPENDIX D

Most Influential Filipina Woman in the World Award™ (Global FWN100™)

AWARD CATEGORIES

☐ **INNOVATOR & THOUGHT LEADER: PIONEER OF PROGRESS**

This award honors the Filipina woman whose groundbreaking contributions have redefined industries and dares to think differently. From disrupting traditional business models to revolutionizing art, literature, and science, these leaders inspire innovation and foster advancements that change the way we live and whose inventive spirit and visionary ideas have created waves of change, touching lives and shaping the future.

☐ **BUILDER: ARCHITECT OF CHANGE**

This award goes to the Filipina woman who not only dreams of a better world but lays the foundation stone by stone, leading with heart, transforming challenges into opportunities for growth, and celebrating a Filipina leader who constructs bridges to the future with her remarkable organizational prowess. Recognized for her spirit and dedication to collaboration, driving measurable results, the Builder awardee reshapes the landscape of corporations, nonprofits, and government agencies. A Builder is redefining the essence of leadership and leaving a lasting impact on her organization and community.

☐ FOUNDER & PIONEER: THE GROUNDBREAKER

This award salutes a Filipina woman who is the chief executive, president, executive director, or founder of a company, a non-profit, or a business venture she helped launch, build, or significantly grow. An entrepreneur who has blazed new trails and groundbreaking ventures that reflect a commitment to innovation and growth. This award recognizes those who harness resources, creativity, and technology and have turned visions into reality, leading by example and inspiring bold, innovative leadership legacy.

☐ POLICYMAKER & VISIONARY: THE STRATEGIST

This award honors the Filipina woman leader at the forefront of change whose strategic and business acumen have significantly influenced policy and innovation, enriching her constituents' lives by sharing her knowledge and experiences driving business, industry, and society progress. She is a leader whose foresight and decision-making sculpt a more prosperous and inclusive future.

☐ EMERGING LEADER: The Trailblazing Catalyst. (below age 30).

She is a young Filipina woman blazing a trail and inspiring others with her powerful mindset and skillsets. This accolade spotlights a Filipina woman under 30 whose leadership sets the stage for a new era. With an indomitable spirit and exceptional skill sets, the Emerging Leader is a beacon of inspiration, driving transformative change across her organizational sphere. This award celebrates the dynamism and potential of young Filipina leaders navigating their path for others to follow. Emerging Leaders who remain influential may be renominated for another award category.

☐ KEEPERS OF THE FLAME

Sustaining Global Pinay Power is quite daunting. As the excitement dies down and the reality of executing FWN's Vision sets in, many drop out, and others pick up the torch. The Keepers of the Flame are the caretakers that ensure the FWN Vision is kept alive.

**This category is reserved for FWN Board Directors and Lifetime Awardees who have demonstrated long-term volunteer work for FWN.*

APPENDIX E

LIST OF FWN AWARDEES
(2007-2014)
100 MOST INFLUENTIAL FILIPINA WOMEN
IN THE U.S. (US FWN100™)

Behind the Scenes Leaders

2007
Asia Yulo-Blume
Aurora Cavosora Daly
Cheely Ann Sy
Cora Basa Cortez Tomalinas
Denielle Palomares
Edna Austria Rodis
Evangeline Buell
Flor Alcantara-Reyes
Kai Delen-Briones
Laarni San Juan
Lolita Kintanar
Lorna Lardizabal Dietz
Maria Jocelyn Bernal
Perla Gange Ibarrientos
Rosalinda Medina Rupel
Susie Quesada

2009
Aileen Suzara
Belle Santos
Cherie Querol Moreno
Daisy Magalit Rodriguez
Dolly Pangan-Specht
Elsie Rose
Helen Marte Bautista
Jian Zapata
Kathleen Davenport
Lorrie V. Reynoso
Lottie T. Buhain
Lovette Rosales Llantos
Lydia Castillo Fontan
Lyna Larcia-Calvario
Mady Rivera
Maria Concepcion Banatao

2009 *(cont.)*
Naomi Tacuyan Underwood
Nerissa M. Fernandez
Nida L. Recabo
Priscilla Magante Quinn
Roselyn Estepa Ibañez
Shirley Orille Brazis
Sunny Dykwel
Tess Ricafort Alarcon

2011
Bennie Lou Quevedo
Cherina Viloria Tinio

2011 *(cont.)*
Mary Ann C. Ubaldo
Pearl Parmelee

2012
Angie Louie
Edcelyn Pujol

Evelyn Javier-Centeno
Evelyn Luluquisen
Francine Villarmia-Kahawai
Gloria Ramil Omania
Gretheline Bolandrina
Henni Espinosa
Julieta Zarate Hudson

Rosario "Puchi" Carrion
Di Ricco

JoAnn Fields
Marian Catedral-King
Maritessa Bravo Ares
Pureza Belza
Theresa Noriega-Lum
Yong Chavez

Builders and Emerging Leaders

2007
Arlene Marie A. "Bambi" Lorica
Bettina Santos Yap
Claire Oliveros
Edna M.Casteel
Genevieve Jopanda
Jennifer Briones Tjiong
Laura Izon Powell
Laureen Dumadag Laglagaron
Lorna Mae DeVera
Lyna Larcia-Calvario
May Nazareno
Melinda Poliarco
Milagros "Mitos" G. Santisteban
Nieves Cortez
Paz Gomez
Polly Cortez
Rachel Buenviaje
Rebecca Samson
Regina "Ging" E. Reyes
Rose-Ann K. Ubarra
Shirley Raguindin
Sonia T. Delen Fitzsimmons
Susan Afan
Sylvia Lichauco
Thelma Boac
Theresa Tantay Wilson
Zenei T. Cortez

2009
Ana Julaton
Cielo Martinez
Cynthia Aloot
Denise Castañeda Miles
Gel Santos Relos
Isabelita M. Abele
Jannah Arivan Manansala
Jennifer Ong
Katherine Abriam-Yago
Katrina R. Abarcar
Maria (Mimi) Amutan
Mivic Hirose
Raquel Cruz Bono
Raquel R. Redondiez
Rebecca Delgado Rottman
Rowena Verdau-Beduya
Stephanie Ong-Stillman
Valerie Pozon-de Leon

2011
Cynthia Rapaido
Diana Reyes
Estela Matriano
Esther Misa Chavez
Genevieve Herreria
Gloria B. Gil

2011 *(cont.)*
Kathleen Quinn DuBois
Keesa Ocampo
Leah Beth O. Naholowaa
Leia Lorica
Maria Africa Beebe
Melanie A. Caoile
Mila M. Josue
Odette Alcazaren Keeley
Selenna Franco-Cefre

2012
Belinda Muñoz
Cora Aragon Soriano
Cynthia A. Bonta
Eleanore Fernandez
Esther Lee
Jacqueline Dumlao Yu
Lili Tarachand
Nadia Catarata Jurani
Natalie C. Aliga
Olivia Finina De Jesus
Prosy Abarquez-Delacruz
Rita Dela Cruz
Rocio Nuyda
Sheryll Casuga
Stefanie Medious
Theresa Chua

Founders & Pioneers

2007
Celia Ruiz-Tomlinson
Connie S. Uy
Cora Alisuag
Ellen M. Abellera
Erlinda Sayson Limcaco
Gina Lopez Alexander
Gloria T. Caoile
Joy Bruce
Linda Maria Nietes-Little
Loida Nicolas Lewis
Ludy Payumo Corrales
Luzviminda Sapin Micabalo
Marietta Aster Nagrampa Almazan
Mary Carmen Madrid-Crost
Nimfa Yamsuan Gamez
Patricia Aldaba Lim-Yusah

2007 *(cont.)*
Rozita Villanueva Lee
Sony Robles Florendo
Tessie Guillermo
Virna S. Tintiangco
2009
Alice Bulos
Adelamar Alcantara
Analisa Balares
Carina Castañeda
Cora Oriel

Delle Sering Fojas
Ethel Luzario
Evelyn Silangcruz Bunoan
Fe Martinez

2009 *(cont.)*
Fe Punzalan
Fely Guzman
Imelda Ortega Anderson
Judy Arteche-Carr
Maria Maryles Casto
Mivic Hirose
Mona Lisa Yuchengco
Nanette D. Alcaro
Nelsie Parrado
Nini RB Bautista de Garcia
Norma Calderon-Panahon
Patricia Espiritu Halagao
Rosie Abriam
Ruthe Catolico Ashley
Sherri Burke
Zenaida Cunanan

Founders & Pioneers

2011	2011	2012
Alma Onrubia	Joy Dalauidao-Hermsen	Betty O. Buccat
Chateau Gardecki	Lillian Pardo	Conchita Bathan
Christina Rodriguez Laskowski	Maria Benel Se-Liban	Constance Valencia Santos
Dellie Punla	Marjan Philhour	Elaine R. Serina
Geri Ferrer-Chan	Perla Paredes Daly	Josie Jones
Herna Cruz-Louie	Rhoda Yabes Alvarez	Kristine Custodio
Janelle So	Soledad Manaay	Victoria J. Santo
Josefina R. Enriquez	Tess Mauricio	
Jossie Alegre	Vellie Sandalo Dietrich-Hall	

Innovators & Thought Leaders

2007	2009	2011
Angelita Castro-Kelly	Brenda Buenviaje	Angel Velasco Shaw
Carissa Villacorta	Cora Manese Tellez	Celia Pangilinan-Donahue
Charmaine Clamor	Esminia "Mia" Luluquisen	Christina Dunham
Connie Mari	Hazel Sanchez	Evelyn Dilsaver
Diana J. Galindo	Jei Africa	France Viana
Edith Mijares Ardiente	Lenore RS Lim	Gemma Bulos
Elena Mangahas	Marlina Feleo Gonzales	Minerva Malabrigo
Elenita Fe Mendoza Strobel	Marissa Aroy	Tantoco
Gemma Nemenzo	Nana Luz Khilnani	2012
Jane Hofileña	Norma P. Edar	A. Fajilan
Leila Benitez-McCollum	Ma Rowena Verdan-Beduya	Cris Comerford
Lilia Villanueva	Robyn Rodriguez Canham	Janet Nepales
Malu Rivera-Peoples	Sokie Paulin	Maricel Quiroz
Marisa Marquez		Penélope V. Flores
Mutya San Agustin		Vivian Zalvidea Araullo

Nicole

2007	2009	2012	2013
M. Evelina Galang	Jessica Cox	Nilda Guanzon Valmores	Annalisa Enrile
		Paulita Lasola Malay	

Policymakers and Visionaries

2007	2007 (cont.)	2007 (cont.)
Christina Arvin Baal	Lillian Galedo	Ruth Asmundson Uy
Eleonor G. Castillo	Lourdes Tancinco	Sonia Aranza
Grace Walker	Marissa Castro-Salvati	Tani Gorre Cantil- Sakauye
Gwen de Vera	Miriam B. Redmiller	Vanessa Barcelona
Irene Bueno	Mona Pasquil	Velma Veloria
Kris Valderrama	Norma Doctor Sparks	Vida Benavides
Kymberly Marcos Pine	Rida T. R. Cabanilla	

Policymakers and Visionaries

2009
Carmelyn Malalis
Carmen Lagdameo Stull
Faith Bautista
Hydra B. Mendoza
Gertrude Quiroz Gregorio
Joanne F. del Rosario
Joselyn Geaga-Rosenthal
Lorraine Roder0-Inouye
Lynn Finnegan
Marissa Garcia Bailey
Myrna L. De Vera

2009
Noella Tabladillo
Rose Zimmerman
Dr. Rozzana Verder-Aliga
Stephanie Ong Stillman

2011
Agnes Briones Ubalde
Amy Agbayani
Arlie Ricasa
Cheryl Nora Moss
Katherine M. Eldemar

2011 *(cont.)*
Mae Cendana Torlakson
Melissa Roxas
Monique Lhuillier Pat
Gacoscos Rosa Mena Moran

2012
Alicia Fortaleza
Rosita Galang
Zenda Garcia-Lat

Keepers of the Flame

2007
Al Perez
Arlene Marie "Bambi" Lorica
Elena Mangahas
Franklin M. Ricarte
Genevieve Herreria
Maria Roseni "Nini" M. Alvero
Marily Mondejar
Maya Ong Escudero
Nida Recabo
Rowena Mendoza Sanchez
Sonia T. Delen Fitzsimmons
Thelma Boac

2009
Al Perez
Arlene Marie "Bambi" Lorica
Elena Mangahas
Ellen Abellera
Franklin M. Ricarte
Gloria T. Caoile
Jocelyn Bernal
Josephine "Jopin" Romero
Lilia V. Villanueva
Marily Mondejar
Mutya San Agustin Shaw
Shirley S. Raguindin
Sonia T. Delen Fitzsimmons
Thelma Boac

2011
Al Perez
Arlene Marie "Bambi" Lorica
Franklin M. Ricarte

2011 *(cont.)*
Gloria T. Caoile
Josephine "Jopin" Romero
Lilia V. Villanueva
Mutya San Agustin Shaw
Shirley S. Raguindin
Susie Quesada
Thelma Boac

2012
Al Perez
Arlene Marie "Bambi" Lorica
Cherina Tinio
Cynthia Rapaido
Elena Mangahas
Esther Chavez
Franklin M. Ricarte
Gloria T. Caoile
Josephine "Jopin" T. Romero
Judy Arteche-Carr
Lilia V. Villanueva
Mutya San Agustin Shaw
Shirley S. Raguindin
Sonia T. Delen Fitzsimmons
Susie Quesada
Thelma Boac

2013
Al Perez
Arlene Marie "Bambi" Lorica
Alicia Fortaleza
Cynthia Rapaido
Edcelyn Pujol
Elena Mangahas

2013 *(cont.)*
Franklin M. Ricarte
Gloria T. Caoile
Marily Mondejar
Maria Roseni "Nini"
M. Alvero
Maya Ong Escudero
Mutya San Agustin Shaw
Shirley S. Raguindin
Sonia T. Delen
Fitzsimmons
Susie Quesada
Thelma Boac

2014
Arlene Marie "Bambi" Lorica
Alicia Fortaleza
Delle Sering Fojas
Edcelyn Pujol
Elena Mangahas
Franklin M. Ricarte
Gizelle Covarrubias
Robinson
Gloria T. Caoile
Marily Mondejar
Maria Roseni "Nini"
M. Alvero
Maria A. Beebe, Ph.D.
Maya Ong Escudero
Mutya San Agustin Shaw
Shirley S. Raguindin
Sonia T. Delen Fitzsimmons
Susie Quesada
Thelma Boac

2013 AWARDS – 100 MOST INFLUENTIAL FILIPINA WOMEN IN THE WORLD (GLOBAL FWN100™)

Behind the Scenes Leaders

Bessie Badilla
Elizabeth Ann Quirino
Emma Cuenca

Genevieve Jopanda
Loisa Cabuhat

Maria Beebe
Regina Manzana-Sawhney

Builders

Carmela Clendening
Imelda M. Nicolas

Jocelyn Ding
Nina D. Aguas

Rebecca Delgado Rottman

Emerging Leaders

Ariel Batungbacal
Christina Luna

Meriam Reynosa
Michele Bumgarner

Patricia Gallardo-Dwyer

Founders & Pioneers

Allyson Tintiangco-Cubales
Bella Aurora Padua-Belmonte
Dawn Bohulano Mabalon
Delle Sering-Fojas
Ernestina de los Santos-Mac
Evelia V. Religioso
Isabelita Manalastas-Watanabe

Joselyn Geaga-Rosenthal
Julieta Gabiola
Librada C. Yamat
Loida Nicolas Lewis
Lydia Cruz
Maria Almia de los Santos

Mariedel Leviste
Marife Zamora
Norma Fulinara Placido
Patricia Zamora Riingen
Rosemer Enverga
Tess Mauricio

Innovators and Thought Leaders

Amelia Duran-Stanton
Annette M. David
Carmencita David-Padilla
Janet C. Mendoza Stickmon

Janet Susan R. Nepales
Lirio Sobreviñas Covey
Lucille Lozada Tenazas
Mary Ann Lucille L. Sering

Mary Jane Alvero-Al Mahdi
Mira Soriano Gillet
Rozita Villanueva Lee
Suzie Moya Benitez

Policymakers & Visionaries

Astrid S. Tuminez
Cora Manese Tellez
Eleanor Valentin

Hydra Mendoza-McDonnell
Imelda Cuyugan
Gloria T. Caoile

Kris Valderrama
Margaret Lapiz
Patricia V. Paez

2014 AWARDS –100 MOST INFLUENTIAL FILIPINA WOMEN IN THE WORLD (GLOBAL FWN100™)

Behind the Scenes Leaders

Consuelo "Chit" Lijauco
Elvie Abordo

Fritzie Igno
M. Evelina Galang

Builders

Aida Garcia, Esq.
Carmen Lamagna Ph.D.
Filomenita Mongaya-Hoegsholm
Ivic Mueco
Judy Arteche-Carr
Ma. Rhodora "Ayhee" L. Campos
Marianne Hontiveros
Marie Claire Lim Moore

Wafa 'Marilyn' R. Qasimieh, Ph.D.
Mary Ann Covarrubias Ph.D.
Milagros Sering
Myrna Obligacion Carreon
Nora Kakilala-Terrado
Olivia Valera Palala
Sarah Songalia
Zenei Triunfo-Cortez RN

Emerging Leaders

Janice Lao-Noche

Melissa Ramoso

Founders & Pioneers

Analisa Balares
Angelica Berrie
Catherine Feliciano-Chon
Conchita "Chit" Bathan
Darlene Marie Berberabe

Delia Domingo-Albert
Edith Villanueva
Karen Batungbacal
Ma. Victoria Añonuevo

Innovators and Thought Leaders

Boots Anson Roa-Rodrigo
Cris Comerford
Grace Princesa
Ida Ramos-Henares
Jennifer Lopez Fernan

Josefina "Chef Jessie" Sincioco
Maria Lourdes (Marides) Fernando, MPS
Maria Ressa
Patricia Espiritu-Halagao
Teresita Pullin

Monique Wilson

PoLicymakers & Visionaries

Delia Rodriguez-Amaya, Ph.D.

Maria Castañeda

Maria Teresa Bonifacio Cenzon

Rida Cabanilla

Ruth Uy Asmundson, Ph.D.

Thetis Mangahas

2015 AWARDS –100 MOST INFLUENTIAL FILIPINA WOMEN IN THE WORLD (GLOBAL FWN100™)

Behind the Scenes Leaders

Agnes Joyce Garlit Bailen
Angelica Ligas
Cheryl Sevegan
Em Angeles
Hazel Dolio Tag'at
Builders

Leonor S. Vintervoll
Leslie Y. Tabor
Lisa Suguitan Melnick
Maria Cecilia "Cecile" Gregorio Ascalon
Susan Bautista Afan

Builders

Aimee Alado
Annabelle Misa Hefti
Aurora Abella Austriaco
Catherine Campbell
Cathy Salceda Ileto
Elizabeth J. Bautista
Grace Trinidad Vergara
Imelda "Emmie" Collado Ortega Anderson

Leticia "Letty" Quizon
Pet Hartman
Salve Vargas Edelman
Sonia Lugmao Aranza,
Stephanie Lomibao
Tess Martillano-Manjares
Tiffany Bohee
Trina Villanueva

Emerging Leaders

Francine Maigue
Juslyn C. Manalo
Kharissa Fernando

Michelle Joyce Florendo
Noelani Sallings
Patricia Quema La Chica

Founders & Pioneers

Ace T. Itchon
Hedy Marie Leuterio Thomas, PE
Irene Sun-Kaneko
Juanita Nimfa Yamsuan Gamez

Maria Nieves
Santos-Greaves
Myrna Tang Yao
Tessa Yutadco

Innovators and Thought Leaders

Glenda Tibe Bonifacio
Melissa Orquiza

Ramona Diaz
Vina Lustado

Policymakers & Visionaries

Lorna G. Schofield

Luisa Vicerra-Blue

Keepers of the Fame

Amar Bornkamp
Alicia Fortaleza
Bambi Lorica, MD, FAAP
Edcelyn Pujol, CFP
Elena Mangahas

Gloria T. Caoile
Maria Beebe, Ph.D.
Maria Roseni "Nini" M. Alvero
Marily Mondejar
Colonel Shirley S. Raguindin

Sonia T. Delen
Susie Quesada
Thelma Boac

2016 AWARDS –100 MOST INFLUENTIAL FILIPINA WOMEN IN THE WORLD (GLOBAL FWN100™)

Behind the Scenes Leaders

Ana Bel Mayo
Belen M. Saramosing- Ramirez
Carlota Hufana Ader
Carmen Garcia
Elena "Jingjing" Villanueva Romero
Imelda Martin Hum

Maria Victoria Jose Cuisia
Melanie C. Ng
Rachel U. Salinel
Rocio Nuyda
Sandy Sanchez Montano
Theresita "Tita" Q. Dumagsa

Builders

Arlene Abe Pulido
Bernadette M. Schlueter
Cristina "Bea" Teh-Tan
Charina Mundo Vergara
Eloiza T.B. Domingo-Snyder
Irene Corpuz
Lorna Patajo-Kapunan
Magnolia Misolas Uy

Maria Cristina "Ginbee" Layug Go
Maria Socorro "Cory" Valenzuela Vidanes
Marites T. Dagdag
Milalin Sarenas-Javellana
Mona Lisa Bautista Dela Cruz
Patricia "Pixie" Javier- Gutierrez
Rosario Cajucom-Bradbury
Stella Solero Bernabe

Emerging Leaders

Anne Quintos
Eva Marie Wang
Mary Lou Flores Cunanan

Founders & Pioneers

Agnes A. Gervacio
Amparito Llamas Lhuillier
Christine Amour-Levar
Cynthia Romero Mamon
Gina Garcia Atienza
Glenda Barretto
Janette Nellie Go-Chiu
Karen Graciles Libarios Remo

Maria Rosa 'Bing' Nieva Carrion, Ph.D.
Malou N. Santos
Marylou Ty Garcia
Nancy Reyes Lumen
Ophelia Mananquil-Bakker
Paulette Deduque-Liu
Raquel Toquero-Choa
Rosalind L. Wee

Innovators and Thought Leaders

Caroline Marian Santos-Enriquez
Cynthia Carrion
Edita A. De Leon
Mylene Romualdez Abiva

Karen Ida Alparce-Villanueva
Marina Durano
Olivia Limpe Aw

Nicole

Leni Robredo

Policymakers & Visionaries

Maria Milagros Fernan Cayosa

Continuing Influencers
Ace Itchon
Annabelle Misa Hefti
Chit Lijauco
Emma Imperial
Josefina "Chef Jessie" Sincioco

Karen Batungbacal
Maan Hontiveros
Myrna Tang Yao
Nora Kakilala Terrado
Pet R. Hartman

Keepers of the Flame

Amar Bornkamp
Bambi Lorica
Delle Sering
Elena Mangahas
Gloria T. Caoile
Josephine Romero
Maria Beebe, Ph.D.

Maria Roseni "Nini" M. Alvero
Marily Mondejar
Colonel Shirley S. Raguindin
Sonia T. Delen
Susie Quesada
Thelma Boac

2017 AWARDS –100 MOST INFLUENTIAL FILIPINA WOMEN IN THE WORLD (GLOBAL FWN100™)

Behind the Scenes Leaders

Ann Mariza Nepomuceno Sanchez- Bensurto
Editha Tijamo Winterhalter, Ed.D.
Cristina Calaguian

Engr. Lilian Maria Soriano Bautista
Rosary Escaño

Builders

Isabelita "Lita" M. Abele
Jacqueline D. Yu, Esq.
Leah L. Laxamana
Lou Olvido Parroco
Mary Ann Gamboa

Myrna P. Young, MSN, RN, CNOR
Rebecca Murry
Rowena Romulo
Roxane Martin Negrillo
Wilma 'Amy' Eisma

Emerging Leaders

Claire Aquino Quito
Joanne Michelle Fernandez Ocampo
Kristina Laranjo Alabado

Founders & Pioneers

Cherry Pua Africa
Claire Navarro Espina, Esq.
Cora dela Cruz
Dina Dela Paz Stalder
Edna Consing Concepcion

Joji Ilagan Bian
Kalika Nacion Yap
Mercedes Muldong Calderon
Nikki Tang

Innovators and Thought Leaders

Anna-Karina Tabuñar
Catherine Teh, M.D.
Fidelina "Faye" Adan Corcuera
Georgitta 'Beng' Pimentel Puyat

Geri Alumit Zeldes, Ph.D.
Gizelle Covarrubias Robinson
Jennifer Marie B. José, M.D.

Policymakers & Visionaries

Hon. Cynthia Alcantara Barker
Jerrilyn Malana, Esq.
HE Junever Melchor Mahilum-West
Lily Torres-Samoranos

Ma. Nieves R. Confesor
Mila Eustaquio-Syme
HE Petronila P. Garcia
Hon. Rosalinda V. Canlas

Continuing Influential
Mary Jane Alvero-Al Mahdi

Keepers of the Flame

Amar Bornkamp
Bambi Lorica, M.D., FAAP
Elizabeth Bautista
Gloria T. Caoile
Leonor Vintervoll
Maan Hontiveros
Maria Beebe, Ph.D.

Maria Roseni "Nini" M. Alvero
Maria Santos Greaves
Marily Mondejar
Rosario Cajucom-Bradbury
Colonel Shirley S. Raguindin
Susie Quesada
Hon. Thelma Boac

2018 GLOBAL FWN100™ AWARDEES

BEHIND THE SCENES LEADERS
Lolita Johansson
Maria Trinidad Manalo Maramba
Marietta Palacio Revilla
Novabel Teves Fossgard

BUILDERS
Cristina Manahan Llamzon, PhD
Elena Francisco Samson
Joy Murao
Joyce Rivera Javier
Maria Victoria M. Acosta
Mary Cheryl Bravo Gloner, MPH
Ruby Canteras Pacis

EMERGING LEADERS
Ann Michelle Bagayna Mondragon
Christen-Leonor Santos Montero
Trish Marie Edar Marco

FOUNDERS & PIONEERS
Angela Katrina Adams
Conchita Labao Manabat, PhD
Crystal Dias LLB
Mildred Christine Flores Piad, Ph.D

INNOVATORS & THOUGHT LEADERS
Alexandra Noelle Cuerdo
Angie Go Flaminiano
Marissa Estiva Magsino, MD, FAARFM
Pamela Gotangco
Hon. Susan Pineda Mercado, MD, MPH

"NICOLE"
Hon. Gwendolyn Fiel Garcia

POLICYMAKERS & VISIONARIES
Hon. Rachelle Sumagaysay Pastor Arizmendi
Hon. Wendy Lee Ho

CONTINUING INFLUENTIAL
Hon. Juslyn Cabrera Manalo

KEEPERS OF THE FLAME
Amar Bornkamp
Dr. Caroline Marian Enriquez
Georgitta "Beng" Pimentel Puyat
Leonor Vintervoll
Maria Beebe, Ph.D.
Maria Roseni "Nini" M. Alvero
Maria Santos Greaves
HON Marily Mondejar
Susie Quesada
HON Thelma Boac

2019 GLOBAL FWN100™ AWARDEES

BEHIND THE SCENES LEADERS
Corazon De Jesus Manimbo
Corazon Sobrevega Laraya-Coutts
Gemalin Batino Diaz
Lorena Domanog Clerc
Maria Consolacion P. Geroche
Maria Paz Rosales Alberto
Maria Zelda Magistrado Rojas
Pauline Plata Bondad
Dr. Yasmin Balajadia Cortes
Zarah Jane D Juan

BUILDERS
Dr. Aileen Mariategue Villanueva
Ana Margarita Navarro Hontiveros
Erlinda Lacson Olalia-Carin
Madelene Eloisa Labandilo Ortega
Atty. Margarita Navarro Gutierrez
Maria Amparo Victoria Trinidad Yee
Maria Fides Lagamon Balita
Maria Jacinta Victoria Torino Lualhati Ph.D.
Teresita Ignacio Batayola

EMERGING LEADER
Nicola Louise Negapatan Paclibar

FOUNDERS & PIONEERS
Dr. Bernadette Jardiolin Madrid
Carmina Montesa Aldana
Charina Palomares Garcia
Ellen Ferrer Samson
Fe Odsigue Punzalan
Mildred Vande Vusse Vitangcol
Dr. Ninez Ponce

Nora G Galleros-Tinio
Rhodora Perpetua Palomar-Fresnedi
Atty. Rosario Calixto Chavez

INNOVATORS & THOUGHT LEADERS
Anna Isabel Crisostomo Sobrepeña
Arlene Oliveros
Charlene Consolacion
Ildeme Mahinay Koch
Kristen Nicole Brillantes
Maria Ester Follosco Bautista
Maria Francesca Dela Fuente Tan
Ma. Kristina Grace Penalosa Carpio
Maria Victoria B Garcia
Nerissa Mendoza Gerial
Rose Anne de Pampelonne

POLICYMAKER & VISIONARY
Clarissa Eleanor Bravo

CONTINUING INFLUENTIAL: INNOVATOR & THOUGHT LEADER
Maria Africa Beebe, Ph.D.

KEEPERS OF THE FLAME
Amar Bornkamp
Caroline Marian Enriquez, MD
Georgitta "Beng" Pimentel Puyat
Leonor Vintervoll
Maria Roseni "Nini" M. Alvero
Maria Santos Greaves
Marily Mondejar
Susie Quesada
Hon. Thelma Boac

2021 GLOBAL FWN100™ AWARDEES

BUILDERS
Alicia del Prado, Ph.D.
Arlene Tordecilla Ferrolino
Charity Nicolas
Cynthia CK Suero-Gabler
Holly Vocal
Joanne De Guzman Rico
Kathy V. Lai
Melissa Sanvictores

EMERGING LEADERS
Carla Laurel
Korina Alvarez Mercado

FOUNDERS & PIONEERS
Grace Reyes
Marla D. Rausch
Dr. Mary Joy Canon Abaquin
Rhoda Castro Caliwara

INNOVATORS & THOUGHT LEADERS
Annabelle Manalo-Morgan, Ph.D.
Denise Lopez, Ph.D.
Giovannie Espiritu
Jaclyn Tolentino, Ph.D.
Lucia Olalia Reyes
Paula Rosales

POLICYMAKERS & VISIONARIES
Jessica M Caloza
Natalie Garcia Lashinsky
Nikki Fortunato Bas

KEEPERS OF THE FLAME
Benel Se Liban
Carol Enriquez ,M.D.
Charina Garcia, Esq.
Fe Punzalan
Genevieve Jopanda
Georgitta "Beng" Pimentel Puyat
Gina Atienza
Juslyn Manalo
Leonor Vintervoll
Lorna Kapunan, Esq.
Maria Beebe, Ph.D.
Marily Mondejar
Marla D. Rausch
Mica Tan
Susie Quesada

2022 GLOBAL FWN100™ AWARDEES

BUILDERS
Abby Watabe
Catalina Manarin Bagsic
Dr. Eileen P. de Villa
Gwendolyn T. Pang

Jane Po Panganiban
Joanne de Asis-Benitez
Judis Guintu Santos
Kristine Custodio Suero
Malve Peralta Ildefonso
Patricia Kaye Yeh Choa
Patricia Quebada Clerkin

FOUNDERS & PIONEERS
Annaflor Feliprada-Patrizio
Cymbeline Tancongco Culiat, Ph.D.
Elena Cacho Tesoro, Ph.D.
Ma. Cristine Caringal Melad
Maria Regina A. Alfonso
Ma. Teresa Beltran Chan
Melesa Dy Chua
Myra Colis

INNOVATORS & THOUGHT LEADERS
Grace Gorospe-Jamon, Ph.D.
Jenette E. C. Ramos
Dr. Jennifer Camota Luebke
Joycelyn David
Judy Anne Santos-Sierszula
Regina Pascua Berba

POLICYMAKERS & VISIONARIES
Mayor Maria Sheilah Honrado Lacuna-Pangan
Deputy Mayor Myla Arceno
MP Rechie Valdez
Mayor Sofia Asuncion Anis Aragon

KEEPERS OF THE FLAME
Benel Se Liban
Carol Enriquez
Fe Punzalan
Georgitta Pimentel Puyat
Gina Atienza
Juslyn Manalo
Leonor Vintervoll
Lorna Kapunan
Maria Beebe, Ph.D.
Marily Mondejar
Mica Tan
Susie Quesada

GLOBAL FWN100™ 2022 AWARDEES

☐ **Annaflor Feliprada-Patrizio**, Owner, Schomberg Village Pharmacy. CANADA

☐ **Catalina Manarin Bagsic**, President, First Integrity Bank, Inc. PHILIPPINES

☐ **Cymbeline Tancongco Culiat, PhD.**, President, NellOne Therapeutics Inc. UNITED STATES

☐ **Dr. Eileen Patricia De Villa**, Medical Officer, Toronto Public Health, City of Toronto. CANADA

☐ **Elena Cacho Tesoro, PhD.**, Executive Director, AEK Training and Review Center. PHILIPPINES

☐ **Grace Gorospe-Jamon, PhD**, President, Lapu-Lapu Cebu International College. PHILIPPINES

☐ **Jane Po Panganiban**, CFO, Cebu Advent Development Corporation. PHILIPPINES

☐ **Jenette Ramos**, Member, Board of Regents Washington State University. UNITED STATES

☐ **Jennifer Camota Luebke, EdD, MBA**, Senior Vice President and Chief Workforce Inclusion Officer, PRIDE Industries. UNITED STATES

☐ **Joycelyn Espiritu David**, CEO, AVCommunications Inc. CANADA

☐ **Judis Guintu Santos**, Equity Officer, Metropolitan Transportation Commission/Association of Bay Area. UNITED STATES

☐ **Judy Ann Santos-Sierszula**, Manager, Nike EMEA. NETHERLANDS

☐ **Kristine Custodio Suero**, Legal Professional, Butterfield Schechter, LLP. UNITED STATES

☐ **Ma. Cristine Caringal Melad**, Partner, Dampa Seafood and Spice Grill. UNITED ARAB EMIRATES

☐ **Malve Peralta Ildefonso**, CPA, Partner, BDO USA, LLP. UNITED STATES

☐ **Maria Regina Abella Alfonso, PhD.**, Director, MAGIS Creative Spaces, Inc. PHILIPPINES

☐ **Dr. Maria Sheila Honrado Lacuna-Pangan**, Mayor, City Government of Manila. PHILIPPINES

☐ **Maria Teresa Beltran Chan**, CEO, E-Asia Tech Solutions. PHILIPPINES

☐ **Melesa Dy Chua**, President, CDC Holdings Inc. PHILIPPINES

☐ **Myla Dela Vega Arceno**, Deputy Mayor and Councillor, Stevenage. UNITED KINGDOM

☐ **Myra Colis**, Chair of the Board, MABIKAs Foundation - The Netherlands. THE NETHERLANDS

☐ **Patricia Kaye Yeh Choa**, Director, Google Services, Philippines, Inc. PHILIPPINES

☐ **Dr. Patricia Quebada Clerkin**, Director, Dartmouth-Hitchcock Medical Center. UNITED STATES

☐ **Rechie Valdez**, Member of Parliament, House of Commons, Canada. CANADA

☐ **Regina Pascua Berba**, Head of the Hospital Infection Control Unit, University of the Philippines Manila - Philippine General Hospital. PHILIPPINES

☐ **Sofia Asuncion Anis Aragon**, Mayor, City of Burien, Washington; Executive Director, Washington Center for Nursing. UNITED STATES

KEEPERS OF THE FLAME

☐ **Benel Se Liban**, Managing Partner, JBC Group Los Angeles, California. UNITED STATES (US FWN100™ 2011)

☐ **Carol Enriquez MD**, President and CEO of Our Lady Fatima University, Valenzuela City. PHILIPPINES (Global FWN100™ 2016)

☐ **Fe Punzalan**, President, Silver Punzalan Inc. San Jose, California. UNITED STATES (US FWN100™2011; Global FWN100™ 2019)

☐ **Georgitta "Beng" Pimentel Puyat**, Chairman, Philippine Orchard Corporation, Makati. PHILIPPINES (Global FWN100™ 2017)

☐ **Gina Atienza**, President, SunStar Management Inc., Cebu. PHILIPPINES (Global FWN100™ 2016)

☐ **Juslyn Manalo**, Mayor, City of Daly City, California. UNITED STATES (Global FWN100™ 2015; Continuing Influential Global FWN100™2018)

☐ **Leonor Vintervoll**, Chair of the Board, European Network of Filipino Diaspora (ENFiD), Oslo. NORWAY (Global FWN100™ 2015)

☐ **Lorna Kapunan, Esq.** Partner, Kapunan & Castillo Law Offices, Bonifacio Global City, Taguig. PHILIPPINES. (Global FWN100™ 2016)

☐ **Marily Mondejar**, Founder & CEO, Filipina Women's Network, San Francisco, California. UNITED STATES

☐ **Maria Beebe, PhD**, President, Kaisipan, Naples, Florida. UNITED STATES (Global FWN100™ 2013; Continuing Influential Global FWN100™2019)

☐ **Marla D. Rausch**, CEO, Animation Vertigo, Inc. UNITED STATES; Animation Vertigo Asia PHILIPPINES (Global FWN100™ 2021)

☐ **Mica Tan**, CEO, MFT Group of Companies, Bonifacio Global City, Taguig. PHILIPPINES, HONG KONG, SINGAPORE, UNITED STATES (Global FWN100™ 2019)

☐ **Susie Quesada**, President, Ramar Foods International, Pittsburg, California. UNITED STATES (US FWN100 '07, Global FWN100™ '13)

GLOBAL FWN100™ 2023 AWARDEES

☐ **Charina Amunategui**, Executive Director, MUFG Investor Services, Business Execution Fund Finance. **UNITED STATES**

☐ **Consuelo Lacson**, President, Seven Oaks Properties Inc., Jelac Construction and Development Corporation. **CANADA**

☐ **Dr. Denise Marie Koh, MD,** Director, Dr. Denise Koh Medical Corporation. **CANADA**

☐ **Donna May Künzler**, Director, ABB Switzerland Ltd. **SWITZERLAND**

☐ **Elaine Antonio Bordeaux**, Lawyer Sculptor, Dr. Jose Rizal Legacy International Foundation. **UNITED STATES**

☐ **Jennifer Lee Mah**, Academic Dean, NorQuest College. **CANADA**

☐ **Joanne De Asis Benitez**, Senior Advisor, Morgan Stanley & Co. **UNITED STATES**

☐ **June Cheryl A. Cabal-Revilla**, CFO, Metro Pacific Investments Corporation. **PHILIPPINES**

☐ **Kareen Mills**, Founder, MULTIPLY Influence LLC. **UNITED STATES**

☐ **Kat Abejuela Morse**, Senior Manager, Innovation and Partnerships, International Air Transport Association. **SWITZERLAND**

☐ **Kathleen Nolasco Lior-Liechtenstein**, President, KSL Development Corporation. **PHILIPPINES**

☐ **Lumina Lawangen Peil**, CFO, AIP Construction. **PHILIPPINES**

☐ **Dr. Pamela Rama-de Padua**, Baptist Heart Specialist. **UNITED STATES** [Economic Sector: Healthcare, Science & Technology]

☐ **Judge Rohanee Zapanta Casillan**, San Diego Superior Court. **UNITED STATES**

☐ **Dr. Rosannette Hernandez Rimando-Chareunsap**, CEO, Seattle Colleges. **UNITED STATES**

☐ **Rosemarie Pay Rafael**, Chair of the Board, AIC Group of Companies Holding Corp. **PHILIPPINES**

KEEPER OF THE FLAME

☐ **Benel Se Liban**, Managing Partner, JBC Group Los Angeles, California. UNITED STATES (US FWN100™ 2011 and Global FWN100™ 2022)

☐ **Carol Enriquez MD**, President and CEO of Our Lady Fatima University, Valenzuela City. PHILIPPINES (Global FWN100™ 2016)

☐ **Georgitta "Beng" Pimentel Puyat**, Chairman, Philippine Orchard Corporation, Makati. PHILIPPINES (Global FWN100™ 2017) and Global FWN100™ 2022

☐ **Gina Atienza**, President, SunStar Management Inc., Cebu. PHILIPPINES (Global FWN100™ 2016 and Global FWN100™ 2022)

☐ **Juslyn Manalo**, Mayor and Councilmember, City of Daly City, California. UNITED STATES (Global FWN100™ 2015; Continuing Influential Global FWN100™2018 and Global FWN100™ 2022)

☐ **Lorna Kapunan, Esq.** Partner, Kapunan & Castillo Law Offices, Bonifacio Global City, Taguig. PHILIPPINES. (Global FWN100™ 2016 and Global FWN100™ 2022)

☐ **Marily Mondejar**, Founder & CEO, Filipina Women's Network, San Francisco, California. UNITED STATES

- ☐ **Marla D. Rausch**, CEO, Animation Vertigo, Inc. UNITED STATES; Animation Vertigo Asia PHILIPPINES (Global FWN100™ 2021)

- ☐ **Mica Tan**, CEO, MFT Group of Companies, Bonifacio Global City, Taguig. PHILIPPINES (Global FWN100™ 2019)

- ☐ **Maria Beebe, Ph.D.**, President, Kaisipan, Naples, Florida. UNITED STATES (Global FWN100™ 2013; Continuing Influential Global FWN100™2019)

- ☐ **Susie Quesada**, President, Ramar Foods International, Pittsburg, California. UNITED STATES (US FWN100 '07, Global FWN100™ '13)

GLOBAL FWN100™ 2024 AWARDEES

BUILDER: ARCHITECT OF CHANGE

Jackie Cezar Dela Cruz
COO, Innovention Food Resources Inc.
PHILIPPINES

Michelle Baltazar
Executive Director
ISS MI (PART OF ISS STOXX)
AUSTRALIA

Nadia Bint Rafael
Director, Nadia Bint Rafael Personal Real Estate Corporation
CANADA

Sheilani Cruz Alix
Owner, Sandigan Consulting
UNITED STATES

Tina Bailon Lindres
CEO-Co-Founder, Manitoba LTD DBA The Green Apron
CANADA

FOUNDER & PIONEER: THE GROUNDBREAKER

Evangeline Rivera Powell
CEO, Rockwell Healthcare LLC
UNITED STATES

Maricor Mendoza Akol
President and Founder, Philippine National IT Standards (PhilNITS)
PHILIPPINES

INNOVATOR & THOUGHT LEADER: PIONEER OF PROGRESS

Dr. April Joy Guiriba Damian
Vice President, Moses/Weitzman Health System
UNITED STATES

Mary Lizabeth Lu
CEO, Leveret Pte Ltd.
PHILIPPINES

Marylou Ngo Ang
President
MAGNA CMGN Solutions
PHILIPPINES

POLICYMAKER & VISIONARY: THE STRATEGIST

Jeannie Ng Sandoval
Mayor of City of Malabon
PHILIPPINES

Mary Massina
CEO, Mary Ann Island P/L
AUSTRALIA

BIOGRAPHIES

Marily Mondejar is a Filipina American nonprofit executive, a community organizer, and an untiring advocate against domestic violence and the trafficking of Filipina women. She is passionate about women's rights and primarily works to ensure the representation of Filipina and Asian women's voices.

She has parlayed her success as a business leader and image consultant into founding the Filipina Women's Network. FWN has members in 31 countries and has steered the organization to a leading position in the Filipino community worldwide by reshaping the Filipina image, highlighting the leadership roles and economic contributions of Filipina women in the public and private sectors after a 2001 internet search for "Filipina" returned millions of hits as "mail-order brides, sluts, exotic, sexy and submissive wives."

Ms. Mondejar is recognized for the Image 360°-degree assessment questionnaire she developed, measuring an executive's image performance and corporate reputation. She has delivered international business, career, and image presentations in various formats.

Ms. Mondejar balances her professional life by serving on multiple public service, community, philanthropy, and professional development boards. Appointed by the late San Francisco Mayor Edwin Lee, Marily has served as chair and president of the Commission on Community Investment and Infrastructure (CCII), the Successor Agency of the San Francisco Redevelopment Agency, which exercises land use, development and design approval authority for projects representing $20 billion in assets that create jobs, affordable housing, commercial space, parks, art installations and open space areas.

A resident of San Francisco, she has raised two wonderful sons as a single mother, is a proud grandmother of three boys, and adores her new great-granddaughter.

MARIA AFRICA BEEBE, PH.D.
Introduction
Fractals: Recursive. Non-Linear. Ever-changing

Synthesis ☙ Global ☙ Educator ☙ Katipunera

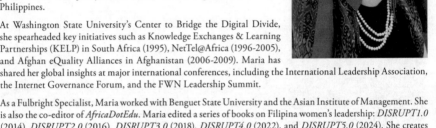

Maria Beebe, a pioneering leader in her field, is an expert in fostering women's leadership in international development, discourse analysis, and digital capabilities development to enhance education quality. She holds a Master's in Anthropology and a Ph.D. in Education from Stanford University. With over 30 years of experience, Maria has successfully led large multistakeholder programs that unite academics, industry practitioners, and policymakers across Africa, Afghanistan, and the Philippines.

At Washington State University's Center to Bridge the Digital Divide, she spearheaded key initiatives such as Knowledge Exchanges & Learning Partnerships (KELP) in South Africa (1995), NetTel@Africa (1996-2005), and Afghan eQuality Alliances in Afghanistan (2006-2009). Maria has shared her global insights at major international conferences, including the International Leadership Association, the Internet Governance Forum, and the FWN Leadership Summit.

As a Fulbright Specialist, Maria worked with Benguet State University and the Asian Institute of Management. She is also the co-editor of *AfricaDotEdu*. Maria edited a series of books on Filipina women's leadership: *DISRUPT1.0* (2014), *DISRUPT2.0* (2016), *DISRUPT3.0* (2018), *DISRUPT4.0* (2022), and *DISRUPT5.0* (2024). She creates personalized 'About Me' stories for her grandchildren, incorporating photos she's taken, and shares these stories with them during special reading sessions.

Maria's latest pro bono initiative, Kaisipan, launched during the COVID-19 pandemic, seeks to enhance digital capabilities for educators and learners in the Philippines, contributing to Sustainable Development Goal 4: inclusive and equitable quality education for all. Maria is a remote work consultant focused on co-creating the Asia Open RAN Academy. This initiative aims to open the radio access network for improved connectivity to foster digital inclusion in the Philippines and India.

CHARINA AMUNATEGUI, MBA
I AM ENOUGH
Passionate Leader ∾ Relationship Builder ∾ Global Advocate

Charina Amunategui, an accomplished finance professional, embodies resilience, determination, and success. With over 20 years of experience in asset management operations across the United States, Canada, the United Kingdom, and Bermuda, she currently serves as Executive Director of Fund Finance Business Execution at MUFG Investor Services, a subsidiary of Mitsubishi UFJ Financial Group, one of the world's largest banks.

Born and raised in Tondo, Manila, Charina is a testament to dreaming big despite humble beginnings. She and her family immigrated to Canada when she was 14. Charina recently graduated with an MBA from Yale University in May 2024, specializing in Asset Management.

Charina has engaged with large audiences and empowered hundreds, speaking about personal branding, self-advocacy, and confidence building. As Treasurer of the Board of Inspiring Girls USA, she supports development and leadership programs for young girls nationwide. She has been featured in Forbes, Global Investor Group, and Thrive Global. Beyond her professional endeavors, Charina demonstrates her determination and resilience as a fitness competitor in the Wellness division of the North American bodybuilding scene.

In 2023, the Foundation for Filipina Women's Network honored her with the "Most Influential Filipina Woman in the World" award, recognizing her leadership and influence in advancing women of Philippine heritage. In 2024, she proudly served as the Grand Marshal of the Philippine Independence Day Parade in New York City, honoring her roots and inspiring the community.

SOFIA ARAGON
Wandering off the Plantation:
Racism and Gender Bias in Incivility
Advocating ∾ Representing ∾ Leading

Sofia Aragon, JD, BSN, R.N., FAAN, is the Executive Director of the Washington Center for Nursing and former Mayor and City Council member for Burien, Washington.

She earned a B.A. in Economics from the University of Washington-Seattle, a B.S. in Nursing from Seattle University, and a law degree from Loyola University — Chicago.

Sofia immigrated to Seattle from the Philippines with her parents in 1975. She credits her advocacy journey to her mother, a Philippine-educated nurse.

As the Senior Governmental Affairs Advisor for the Washington State Nurses Association, Sofia was instrumental in managing legislative and political affairs. Her current role as the Executive Director of the Washington Center for Nursing is a significant milestone, as she is the first woman of color to lead a statewide nursing organization in Washington.

In 2019, Sofia's leadership was recognized when she was elected to the Burien City Council. In 2022, she made history as the first woman of color to be elected as the city's mayor. Her proactive stance against hate crimes due to COVID-19 was evident when she passed the first Proclamation Against Anti-Asian Hate. Her commitment to public health was further solidified when she was appointed to the Public Health Advisory Board to represent the Association of Washington Cities. In the same year, she was honored with an induction into the Washington Nurses Hall of Fame. The following year, her contributions to the nursing field were acknowledged when she was awarded the prestigious title of Fellow of the American Academy of Nursing.

MARIA SANTOS-GREAVES
Mastering the Mind
Courageous ৩৩ Resilient ৩৩ Charismatic

Maria Santos-Greaves is a seasoned entrepreneur with 30 years of expertise in the hearing industry. She founded Surrey Hearing Care to improve the lives of those with hearing impairments. Over the years, her clinic has served more than 16,000 clients across the Lower Mainland and the Philippines, offering expert care and compassionate service. Through the clinic, Maria and her team have collaborated with numerous care facilities and organizations in Canada, tirelessly advocating for the importance of hearing health, especially among older people.

In recognition of Maria's outstanding contributions, she was named Entrepreneur of the Year (2022) by the Surrey Board of Trade, making her the first Filipino to receive this prestigious award. That same year, Maria expanded her entrepreneurial pursuits by founding MinaMar Janitorial Services. This new venture provides top-quality cleaning services to households and commercial spaces across Metro Vancouver. Under her leadership, Minamar has quickly gained a reputation for excellence, known for its meticulous attention to detail and commitment to customer satisfaction.

ISABELITA "LITA" T. MANALASTAS-WATANABE
Navigating The Labyrinth of Race and Gender in Japan
Warrior ৩৩ Kind ৩৩ Fierce Enemy

Isabelita "Lita" T. Manalastas-Watanabe was an economist and diplomat and is now a businesswoman. She holds a B.S. in Economics from the University of the Philippines UP) at Diliman; an M.A. in Economics from Tsukuba University, on full scholarship from the Japanese government; a Diploma in Japanese language from Osaka University; and completed an Executive Program for Leaders in Development at Harvard University's Institute for International Development.

Lita was Youth Ambassador of Goodwill to Japan and the ASEAN countries, UP Most Outstanding Alumna in 2022 (Banking and Corporate Responsibility), and received the Most Outstanding Kapampangan Award (Entrepreneurship) in 2022.

Lita's career is a testament to her leadership and strategic acumen. She has held significant roles in various organizations, serving as the top investment official at the ASEAN-Japan Centre in Tokyo, leading the Philippine National Bank Tokyo Branch as the Senior Vice President and Managing Director/Head of Asia-Pacific, and later, being assigned to Rome as the First Senior Vice President/Head of Europe, Israel, and Africa.

Even today, Lita's entrepreneurial spirit continues to thrive. She is the President of a money transfer/international finance company in Japan, which is a testament to her business acumen. Additionally, she is at the helm of a consulting company in the Philippines, both of which she established and continues to lead.

Looking ahead, Lita envisions a life of tranquility and reflection. She plans to retire as a farmer at her Thanks Nature Integrated Farm in Pampanga, a learning farm/resort far from the hustle and bustle of the modern world. Here, she hopes to share her love for nature and the importance of sustainable living.

Lita continues to give back and share with others the many blessings she has received so far.

PROFESSOR GRACE R. GOROSPE-JAMON, PH.D.
By Grace, Through Grace
Faith & Grit & Grace

Professor Grace Gorospe-Jamon is the President of Lapu-lapu Cebu International College (LCIC). Professor Grace holds a Doctorate in Political Science, a Master of Arts, and a Bachelor of Arts in Political Science from the University of the Philippines in Diliman, Quezon City. Grace built a career in education spanning 40 years in various roles, from being a faculty member to Director of the premier state university's extension program. As a university professor, she consistently topped the university's annual Student Evaluation of Teachers (SET), mentoring and advising a generation of doctoral, master's, and undergraduate students. As Director of the state university's extension program, Professor Grace implemented many internationally funded extension program partnerships with the UN and various international private social enterprise groups, showcasing her global impact and influence. She has been a public policy advocate as a fellow and mentor at the Asia Foundation and the Geneva Institute for Leadership and Public Policy. Gorospe-Jamon's remarkable career includes being Dean of the Development Academy of the Philippines (DAP), Director of the University of the Philippines Extension Program in Clark and Olongapo, Executive Director of the Philippine Social Science Council, and president of the Association of Schools of Public Administration in the Philippines.

REGINA P. BERBA, MD
People Giving Hope: Ten PGH Champions during COVID-19
Committed & Courageous & Congenial

Dr. Regina Berba is an Infectious Disease physician, clinical epidemiologist, and the head of infection control at the Philippines' most prominent government tertiary referral hospital, the Philippine General Hospital (PGH). She is also the Head of ID at The Medical City, the main hospital of the largest private healthcare network in the country.

During the COVID pandemic, Dr. Berba guided the PGH transformation into a Covid-19 Referral Center for the country and spearheaded several COVID researches. Since then, she has been recognized with several national awards: Outstanding Filipino Physician 2022, People of the Year 2022, Dr. Lourdes Campos Award for Public Health 2023, and international awards, including the UP International Health Professional Award for Excellence 2024 and the Society for Healthcare Epidemiology in America (SHEA) International Scholarship Award 2024.

Dr. Berba was named an FWN Global 100 in 2022 for the Innovators and Thought Leaders Category. As her global pitch project, she launched the Project PROMISE book with the Mu Sigma Phi Sorority to empower Filipino mothers to fight the ominous global threat of antimicrobial resistance (AMR).

Dr. Berba now serves on the boards of the Philippine College of Physicians(PCP), the Philippine Society for Microbiology and Infectious Diseases(PSMID), and the International Society of Antimicrobial Chemotherapy(ISAC).

Regina Berba MD MSc FPCP FPSMID

University of the Philippines Manila-Philippine General Hospital

rpberba@up.edu.ph

KRISTINE CUSTODIO SUERO
OVERCOMING "Just": Being Underestimated is a Superpower
Consultant &/> Coach &/> Educator

Kristine Custodio Suero, ACP, is an award-winning legal professional, a published author, and a highly sought-after speaker. A true servant leader, she has led the San Diego Paralegal Association and California Alliance of Paralegal Associations as President. Kristine serves as the Vice Chair/Commissioner of the San Diego County Commission on the Status of Women & Girls, teaches legal courses for the University of San Diego School of Law Paralegal Program, and lends her time to the program's advisory board. Kristine serves as a member of the California Judicial Council Center for Judicial Education and Research Advisory Committee as well as NALA – The Paralegal Association's Board of Directors as the Area 3 Director and is the immediate past Chair of the Diversity, Equity, and Inclusion Committee and past member of the NALA Professional Development Committee and Continuing Education Council as well as past Ethics Chair. She is a co-host for the American Association for Paralegal Education Legal Luminaries podcast. Kristine is also a Senior Paralegal/Business Development Director for Butterfield Schechter LLP. Kristine may be reached at kristine.custodio@gmail.com.

ELLEN SAMSON
From Harried Child to Resilient Leader
Strong &/> Ambitious &/> Caring

Ellen Samson is a dedicated entrepreneur and community leader with a passion for making a difference behind the scenes. She is the CEO and owner of two companies: American Geriatric Care Management and My Own EVA, both focused on serving others through innovative solutions. A Certified Dementia Practitioner and Trainer, Ellen has built a reputation for her hands-on approach to Dementia care. Her workshop, Dementia: Up Close and Personal, has touched countless lives, offering families practical techniques to preserve relationships amidst the challenges of caregiving. As a John Maxwell Certified Coach, she also specializes in helping families navigate the complexities of Dementia with compassion and understanding.

Ellen's efforts earned her the prestigious Most Influential Filipina Award in Paris in 2019, recognizing her advocacy for Dementia awareness. As a co-founder of the Coalition of Filipino American Chambers of Commerce (COFACC) and the founding president of the Filipino American Chamber of Commerce Foundation, Inc., she has played a pivotal role in empowering Filipino entrepreneurs and promoting unity within the community. Ellen's drive is rooted in her belief in the power of service, and she always strives to uplift others through her work.

JUDGE ROHANEE ZAPANTA
Identity, Law, and Justice
Faith. Family. Filipina-American

Judge Rohanee Zapanta was appointed in 2018 by California State Governor Jerry Brown as the second Filipina American to serve as Superior Court Judge for San Diego County. Judge Zapanta was recently awarded in October 2023 the FWN 100™ Most Influential Filipina Women in the World Builder Award. She believes in empowering students of diverse backgrounds through celebrating their cultural core values. Judge Zapanta is co-chair and co-founder of the youth project - *Brown Faces to the Sun*, which celebrates Filipinx-American core values through student workshops and music. She is also co-chair and co-founder of the California Judges Association's Ethics & Wellness Workshops for first-generation law students. Judge Zapanta sits on the Diversity Equity and Inclusion Task Force for the University of San Diego Alumni Board of Directors. She is also the Chief Managing Editor of *The Bench* - the official journal of the California Judges Association, where she regularly contributes a self-assessment column on identity and wellness.

MYLA ARCENO
The King and I
Amiable ☙ Resilient ☙ Trustworthy

Myla was born and raised in Pulupandan, Negros Occidental, a town where everyone knows everyone. At a young age, she was already aware of the importance of community and the people around her. She graduated salutatorian from Pulupandan Elementary School and valedictorian from Our Lady of Lourdes Academy in high school. She always held elected positions as the class and school president. She graduated from Riverside College, Bacolod City, with a Bachelor of Science in Physical Therapy degree and full academic scholarships. She has postgraduate units in Masters in Public Administration and Education.

She lives in Stevenage, Hertfordshire, UK, with her husband Joseph and her children John Benedict and Mary Sophia. She was the first Filipina Mayor in Stevenage, Hertfordshire. UK.

DR. DENISE VIARDO KOH
Finding Filipina, Embodying Intsik: -Isms of Intersectionality

Outrageous ♻ Relentless ♻ Healer.

Dr. Denise Viardo Koh is an award-winning Canadian Tsinay Public Health and Occupational Medicine specialist, hypnotherapist, life coach, speaker, author, assistant professor, and President of the new Manitoba Branch of the Federation of Medical Women of Canada. She has consistently used her training, analytical skills, broad systems thinking, story-telling, and connections through action, advocacy, and leadership.

As Manitoba's former Chief Occupational Medical Officer/Medical Officer of Health, Dr. Denise Viardo Koh led the Workplace COVID Unit and the response for Food Processing, Temporary Foreign Workers, and other high-risk/racialized worker groups. Her leadership in these challenging times reassured many about her capabilities. She founded MedResRx, which runs a Facebook Canadian physician support network for medical learners and an informal Canadian Physician Suicide Log. Her MedResRx Hypnotherapy App and virtual group therapy allows anyone to access her motivational, Burnout Blaster, and other wellness programs anytime anywhere.

Dr. Denise Viardo Koh's commitment to promoting equity, diversity, inclusivity, and representation is inspiring. She shares her experiences with anti-Asian racism and sexism in Medicine and the workplace, her insights into what makes racialized workers sick, and the pandemic learnings that could be put into practice. Her healer superpower is turning patients into powerhouses in record time. Using innovative approaches, she heals systems by assessing risk and championing complex issues in dynamic systems.

DONNA AVELLANA KÜNZLER
Overseas Fabulous Pinay

Overseas ♻ Fabulous ♻ Pinay.

DONNA AVELLANA KÜNZLER was born and raised in Cavite, Philippines. She is a Process Improvement and Digital Transformation Leader by profession. She has a postgraduate degree in Strategy and Innovation from the University of Oxford and an Accountancy degree from De La Salle University, Manila. She is a Certified Public Accountant, Certified Information Systems Auditor, and Certified MSP Program Manager.

For most of her career, she has been an information systems auditor. She has worked for E&Y and Singapore Airlines in Singapore and PricewaterhouseCoopers in the Philippines, US, UK, and Switzerland.

She is currently the Head of Procurement Process Excellence and Digital Transformation for global technology leader ABB's Robotics and Discrete Automation business; a Board member of BSM Global Association, a non-profit that aims to advance the fight against Gender-Based Violence (GBV); the Swiss Bureau Editor of Roots & Wings magazine, an award-winning bi-monthly Filipino expat e-magazine; and an award-winning author of "The Overseas Fabulous Pinay: A modern Filipina's Handbook on How to Thrive Abroad", an Amazon bestseller non-fiction self-help book.

Donna received the Filipina Women's Network's (FWN) Most Influential Filipina in the World Award in 2023. She lives in Zurich with her husband and daughter.

MARLA DE CASTRO RAUSCH
Navigating Dual Worlds: A Filipina leader's Journey of Resilience and Creativity
Formidable ✢ Passionate ✢ Multi-faceted.

Marla de Castro Rausch is the founder and CEO of Animation Vertigo, a motion capture animation company with locations in the US and the Philippines. Since its founding almost 20 years ago, Marla's been considered a trailblazer in the motion capture outsourcing industry; her roster of titles in leading video games franchises such as *Activision 's Call of Duty, NetherRealm's Mortal Kombat, Quantic Dream's Detroit: Becoming Human* as well as Triple A sports titles like **NBA2k, FIFA,** and **Madden** to mention a few that became blockbuster films. It is not a small feat for a woman in a highly competitive, fast-paced, male-driven game and 3D animation industry.

Marla's entrepreneurial spirit extends beyond outsourcing. She is also the Managing Partner of Kampilan Productions, where she focuses on bringing to light the hidden and untold stories of culture, values, and people from Asia. In addition, she is the writer and director of a 3D animated feature, where she is developing her own IP featuring a Filipino hero.

As passionate about growing businesses and helping organizations thrive, Marla is also a mentor, sharing her lessons and experiences through talks and panels. Her goal is to inspire, encourage, and motivate women.

Marla's commitment to the growth of the industry is evident in her ongoing efforts to start new ventures. These ventures are specifically designed to foster capability growth and create more opportunities in the Philippines.

DR. MARY JOY CANON-ABAQUIN
Leading with Purpose: Shaping a More Just and Equitable Future
Visionary ✢ Passionate ✢ Purpose-driven

Dr. Mary Joy Canon-Abaquin, "Teacher Joy," is a pioneer and educational reform advocate. She founded the Multiple Intelligence International School (1996), a progressive international school (preK-12) to make Filipino children globally competitive. Dr. Howard Gardner, the Harvard-based theorist of Multiple Intelligences, cites the MI School in the Philippines for piloting MI and Good Work to "use one's intelligences to make a difference." Gardner cites this significant work in international publications Multiple Intelligences New Horizon, Multiple Intelligences Frames of Mind, and Multiple Intelligence Around the World.

Abaquin's advocacy for Youth Entrepreneurship is evident in her creation of Kids Can, the only For Kids, By Kids bazaar in the country, and her bestselling book, Go Negosyo's "8 Simple Secrets to Raising Entrepreneurs". She also founded the national Youth Innovation Challenge, encouraging students to design-think solutions to real-world problems. Her leadership in the MI Awards, a biennial search for youth role models who make a difference through their intelligences, further demonstrates her Commitment to nurturing the next generation of changemakers. Through her work as an educator, author, womanprenuer, parent-advocate, and teacher-trainor, Abaquin is building a brighter future for all.

RHODORA FRESNEDI
What Will My Mother Say?
Mother & Sunshine Maker & Lifelong Learner.

Rhodora is a mother to three adult kids, dozens of people she coaches through their lives, hundreds of adopted mentees and people she has led in her various senior executive positions globally, and many innovations she has created and sustained throughout her multi-faceted life and career. Rhodora has lived and worked in the U.S., Europe, and Asia, in a professional journey that includes being a teacher, financial controller, HR professional, corporate communications and branding head, general manager, international business leader, consultant, executive coach, entrepreneur, NGO founder, and DEI advocate. She has skillfully held senior executive roles and advised top CEOs on global leadership, strategy, and corporate responsibility. She caps her business career with NGO leadership. As the Founding President and CEO of the Center for Growing and Giving Foundation, Inc., she established Sunshine Farm Philippines, a sunflower farm providing employment and livelihood opportunities for persons with disabilities. She also chairs Best Buddies Philippines and advocates for Arte Autismo Filipino, an organization of gifted artists with autism. On top of all those, she is building on her expertise in the field of inclusion with academic grounding. She is a Global Executive Doctor of Education doctoral candidate at the University of Southern California.

ATTY. LORNA PATAJO-KAPUNAN
Been There, Done That
Courage & Competence & Integrity

Atty. Lorna Patajo Kapunan, founding Partner of Kapunan & Castillo Law Offices, has been a practicing lawyer for 46 years. She has been recognized among the Top 100 Lawyers in the Country for three consecutive years (2019-2021) and was recently awarded the global "Women In Law Awards" for Corporate Law-Philippines, "Asias' Iconic Award for Law," and Linguistic Intelligence Award. She is an awardee of TOWNS (1995), Outstanding Women of the University of the Philippines (1998), and Global FWN 100 (2016).

Atty. Kapunan, while known as a leading litigator due to her involvement in high-profile cases, possesses a breadth of legal expertise. Her areas of practice include intellectual property law, corporate and commercial law, international humanitarian law, family law, estate law, and succession. This extensive knowledge base ensures that she is well-equipped to handle a wide range of legal matters.

Atty. Kapunan was a columnist for Business Mirror with a weekly "Legally Speaking" column and a regular Saturday tele-radio program, "Laban Para Sa Karapatan" (Fight for your Rights) 11-12 at DWIZ 882 AM radio. She has a daily program 'Face2Face' (aired on TV5, I TV, and YouTube), which is a public affairs program settling barangay disputes on air. She is actively involved in socio-civic organizations. Among them are the Philippine Red Cross, Cultural Center of the Philippines, World Wildlife Fund, Rotary International, Zonta Foundation, Women's Business Council, Management Association of the Philippines, Ballet Philippines, Kilusang Makabansang Ekonomiya and People for the Ethical Treatment of Animals.

ROSEMARIE P. RAFAEL
Lead Like a Bamboo
Visionary ✧ Empowered ✧ Courageous.

Rosemarie P. Rafael is the Chairwoman and President of several Philippine companies, including Airspeed Group of Companies and Linex Corporation. She founded Airspeed in 1985, a corporate logistics company now operating worldwide, offering freight forwarding, storage solutions, specialized logistics, e-commerce fulfillment, and customs clearance. As an innovative entrepreneur, she initiated new digital products like UnboxMe, Pinaspeed, and KHPinas. A prominent figure in logistics, Rosemarie was the first woman President (1996-1997) of the Aircargo Forwarders of the Philippines, Inc., recognized by the Civil Aeronautics Board (CAB). With her passion, she has led several companies in consultancy, training, travel, and food.

Mrs. Rafael has received numerous accolades, including the Circle of Excellence for PLDT Enterprise Global Filipino Executive of the Year at the Asia CEO Awards 2022, the ASEAN Special Awards for Women Entrepreneurs 2022, and the ASEAN Women Entrepreneurs Network Award 2022. Additionally, she was recognized as the Woman Leader of the Year Circle of Excellence 2023 by the ASIA CEO Awards. She was named one of the Global FWN100 Awardees 2023 by the Philippine Women's Network.

She actively participates in projects committed to giving back to society, including supporting MSMEs, promoting sustainability, and championing women's empowerment.

NORA KAKILALA TERRADO
Fifty Years of Pivots and Strategies
Leader ✧ Builder ✧ Visionary.

Nora Terrado is a prominent leader in the IT and Business Process Management sector in the Philippines. She founded and led Carelon Global Solutions Philippines (formerly Legato Health Technologies Philippines) as Chief Country Executive. Previously, she was President and Country Manager of Headstrong Philippines and held senior roles at James Martin & Co. and Circle Freight International of the Harper Group USA. Her career began at SGV & Co.

Nora has been active in industry organizations, serving on the boards of the Health Management Association of the Philippines, the IT & Business Process Association of the Philippines, and the Philippine Software Industry Association. She is also a Fellow at the Institute of Corporate Directors.

As Undersecretary of the Department of Trade and Industry (DTI) for over five years, she oversaw management services operations and later led the trade and investment promotion group.

Nora's dedication to mentoring women and her commitment to a sustainable and inclusive future is evident in her extensive contributions to the industry and community. Her efforts have been recognized globally, as she was listed in the Global FWN100™ in 2014 and 2016.

Outside of her professional life, Nora has been married to a business owner for over forty years. They have two sons who have pursued careers as sports journalists and content creators.

MARIA BENEL CORAZON G. SE
Life Unnoticed: Legacy Built
Spiritual ❧ Visionary ❧ Positive

Maria Benel Corazon G. Se is the Managing Partner of JBC Group, LLC (www.wyjbcgroup.com), a full-service minority and women-owned business consulting firm whose partners have provided more than 60 combined years of unparalleled commitment to customer satisfaction in resource efficiency, business consulting, cleantech, sustainability, and human capital fields. Benel is a CPA with over 25 years of experience in audit, tax, accounting, financial planning, and consulting services.

Benel is one of the pioneering leaders in the Los Angeles Filipino-American community. She is the Founding President of the International Society of Filipinos in Finance and Accounting (ISFFA, http://isffa.org/), whose mission is to assist, educate, train, and mentor emerging professionals domestically and globally. She is a board member of the Life Steps Foundation (www.lifestepsfoundation.org), dedicated to meeting the health, psychological, and socioeconomic challenges of people experiencing mental, developmental, or physical disabilities throughout their lifespan. She is a Board Member of the Foundation of Filipina Women Network (FFWN).

Benel is an active member of the Women Presidents Organization (WPO). She is a member of the City Club and is actively involved as an Ambassador of the Club. She is a member of the American Society of Certified Public Accountants.

Her recognitions include one of the 100 Most Influential Filipina Women (2011) award by the Filipina Women's Network, Women Making A Difference Nominee (2012) by Los Angeles Business Journal; and 100 Outstanding Agnesians Awardee (2012) by her Alma Mater High School St. Agnes Academy during its Centennial Celebration.

Benel is a proud wife and mother. Her husband, Dr. Cris B. Liban, is the first Chief Sustainability Officer at LA Metro and President of the City of LA Board of Transportation Commissioners. He was a former US Environmental Protection Agency adviser on national environmental policy and technology. Benel is also the mother of JP. He has a bachelor's and master's degree from Purdue University and is a certified sustainability professional. He is an environmental engineering consultant in New York, NY. This strong family background has been a source of inspiration and support in Benel's professional journey.

FRANCIS TSANG
Preface
Innovative ❧ Collaborative ❧ Resourceful

Francis Tsang, a lifelong San Francisco native, has dedicated 17 years to public service within the City and County of San Francisco. His roles have included Deputy Press Secretary under Mayor Gavin Newsom and Deputy Chief of Staff to Mayor Ed Lee. Currently, he serves as a Strategic Communications Advisor in External Affairs at San Francisco International Airport (SFO), a position he has held since Mayor Lee's passing. Francis earned his Bachelor's degree in Molecular Cell Biology & Biochemistry from UC Berkeley and his Master's in Public Health from Columbia University. Recently, he has triumphed over cancer, adding a personal victory to his distinguished career.

ADELA "DELLE" SERING
CEO and Co-Founder, Seven Seven Softwares, Inc
Global FWN 100™ 2013

In the male-dominated Information Technology (IT) industry, I, Adela "Delle" Sering[66] have been recognized as an unstoppable force, not just in the boardroom, but on a global scale. As a woman of Filipino descent leading in an industry dominated by men and Western norms, I have navigated a unique intersection of gender, race, and cultural expectations. Overcoming these challenges, as the Chief Executive Officer and co-founder of Seven Seven Softwares Inc., I've had the privilege of leading an organization that offers a wide range of IT services to clients worldwide. Together with my co-founder, Seven Seven President Mac Fojas, we built this company from the ground up, turning a modest start-up into a trusted name by creating opportunities for our talented IT professionals to work with Fortune 500 companies and leading firms across the globe.

---

66   Sering D. (2015) Pakikisama: Building Relationships, Building an Industry. In M. Beebe and Maya Escudero (Eds.) Disrupt. Filipina Women. Proud. Loud. Leading without a Doubt. Filipina Women's Network. San Francisco, CA.

It all began with tireless work for the IT-BPM company to gain attraction and entice major clients since Seven Seven was just an unfamiliar start-up in its early days. Our combined passion, resilience, and expertise paid off when we secured key partnerships and established credibility, transforming the start-up from a humble venture into a trusted name in the industry. We built a reputation reflecting the innovative solutions we were determined to deliver.

Fast forward to today, Seven Seven has expanded its footprint internationally, with operations in Singapore, Hong Kong, Japan, and Australia. This global expansion required us to invest in cutting-edge technologies and career development for our IT resources, ensuring they could deliver on global projects. I'm proud that we've created an environment where our employees can thrive by learning and working on advanced technologies like cloud solutions, Machine Learning (ML), Artificial Intelligence (AI), and our Resource Sustainability Solution (RSS), providing employees with the training and hands-on experience they need to excel in these fields. Seven Seven enhances its technological capabilities and fosters a culture of continuous learning and adaptation.

At the core of Seven Seven's success is our unwavering commitment to excellence. We align client needs with our technological capabilities and focus on maintaining quality and adapting quickly to the ever-changing IT landscape. Every project we take on must not only meet but exceed the high standards of our clients, and that is a principle I stand by.

My relational leadership style has played a significant role in creating a welcoming and growth-oriented environment at Seven Seven. By fostering professional development, we attract top talent and enhance operational efficiency through advanced technology and a dedicated, skilled workforce. I am committed to excellence, and this determination has driven Seven Seven to deliver cost-effective, high-quality services to our clients continuously.

Recently, we celebrated Seven Seven's 27th anniversary—a milestone that truly belongs to the employees who have been instrumental to the company's success. I believe wholeheartedly that without their hard work and dedication, we would not be where we are today. As a leader, I understand the significance of representation and the importance of providing pathways to advance in an industry that historically hasn't been designed with us in mind. Together, we have achieved so much and have every reason to be proud.

Despite the company's many achievements, I remain deeply grateful for the opportunities that have come my way. I'm committed to giving back and providing holistic programs meant for the long-term sustainability of different communities in need in the United States and the Philippines, including youth, women, education, and disaster relief. We go beyond delivering IT services by focusing on community development and philanthropy. From sponsoring medical missions and community events to providing educational support for employees' children, Seven Seven has always aimed to make a positive impact.

Our commitment to social causes also extends to fundraising efforts for cardiovascular care and promoting diversity and inclusion within the company. Celebrating Pride Month and actively supporting LGBTQIA++ employees and their allies through participation in Pride Marches is just one example of how we foster an inclusive culture at Seven Seven. Our "Green Sustain" campaign further demonstrates our dedication to environmental stewardship, with activities like mangrove planting and coastal cleanups in the Philippines that promote sustainability and community welfare.

Through all these efforts, I've worked hard to ensure that Seven Seven not only stands out in the IT industry but also pays it forward by making a lasting difference in the communities we serve. My journey with this company has been enriching and shaped by the intersections of my identity as a woman, a Filipina, and a leader in a male-dominated field. I'm excited about what the future holds for Seven Seven—continued innovation, growth, and a positive impact both in our industry and society.

LIFETIME MEMBERS: UPDATES

ANGELICA BERRIE, PRESIDENT,
The Russell Berrie
Foundation https://www.russellberriefoundation.org/
Global FWN 100™ 2014

My story of becoming in Disrupt 4.0[67] related to my journey as a Filipino American, my transformation from a Catholic convent-educated girl to a Jew who took the Hebrew name Ruth when I embraced Judaism.

Since October 7, 2023, it has been a particularly painful year for me as a Jew. HAMAS attacked Israel, slaughtering over 1200 people, raping women, torturing children, kidnapping, and taking hostages to Gaza, including Filipinos.

---

67   Berrie, A. (2023). Becoming Ruth: A Transformational Journey. In M. Beebe (Ed.) Disrupt 4.0, Filipina Women: Being. Filipina Women's Network, San Francisco, CA.

I met Camille Jesalva, a Filipina caregiver in Israel who saved her 95-year-old employer by offering the Palestinian terrorist who entered their home her savings of $ 370. Miraculously, he took her money and spared their lives.

President Herzog of Israel recognized Camille's incredible courage. Her story is included in the book One Day in October: Forty Heroes, Forty Stories, which features the stories of 40 real-life heroes who endured the October 7, 2023, attack.

Thanks to the Filipina Women's Network, Camille received a grant in recognition of her leadership in the face of such horror.

Since October 7, the sympathy of the world for Israel changed to hatred towards Jews as the death toll in Gaza mounted. Jewish students on US campuses received death threats and were subjected to hate speech from pro-Palestinian sympathizers. In response to anti-Semitism on Columbia's campus, the Russell Berrie Foundation issued a statement announcing our intention to pause funding for Columbia, where we founded the Naomi Berrie Diabetes Center in New York.

At the height of the campus occupation, my remarks appeared on the front page of the New York Times: The Russell Berrie Foundation, which had donated some $ 86M to Columbia over the years, also suspended gifts. *"It's a painful decision for us to have come to this point where we have to tell them, 'There's a disconnect between your values and ours,'"*

Angelica Berrie, the president of the foundation's board, said in an interview earlier this year, explaining that *"our Jewish values infuse our philanthropy."*

In the Biblical story of Queen Esther, she reveals her identity as a Jew after an edict to kill all the Jews is issued by her husband, the King, who does not know she is Jewish. In a moment of moral courage, Esther faces a historic choice; *"Do I reveal my identity and face certain death, or should I cast fear aside to stand with my people?"* It is a story that resonates in this moment when my identity as a Jew puts me in the crosshairs of hate.

When I decided to convert, a prominent Jewish philanthropist asked me: *"Why are you doing this? Don't you know Jews are the most persecuted people on earth?"* I never imagined that the day would ever come when this would be borne out, of all places, in America.

The climate of hate has not diminished my passion for building bridges between faiths, in our local New Jersey community and globally, through 140 Russell Berrie Fellows in 47 countries who are alumni of the Pope John Paul II Center for Inter-Religious Studies at the Angelicum, a Pontifical university in Rome.

In my philanthropic work in Israel, I learned that peace is not a utopia but a foundation built by people who believe they have a shared destiny. I encountered changemakers like:

> Zahia Abu Zarmeliah, one of 150 Palestinian women beekeepers whose rooftop hives in East Jerusalem provide economic opportunities through this innovative women's empowerment program;

> Vivian Silver, a peace activist murdered on October 7, who co-founded Women Wage Peace, the largest grassroots peace movement in Israel with 44,000 Palestinian and Israeli members;

> Nabeel Abboud Ashkar, an Arab from Nazareth, founded Polyphony Galilee Chamber Orchestra, the first professional orchestra in Israel that consisted of Arab and Jewish musicians.

In this moment of global challenges, the Filipina Women's Network is a light for women by creating positive change where we are, with what we have. We have to stand up, speak out, and step forward on issues that matter: democracy, peace, women's rights, climate change, and freedom.

Let us be intentional in how we exercise our agency to be a blessing!

FE ODSIGUE PUNZALAN
-- Founder and CEO, Punzalan Homes of Fe Odsigue Punzalan

Early Beginnings

My journey from a little girl selling peanut brittle to becoming an exceptional registered nurse and eventually a successful entrepreneur has been nothing short of extraordinary. Growing up in a family of 11 siblings in Antique, Philippines, financial hardship was a constant companion. My parents worked tirelessly as farmers, but despite their efforts, there were many nights when I went to bed hungry. Those difficult times, paired with the ridicule I faced, only fueled my determination to ensure that my circumstances would not define my future. Today, as a philanthropist, CEO, and multimillion-dollar entrepreneur, my story is one of triumph over adversity.

Graduating 5th out of 75 top-notch University of the Philippines - Philippine General Hospital School of Nursing (UP-PGH SON) students, I was eager to make a difference in the world of nursing. My success has been a blend of academic strength, a strong sense of service, and a natural inclination toward risk-taking. In 1977, I made my way to the United States, determined to chase the American dream and lift my family in the Philippines out of poverty. Chicago, Illinois, was my first stop, but it wasn't long before I found my way to San Francisco, California, where I would begin my entrepreneurial journey.

As a newcomer with an accent and an immigrant background, I experienced moments of doubt and feelings of non-acceptance. This intersectionality of being a Filipina woman in a male-dominated field, coupled with my immigrant status, made the journey more difficult. Yet, the seal of honor and excellence I carried from the University of the Philippines reignited my resolve. I worked diligently in acute care settings, spearheading several patient-centered initiatives. Always seeking to improve, I completed my Bachelor of Science in Nursing and my Master of Science in Nursing, both focusing on Nursing Administration while raising my young children. My career flourished, and I held several management positions, all of which prepared me for my future ventures as an entrepreneur. I was certified as a **Group Home Administrator by the State of California in 2000** and became a **Qualified Intellectual Disability Professional (QIDP) by the California Department of Developmental Services in 2007**. Additionally, my professional credentials were reinforced by my continued certification as an **ANCC Med-Surg Nurse (RN-BC), a distinction I've held since 1989**.

Envisioning the Future

In 1997, my husband German suggested that I reduce my long work hours to spend more time with our family. He believed my talents and abilities were well-suited to running residential care facilities. With his encouragement, I embarked on the rigorous journey of meeting training, licensing, and certification requirements. After we purchased and renovated a house to serve as a home for individuals with intellectual disabilities, we found ourselves with only $200 left in the bank. Yet, I was unwavering in my resolve. Over the next 18 months, I secured permits, financing, and ensured compliance with regulatory mandates, setting the stage for our first resident.

Navigating the Journey of Entrepreneurship

With German's vision in mind, we formalized our partnership, with me assuming the primary administrator role. My two decades of experience in nursing, both clinical and managerial, were essential to laying the foundation for what would become an award-winning residential care facility. Punzalan Homes started with just one resident, with only German and myself as staff. Within a year, we had four residents. I applied for and secured a highly competitive government grant focused on developing residential care facilities, which allowed us to expand further.

I cultivated a culture of professionalism, mutual respect, and service. My leadership style encouraged dynamic dialogue, where team members, residents, and their families could express concerns. With a strong focus on empathy, care, and behavioral programming, our residents saw remarkable improvements in their quality of life. By 2007, I employed 24 residents and 25 staff, supported by an interdisciplinary team of psychologists, behaviorists, therapists, nutritionists, and educators.

My experiences as an immigrant woman deeply informed how I built my business. The intersectionality of my immigrant status and my role as an entrepreneur meant that I was not just navigating the challenges of starting a business, but also adjusting to cultural and social dynamics that often placed me on the margins. This allowed me to foster a deeper understanding and empathy for my residents, many of whom experienced their own struggles with marginalization. As my facilities grew, so did recognition of the quality of care we provided. In **2002, I was honored with the Service Provider of the Year award by the California State Assembly**, an accolade that affirmed the excellence we had cultivated. The following years brought further validation of my leadership and service, with **The Filipina Women's Network recognizing me in 2009 as one of the 100 Most Influential Filipina Women in the US** and later, in **2019, I was named one of the 100 Most Influential Filipina Women in the World**. Each award was a testament to the dedication and perseverance that German and I poured into our work.

Sharing the Blessings

Despite my success, I have always believed in giving back. Rather than expanding my business further, I chose to become a pro-bono consultant to seven Filipino couples, helping them establish their own residential care facilities in California. I have also remained deeply involved in the Filipino community and the UP-PGH SON Alumni Association. I was honored to receive the **Outstanding Alumna for Community Service from UP-PGH SNAA in 2020**, which reflected my deep commitment to my community. As a lifetime member of the Filipina Women's Network, both in the USA and globally, I take pride in knowing that I am making a difference.

Family has always been at the heart of my journey. German and I shared 40 wonderful years together until his untimely passing in 2018. His loss was devastating, but the love and devotion of our daughters, Clarisse, Christina, and Maureen, continue to light my way. German's voice still echoes in my mind, saying:

"Ginahigugma ko ikaw tuod gid"

(*I love you very much*)

These words fill my heart with gratitude for a life full of amazing and fulfilling moments. To those I have helped on their own journey to achieve the American dream, my words of wisdom are simple:

"I would have spent my life planting kangkong with my Nanay if I had not dared to believe in something more."

Through this journey, the intersectionality of my gender, cultural background, and immigrant experience became my most significant challenges and profound strengths, shaping the entrepreneur and leader I am today.

LOIDA NICOLAS-LEWIS
Chair and CEO of TLC Beatrice, LLC
Global FWN 100™ 2013[68]

As Chair and CEO of TLC Beatrice, LLC, a family investment firm, I have navigated a path shaped by the intersections of gender, race, and cultural heritage. My journey as a Filipino woman in both the legal and business worlds has required resilience, adaptability, and a steadfast belief in the possibility of breaking through barriers that have historically held back people like me. I am a lawyer by profession, admitted to practice in both the Philippines and New York. One of my proudest accomplishments was becoming the first Filipino woman to pass the New York bar without attending law school in the United States, a significant milestone that challenged the norms of legal practice in a foreign land.

---

68   Nicolas-Lewis, L. (2015). Ora et Labora: A Girl Named Loida of Sorsogon. In M. Beebe and Maya Escudero (Eds.) Disrupt. Filipina Women. Proud. Loud. Leading without a Doubt. Filipina Women's Network. San Francisco, CA.

My legal career took on a deeper meaning when I won my discrimination case against the U.S. Immigration and Naturalization Service. This victory allowed me to integrate the agency and serve as General Attorney in its New York Federal office from 1978 to 1988. I later co-authored *How to Get a Green Card*, a resource that has become a bestseller and helped countless immigrants navigate a complex and often intimidating system. This achievement speaks to my commitment to making legal knowledge accessible, especially for immigrants like myself who must overcome numerous obstacles to achieve their dreams.

In 1994, my life took another pivotal turn when I assumed the leadership of TLC Beatrice International, a $2 billion multinational food company, after the sudden death of my husband, Reginald F. Lewis. Reginald was a brilliant Wall Street financier who, in 1987, made history by engineering a leveraged buyout of Beatrice International Foods for $985 million, making him the first African American to create a billion-dollar company. Stepping into the role of Chair and CEO after his passing was both an honor and a challenge. I was not only a woman leading a multinational business but also an Asian woman succeeding an African American icon. Despite cultural expectations and racial stereotypes, I knew that my leadership would defy the assumptions of what a CEO should look like.

For 13 years, from 1994 to 2007, I led TLC Beatrice International, navigating the complexities of a global business, with operations across Europe. My experience managing a multinational corporation in a male-dominated industry required me to continually assert my presence and expertise, as an Asian American woman, a widow, and a mother—each influencing the way I approached leadership.

I recently launched my memoir, *Why Should Guys Have All The Fun? An Asian American Story of Love, Marriage, Motherhood, and Running a Billion Dollar Empire*, where I reflect on these experiences. The book's success, landing on Amazon's Number 1 list of recent releases in business and finance for eight weeks, tells me that my story resonates with many people.

My commitment to honoring my late husband's legacy continues through the work of the Reginald F. Lewis Foundation, where I serve as Chair. The foundation is a benefactor of several prestigious institutions, including Harvard Law School, the Museum of Maryland African American History & Culture, Virginia State University, and the Lewis College in my hometown of Sorsogon, Philippines. These institutions have honored Reginald's contributions to history, and through the foundation, we ensure that his impact continues. The foundation is also a major donor to the National Museum of African American History and Culture in Washington, D.C., where the story of African American excellence, including my husband's, is told for generations to come.

In addition to my business and philanthropic work, I serve on the Board of Directors of several organizations that are close to my heart, including the Children's Orchestra Society, The National Judicial College, and the USC Center on Public Diplomacy. I am particularly proud of my involvement with *Kinding Sindaw*, an organization dedicated to preserving Indigenous cultures and advocating for political strength, especially for marginalized communities.

Throughout my life, I've been driven by the need to advocate for those who often do not have a voice. I co-founded several advocacy organizations, including the Asian American Legal Defense & Education Fund, the National Federation of Filipino American Associations, US Pinoys for Good Governance, and the Global Filipino Diaspora Council. These organizations are central to my mission of ensuring that the voices of Asian Americans, Filipinos, and other marginalized communities are heard and empowered towards creating a more equitable world.

Fluent in Filipino, English, French, and Spanish, I have embraced the richness of my multicultural background, using language and culture as tools to bridge gaps and connect with diverse communities. My greatest joy, however, comes from my family. I have two wonderful daughters and five grandchildren, and they remain at the center of my life.

BENEL SE-LIBAN WITH CRIS LIBAN
Managing Partner
JBC Group, LLC
Global FWN 100™ 2011

Since the publication of our Disrupt 2.0 Chapter, *A Life That Matters*[69] my family and I have had a decade of life-changing stories. We have undergone transformational change, and there was no shortage of inspirational outcomes as we practiced the 16 principles we laid out.

We reflect on the value of life, building a strong legacy, and timeless memories.

---

69   Se-Liban, B. with Cris Liban (2016). A Life That Matters. In M. Beebe (Ed.) Disrupt 2.0, Filipina Women: Daring to Lead. Filipina Women's Network, San Francisco, CA.

Value of Life

Exacerbated by the worldwide pandemic, we lost many of our relatives and friends, including my parents and my eldest sister. However, seeing my husband Cris' parents both still alive, we are reminded to celebrate what we have in the moment rather than dwell on the losses of the past. As we have traveled to multiple continents this past decade, we celebrated every fleeting moment of life's journey. Setting sights to Africa and Antarctica next, we continually savor the companionship and friendship of everyone we meet, learning from those lives to improve our lives and the communities we serve.

Building A Strong Legacy

The last decade has taken us to explore and overcome the challenges of entrepreneurship. Since 2017, JBC Group, LLC has grown from a staff of two to a global network of strategic partners that provide business consulting, sustainability, and financial services to small entrepreneurial ventures and some of the largest global companies and organizations. "Just Be Christ" is the meaning of JBC. The faith reference provides context on our delivery of service to our clients.

We also extend our servant leadership, guided by our faith, through the non-profits we founded, the International Society of Filipinos in Finance and Accounting and Engineer Action Rising, uplifting everyone through leadership, mentorship, and scholarship programs.

Timeless Memories

As we look back on the last decade, we realize the endless images of where we have been, our decisions, and, ultimately, the outcomes we faced. Most of them reinforced our innate values: deep faith in God, the importance of family and community, the value of education, having enough savings for the future, experiencing life vs. buying stuff, and being the best in our careers.

JP has an advanced engineering degree from Purdue University and is on his way to becoming a licensed environmental engineer. My husband Cris is at the top of his game as the Chief Sustainability Officer of his agency. JBC Group, LLC is thriving very well globally. Cris and I also celebrated our Silver Wedding Anniversary. In addition to Los

Angeles and Lake Arrowhead, we planted additional roots in New Jersey, New York, Manila, and Bicol.

Looking back at this decade, we see the faces of the friends, family, and communities we worked with. We also see significant progress in the lives of people we help. We have all grown up together with them, on a journey that has not always been pleasant, but whose lessons sharpened our outlook.

Thirty years from now, the next generation of leaders will lead us. We cannot predict what the future looks like. However, we hope that we have contributed well to preparing JP and all the lives we touched to build a better world for all *in a life that matters*. We did!

COLONEL SHIRLEY RAGUINDIN
Defense Advisory Committee on Diversity & Inclusion
Global FWN100™ 2007[70]

Leadership Journey

My journey within the U.S. Air Force, the National Guard Bureau, and my broader career as a Federal Government director in the Department of Defense has been a testament to the power of intersectional leadership. Since 2012, when I was honored as a Lifetime Member of the 100 Most Influential Filipinas in the United States, my career has been filled with opportunities to break barriers and set new standards. In my current role as Director of Military Equal Opportunity in the Office of Diversity Management and Equal Opportunity at the Defense Pentagon, I continue to uphold the values of inclusion and diversity. Over the years, I have been fortunate to receive

---

70   [1] Raguindin, S. (2015). Beating the Odds. In M. Beebe and Maya Escudero (Eds.) Disrupt. Filipina Women. Proud. Loud. Leading without a Doubt. Filipina Women's Network. San Francisco, CA.

prestigious recognitions, including being named one of the Global 100 Most Influential Filipinas in 2012 and the Most Influential Filipinas in the United States in 2007. These accolades reflect my deep commitment to fostering diversity and pursuing excellence.

Following my recognition in 2012, I stepped into a critical leadership role as Chief Diversity and Inclusion Advisor to the Chief of the National Guard Bureau and the Director of the Air National Guard, representing over 458,000 Soldiers and Airmen. This role allowed me to influence and shape the organizational culture, ensuring that diversity and inclusion were integrated into operational frameworks. Serving as Chief Diversity Officer to both a 3- and 4-star General Officer for over six years, I worked to create an inclusive environment that enhanced mission readiness and lethality by addressing systemic inequalities and promoting representation.

As Director of Military Equal Opportunity, I developed and implemented transformational approaches to military equal opportunity policies, overseeing training programs for over 2.3 million service members. This position allowed me to advocate for equality within the Pentagon and across the broader military community. In 2007, I was recognized with the Global Thought Leader - Diversity Officer Leadership Award by Diversity Best Practices, Inc., which highlighted the work I had been doing to champion diversity and inclusion at the highest levels.

Throughout my career, my leadership has been shaped by my intersectional identities. As a Filipina woman in a predominantly male military environment, I have faced and navigated multiple layers of bias and discrimination. Yet, these challenges have fueled my drive to advocate for those who, like me, are often underrepresented. In 2013, I was one of 15 leaders nationwide selected by the American Psychological Association to redefine leadership competencies at a Diversity Leadership Summit (LDS). The summit explored how our identities, lived experiences, and cultural backgrounds influence our leadership styles, and it further solidified my belief that intersectional leadership is crucial in today's diverse, globalized world. We discussed the following questions:

- How do you view leadership?

- How is your exercise of leadership influenced by the context in which you lead, the multiple dimensions of your identity, and your lived experiences associated with culture and minority status?

- How do you project the kind of leadership needed for the future, given the rapid change, growing diversity, and increased globalization in society?

Each question was covered in a roundtable session, and discussions were recorded, transcribed, and content analyzed. The LDS identified 4 competencies (with 16 dimensions) that are likely to be crucial to leadership in the coming years as organizations become increasingly diverse: leveraging personal and social identities, utilizing a global and diverse mindset, leveraging community and organizational contexts, and promoting a diversity-supportive and inclusive climate. As a result, this study gained a better understanding of the new leadership challenges that diversity brings to organizations.[712]

As a woman in the military, I have worked tirelessly to dismantle gender biases that limit opportunities for women in this traditionally male-dominated institution. My rise to senior leadership roles in diversity and inclusion reflects my dedication to challenging and redefining gender norms within the military. Likewise, as a Filipina, I have experienced the challenges faced by people of color in the military firsthand. My experiences have reinforced the importance of representation and the need for leadership that addresses the unique challenges of racial and ethnic minorities.

Cultural competence has always been central to my leadership. My work as Chief Diversity and Inclusion Advisor, and later as Director of Military Equal Opportunity, has focused on creating policies that not only promote diversity but also ensure that service members are equipped to engage with the diverse cultures and communities they encounter, both within the military and in their global operations. In my published story *Disrupt 1.0*, I discuss how cultural barriers can either help or hinder the development of leadership competencies for minority women, particularly from my perspective as a Filipina woman in the military.

My pursuit of continuous professional development has also been integral to my leadership journey. In 2019, I completed the Global Executive Leadership Program at the Yale School of Management, equipping myself with the knowledge and tools to lead meaningful change. I also graduated from the Federal Executive Institute, which

---

71   Chin, J. L., Desormeaux, L., & Sawyer, K. (2016). Making way for paradigms of diversity leadership. Consulting Psychology Journal: Practice and Research, 68(1), 49–71. https://doi.org/10.1037/cpb0000051

broadened my understanding of leadership in complex, diverse environments and has greatly influenced my approach to my current role.

Mentorship and advocacy have been at the heart of my work. Throughout my career, I have mentored countless junior officers, cohorts, and federal employees, guiding and supporting them as they navigate their careers. My advocacy has always extended beyond policy work to include personal mentorship for women and people of color who face additional obstacles in advancing their careers within the military.

Of course, my path to leadership has not been without its challenges. As a Filipina woman in senior military roles, I have had to contend with both gender and racial biases. These challenges have required me to develop resilience and a strategic approach to overcoming barriers. However, the ability to persevere and excel in the face of adversity has been a defining aspect of my leadership.

Looking back, I'm proud of the legacy I've built in the military and the broader Department of Defense. My unwavering commitment to diversity, inclusion, and leadership excellence has had a profound impact on policies and practices, ensuring that the values of a diverse and inclusive environment are upheld at the highest levels. Through my resilience, advocacy, and continuous professional development, I have set a new standard for leadership—one that embraces intersectionality as a source of strength and innovation.

To emerging leaders from diverse backgrounds, I always share this important message: the only barriers to your goals in life are not those created by others, but the ones you create yourself. And with my favorite quote by Nikosi Johnson, *"Do what you can, in the time that you have, in the place that you are,"* I hope to inspire others to give their best every day, just as I continue to strive to do in my journey.

SONIA T. DELEN
Director, Bank of America- Global Leasing
US FWN 100™ 2007
Global FWN 100™ 2013
Keeper of the Flame, 2007, 2009, 2011, 2013

My journey is a *hinabi* woven from intersecting identities that have shaped who I am today: a Filipina-American immigrant, mother, corporate leader, advocate, and cultural ambassador. In 1982, I migrated to the U.S. as a single mother with my son, David, who is blind and hearing-impaired. Navigating the challenges of raising a child with disabilities in a new country laid the foundation for my lifelong advocacy. My experiences as David's mother and an immigrant have profoundly influenced both my personal and professional paths.

In 1990, I married Christopher Fitzsimmons, and together, we raised three sons: David, who continues to inspire my advocacy; Justin, a lawyer; and Matthew, a U.S. Army captain. Balancing motherhood, especially raising a child with special needs, alongside a demanding corporate career shaped me in unexpected ways. I thrived in the corporate world, rising to Director at Global Leasing, a division of Bank of America, and eventually reaching senior leadership positions. As the highest-ranking Filipina in Global Leasing, I experience the intersection of gender and ethnicity in corporate America, where being a woman of color presents both challenges and opportunities. These challenges have only fueled my drive to excel.

My advocacy for children with disabilities is deeply personal. I served on the boards of the Blind Babies Foundation and Families of Children with Special Needs, not just as community work, but to advocate for my son and others like him. I've witnessed the struggles families face when navigating systems that often overlook children with disabilities, particularly as an immigrant learning to navigate the complexities of the American healthcare system.

Professionally, I expanded my advocacy for women's rights and leadership, especially within the Filipina community. My involvement with the Filipina Women's Network (FWN) connected me with a powerful group of women who, like me, are passionate about ensuring our voices are heard and our faces seen in spaces that haven't always welcomed us. In 2022, being named one of The Top 50 Women Leaders of San Francisco was a powerful reminder of how far I've come as a Filipina in a male-dominated corporate world.

In 2018, I became the first Filipina-American and Asian-American to serve as a non-lawyer public member of the State Bar of California's Board of Trustees. This appointment by then-Governor Jerry Brown was a significant milestone for me—reflecting the intersection of my ethnicity, gender, and commitment to public service. My earlier appointment in 2016 was with the Health Professions Education Foundation, the state-created foundation that provides scholarships and loan repayment for health professionals serving in underserved institutions in California. These are humbling reminders that also emphasize the importance of representation, especially in regulatory and public policy spaces where women of color are often underrepresented.

Healthcare equity has always been a key focus of mine. As chairperson of the Apl.de.ap Foundation International (APLFI), I work to eradicate preventable blindness in the Philippines through the Campaign for Filipino Children, which brings cutting-edge medical technology to underserved hospitals, ensuring that babies born with conditions like Retinopathy of Prematurity (ROP) have a fighting chance at sight. Working with the Philippine Academy of Ophthalmology, ROP still affects over 4,000 premature babies in the Philippines annually. Select Philippine regional hospitals, including Southern Philippines Medical Center in Davao City and J.B. Lingad Memorial

Regional Hospital in Angeles City, Pampanga, are the beneficiaries. I spearheaded the collaboration as director of the University of the Philippines Alumni Association of San Francisco (UPAASF) and APLFI. I've also led efforts to secure donations, including 300,000 COVID-19 test kits valued at U.S. $2,850,000 to the University of the Philippines-Philippine General Hospital, and assisted in fundraising initiatives to help the university during the pandemic towards PPEs, food for the stranded UP students, *Kaagapay Sa Pag-Aaral* to provide computers to enable remote learning during the pandemic; and the UPgrade project in refurbishing the UP Main Library. This work isn't just about healthcare—it's about giving back to my home country and ensuring that even the most vulnerable have access to the care they deserve.

Cultural preservation is another passion of mine. In 2013, I co-founded the UPAASF Filipino Cultural Immersion Camp to help children learn about and connect with their heritage, language, and traditions.

I'm particularly proud of my efforts to elevate Filipino cuisine. In 2010, I co-founded the Kulinarya Showdown in partnership with the Philippine Department of Tourism, showcasing talented chefs and celebrating Filipino food across the U.S. In 2014, I co-founded the Filipino Food Movement with a group of passionate volunteers with the mission to preserve, promote, and progress Filipino cuisine worldwide. As president, I've dedicated myself to promoting Filipino cuisine on the global stage through education and community building, and I've been fortunate to help make that happen.

Filmmaking has also given me a unique platform to tell stories that matter. As an executive producer for critically acclaimed films, I've had the privilege of bringing narratives about the Filipino lost art of serenade in HARANA (www.haranathemovie.com), about Filipino culture in LAHI, and about transgender rights in *LABELED: THE ROAD TO SYDNEY* to a wider audience. I was also an Associate Producer for the Netflix TV series "1N7K" for two episodes (Food and Surfing). Through storytelling, I've been able to advocate for marginalized communities, whether preserving our cultural traditions or fighting for equality and representation to broader audiences.

In recognition of my contributions, President Biden honored me with the Presidential Lifetime Achievement Award at The Outstanding Filipinos in America (TOFA) in 2023 and Asia's Remarkable and Multidimensional Leader Award in 2024. I also received the Gawad Oblation Award from the University of the Philippines in 2022, the institution's highest honor awarded every six years to friends and alumni who have contributed significantly to UP.

I've channeled my experiences into writing and co-authoring leadership books addressing Filipina women's unique challenges, including From Boondock to the Boardroom in *DISRUPT. Filipina Women. Proud. Loud. Leading without a Doubt* (2015)[72], Power of Connection in *DISRUPT 4.0. Filipina Women: Being (2023)*[73], *Rooted In Practice* (Pinays in Law)_in_ PinayPowerHouse anthology book (2023), and *Iconic Pinoy*, a Maharlika Inaugural book (2023). These books aren't just about leadership—they're about what it means to be a woman, a minority, and a leader all at once. Through my writing, I aim to inspire women to embrace their identities and find strength in their intersections, just as I have.

My life reflects the many intersecting identities that define who I am—an immigrant, mother, corporate leader, mentor, advocate, filmmaker, motivational speaker, and proud Filipina. Each of these roles shapes how I navigate the world, fueling my passion for creating positive change in both corporate and community spaces. Above all, I am most proud of my family and grateful for the unwavering support of my husband, Chris; my sons David, Justin, and Matthew; my sister, Ester; and my 99-year-old father, Aquilino Delen, who instilled in me the importance of giving back from an early age. I take immense pride in my sons, who are passionate leaders dedicated to serving their communities through their professions. In my personal time, I enjoy playing golf, traveling, and immersing myself in classical music and the opera.

---

72   Delen, S. (2015). From Boondock to the Boardroom. In M. Beebe and Maya Escudero (Eds.) Disrupt. Filipina Women. Proud. Loud. Leading without a Doubt. Filipina Women's Network. San Francisco, CA.

73   Delen, S. (2023). Power of Connection. In M. Beebe (Ed.) DISRUPT 4.0. Filipina Women: Being. Filipina Women's Network, San Francisco, CA.

SUSIE QUESADA
President and CEO of Ramar Foods
Global FWN 100™ 2014

My Journey: A Five-Year Reflection on Professional and Personal Growth

Over the past five years, my journey has been one of dynamic transformation, marked by significant professional achievements and profound personal developments[74]. As a leader in the CPG (Consumer Packaged Goods) industry, particularly within the food manufacturing sector, I've experienced both the challenges and rewards of navigating this path. My story is one of resilience, innovation, and a deep commitment to diversity and inclusion, shaped by the complex interplay of various social identities—what we often refer to as intersectionality.

Professional Achievements: Innovating in the CPG Industry

Professionally, the last five years have been incredibly fulfilling. As the President and CEO of Ramar Foods, a family-owned business specializing in Filipino cuisine, I've had the privilege of leading my family's company through significant growth and transformation. One of my most notable accomplishments during this period was

---

74   Quesada, S. (2015). Mommyla, Popsy, and Me: Leading by Example through Generations. In M. Beebe and Maya Escudero (Eds.) Disrupt. Filipina Women. Proud. Loud. Leading without a Doubt. Filipina Women's Network. San Francisco, CA.

navigating the uncertainty of the COVID-19 Pandemic. As an essential business, my leadership team and I created a new playbook for dealing with public health crises as we kept our lines running to provide much-needed subsistence to the communities we serve around the world. With daily huddles to stay connected, we were able to support our three hundred team members and their families. With federal, state, and county regulations changing almost daily, my team was able to persevere by helping each other and the community.

Another area of focus has been expanding our distribution network. By forging strategic partnerships with major retailers and exploring e-commerce opportunities, we've significantly increased our domestic and international market reach. This expansion has not only boosted our revenue but also solidified Ramar Foods' position as a leader in the Asian-American foods category.

Sustainability has also been a major priority for me. Under my guidance, we've implemented various initiatives to reduce our environmental footprint, such as sourcing ingredients from sustainable suppliers, reducing packaging waste, and increasing energy efficiency in our manufacturing processes through massive solar and hydrogen fuel cell investments, as well as EV charging infrastructure. These efforts have earned us recognition within the industry, the California Air Resources Board (CARB), and have resonated with today's sustainability-conscious consumers.

Leadership in Diversity and Inclusion: A Commitment to Intersectionality

While my professional accomplishments are important, my commitment to diversity and inclusion is equally significant. As a Filipina-American woman leading a family-owned business in a predominantly male-dominated industry, I've long understood the importance of intersectionality. My unique perspective has driven me to create a more inclusive workplace and to champion diversity within the broader business community.

My approach to leadership is deeply rooted in my identity, and in doing so, inspiring my teams to tap into theirs. I've worked hard to ensure that Ramar Foods reflects the diversity of the communities we serve, both in our workforce and in our leadership team. By fostering an inclusive culture, I've empowered employees from various backgrounds to bring their whole selves to work, resulting in a more innovative and dynamic organization. More so, through the Ramar Scholarship Foundation, a non-profit for post-secondary scholarships in the USA and the Philippines, our company has made a meaningful impact on hundreds of students in both countries, positively altering their trajectory as productive members of society.

Separate from leading Ramar Foods, I'm a vocal advocate for diversity and inclusion in the wider business world. I've participated in numerous panels, conferences, and workshops that are male-dominated, sharing my insights on the importance of intersectionality in leadership. Through these platforms, I aimed to inspire other business leaders to recognize and embrace the value of diverse perspectives in driving innovation and growth.

My commitment to intersectionality extends beyond the workplace as well; I've been actively involved in community organizations that support underrepresented groups, particularly women and people of color. By mentoring young professionals and supporting initiatives that promote education and economic empowerment, I've tried to make a tangible impact on the lives of others. I believe that true leadership involves not only achieving business success but also uplifting others along the way.

Personal Growth: Navigating Life's Challenges

While my professional life has been filled with accomplishments, my personal journey over the past five years has been equally transformative. Balancing the demands of leading a growing business with personal responsibilities has required resilience, adaptability, and a deep sense of purpose. One of the most significant personal developments in my life during this period was my decision to prioritize my mental and physical well-being. As a business leader, the pressures of the job can be overwhelming, and I recognized the importance of self-care in maintaining my effectiveness. I've since incorporated regular exercise, mindfulness practices, and a balanced diet into my daily routine, leading to improved health and well-being. I have also invested time in business organizations that support my personal growth and development, similar to FWN, like the Women's Presidents Organization and Tugboat Institute.

Moreover, I've embraced the concept of work-life integration, understanding that true success is not just about professional achievements but also about maintaining meaningful personal relationships. I've prioritized spending quality time with my family and husband, who have been a source of inspiration and motivation. By setting boundaries and being intentional about my time, I've found a way to nurture my personal life in meaningful ways that further increase my effectiveness in my professional life.

Spending time coaching and mentoring others has been extremely fulfilling. Although my Femtee from FWN's Femtormatch has ended, I have continued this practice. Connecting with others from different generations and backgrounds is a two way street. While I have much to offer from my experiences as a coach, business leader and teacher, I find that it is reciprocated ten-fold from each femtee,or mentee, that I meet.

Intersectionality in Action: Bridging Professional and Personal Life

My journey over the past five years illustrates the power of intersectionality in shaping both professional and personal experiences. My ability to navigate the intersections of my identity—as a Filipina-American woman, a business leader, and a community advocate—has informed my approach to leadership and fueled my passion for diversity and inclusion, climate change, and supporting the growth and development of women and girls.

Intersectionality has driven my efforts to create a more inclusive and equitable workplace at Ramar Foods. By recognizing and embracing the diverse experiences and perspectives of my employees, I've fostered a culture of belonging that has not only improved employee morale but also driven innovation and business success. My leadership serves as a model for other companies in the CPG industry and beyond, demonstrating the value of diversity in achieving sustainable growth.

At the same time, my personal experiences have enriched my professional life. My journey as a coach and mentor has provided me with a deeper understanding of the challenges faced by employees with caregiving responsibilities. This understanding has led to the implementation of more flexible work policies at Ramar Foods, ensuring that employees have the support they need to balance their personal and professional lives.

My commitment to intersectionality also extends to my advocacy work. By speaking out on issues related to diversity, inclusion, and work-life balance, I've contributed to a broader conversation about the importance of recognizing and addressing the unique challenges faced by individuals with intersecting identities. My voice has been instrumental in advancing these issues within the business community, and I hope that my efforts have had a lasting impact on the industry.

Looking Ahead: The Future of Leadership and Intersectionality

As I look to the future, I'm committed to continuing my work as a leader who champions diversity, inclusion, and intersectionality. I'm passionate about mentoring the next generation of leaders and empowering them to embrace the complexities of their identities as they navigate their careers.

I also plan to expand my efforts to promote sustainable business practices and innovation within the CPG industry. I believe that by staying true to my values and leveraging the power of intersectionality, I can drive positive change that benefits both my company and the broader community.

In my personal life, I focus on maintaining the balance I've worked hard to achieve. I'm committed to being present for my family while continuing to grow as a leader and advocate. As I embark on the next chapter of my journey, I'll remain guided by my core values of curiosity, resilience, and a deep commitment to making a difference.

Conclusion

The past five years have been a period of tremendous growth and transformation for me, both professionally and personally. My journey is a powerful example of how intersectionality can shape and enrich our experiences, driving us to achieve success while staying true to our values.

As a leader in the CPG industry, my work in diversity and inclusion and my dedication to my family and community reflect the unique and complex intersections of my identity. As I continue to lead with compassion and purpose, I hope my story inspires all who seek to make a meaningful impact in their work and lives.

FWN AMBASSADOR

A Mosaic of Filipina Women DISRUPT the Status Quo in Canada

ROSARY ESCAÑO
Global FWN 100™ 2017, Canada Ambassador (2022-2024)

NEW FWN CANADA MEMBERS

The FWN Summit 2023 in Prague, Czech Republic awarded and welcomed 3 Filipino-Canadians as new FWN members:

1. **Dr. Denise Koh from Manitoba**: Public Health/Occupational Medicine specialist, hypnotherapist, life coach, motivational speaker, mentor, social justice advocate, and leader in the ethnocultural community. Dr. Denise founded MeResRX, created the MedResRX Hypnotherapy App, and co-authored two book collaborations (Artificial Intelligence in Medicine and Canada's Family Doctor Crisis)

2. **Consul Connie Lacson from Nova Scotia**: Philippine Consul ad honorem to Nova Scotia, with oversight to New Brunswick. She holds a special place in the hearts of more than 15,000 Filipino immigrants in Atlantic Canada, with her most notable achievement having a pivotal role in the credential recognition of Philippine-educated nurses in Nova Scotia, empowering these Filipino nurses while addressing the country's healthcare shortage crisis.

3. **Jennifer Mah from Alberta**: Dean for the Faculty of Health Studies at NorQuest College. As a Registered Nurse with a master's degree in nursing, she led the Practical Nurse Program through tremendous growth, the development of over 20 programs, a new Provincial Health Care Aide Curriculum, building the first award-winning virtual reality medication administration, developing initiatives in China, the Philippines, and Jamaica and securing a $12.8M grant.

FWN CANADA ROUNDTABLE DISCUSSION

The FWN Canada Roundtable Discussion, held during Women's Month of 2023, brought together eight members of the Filipina Women's Network (FWN) to share their insights and experiences regarding the significance of being recognized as one of the Most Influential Filipina Women in the World, representing Canada. This material continues to serve as an introduction to the Filipina Women's Network, highlighting the award's importance and its impact on empowering Filipina trailblazers. Those who participated were Coria Laraya-Coutts (Global FWN100™2019), Joycelyn David (Global FWN100™2022), Dr. Eileen de Villa (Global FWN100™2022), Rosary Escano (Global FWN100™2017), Mary Ann Gamboa (Global FWN100™2017), Maria Geroche (Global FWN100™2019), Anna Patrizio (Global FWN100™2022), and Minister Rechie Valdez (Global FWN100™2022).

DISRUPT 4.0 BOOK LAUNCH

The Disrupt 4.0 Book Launch and Disrupt Series promotions in August 2023 drew around 90 dynamic Filipina women and supportive male allies to the Philippine Consulate General in Toronto for an inspiring evening celebrating powerful Filipina narratives. Attendees were immersed in a vibrant atmosphere of storytelling, networking, and engaging activities that fostered connections across generations. The event featured four distinguished Disrupt authors, namely Cora dela Cruz (Global

FWN100™2017) and Lucy Reyes (Global FWN100™2021) from Canada and FWN Founder & CEO Marily Mondejar and Laarni San Juan (US FWN 2007), both from the USA. Nine members of the Filipina Women's Network (FWN) attended the launch and participated in the chapter reading. They were Erlinda Carin (Global FWN100™2019), Coria Laraya-Coutts (Global FWN100™2019), Joycelyn David (Global FWN100™2022), Dr. Eileen de Villa (Global FWN100™2022), Rosary Escano (Global FWN100™2017), Maria Geroche (Global FWN100™2019), Agnes Miranda (Global FWN100™2018), Anna Patrizio (Global FWN100™2022), and Minister Rechie Valdez (Global FWN100™2022). Additionally, a male ally joined the lineup to read, while enthusiastic attendees stepped up to share excerpts from select chapters, creating a collaborative and uplifting experience for all.

2024 FWN CANADA EVENTS

She Matters: Prioritizing Women's Health and Wellbeing will gather Filipina women who would like to participate in a get-together and open discussion on pressing women's health issues in October, timing it during Breast Cancer Awareness Month. Headlining this will be FWN members who are in the healthcare industry sharing their expertise and insights, together with guests who will share their survival stories and experiences.

She Connects: An Evening of Empowerment and Inspiring Conversations in November will gather Filipina women and FWN Members over speed networking, a woman leader speaker to discuss resilience and empowerment, a panel discussion to career challenges, work-life balance and leadership with Q&A session and participants sharing. Networking break and sharing of personal stories, lessons learned, and fostering a sense of community.

Strengthening Global Filipina Leadership: A Report on Community Building, Advocacy, and International Collaboration as the Philippine Ambassador of the Filipina Women's Network

MARY JOY CANON-ABAQUIN
Ed.D., FWN100™ Philippine Ambassador (2022-2024)

As the founding Philippine Ambassador of the Filipina Women's Network (FWN) of influential Filipinas, my primary objective was to foster a sense of community, create opportunities for meaningful dialogue, and provide unwavering support for various advocacies and initiatives that resonate with Filipina Leaders worldwide, as the Philippines has been a busy hub for women who want to impact the country. In this capacity, I have had the privilege of promoting FWN's mission and vision, extending support to FWN Sisters beyond the geographical boundaries of the Philippines, as we support the intersectionalities of the advocacies of Philippine-based FWN Sisters and Global FWN Sisters who come home to the Philippines, to share their initiatives and aspirations. The position of the FWN Philippine Ambassador is unique because our role as Filipina leaders is deeply rooted in our shared identity and commitment to the Philippines, regardless of where we are based. Thus, my role as the founding ambassador was to set a strong foundation for FWN to thrive in the Philippines based on relationships, mutual support, and respect, and re-igniting in each FWN Sister the identity of being part of a global network of influential Filipinas. Over the past 2 years, I was engaged in much groundwork, which reaped highly attended FWN Manila events. I want to share key events and the beginning of DISRUPTing in Philippine soil. After building a stronger FWN Network of Leaders, I pass on to my successor, a community of Filipina Women Leaders and Influencers ready to continue to do transformative work as we continue to promote the vision of FWN.

FWN DISRUPTing Philippines, February 16, 2023, Marriot Hotel

The FWN DISRUPT Movement comes home to the Philippines as 16 authors of DISRUPT 4.0 and guest authors from DISRUPT 1.0, 2.0, and 3.0 join forces for an afternoon of sharing stories of Pinay Power: Liberation, Transformation, and Change. It was my privilege to host the fun format of round theater as we gave women the spotlight in the ballroom to read from their chapters. It was a full house of authors who moved the audience from teary-eyed to laughing their eyes out with their stories.

We were privileged to hear from Disrupt 4.0 Authors who represented the different sections of the book: a) Liberation - Anna Sobrepeña, Cora dela Cruz, Isabelita Manalastas-Watanabe, Chito Chavez; b) Transformation - Denise Lopez; c) Change - Georgitta Puyat, Gina Atienza, Marla Rausch, Rhoda Caliwara, Marivic Lualhati, Rhodora Palomar-Fresnedi, Mitzi Piad, and Lorna Kapunan. It was even more fun when the Disrupt Authors' 1.0, 2.0, and 3.0, Bing Carreon, Jennifer Jose, and Leonor Vintervoll, represented the DISRUPT Leadership Series.

PINAY Power that brings about Liberation, Transformation, and Change is much needed in the Philippines. When powerful PINAY leaders come together to inspire each other, it is just the beginning of DISRUPTing the Philippines as FWN Sisters create change in big and small ways.

FWN DISRUPTing Manila: Mayor Honey Lacuna Hosts Binondo Food Crawl, March 2, 2023

At the heart of Manila, the capital of the Philippines, our very own FWN Sister, Mayor Honey Lacuna (Global FWN 2022), leads as City Mayor and rolls out the red carpet, complete with a marching band, to welcome "The Most Influential Filipinas of the World Awardees and Global Filipina Leaders". It was an eye-opening experience to see Manila City Hall in action as the Mayor explained the vision for the city and the historical importance of paintings and the building. FWN Sisters were given the privilege to tour the newly renovated Manila City Hall Clock Tower which was an opportunity for discussion of history, art, and the hopes for Manila. The Mayor hosted lunch at 1919 Grand Cafe, one of the oldest heritage gems, a 97-year-old building at the corner of Juan Luna and Escolta.

32 FWN Sisters, learned about the streets of Manila, its historic landmarks, and most of all experienced the famous Binondo Food Crawl. The famous saying that the way to a man's heart is through the stomach resounded to FWN Sisters as bonding, stories, laughter, and a renewed appreciation for Filipino history and culture became a shared experience. The streets of Manila equally opened our eyes to the challenges that Filipinos face every day. The street vendors, children in the street, and the state of the city's streets less trodden reminded us, as Filipina leaders, to ponder on the possibilities for change, transformation, and liberation from poverty. Some FWN Sisters have lived in Manila but have never roamed the streets of Binondo, other FWN Sisters who joined the event live in other developed countries. Regardless, DISRUPTing Manila opens one's eyes on many levels. It raises questions of equity, roles we can play in creating opportunities for others and improving lives, which begs the true question of why we are recognized as FWN Global Influencers. How do we as FILIPINA WOMEN, no matter where we are from, DISRUPT Manila, because we are all FILIPINAS?

FWN New Year 2024 Pinay Global Pinay Power, Marriot Hotel, January 11, 2024

FWN Sisters open a New Year with the Power of Miracles and Courageous Intentions. In partnership with Megaworld, FWN Sisters donned their hats and fascinators for an Unstoppable 2024: Global Pinay Power Tea at Marriot Hotel Manila. As a new year began, it was timely to launch the Face of Global Pinay Power, Chaye Cabal-Revilla (Global FWN100 2023), President and Chief Executive Officer of mWell. The event was graced by FWN Founder Marily Mondejar, Benel Se-Liban (US FWN100 2017, Global FWN100 2022), Board Member, and Editha Winterhalter (Global FWN 100), Southern California FWN Ambassador. The afternoon was a time for New Year's Courageous Intentions for 2024, led by Marily Mondejar. It was a wonderful opportunity for sisterhood as 25-30 FWN Sisters were encouraged to share and support each other's courageous intentions. As the Philippine FWN Ambassador, it was a privilege to lead a reflection on what Global PINAY Power means in terms of Power of Ideas, Power of Words, and Power of Actions. We took a moment of gratitude to think of a STRONG PINAY WOMAN in our lives that paved the way for us. Women supporting women become Unstoppable in 2024 was a key take-away and cause for celebration. FWN Sisters renewed our commitment to answer the call of Chey Cabal-Revilla, "Everybody in the FWN sisterhood is a face of Global Pinay Power for good." Together, we can be UNSTOPPABLE in 2024!

FWN Sisterhood Beyond Borders: Supporting Global Pitches, INTERSECTIONALITY, and DISRUPTIONS

As founding FWN Philippine Ambassador, over the past 2 years, I wanted to foster belongingness, a sense of identity as being part of the FWN elite sisterhood of women leaders, and give genuine support to each person by meeting them where they are in terms of their needs. I wanted all FWN Sisters to know that coming home to the Philippines, was like coming home to the FWN Sisterhood. It is with full support and open arms that I have found myself responding to the needs and aspirations of FWN Sisters from different parts of the world as they find intersectionality with FWN Sisters in the Philippines. FWN as a GLOBAL organization is alive in the Philippines. What is unique about the FWN Philippine Ambassador position, is that since all FWN Sisters are Filipina, the lines are blurred because every FWN Sister that comes to the Philippines, is part of the FWN Philippine Sistershood.

There have been many informal gatherings, community-building activities, and opportunities to support each other's work and advocacies. I want to share some key initiatives that were supported through the FWN Philippine Ambassador position:

a. **DISRUPTing Benguet, October 6, 2023, Benguet State University, La Trinidad, Book Launch of the 4th Filipina Leadership Series Book, Maria Beebee.**
   Taking DISRUPT to the mountains in Benguet State University, as the well-loved DISRUPT editor, Maria Beebee (US FWN 100 2011, Global FWN 100 2013, 2019), engaged college students with the reading of DISRUPT 4.0. Marivic Lualhati (Global FWN 100, 2019) trooped to Benguet to support the reading at Benguet State University.

b. **FWN Supports I.D.E.A.(Inclusion, Diversity, Equity, Anti-Discrimination), February 9, 2024, Julyan's Cafe, Makati.**
FWN Sisters gather together at Julyan's Cafe, a space and business that supports children with autism. It was a perfect reminder for the sharing and dialogue of 23 FWN sisters about their respective initiatives and intersectionality with I.D.E.A. Keeping abreast with possible ways sisters can support each other's projects made the Power Lunch with great food by Chef Sau, a great reminder of the benefits of keeping oneself an active and updated FWN Member. All events of FWN are an open opportunity for sisters to showcase and get support for their Global Pitches. We were happy to support the trunk show of Pamela Gotangco (Global FWN 100 2018), as most of us went home proudly wearing PAMPINAY. It is inspiring to witness how helping and success can be borderless. Swiss-based Pam's small initiative over the pandemic to help provide livelihood to women sewers with her creations has now grown to being featured in fashion-shows around the world bringing Filipino pride and fashion to being accessible in the Kultura local market.

c. **DISRUPTing Philippine Wines and Coffee - February 22, 2024, Olive Rose, The Farmhouse Table, Manila**
Arlene Oliveros (Global FWN 2019) opens Olive Rose with FWN Sisters who are treated to an educational lunch, to expand their knowledge and understanding of the state of Philippine Coffee and the dream of creating Philippine Vinyards. Arlene's passion for putting the Philippines in the map with coffee and wine was well supported by 13 FWN Sisters. Dialogue and education created the space for intersectionality.

d. **Celebrating Women's Month with FWN Featured Artist in the National Museum, March, 22, 2024, National Museum Manila.**
FWN Artist, Lenore RS Lim (US FWN 100 2009), takes center stage with her solo exhibit that kicks off Women's Month. Director General of the National Museum, Jeremy Barns, opens Leaves, Lace, and Legacy The Art of Lenore RS Lim. As a student of Philippine National Artists, Jose Joya, Napoleon Abueva, and Federico Alcuaz, our FWN Sister has brought pride to the Philippines in Canada, New York, and Manila where she exhibits. It was a pleasure for FWN Sisters to celebrate women's month at the National Museum. She will hold another artist talk with exclusive invitations to FWN Sisters in November 2024.

e. FWN Femtors at the Youth Innovation Challenge, April 13, 2024, Manila

Around 500 High School Students around the Philippines gather online for the Youth Innovation Challenge to solve prevalent societal problems by creating solutions or innovations. Mentors play an important role in sharing their knowledge and stories to help students create solutions. FWN Sisters Lorna Kapunan (Global FWN100 2016), Pamela Gotangco (Global FWN 100 2018), Marla de Castro Rausch (Global FWN100 2021), Christine Amour-Levar (Global FWN100, 2016), inspired and helped guide students.

f. FWN Reception for Minister Rechie Valdez, MP, Minister of Small Business, July 21, 2024, Manila Peninsula, Makati

FWN Philippines welcomes Minister Rechie Valdez, Canadian Member of Parliament and Minister of Small Business. An intimate and exclusive reception at the Manila Peninsula was hosted by FWN Sisters, Marla Rausch (Global FWN100 2021), Marivic Lualhati (Global FWN100 2018), Fe Punzalan (US FWN100 2009, Global FWN100 2019), Bing Carrion (Global FWN100 2014), Georgitta Puyat (Global FWN100 2017), Chito Calixto Chavez, Cora DJ Manimbo, Catalina Bagsic (Global FWN100 2022), Arlene Oliveros (Global FWN100 2019), and Joy Abaquin (Global FWN100 2021).

Minister Rechie Valdez and the FWN Sisters had a round table discussion about the state of Philippine-Canadian relations, and on a personal level, shared intersectionalities in the current advocacies of every FWN Sister. Minister Rechie Valdez shared her inspiring story of the struggles and triumphs of reaching the pinnacle of representation to be a Member of Parliament. Discussion on inclusivity, equity, resilience, and creating opportunity, filled the evening with learning, reflection, and shared aspirations. We all went home with loot bags from the global pitch food processing and agriculture Philippine project of Canada-based, Annaflor Patrizio (FWN Global100, 2022), as a testament to the success of her initiative.

Thank you for the privilege of serving as FWN Philippine Ambassador to an inspiring group of Filipina Women. Through this work, we have strengthened global connections, empowered Filipinas in diverse fields, and ensured that our collective voice continues to inspire and impact communities around the world.

Empowering Filipina Leadership: Disrupting the Status Quo, Amplifying
Voices, and Protecting the Environment

EDITH WINTERHALTER,
Ed.D., FWN100™ Southern California Ambassador 2023-2024

As the Southern California ambassador of the Filipina Women's Network (FWN), my mission has been to engage FWN awardees in the region and showcase FWN's credo: disrupt the status quo, amplify Filipina women's voices, be invincible for the FWN sisterhood, and say "yes" to every opportunity. Over the past two years, I've had the privilege of leading activities that reflect these values, shaping impactful experiences that elevate Filipina leadership and build community. Here are four memorable events that have embodied this mission.

1. FWN Goes to the Beach: Santa Monica Beach Clean-Up, a Collective Stand for Our Environment (August 12, 2023)

On August 12, 2023, we gathered on the shores of Santa Monica with a team of 8 committed FWN volunteers for a beach clean-up. Under the California morning sun, we removed over 442 pieces of trash, knowing that every plastic bottle and discarded wrapper we picked up was a step toward a cleaner, healthier planet. But this was more than just an environmental effort—it was a chance to educate volunteers about the long-term damage plastic and trash causes to our oceans and wildlife. We said "yes" to this opportunity to disrupt the neglect that our environment faces and to take action, demonstrating that Filipina leadership extends far beyond boardrooms. It's about leading by example, even on the beach, and taking a stand for what matters most. Kudos to the following FWN sisters who volunteered for this clean-up: Maria Fides Balita (Global FWN100™ 2019), Marily Mondejar, Benel Se-Liban (US FWN100™ 2017, Global FWN100™ 2022), Ninez Ponce (Global FWN100™ 2021), Joycelyn Geaga-Rosenthal (Global FWN100™ 2013), Joy Murao (Global FWN100™ 2018), and Jaclyn Tolentino, DO (Global FWN100™ 2021).

2. FWN DISRUPTed Los Angeles: DISRUPT 4.0 Book Launch (September 22, 2023)

On September 22, 2023, the Philippine Consulate General in Los Angeles became the stage for an evening of inspiration, as we launched FWN's DISRUPT 4.0 book. This wasn't just a celebration of literature; it was a moment to amplify Filipina voices in leadership globally. The room was filled with students, young professionals, and seasoned Filipina leaders, eager to hear from the authors—women who have broken barriers in their respective industries. This event was a testament to the power of storytelling. By sharing our journeys, we disrupt the status quo that often excludes Filipinas from leadership narratives. The energy in the room was electric, as everyone in attendance felt the deep resonance of what it means to be invincible for the FWN sisterhood and to be part of a larger movement that champions Filipina empowerment.

With much appreciation to the Philippine Consul General Edgardo B. Badajos, Jr., Deputy Consul General Maria Alnee A. Gamble, Consul Marie Cris Chieng, and Cultural Officer Edel Valencia for collaborating with FWN in launching this event. Gratitude to Island Pacific for sponsoring this event. And deep thank you to the following FWN sisters/authors who volunteered for this book launch: Arlene Ferrolino (Global FWN100™ 2021); Johana Melissa Disini Orquiza (Global FWN100™ 2015); Jaclyn Tolentino, DO (Global FWN100™ 2021); Laarni San Juan (US FWN100™ 2007); Joyce Javier, MD (Global FWN100™ 2018), Patricia Denise Lopez, Ph.D. (Global FWN100™ 2021); Marily Mondejar, and Benel Se-Liban (US FWN100™ 2017, Global FWN100™ 2022).

3. Homage to Filipina Voices: In Celebration of Women's History Month (March 31, 2024)

On March 31, 2024, in celebration of Women's History Month, we hosted *"Homage to Filipina Voices"* at the Los Angeles Athletic Club, bringing together Filipina leaders to engage in powerful conversations on diversity, equity, inclusion, and belonging. Judge Rohanee Zapanta (Global FWN100™ 2023), the second Filipina to be appointed to the San Diego Superior Court, and Bianca Nicole Nepales, Lionsgate's vice president of Diversity, Equity, and Inclusion, were the featured speakers. These two incredible women shared their personal journeys, challenges, and triumphs, each one embodying the spirit of Filipina leadership.

Nepales emphasized, "I am not trying to bring you into a racist system or asking you to assimilate. I am trying to co-create new models of freedom for us all." She reminded the audience of how far we've come, yet how essential it is to recognize who is at the table and who is still being left out. In her deeply thought-provoking words, she called us to action: to not only navigate inclusion but to actively open doors for future generations.

Zapanta echoed this call to disrupt the internal barriers we often face. She shared her struggles with self-doubt, asking herself, "Am I good enough?" but recognizing that if she didn't take her place at the table, the opportunity might be lost for others. "I am because you are," she said, expressing the value of *kapwa*—a deep connection and shared identity. Together, we filled the room with not just conversation but action, encouraging everyone to push forward and embrace their unique voice.

This event honored the remarkable dynamism of Filipina leaders, reinforcing FWN's credo to disrupt the status quo and amplify voices that deserve to be heard, on our terms and in our authentic voices.

4. FWN Pinay Speed FEMtoring: Lifting Future Filipina Leaders (September 14, 2024)

On September 14, 2024, we held Southern California's first FWN Pinay Speed FEMtoring in Eagle Rock, California. This proved to be an exhilarating and inspirational event that brought together students, young professionals, and women at various stages of their careers. The mentors—each a recipient of FWN's Global *100 Most Influential Women in the World* awards—offered their time, wisdom, and guidance to help the next generation of Filipina leaders thrive. This event was not just about career advice; it was about creating opportunities for meaningful connections and mentorships that will shape the future of Filipina leadership. The energy was contagious, as attendees absorbed invaluable insights from leaders who've blazed trails before them. This event embodied FWN's credo of saying "yes" to opportunity, lifting as we climb, and ensuring that the next wave of Filipina leaders is prepared and supported.

I would like to express my appreciation to Crowe LLP, spearheaded by Kathy V. Lai, for sponsoring this event. And heartfelt thanks to the following FEMtors: Laarni San Juan (US FWN100™ 2007), Jessica Caloza (Global FWN100™ 2021), Joyce Javier, MD (Global FWN100™ 2018), Ellen Samson (Global FWN100™ 2019), Kathy V. Lai (Global FWN100™ 2021), Malve Ildefonso (Global FWN100™ 2022), Benel Se-Liban (US FWN100™ 2017, Global FWN100™ 2022), Kalika Yap (Global FWN100™ 2017), Vina Lustado (Global FWN100™ 2015), Arlene Ferrolino (Global FWN100™ 2021), Marily Mondejar, and Patricia Denise Lopez (Global FWN100™ 2021).

These four events serve as meaningful capstones as I transition out of my role as the Southern California ambassador for FWN. While this chapter of my journey comes to an end, I know that this is only the beginning. The mission to disrupt the status quo, amplify Filipina voices, and create opportunities for future leaders will continue to grow stronger. I am filled with excitement and pride as I look forward to supporting the next ambassador in carrying on this wonderful journey, ensuring that the spirit of the FWN sisterhood remains invincible for generations to come.

2021 GLOBAL FWN100™ AWARDS SELECTION COMMITTEE

Cherina Viloria Tinio, PhD
US FWN100™ 2011

Cristina Calaguian
Global FWN100 ™ 2017

Edith Winterhalter EdD
Global FWN100 ™ 2017

Janice Lao
Global FWN100™ 2014

Maria Beebe, PhD
US FWN100™ 2011
Global FWN100™ 2013
Global FWN100™ Continuing Influential 2019

Maria Fides L. Balita
Global FWN100™ 2019

Roxane Magbanua
Global FWN100 ™ 2017

Teresita Ignacio Batayola
Global FWN100™ 2019

2022 GLOBAL FWN100™ AWARDS SELECTION COMMITTEE

Carmina Montesa Aldana
Global FWN100™ 2019

Cora Dela Cruz
Global FWN100™ 2017

Cristina Calaguian
Global FWN100™ 2017

Pamela Gotangco
Global FWN100™ 2018 Awardee

Rosary Saldaña-Escaño
Global FWN100™ 2017

Rhodora Palomar-Fresnedi
Global FWN100™ 2019

Teresita Batayola
Global FWN100™ 2019

2023 GLOBAL FWN100™ AWARDS SELECTION COMMITTEE

Annabelle Manalo-Morgan PhD
Global FWN100™ 2021

Bernadette Schlueter EdD
Global FWN100™ 2016

Edith Winterhalter EdD
Global FWN100 ™ 2017

Ellen Samson
Global FWN100 ™ 2019

Kristine Custodio-Suero
Global FWN100 ™ 2022

Leonora Galleros CPA
Global FWN100 ™ 2019

Maria Fides Balita CPA
Global FWN100™ 2019

Marivic Lualhati PhD
Global FWN100 ™ 2019

Rosario "Chito" Chavez
Global FWN100 ™ 2019

Rosary Escaño
Global FWN100 ™ 2017

Teresita Batayola
Global FWN100™ 2019

2024 GLOBAL FWN100™ AWARDS SELECTION COMMITTEE

Bernadette Schlueter EdD
Global FWN100™ 2016

Donna Küenzler
Global FWN100™ 2023

Kristine Custodio Suero
Global FWN100 ™ 2022

Leonora Galleros CPA
Global FWN100 ™ 2019

Rhodora Palomar Fresnedi
Global FWN100™ 2019

Teresita Batayola
Global FWN100™ 2019

FILIPINA∘WOMEN'S∘NETWORK

FILIPINA WOMEN'S NETWORK: SIGNIFICANT MILESTONES

440

Memories from the 5th Filipina Leadership Global Summit 2007
in Washington DC, USA

FILIPINA·WOMEN'S·NETWORK

443

MEMORIES FROM
THE 6TH FILIPINA LEADERSHIP GLOBAL SUMMIT 2009
IN BERKELEY, CALIFORNIA, USA

FWN Board Members

444

(L to R) Josephine Romero,
Philippine Trade Commissioner,
Dolly Pangan-Specht, US FWN100™ 2009,
Ana Julaton, USFWN100™ 2009
first Filipina woman to win the
Women's WBO Super Bantamweight
and IBA Super Bantamweight titles

445

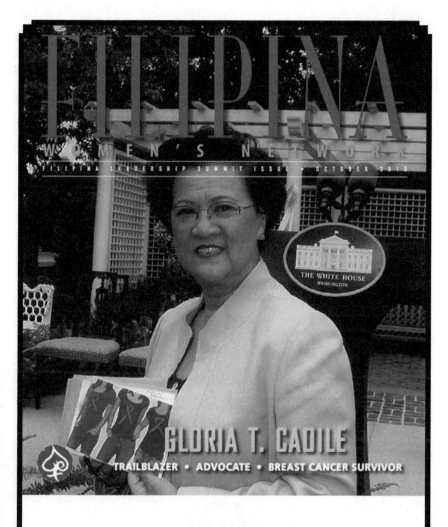

Gloria T. Caoile FWN Magazine Cover
for the 7th Filipina Leadership Global Summit 2010
in Las Vegas, Nevada, USA

Memories from the
8th Filipina Leadership Global Summit 2011
in San Francisco, California, USA

FILIPINA·WOMEN'S·NETWORK

Memories from the
9th Filipina Leadership Global Summit 2012
in San Francisco, California, USA

Memories from
the 10th Filipina Leadership Global Summit 2013
in San Francisco, California, USA

452

Apl.de.Ap receiving the FWN Kapuso
(Good Guy) Award

Memories from the
11th Filipina Leadership Global Summit 2014
in Makati, Philippines

454

Memories from the
12th Filipina Leadership Global Summit 2015
in San Francisco, USA

FILIPINA·WOMEN'S·NETWORK

Colonel Shirley Raguindin on the
cover of FWN Magazine 2015

FILIPINA·WOMEN'S·NETWORK

457

Memories from
the 13th Filipina Leadership Global Summit 2016
in Cebu, Philippines

458

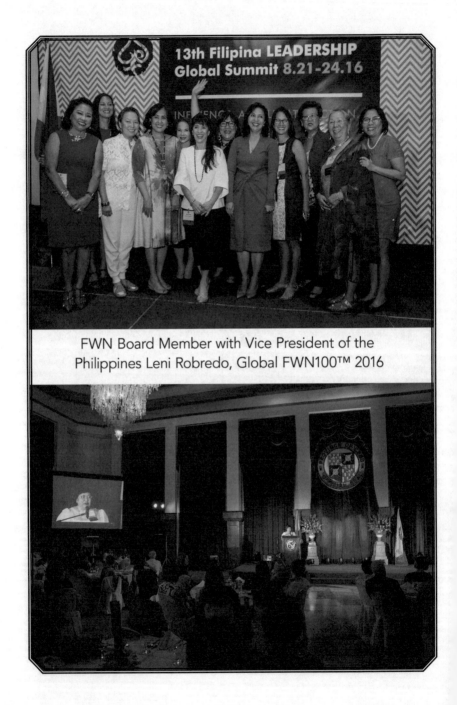

FWN Board Member with Vice President of the
Philippines Leni Robredo, Global FWN100™ 2016

Vice President of the Philippines Leni Robredo,
Global FWN100™ 2016

FILIPINA•WOMEN'S•NETWORK

Memories from
the 14th Filipina Leadership Global Summit 2017
in Toronto, Canada

FILIPINA·WOMEN'S·NETWORK

FWN Board Members

Atty. Wilma "Amy" T. Eisma, Global FWN100™ 2016,
first woman Administrator and Chairman
of the Subic Bay Metropolitan Authority and the newly appointed
President and COO of PAGCOR (2024)

FILIPINA•WOMEN'S•NETWORK

FWN Board Members with Deputy Speaker
of the Philippines' House of Representatives Gwen Garcia,
currently (2024) the Governor of Cebu

Memories from the 15th Filipina Leadership
Global Summit 2018 in London, United Kingdom

Memories from the 16th Filipina
Leadership Global Summit 2019 in Paris France

Memories from
the 17th Filipina Leadership Global Summit 2021
in San Francisco, California, USA

FILIPINA·WOMEN'S·NETWORK

100 Pinay Girls Who Will One Day Influence The World Book Club

Finalists for the 2021 Faces of Global Pinay Power

FWN Political Panel (L-R):

Marjan Philhour, US FWN100™ 2012,

Candidate for D1 San Francisco Supervisor,

Jessica Caloza, Global FWN100™ 2021,

Candidate for D52 California State Assembly,

Nikki Fortunato Bas, Global FWN100™ 2021,

President, Oakland, California City Council,

Candidate for Supervisor of Alameda County Board of Supervisors

FILIPINA·WOMEN'S·NETWORK

Memories from the 2022 Post-Summit Tour in Fatima, Portugal

469

FILIPINA∘WOMEN'S∘NETWORK

FILIPINA°WOMEN'S°NETWORK

FILIPINA·WOMEN'S·NETWORK

Memories from
the 18th Filipina Leadership Global Summit 2022
in Lisbon, Portugal

The amazing FWN Team (L-R): Genevieve Dwyer, Franklin Ricarte, Marily Mondejar, Isabelle Santiago

474

Memories from FWN's last show after 18 years of production. "The Vagina Monologues" 2022 show at the Herbst Theatre.

(L-R)
Caifornia Attorney General Rob Bonta,
California State Treasurer Fiona Ma,
San Francisco City Attorney David Chiu

FILIPINA·WOMEN'S·NETWORK

Memories from the 2023 Post-Summit Tour in Prague, Czech Republic

A visit to a Jewish cemetery

FWN Graffiti Experience

A visit to Petrof, the oldest piano manufacturer in Europe

480

FILIPINA WOMEN'S NETWORK

Memories from
the 19th Filipina Leadership Global Summit 2023
in Prague, Czech Republic

Great Gatsby Soiree

Great Gatsby Soireé FWN Awardees Performance

Women Who Rock Reception with
The Influential Women of Prague

Prince William Lobkowicz with (L-R): Franklin Ricarte,
Marily Mondejar,
Philippine Ambassador to Czech Republic Eduardo Meñez
at the Lobkowicz Palace

FWN Board Members with
the Philippine Ambassador to Czech Republic
Eduardo Meñez invited by the Women Members
of the Czech Republic Parliament at the Assembly Hall

FWN 2024 Awardees and Board Members
with Philippine Ambassador to Czech Republic
Eduardo Meñez and Prince William Lobkowicz
at the Lobkowicz Palace

FWN Board Members Visit Philippine
Embassy in Washington DC to Launch
DISRUPT. Filipina Women: Proud. Loud. Leading Without A Doubt.

Memories from the Book Launch of
DISRUPT 2.0: Filipina Women: Daring to Lead in Cebu, Philippines

Nellie Chiu, Global FWN100™ 2016 with
Maria Beebe, PhD, Global FWN100™ Continuing Influential 2018

DISRUPT 3.0: Filipina Women: Rising in London, United Kingdom at the House of Lords

The authors of
DISRUPT 3.0

FWN Board Member Georgitta Puyat,
Global FWN100™ 2017
sponsored the first edition printing of
DISRUPT 3.0 as her legacy

FILIPINA•WOMEN'S•NETWORK

Memories from the Book Launch of DISRUPT 4.0:
Filipina Women: Being in Lisbon, Portugal at the Grémio Literário, housed in the Palacete de Loures in the Chiado area of Lisbon

FILIPINA·WOMEN'S·NETWORK

The authors of DISRUPT 4.0:
Filipina Women: Being

The first woman president of
Grémio Literário in Lisbon, Portugal

496

Memories from
the D4.0. Filipina Women: Being Book Launch
at the Marriott Hotel, Philippines in February 16, 2023

497

Meet the 2021 Faces of Global Pinay Power (from the left):
Joyce Javier, MD (Global FWN100™ '18),
Natalie Garcia Lashinksy (Global FWN100™ '21),
Giovannie Espiritu (Global FWN100™ '21),
Jessica Caloza (Global FWN100™ '21),
Ninez Ponce, PhD, MPP (Global FWN100™ '19),
Alicia del Prado (Global FWN100™ '21),
Katherine Lai CPA, CGMA (Global FWN100™ '21).

FILIPINA•WOMEN'S•NETWORK

2021 Faces of Global Pinay Power strike
the iconic "Rosie the Riveter" pose

2021 Faces of Global Pinay Power unite to
#BreakTheBias for FWN's Against Hate campaign

Made in United States
Troutdale, OR
11/07/2024

24520093R00294